The Law of Road Traffic in the Republic of Ireland

The
Law of Road Traffic
in the
Republic of Ireland

Robert Pierse *BCL LLB, Solicitor*

Butterworths (Ireland) Limited
Dublin
1989

Ireland	Butterworth (Ireland) Ltd, DUBLIN
Australia	Butterworths Pty Ltd, SYDNEY, MELBOURNE, BRISBANE, ADELAIDE, PERTH, CANBERRA and HOBART
Canada	Butterworths Canada Ltd, TORONTO and VANCOUVER
Malaysia	Malayan Law Journal Sdn Bhd, KUALA LUMPUR
New Zealand	Butterworths of New Zealand Ltd, WELLINGTON and AUCKLAND
Singapore	Butterworth & Co (Asia) Pte Ltd, SINGAPORE
United Kingdom	Butterworth & Co (Publishers) Ltd, 88 Kingsway, LONDON WC2B 6AB and 4 Hill Street, EDINBURGH EH2 3JZ
USA	Butterworths Legal Publishers, ST PAUL, Minnesota, SEATTLE, Washington, BOSTON, Massachusetts, AUSTIN, Texas and D & S Publishers, CLEARWATER, Florida

First Published 1989

ISBN Hardback 1 85475 055 0

Typeset by Kerrypress, Luton
Printed by and bound in Great Britain by Billing & Sons Ltd, Worcester

Contents

Foreword

It is now some hundred years since the motor car commenced its invasion of the lives of the people of this country.

As can be seen from the following pages there are approximately one million vehicles on the roads, and whether or not a citizen is a car owner, he cannot fail to be affected by the ever increasing number of motor vehicles. Commensurate with this increase in numbers, and practically in direct ratio thereto, an extraordinary body of laws has developed throughout the years to deal with the dangers and problems consequently created. The laws to which I refer, of course, are related to developments on the old common law of tort, together with a large body of statutes, statutory instruments and bye-laws which have been implemented and interpreted by numerous decisions of the courts.

In fact, the impact of the motor car can scarcely have hit any part of society more than the courts, where in the past eighty years it has been a major cause of litigation on both the criminal and civil sides. The provision of such legislation, statutory instruments and local authority legislation, together with roads and parking places, has involved a vast amount of time and money. I think it can be said that the whole environment of the country has been altered to accommodate the motor car in a manner which no other invention in history would appear to have demanded.

Under these circumstances it is somewhat strange that no major work encapsulating all the legislation and case-law in relation to the motor car (other than tort) has been produced so far. The work which follows is a thorough demonstration, not only of the great volume of law which has grown up, but also of the manner in which the law relating to the motor car penetrates into almost every aspect of our daily lives. It is clear that a great deal of well ordered industry has gone into the production of this book. This relates not simply to the volume of material which has been gathered but to the manner in which it has been laid out and in particular to the manner in which it has been indexed and cross-indexed, which will facilitate all users in the extraction of the information contained therein.

The book itself I anticipate will prove of use not only to lawyers but also to many others who wish to ascertain with precision and ease the rules and regulations which govern an extremely important part of their lives. The author is to be congratulated in having harnessed his well known academic ability and diligence to produce a volume which will be of real use to all those engaged in the practice of law.

Richard Johnson BCL, LLB, SC
Judge of the High Court
Dublin

Preface

The past

Man's age old obsession for a 'horseless carriage' is now a reality, approximately a century old. Possibly no other single invention has impinged on the social scene as much as the motor vehicle. Wishes for better cars now contend with anxieties about safety, congestion and pollution. The social importance of the dimensions brought to man—freedom or decay—are not our concern here, though they merit serious consideration in the Irish context.

Mechanically propelled vehicles made their appearance on the roads for the first time in the 1850s. The Locomotive Acts 1861–1865 dealt with them first. The 1903 Motor Act initiated the basic Rules of the Road as we know them to-day.

The present

This book attempts within narrow confines to state in outline the present law on Road Traffic in the Republic of Ireland. It is not possible to deal with it exhaustively, as to do so would produce a three-volume tome unsuited to the market available. Concentration is on Irish statute law and case-law. Civil liability is not dealt with.

The Irish law deals with this masterful servant, known to the law as 'the mechanically propelled vehicle', by an interlocking series of controls and enforcement provisions. It seeks to govern who can drive and how he or she does it; also the vehicle used and the places used. These controls are reinforced by stringent enforcement provisions and supplemented by an insurance system to compensate victims of so-called road 'accidents'.

This field of law is one of the most dynamic in modern times. Dealing as it does with an area of often apparently conflicting objectives, it must be flexible in its operation. At present there are five major statutes covering the period from 1961 to date and much delegated legislation. Considerable case-law also exists.

The changing nature of the law makes it difficult to produce a book of long lasting value. There is a view, however, that a modern book is better than none. It is hoped that the busy lawyer, administrator or Garda searching for a reference may be helped by this one.

The Law is stated as far as possible as at 1 January 1989.

The future

It is self evident that Road Traffic Law is a continuously developing process. The existing legislation allows for this in many respects by permitting changes by regulations. Presumably amending and consolidating legislation of a domestic kind will become necessary. An amending bill in 1989 was promised in the Dail on 25 February 1988 to enable an uninsured vehicle to be impounded and possible to introduce vehicle testing extensions.

Undoubtedly major changes will continue to result from our participation in the EEC. The Community aims at a common transport policy to meet the needs of the rapidly expanding internal trade. At present the common policy covers road, rail, air and waterways transport. Other fields are being investigated. In 1961 the Commission drafted the basic principles of the Common Transport policy, which was adopted by the Council of Ministers. Rules have existed since 1961 to supress discrimination in rates and conditions of transport. Harmonization of conditions of competition in road transport has been only partially completed. The most important of the measures so far adopted concerns working hours and conditions of drivers—Ireland had a three-year adjustment period to these. The aim of freeing trade and uninformity on conditions is the basic consideration in all rules. The operation of EEC. Regulation will primarily be in the transport field. The Road Transport Act, 1986 (No 16) is a major step in that direction. (See Chapter 1.35.)

Acknowledgements

I dedicate this book to my wife, Olive, and to our children. They bore my absence from them with cheerfulness and encouraged the long hours in a way that made the work easier.

Judge Richard Johnson was good enough to write the Foreword. My friend Frank Duggan BL read the script and made some corrections to the text, as did my son, Risteard. The Department of the Environment and many of its officers gave me much valuable assistance.

I am grateful, but the mistakes remain mine.

Richard F. Humphreys generously gave me a List of Statutory Instruments in advance of his three volumes on Statutory Instruments now published by Butterworths. This is an invaluable source work for practitioners. Thanks to him.

Many others helped and gave permissions. Thanks to them.

Disclaimer

Every effort has been made to ensure that the information and comment given in this book is accurate. Nevertheless, I should be grateful to learn of any errors or omissions. However, no responsibility (legal or otherwise) is accepted by me or the publishers for any errors, omissions, or otherwise in that information or otherwise.

Robert Pierse BCL, LLB
Market Street, Listowel,
County Kerry
1.1.1989

Citation of enactments

Abbreviations

Amended (Am); Repealed by (Rp); Substitutions (Sub); Applied by (Appl).

Road Traffic Act 1961–No 24 of 1961

Section	*Subject matter*	*Notes*	*Paragraph*
Part I Preliminary and General			
1	Short title		
2	Commencement	The Act in full operational (except as amended and repealed)	7.5.8
3	Interpretation	Am by Schedule 1968 Act (No. 25) amends various definitions; also s 2 1968 Act	1.7.6; 1.12 7.9
4	Application to state employees' vehicles		6.3.7; 7.8
5	Regulations	Extended by 1968, 1978, 1987 Acts	7.5
6	Approval of bye-laws		1.17; 7.6.2
7	Proof of bye-laws and rules		7.6.3
8	Finance	Am by SI 230 of 1980, Reg 2, Sch and deletes subs (2)–(5)	5.16.2; 7.7.1
9	Disposal of fees and fines	See s 7/1968 Act	7.7.1; 7.7.2
10	Repeals		7.5.3; 7.6.1
Part II General Provisions (relating to vehicles)			
11	Regulations as to use of vehicles	See s 8 1968 Act Am schedule 1968 Act	1.5; 1.7.2; 4.6

Section	*Subject matter*	*Notes*	*Paragraph*
12	Maximum weights	See s 8 1968 Act Am schedule 1968 Act Penalty s 4 1964 Act Sub s 12(4) by s 3(2), 1984 Act	1.7
13	Special permits		1.5; 1.5.5.2; 1.5.7.2.4
14	Weight unladen		1.7.3
15	Weighbridge	Am schedule 1968 Act	1.7.6
16	Weighting	Am schedule 1968 Act and s 16(1) 1968 Act Sub s 16(5) by s 3(3) 1984 Act	1.7
17	Extraordinary traffic expenses	Am schedule 1968 Act	1.7.8
18	Vehicle tests	Am schedule 1968 Act Penalty increase–s 3 1984 Act and Table	1.8
19	Production of test certificates	Am schedule 1968 Act	1.8.3
20	Power to test Examine and inspect	Am schedule 1968 Act Am s 3 1984 Act Penalty increase 1984 Act	1.8.5; 1.20
Part III Driving Licences (Am by Part III of 1968 Act)			
21	Licencing authority		2.3.1
22	Application for driving licence		2.3
23	Grant of driving licence		2.3.4
24	Signing of driving licence		2.3.7
25	Duration of licence		2.3.6
26	Consequential disqualification orders	Am Schedule 1968 Act Am s 25 1978 and s 3A of 1984 Act See also SI 234/1984	2.9.3
27	Ancillary disqualification orders	Appl SI 234/1984	2.9.4
28	Special disqualification orders	Appl SI 234/1984	2.9.5
29	Removal of disqualification orders	Sub s 29(1) by s 19 1968 Act and Add s 5(8) by s 19 1968 Act Appl SI 234/1984	2.9.7
30	Operation of disqualification orders	Sub by s 20 1968 Act Appl SI 234/1984	2.9.6
31	Age disqualification	Appl SI 234/1984	2.3.4

Section	*Subject matter*	*Notes*	*Paragraph*
32	Health disqualification	Appl SI 234/1984	2.3.4
33	Certs of competency	Am s 21/1968 Act	2.5
34	Certs of fitness		2.6
35	Provisional licences		2.4
36	Endorsements	Am Schedule 1968 Act Appl SI 234/1984	2.10
37	Transfer of endorsement to new licence	Appl SI 234/1984	2.10.6
38	Prohibition of driving without licence	Appl SI 234/1984 Am by s 3 1984 Act– penalty increase	2.2
39	Applying when disqualified for licence	Appl SI 234/1984; Penalty increase – s 3 1984 Act	2.9.9
40	Production of licence	Am schedule 1984 Act Appl in Pt SI 234/1984	2.7.1
41	Signature on demand	Appl SI 234/1984	2.7.2
42	Regulations	Am schedule 1968 Act	2.1.3
43	Transitional provisions	now spent	
Part IV Speed Limit (Am by Part IV 1968 Act)			
44	Ordinary speed limits	Am s 44 1968 Act which	3.1.3
44A	General speed limits	inserts s 44A	3.1.4
45	Built up speed limits		3.1.5
46	Special speed limits	Am s 25 1968 Act; s 5(2) deleted	3.1.6
47	Speed limit offences	Am s 26 1968 Act	3.3
Part V Driving Offences (Am by Part V, 1968 Act and Part III, 1978 Act)			
48	Driving MPV while unfit	Sub subs (2) by s 3(5) 1984 Act	4.5
49	Drunk/drugs/ intoxicated driving MPV	Sub by s 10 1978 Act See Part III 1978 Act (procedure, etc) Am s 3 1984 Act– penalty increase	4.9.3; 4.9.5; 4.9.6
50	Intoxicated in charge MPV	Sub by s 11 1978 Act See Part III 1978 Act (procedure, etc) Am s 3 1984 Act– penalty increase	4.9.3; 4.9.5; 4.9.6
51	Drunk/drugs animal-drawn vehicles	Add s 51A by s 49 1968 Act Sub s 5(2) by s 3(6) 1984 Act	4.9.5.

Section	*Subject matter*	*Notes*	*Paragraph*
51A	Driving without reasonable consideration	Inserted by s 49 1968 Act Add by s 49 1968 Act	4.4.
52	Careless driving	Sub by s 50 1968 Act Am s 3 1984 Act– penalty increase	4.3
53	Dangerous driving	Am s 51 1968 Act– Am s 3 1984 Act– penalty increase	1.9.2; 4.2
54	Dangerously defective vehicle	Delete s 5(1) by Sch, 1968 Act Am Schedule, 1968 Act Am s 3 1984 Act– penalty increased	1.9.1; 4.6
55	Dangerous parking	Am s 52/1968 Act Am s 3/1984 Act– penalty increase	4.7

Part VI Insurance (Am by Part VI, 1968 Act)

56	Insurance, obligation to have	Am s 53/1968 Act New subs (2) by SI 322/1987 Am s 3(8)/1984 Act– penalty increase New subs (7) (8) (9) by SI 178 of 1975 R 3 and SI 322/1987	6.3.1
57	Fine in lieu of damages	Partly unconstitutional by *Cullen v AG* 1979 IR 394	6.3.3
58	Vehicle insurer	Am Schedule 1968 Act	6.5
59	Vehicle guarantee	Rp s 53/1968 Act	
60	Exempted persons	Am Sub by s 54/1968 Act	6.6.1
61	Deposits	Sub by s 55/1968	6.6.1
62	Approved policy	Am SI 178/1975 Am SI 322/1987	6.4
63	Approved guarantee	Rp by s 53/1968 Act	
64	Fraud in obtaining	Am schedule 1968 Act Am s 3/1984 Act– penalty increase	6.4.3
65	Excepted persons	Am Schedule 1968 Act	6.7
66	Certificates of insurance		6.4.4
67	Effect of certificate	Rp subs (2) by s 53/1968 Act as to guarantee	6.4.5
68	Certificate of exemption		6.6
69	Production of	s 69A inserted by Reg	6.4.6
69A	certificates	6 of European Communities (Road Traffic) (Compulsory Insurance) Regulations SI 178/1975 and s 3/1984 Act– penalty increase	6.4.6
70	Obligation to deliver up certs	Am s 53/1968 Act Rp subs (2) by 53/1968 Act	6.4.4

Section	*Subject matter*	*Notes*	*Paragraph*
71	Obligation of insured to give notice of accident	Am s 53/1968 Act as to guarantee	6.5.2
72	Obligation of user to give notice of accident	s 72A inserted by SI 178/1975	6.5.2
72A		Am s 53/1968 Act as to guarantee	6.5.2
73	Obligation to give information as to insurance	Am s 53/1968 Act as to guarantee	6.10
74	Amendment of Assurance Companies Act 1909		6.5.1
75	Regulation as to certs and giving information	Am s 53/1968 Act as to guarantee	6.2.2
76	Provisions as to insured moneys	Am schedule 1968 Act and sec 53/1968 Act as to guarantee Rp subs (4) by Civil Liability Act 1961	6.4.7
77	Repayments of deposit	Am s 53/1968 as to guarantee and Schedule 1968 Act	6.6
78	Provisions as to MIB of Ireland	Am s 53/1968 Act as to guarantee	6.8
79	Exception of pedestrian controlled vehicles		6.3.6
80	Provision for non-residents		6.9
81	Transitional provisions (Part VI)		6.8.3

Part VII Control of Public Service Vehicles (Am by Part VII 1968 Act)

82	Regulations	a. s 57/1968 Act	1.12.3
83	Taximeter inspections	a. s 7/1987 Act	1.15
84	Street stands	Am Schedule 1968 Act Power to transfer function – S 62/1968 Act	1.16 7.6.1
85	Bus stops	Power to transfer functions – s 62/1968 Act	1.17
86	Bus stop regulation	Am s 58/1968 Act Power to transfer functions – s 62/1968 Act	1.17
87	Lost property on PSVs	Am subs (8) and (9) by Schedule 1968 Act	1.18

Section	*Subject matter*	*Notes*	*Paragraph*
Part VIII Regulations of Traffic (Am by Part VIII, 1968 Act)			
88	Bye-laws for control of traffic	Rp but bye-laws contd by s 4, 5, 60(4) Sch 1968 Act. New section by s 60/1968	5.3
89	Bye-laws for specified area	Am Schedule 1968 Act Power to transfer functions– s 62/1968 Act	5.4; 7.6.1
90	Parking	Am Schedule 1968 Act Power to transfer functions s 62/1968 Act	5.5; 7.6.1
91	Large assemblies	Am Schedule 1968 Act	5.6
92	Fairs and markets	Am Schedule 1968 Act	1.31.3; 5.7; 7.6.1
93	Protection of bridges	Am s 61/1968 Act Power to transfer functions– s 62/1968 Act	1.7.10
94	Closing roads	Power to transfer functions– s 62/1968 Act	5.10
95	Traffic signs	Am Schedule 1968 Act Power to transfer functions– s 62/1968 Act	5.8
96	School crossings	Am Schedule 1968 Act– Power to Transfer Functions– s 62/1968 Act	5.9
97	Abandoned vehicles	Sub by s 53 of 1968 Act	1.24; 5.12
98	Obstruction of traffic		4.8
99	Prohibition of holding on to vehicles		4.11.5
100	Holding on by cyclists		4.11.5
101	Car parks	Subs (11) Am by SI 230/ 1980 R 2 and Schedule Am Schedule 1968 Act Rp of subs (4) and (5) by Sch 1968 Act	5.14
101A	Bollards and ramps	Inserted by Dublin Transport Authority (Dissolution) Act 1987 (No 34/1987)	5.14.5
101B	Immobilisation of vehicles		5.5.9
101C	Construction site control	ditto	5.14.6
101D	Road works	ditto	5.14.7
Part IX Miscellaneous			
102	General penalty	Am s 2/1984 Act– penalty increase	7.1
103	On the spot fines	Am s 64/1968 Act and Schedule 1968 Act s (2)(3) (5); s 10 of Act No 34/1987 Appl s 16/1976 Act; ss 64(3), 74(1)	1.7; 1.11; 1.16; 1.17; 5.4.3; 5.5.6 5.11
104	Notice of prosecution	Am Schedule 1968 Act	3.3.3; 7.3

Section	*Subject matter*	*Notes*	*Paragraph*
105	Evidence of speed		3.4
106	Duties on occurrence of accident	Am Schedule 1968 Act Am s 3/1984 Act–penalty increase	4.13
107	Duty to give information	Am s 3/1984 Act–penalty increase	4.13; 7.2.2
108	Name of pedal cyclists		7.2.2.2
109	Obligation to stop	Am Schedule 1968 Act	7.2.3
110	Disposition of vehicle		7.2.4
111	Identification of Garda		7.2.6
112	Taking without authority	Sub of subs (1) by Am s 65/1968 Act	4.10
113	Interference with mechanism, etc	Am Schedule 1968 Act Am s 3(8)/1984 Act	4.11
114	Continuous driving periods	Am Schedule 1968 Act Application restricted by SI 16 of 1979 R 10 Transfer of functions SI 164/1966 and 417/1981 EEC Regulations also Limit	4.12
115	False declarations	Am Schedule 1968 Act Am s 3/1984 Act; s 40 of No 15/1986 Act and s 10 of No 34/1987 Act– penalty increase	1.7.2; 1.8.1; 1.12.4 7.4
116	Negligent use–state vehicles	Rp Civil Liability Act 1961 (No 41) and Sub provisions s 59/1961 C.L.A	7.8.3
117	Personal liability for negligent use	Rp Civil Liability Act 1961 (See Part 2 of that Act (No. 41))	
118	Liability and consent		6.4.7
119	Reimbursement of hospitals	Rp. s 5 1968 Act See 1986 Health (Amend ment) Act No. 10	
120	Promotion of road safety	Am of subs (2) by SI No 230/1986 R 2 and Schedule	5.16
121	Calculation of passenger accommodation		1.12.2
122	Keeping petrol	Rp by Act 10/1972, ss 1(2), 7(1), Sch	1.33
123	Regulations	Am Schedule 1968 Act	7.5.3
124	Restriction on disqualification remission		2.9.12; 7.9
125	Saving re nuisance		1.29

Citation of enactments

Section	Subject matter	Notes	Paragraph
126	General power of Commissioner		2.6.7; 7.9
127	Motor Car International Circulation Act 1909	Spent as 1909 Act, repealed by Act 9/1955	

First Schedule (Am by 1968 and 1978 Acts)

Deals with enactments repealed. It is now completely operational. Repeals are

(1) The Public Roads (Ireland) Act, 1911
(2) Road Traffic Act 1933
(3) Section 10, Fire Brigades Act 1940; s 69 Local Government Act 1946; ss 36 and 37, Local Government Act 1955
(4) Section 7, Fatal Injuries Act 1956 (now fully repealed by the Civil Liability Act 1961).

Second Schedule (amended by 1968 Act and 1978 Act)

Lists the offences which under s 26 involve consequential disqualification. Commenced to operate on 1 October 1961. It was amended by Schedule 1968 Act. These are listed under s 26 (Chapter 2.9) and referred to in the text at relevent places.

Road Traffic Act 1968–No 25 of 1968

Section	Subject matter	Notes	Paragraph
Part I Preliminary and General			
1	Short title		
2	Interpretation		
3	Collective citation & construction		
4	Commencement		7.5.8
5	Repeals		
6	Minor amendments of 1961 Act		
7	Non-application of Public Offices Fees Act 1879		7.2.1
Part II General Provisions Relating to Vehicles (Amends Part II 1961 Act)			
8	Control of supply of vehicles		1.2
9	Control of imported parts		1.4; 3.4.2
10	Control of trailers		1.5.2
11	Determining maximum weights	Am s 4/1984 Act–penalty increase	1.7.2; 1.7.4
12	Inspection of vehicles	Am s 4/1984 Act–penalty increase	1.8.5.2 1.8.5.3
13	Inspection of fleets of vehicles	Am s 4/1984 Act	1.8.5.2

Section	*Subject matter*	*Notes*	*Paragraph*
14	Approved marks		1.25
15	Penalty for excess weights	Am s 4/1984 Act	1.7.11
16	Powers of authorised officers		1.7.7
17	Powers of regulation re Excise Acts Extended		1.8.1; 1.11 7.5.3
Part III Driving Licences (Amends Part III 1961 Act)			
18	Control of driving instructions	Am s 4/1984 Act	2.4.4
19	Amends s 29/1961 Act re removal of disqualification		2.9.7
20	Substitutes s 30/ 1961 Act as to operation of disqualification order		2.9.6
21	Amends s 33/1961 Act—certs of competency		2.5
22	Limited certificates of competency		2.5.8
23	Penalty re certain tests	Am s 4(6) 1984 Act	2.5
Part IV Speed Limits (Amends Part IV, 1961 Act)			
24	General speed limit		3.1.4
25	Amends s 46/1961 Act.		3.3
Part V Driving Offences (Amends Part V of 1961 Act; see Part III, 1984 Act)			
27	Definitions	Sub s 6/1978 Act	
28	Provision of preliminary specimen	Rp s 5/1978 Act	
29	Am s 49/ 1961 Act drunk driving	Rp s 5/1978 Act Rp s 5/1978 Act	
30	Provision of specimen	s 3O(3) – effect of previous conviction under ss 4, 11(7) 14(4)(a), 25 of 1978 Act	
31	Bar on defences	Rp s 5/1978 Act	
32	Amends s 50/ 1961 Act—drunk in charge	Rp S 5/1978 Act	
33	Provision of specimen	Section 33(3) effect of previous conviction under – ss 4, 11(7) of 1978 Act	
34	Bar on defences	Rp s 5/1978 Act	

Citation of enactments

Section	*Subject matter*	*Notes*	*Paragraph*
35	Evidence	Rp s 5/1978 Act	
36	Defence to refusal of specimen	Rp s 5/1978 Act	
37	Establishment of Bureau	Rp s 5/1978 Act	4.9.12
38	Functions of Bureau	Sub subs (1) and (2) by s 7/ 1978 Act	4.9.6.12
39	Director of Bureau	Sub s 5(2) by s 8/1978 Act	4.9.6.12
40	Establishment Order		4.9.12
41	Expenses of Bureau	Am by s (1) by SI 230/1980 R 2 and Sch	4.9.12
42	Protection of directors	Del (2) by SI 230/ 1982 R 2 and Sch	4.9.12
43	Procedure re specimen	Rp s 5/1978 Act	
44	Certificate of evidence	Rp s 5/1978 Act	
45	Right to further analysis	Rp s 5/1978 Act	
46	Additional specimen	Rp s 5/1978 Act	
47	Regulations	Rp s 5/1978 Act	
48	Animals, etc vehicles – drunk	Sub subs (2) of s 51/1961 Act	4.9
49	Driving without reasonable consideration	Adds s 51A to 1961 Act	4.4
50	Careless driving	Substitutes s 52 in the 1961 Act	4.3
51		Am s 53/1961 Act re dangerous driving	4.2.2
52	Dangerous parking	Sub, Am s 5/1961 Act	

Part VI Compulsory Insurance (Amends Part VI 1961 Act)

53	Approved guarantee	Repeals concept	6.1
54	Exempted persons		6.6
55	Deposits by exempted persons		6.6

Part VII Public Service Vehicles (Amends Part VII 1961 Act)

56	Damaging public service vehicles		1.19
57	Amend s 83/1961 Act – Control of public service vehicles		1.12.7
58	Transfer of functions		1.17.2

Part VIII Regulation of Traffic (Amends Part VIII 1961 Act)

59	Drunk in public places		4.9.3; 4.9.5.9

Section	Subject matter	Notes	Paragraph
60	Regulations to control traffic	Replaced s 88/1961 Act	5.3
61	Amends s 93/1961 Act - Bridges		1.7.10
62	Transfer of functions		1.7.10;1.16; 1.17;5.4; 5.5; 5.8;5.9;5.10; 7.6
63	Removal of vehicles		5.12
64	Amends s 103/1961 Act by sub new section as to fines on the spot		5.11
65	Taking without authority	Amends s 114/1961 Act	4.10
66	Investigations of accident		5.13

Schedule

Section 6 and the Schedule, which contain minor amendments of the 1961 Act, are almost wholly in operation. They operate to amend ss 3, 11, 12, 15 to 20, 26, 36, 40, 42, 54, 58, 64, 65, 76, 77, 84, 87, 89 to 92, 95, 96, 101, 103, 106, 109, 113, 114, 115, 123, and Schedule of the 1961 Act.

Road Traffic (Amendment) Act 1978–No 19 of 1978

Section	Subject matter	Notes	Paragraph
Part I Preliminary and General			
1	Short title		
2	Interpretation		
3	Collective citation and construction		
4	Commencement	SI 192/1978– commenced on 20/7/1978	7.5.8
Part II Repeals and Amendments			
5	Repeals	Much of 1968 Act, Part V repealed	
6	Re-enacts new s 27 of 1968 Act	Definitions	4.9; 7.9
7	Functions and duties of Bureau		4.9.6.12
8	Functions of director		4.9.6.12
Part III Driving Offences (Amends Part III of 1961 Act and 1968 Acts)			
9	Interpretation of Part III		
10	Prohibition of driving while intoxicated	New s 49/1961 Act Penalty increased by 1984 Act	4.9.3; 4.9.5 4.9.6

Section	*Subject matter*	*Notes*	*Paragraph*
11	Prohibition of being in charge while intoxicated	New s 50/1961 Act Penalty increased by 1984 Act	4.9.3; 4.9.5 4.9.6
12	Obligation to provide preliminary breath specimen	Am – penalty increase s 5/1984 Act	4.9.6.4
13	Obligation to provide specimen in Garda Station (s 49)	Am – penalty Increase s 5/1984 Act	4.9.6.5
14	Obligation to provide specimen in Garda Station (s 50)	Am – penalty increase s 5/1984 Act	4.9.6.5
15	Obligation to provide breath specimen	Am – penalty increase s 5/1984 Act	4.9.6.4; 5.9
16	Procedure following provision of specimen under s 15	Am – penalty increase s 5/1984 Act	4.9.6.4
17	Obligation to provide urine specimen in Garda Station	Am – penalty increase s 5/1984 Act	4.9.5.6
18	Evidential provision in prosecutions under s 49 and 50	Am – penalty increase s /1984 Act	4.9.6.10
19	Refusal of blood sample		4.9.6.8
20	Bar on defences		4.9.6.9
21	Procedure at Garda Station		4.9.6.6
22	Procedure at Bureau		4.9.6.7
23	Presumptions in proceedings		4.9.6.6; 4.9.6.7
24	Amendments to disqualifications – 2nd Sch 1961 Act	Am by s 3(4)/1984 Act	2.10; 4.9.6.7
25	Consequential disqualifications	Am s 26/1961 Act	2.9.3
26	Regulations		4.9.6.12

Road Traffic (Amendment) Act 1984–No 16

1	Definitions	
2	Increase in penalties – s 102/1961 Act	7.1
3	Increase in penalties – 1961 Act	4.5.13
4	Increase in penalties – 1968 Act	Noted in text
5	Increase in penalties – 1978 Act	4.9, etc
6	Offences to which ss 2–5 apply	7.3
7	Short title	

Dublin Transport Authority (Dissolution) Act 1987–No 34

7	Am s 82 of the 1961 Act	1.12.7
8	Powers to Garda Commander 1961 Act	7.2
9	Amendments to Part VIII of the 1961 Act- Inserts s 101A, 101B, 101C, 101D	5.14
10	Miscellaneous Amendments of 1961 Act- Am s 103; s 115	5.11
11	Am Local Government (Roads & Motorways) Act 1974	7.4

Section	*Subject matter*	*Notes*	*Paragraph*
12	Am Local Authorities (Traffic Wardens) Act 1975		5.15
13	Collective Citation – i.e. Road Traffic Acts 1961–1987		7.2

Table of legislation

Table of statutory instruments

EEC Directives and Regulations (R)

Note: Many other Directives are incorporated into Irish Law through Irish Regulations or are inoperative here as we have no motor car assembly plants in Ireland. The list above is incomplete and refers only to those specifically mentioned in the text.

Table of cases

PARA

[B]

PARA

[C]

PARA

PARA

PARA

[I]

[J]

[K]

PARA

[O]

[P]

PARA

[T]

PARA

Chapter 1

Control of vehicles

'With all the law's faults it had one great virtue. It was there.'
Arthur Haley – 'In High Places'

1.1 General

1.1.1 Introduction

There are almost one million vehicles on Irish Roads. Their use is controlled by law, mostly by the Road Traffic Acts. These are the Road Traffic Acts of 1961, 1968, 1978 and 1984, as amended by the Dublin Transport Authority (Dissolution) Act 1987, and are known collectively as the Road Traffic Acts 1961–87.

The Road Traffic Acts approach the important question of controlling these vehicles on the road firstly by regulating vehicles generally and then by dealing specifically with public service vehicles. The latter, which are vehicles plying for hire, are obviously particularly important for the safety of the fare-paying public, often carried in large numbers.

It will be noticed that the 1968 Act altered the basis and nature of control of vehicles very substantially in line with modern thinking. Since joining the EEC in 1972, the impact of Community legislation has been substantial in Ireland. Now the manufacturer must make, the supplier supply, and the owner and user maintain, a safe vehicle. There are provisions in Irish Acts for the control of a vehicle's use, construction and equipment and lighting, and of its weight for road safety purposes and also for the protection of roads, bridges, etc. and national infrastructure.

1.1.2 Scope of chapter

This Chapter on the control of vehicles is divided into three parts:

PART 1, which applies to all vehicles—Deals with the controls on the manufacture, sale, importation of parts, use, lighting, weight, testing, parts, trailers, unattended vehicles, registration and Road Transport vehicles.

PART 2, which deals with Public Service Vehicles—their control, taximeters, taxi stands, buses, lost property, tests, weight, construction, visiting, driving time and drivers licences. These controls are in addition to or substituted for the Part 1 controls.

PART 3, other Controls—Deals with trailers, unattended vehicles, approved marks, holding on to, taking vehicles, nuisances, animals, fuels, etc.

1.1.3 Legal provisions

The basic legal provisions are as follows:

(a) Part II of the 1961 Act, ss 11 to 20 inclusive, which is headed 'General Provisions relating to Vehicles' and Part II of the 1968 Act, ss 8 to 17 again, headed 'General Provisions relating to Vehicles', as amended (see text). These provisions and the regulations thereunder affect all vehicles and are dealt with in Part 1 of the Chapter.

(b) Parts VII of both the 1961 Act (ss 82–87) and 1968 Act (ss 56, 57, 58), as amended, and the Regulations thereunder. These specifically relate to public service vehicles as well.

(c) The numerous regulations under these statutory provisions. These are listed in the appropriate places in the text.

By virtue of s 4 of the 1961 Act these provisions apply to State Vehicles generally.

In relation to regulations, s 5 of the 1961 Act provides that every regulation has to be laid before the two Houses of the Oireachtas (see para 7.5).

1.1.4 Definitions

See Chapter 7.9 and the text generally as to definitions of various words and phrases used in these Acts and regulations. The regulations referred to in this Chapter themselves often have special definitions. These definitions should be referred to when a problem is being considered in relation to those regulations.

1.2 There is no definition of 'vehicle' in the Road Traffic Acts. Therefore the ordinary meaning applies, i.e. all kinds of vehicles such as mechanically propelled vehicles, trailers, animal-drawn vehicles (see para 7.9 also regarding vehicles and the case-law referred to therein). Many types of vehicles have their own definitions in para 7.9.

PART 1 – CONTROLS ON ALL TYPES OF VEHICLES

1.2 Control of supply/sale of vehicle

1.2.1 Prohibition

Section 8 of the 1968 Act is the main section which affects the motor trade and similar interests, both criminally and civilly. It provides basically that the supply (by sale, hire, loan or otherwise) or alteration of specified vehicles not complying with the prescribed requirements—as to construction in s 11 of the 1961 Act and as to weight under s 12 of the 1961 Act and regulations thereunder (see below)—shall be an offence, unless those vehicles have one of the following:

(a) a test certificate (see Para 1.8.1); or
(b) a certificate of conformity with the requirements of the type of vehicles in question; or
(c) the Minister has issued a type approval certificate showing that this type of vehicle meets the requirements.

The general penalty applies (s 102) (para 7.1).

The control of alteration is included as mentioned above and is important, as reconstruction of the vehicle often would render the vehicle unsafe. Therefore unrestricted alteration is controlled.

1.2.2 Warranty

In Civil Law (i.e. Contract) the section (s 8 of the 1968 Act) implies a warranty in the contract for supply of those prescribed vehicles that they either:

(a) comply with the prescribed construction and weight requirements in ss 11 and 12 of the 1961 Act; or
(b) comply with the prescribed requirements for a type of vehicle in respect of which a type approval certificate is in force.

Such a clause does not appear in corresponding English legislation.

In *Badham v Lents Ltd* [1946] KB 45 a court has held that these provisions as to construction, etc. were criminal sanctions and not for the protection of purchasers. Thus, a civil action for breach of statutory duty would not lie (see also *Vinall v Howard* [1954] 1 QB 375). These decisions will no longer affect the Irish position once the section becomes operational.

1.2.3 Regulations

There are wide powers to make regulations for the purposes of the section which are given to the Minister for the Environment. These can specify:

to what vehicles the section applies; exempting vehicles; the issue of certificates; keeping records, etc.

Regulations can make different provisions for different classes of cases within the same matter. Contravention of the regulations carries the general penalty (see para 7.1) once the regulation is stated to be penal. Ancillary disqualification applies, as does optional endorsement of a drivers licence. No regulations have been made yet under s 8. This has rendered it inoperative to date.

1.2.4 Sale of Good Acts

The Sale of Goods Act 1893, as amended by the Sale of Goods and Supply of Services Act 1980, applies to the sale of vehicles. The general provisions as to time, title, sale by description, sample goods, and, warranties as to quality and fitness therefore are incorporated in the sale contract of a vehicle.

It should be noted that those conditions and warranties applying to sale by sample apply only to contracts in the course of business. Other general provisions of the 1893 Act regarding guarantee and restrictions of rights apply. (See 'Sale of Goods and Supply of Services—A Guide to the Legislation' by Grogan, King and Donelan published in 1983 by the Incorporated Law Society of Ireland.)

There is a particular warranty on the sale of motor vehicles provided for in s 13 of the Sale of Goods and Supply of Services Act 1980. The section makes no distinction between new and second-hand vehicles, as other general sections do.

The section begins with a definition of motor vehicles, which is similar to but less restrictive than that in s 3 of The Road Traffic Act 1961 (see para 7.9) The 1980 definition does not include the exception for 'a tram car or other vehicle running on permanent rail' and does not exclude disabled vehicles as referred to in s 3(2) of the 1961 Act.

Section 13 of the 1980 Act provides that in every contract for the sale of a motor vehicle there must be an implied condition (in addition to any other condition or warranty) that at the time of delivery of the vehicle under the contract it is free from any defect which would render it a danger to the public, including persons travelling in the vehicle. The condition does not arise or apply, however, in respect of the following contracts:

(a) a contract in which the buyer is a person whose business it is to deal in motor vehicles, e.g. on a trade-in to a garage. In other words, the condition applies to sales from business to consumers and to private sales only.

(b) where the seller and buyer agree that the vehicle is not intended for use in the condition in which it is to be delivered to the buyer under the contract, witnessed by a signed document, and it is shown that that agreement is fair and reasonable. This term of 'fair and reasonable' is dealt with in the Schedule of the 1980 Act—one must have regard to the circumstances contemplated by the parties; the bargaining strength of the parties; any inducement; the customer's knowledge of the existence of the term; the reasonableness of any condition that excludes liability; and whether the goods have been specially processed or adapted for the customer.

(c) where two years have elapsed after the cause of action accruing. The Statute of Limitations Act 1957 is amended accordingly but if there is a disability (e.g. minority, insanity) the period of two years is from the end of the disability.

A written certificate on the terms of the condition (as to the form of which the Minister may regulate) is to be given by a dealer in motor vehicles to the buyer. If there is an action for breach of the condition and no such certificate is proven to have been given, then it is presumed until the contrary is shown that the proven defect existed at the time of delivery. This certificate does not arise in private sales. If a dealer gives a certificate that is false he will normally be liable to prosecution under the Merchandise Marks Act 1887, amended by s 3 of the Consumer Information Act 1978, i.e. for giving a false trade description of the goods. However, much of the section regarding certificates is inoperable, as no regulations have been made by the Minister.

Section 13(9) of the 1980 Act renders void any term of a contract exempting from application any provision of the section.

As most vehicles purchased are financed by borrowings, the terms of s 14 of the 1980 Act will apply. This section renders the seller answerable jointly and severally with the Finance House for any breach of contract of sale and any misrepresentations made by the seller. (Also see para 1.3.1.)

An auctioneer does not normally offer to sell vehicles; he invites those present to buy (*British Car Auctions v Wright* [1912] Crim LR 562).

Guilty knowledge of defect is not necessary (*Sandford Motor Sales v Hobgood* [1962] Crim LR 487).

1.2.4 EEC provisions

The EEC authorities have enacted much legislation in this field. It has been enacted to effect conformity and safety throughout the EEC. The provisions of this legislation have been directly incorporated into Irish Law under the European Communities (Vehicle Type Approval) Regulations 1978 (SI 305/1980; SI 41/1980; SI 420/1981; SI 134/1982; SI 70/1983; SI 280/1984; SI 322/1985; SI 320/1986).

As to Tractors, see European Communities (Agricultural or Forestry Tractor Type Approval) Regulations SI 137/1979; SI 101/1980; SI 389/1981; SI 270/1483; 162/1988. This latter gives effect to EEC Directive 86/298 dealing with roll over protection structures.

1.3 Control of hire-purchase transactions

1.3.1 Control

Where the financing of the purchase of a vehicle is done by way of a Hire-purchase Agreement, then under the Hire-purchase Acts 1946 and

1960, as amended by The Sale of Goods and Services Acts 1980, there is control of the terms of the sale also. This is in addition to the control discussed in para 1.2.4. The Guide '*Sale of Goods and Supply of Services Acts 1893–1980*—A Guide to the Legislation, by Grogan, King and Donelan, published by The Incorporated Law Society of Ireland, deals with the provisions extensively (pp 47–85).

In this book it is sufficient to draw attention to the controls effected by implied conditions of title (s 26 of the 1980 Act); compliance with description (s 27); as to quality and fitness (s 28); and as to sale by sample (s 29). It is difficult to exclude these conditions. They help to ensure that the third party (the hire-purchase company) is interested in the fitness of the vehicle.

1.4 Control of imported parts

The Republic of Ireland now has no car manufacturing plant. All vehicles, and therefore almost all their parts, are imported. Section 9 of 1968 Road Traffic Act gives the Minister a specific power to regulate the importation, supply (whether by sale, hire, loan or otherwise) and fitting of vehicle parts. Breach of the regulations is an offence to which the general penalty applies (para 7.1).

A 'vehicle part' means any article made or adapted for use as a part of a vehicle or for use as part of the equipment of a vehicle. It includes any article made or adapted for use as part of the equipment of a driver or passenger on or in a vehicle and any device which is capable of being used to indicate the existence of, or frustrate the operation of, electronic or other apparatus being used to give indications from which the speed at which a person was driving can be inferred.

The section allows the Minister to specify in Regulations the matters referred to in the section (importation, supply, etc.) which can be done absolutely or conditionally by licence, and to regulate the fitting of parts to vehicles; require suppliers to supply instructions for the fitting and use of such parts; and it allows the regulations to apply to different classes of parts and for different circumstances.

The general penalty (para 7.1) also applies to any breach of a regulation made under the section. No regulation has been made in relation to vehicle parts and so the section is of little use at present.

Section 9 does not provide for a warranty in civil law as does s 8 of the 1968 Act (see para 1.2.2). However, the Sale of Goods Act 1893, as amended by the Sale of Goods and Supply of Services Act 1980, applies. Section 12 of the 1980 Act implies a warranty, which cannot be negotiated, that spare parts and adequate after-sales services will be made available by the seller in such circumstances as are stated in the offer, description or advertisement by the seller on his own behalf, or on behalf of the manufacturer, for a stated period or a reasonable period if no period is stated. The Minister for Trade, Commerce and Tourism has power to define a reasonable period for any class of goods. There is control of certain imported types contained in the European Communities (Surveillance of certain motor car type imports) Regulations 1988 (SI 39/1988).

1.5 Control of construction use and equipment

1.5.1 General statutory provision

The provisions of the Acts controlling the construction and use of vehicles and their equipment are designed to be wide and flexible and to be applied through regulation. They are generally divided for convenience into (a) Construction, Use and Equipment Regulations, and (b) Lighting Regulations, which are considered at para 1.6.

Section 11 of the 1961 Act makes it an offence for both the user and the owner to use, or for the owner to allow the use of, a vehicle in a public place which does not comply with the regulations. The general penalty applies (para 7.1). (As to 'public place', 'owner' and 'use' see para 7.9.) A defence is provided for the owner if the use is unauthorised.

The Minister for the Environment is by s 11 of the 1961 Act given wide powers to regulate the use generally of vehicles, their construction and equipment, the condition subject to which vehicles and their equipment can be used, duties of drivers and passengers, the use of loudspeakers on vehicles and particulars to be affixed to vehicles. These powers distinguish between different classes of vehicles, different circumstances and areas. The regulations specify those that are penal and therefore carry the general penalty (see para 7.1).

Exemptions can be given by Special Permit (see para 1.5.3).

1.5.2 Trailers

Special controls of these must be first mentioned.

1.5.2.1 *Statutory provisions.* The Minister in making regulations is specifically empowered by s 10 of the 1968 Act to control vehicles drawn by mechanically propelled vehicles (i.e. trailers). This Ministerial power is widely drawn to allow him to regulate the following matters:

(a) the licensing of trailers;
(b) payment of fees on application for licences on plates and who gets the fees;
(c) conditions for the use of trailers;
(d) keeping records, issue of certificates;
(e) production of records and certificates to Gardai and the Ministers Officers (this is in addition to the other powers of Gardai and officers under the Acts: See para 7.2);
(f) the regulations can differentiate between circumstances and classes of vehicles.

Contravention of a regulation which is stated to be a penal regulation is an offence and the general penalty (para 7.1) applies. If the person contravening the Regulation is not the owner, then the owner is also guilty of an offence.

In a prosecution under section 10 certain presumptions are raised by subs (4) and (5). They are:

(a) that the purported signature of a person signing a certificate under the regulations for a licence is valid until the contrary is shown; and
(b) that the defendant did not hold the material licence under the regulations—again until contrary is shown.

As to what is a trailer, see *Carey v Heath* [1952] 1 KB 62, where it was held that a four-wheeled vehicle being towed in such a way that only the rear wheels of the towed vehicle are touching the road surface is not a trailer 'with more than two wheels'.

It should be noted that EEC law applied by Irish law in relation to Trailers is by directive adapting technical progress and approximating the laws of Member States (see 71/320/EEC and 88/194/EEC).

1.5.2.2 *Regulations.* The present regulations are the Road Traffic (Licensing of Trailers and Semi-trailers) Regulations 1982 (SI 35/1982, as amended by SI 127/1983). They are specific to trailers and semi-trailers, which also remain subject to the general regulations discussed in para 1.5.4.

These regulations set up a special system of annual licensing of trailers and semi-trailers with a maximum permissible unladen weight of over 3,500 Kgs (about 1½ tons).

A semi-trailer means the drawn component of an articulated vehicle or a vehicle constructed or adapted for use as such drawn component.

The licensing authorities are the same as the General Registration and Licensing Authorities under the Road Vehicles (Registration and Licensing) Order 1958 (SI 15/1958) (see the 1982–1987 Regulations (para 1.11) as to these), i.e. normally the local authority (see para 9.7).

The following is a note of main Regulations:

R 4 Application is by declaration by scheduled form. Amended by SI 127/1983 as to the production of a Certificate of Roadworthiness (see para 1.8).
R 5 A weight certificate is necessary on the first application or later modification of vehicle. Penal.
R 6 If the licence is granted the applicant gets a licence card. This is to be available to the Garda. Penal.
R 7 If the vehicle is modified, then the card has to be surrendered for amendment. Penal.
R 8 Any change of address of the owner must be notified. Penal.
R 9 Any sale of the vehicle must be notified and the card given to the new owner, who forwards it to the appropriate licensing authority. Penal.

R 10 If acquisition of the vehicle is by other means (i.e. not on a sale), the appropriate licensing authority must be notified. Penal.
R 11 On the destruction or permanent export of the vehicle the licensing authority must be notified and the card given up. Penal.
R 12 Replacement cards can be issued if the original card is lost, destroyed, etc. Penal.
R 13 Every licensing authority has to maintain a 'Trailer Register'. The first registration and subsequent transfers must to be entered.
R 14 The person whose name is last entered on the register is the registered owner.
R 15 The licensing authority allocates an index mark to the trailer on its first licensing.
R 16 Trailer marks must be exhibited. Penal.
R 17 Licensing authorities must supply information on licensed vehicles.
R 18 Licensing authorities may supply certificates of ownership.
R 19 Declares certain regulations to be penal. These have been denoted 'Penal' in the text. The general penalty applies (para 7.1).

Other regulations operating in relation to trailers are found throughout the Construction, Equipment and Use of Vehicles Regulations 1963–1986, referred to at para 1.5.5.

1.5.3 Special permits

By virtue of s 13 of the 1961 Act, the Minister has power to make regulations allowing the issue of special permits authorising particular vehicles to contravene s 11 regulations on such conditions to such persons as are specified. Use of a vehicle with this permit is lawful despite the fact that the use contravenes s 11 regulations.

These special permits may have inserted in them special limitations, restrictions and conditions, including provisions for compensation for public road damage.

The regulations may specify the persons to whom the special permits may be issued and how the applications are to be made (e.g. see 1.5.5.3 below).

1.5.4 General regulations

The main general regulations under s 11 of 1961 Act are very long and complex, dealing with almost every item of ordinary equipment on or in all vehicles. They have been regularly amended. There is a need for consolidating Regulations, especially as the emphasis has shifted from general construction to part-by-part control and approval, since Ireland entered the EEC particularly, i.e. 1972 onwards.

The series of regulations considered below stem from the provisions of ss 11, 12 and 13 of the 1961 Act, the main controls being under s 11. Additional Public Service Vehicles provisions are discussed in Part 2 of this Chapter with some provisions of the 1968 Act.

The regulations under s 11 of the 1961 Act may be divided into:

1.5.4 *Construction use and equipment*

(a) Construction, Equipment and Use Regulations (para 1.5.5); and
(b) Lighting Regulations (para 1.5.6).

1.5.5 Construction, equipment and use regulations

1.5.5.1 *List of regulations.* The following are the regulations now in force under s 11 of the 1961 Act, dealing with the construction equipment and use of vehicles. These normally apply to all vehicles:

(1) Road Traffic (Construction, Equipment and Use of Vehicles) Regulations (1963 SI 190/1963).
(2) Amending Regulations SI 79/1965; 273/1967; 94/1969; 138/1969; 211/1970; 96/1971; 297/1974; 291/1978; 360/1978; 270/1981; 119/1983; 278/1983; 158/1985; 442/1986.

1.5.5.2 *Notes on Construction, Equipment and Use Regulations.* These Regulations, particularly those of 1963, contain long and complicated provisions running to over 100 pages, and there is a series of substitutions and amendments. The more recent regulations reflect the EEC Rules and are part of the continuing approximation of law between members of the EEC. They contain many special definitions, and these need to be studied in any particular case. Reference will have to be made to the actual regulations and amendments thereto when dealing with any specific problem. This book mentions only in general outline commonly met Regulations from them—largely those that are penal. Amendments, where possible, are noted.

1.5.5.3 *1963 Regulations (SI 190 of 1963).* **(a)** Part I is largely definitional, preliminary and general material. Each regulation must be looked at where appropriate.
It is the duty of the Court to see if the vehicle comes within the class affected (See *Wakeman v Cathlow* (1977) RTR 174).

Definitions include 'Agricultural Vehicle' 'Articulated Vehicle' 'Land Tractor', 'Passenger Vehicle', 'Station Wagon', 'Indivisible Load', 'Tractor', 'Wheel', etc..

(b) Part II deals with weight, dimensions and construction of vehicles and trailers. It places liability for compliance on the owner (R 6).

Weight is covered by R 5 and R 7 and its distribution by R 9 (see para 1.7 weight marking (R 8) at para 1.7.5 and weight plate at para 1.7.4, where s 12 of the 1961 Act as amended is discussed).

Width is specified by R 10. The maximum normally is 8 feet 2½ inches, but for certain tractors it is 9 feet (i.e. certain agricultural machines used in daytime only are excepted). The width of a load cannot exceed 9 feet 6 inches normally. Use must be in connection with agriculture (*Markman v Stacey* [1968] 3 All ER 758). Under EEC Directive 85/3/EEC, as amended by 88/218/EEC, the maximum width of all vehicles is restricted to 2.50m, except for thick-walled refrigerated vehicles where it is 2.60m.

Length R 11 (amended by R 2 of SI 211/1970) is normally 36 feet for any vehicle, although public service vehicles can measure 12 metres;

articulated vehicles, 49 feet; trailers, 23 feet; and combinations, 54 feet. Certain exceptions are detailed with safety conditions. In relation to exceptional lengths, the following judgments may be of help:

(1) *Pealk v Johnson* [1967] 1 All ER 172 held that a vehicle which was used for carrying indivisible loads of exceptional length on 131 out of 177 journeys was not normally used for carrying such loads;
(2) *Cook v Brandon* (1975) RTR 505 held that a load which fitted within the confines of an articulated truck of standard length was not a load of exceptional length.

As to what an articulated truck is, see *Hunter v Towers* [1951] 1 All ER 349, where it was held that a breakdown vehicle and a broken down vehicle on tow is not such a vehicle if no part of the towed vehicle is superimposed on the towing vehicle.

Trailers are covered by R 12. Only one can be drawn by a vehicle, except for a large tractor which may draw with an attendant. A cycle may have only a side car. The drawbar must be safe and not more than 15 feet in length. Maximum rear *overhangs* are fixed by R 13—See *O'Connell v Murphy* (1981) RTR 163 as to the danger and extent of overhangs.

Springs must be fitted (R 14) in most vehicles, although exceptions are listed.

Circular wheels must be the way of transmitting weight to the road (R 15), except in specified track type vehicles.

Pneumatic tyres must be fitted to vehicles (with some exceptions) (R 16). In some cases safety tyres are allowed. All tyres must be free from defect. They must not be excessively worn. A tyre is excessively worn if no portion of the tread pattern is clearly visible on the contact wearing area of the tyre under normal operating conditions, or where any portion of the fabric or canvas of the tyre is visible at any point on the contact wearing area under normal operating conditions. It is not excessively worn if the tread of the tyre displays throughout its breadth and around its entire circumference a pattern, the relief of which is clearly visible and is at least 1 millimetre in depth (See *Coote v Parkin* (1977) RTR 61). In *R v R Millar (Contractors) Ltd* [1970] 1 All ER S 77 conviction for dangerous driving causing death was upheld where the accused set out on a journey with a known dangerous tyre which subsequently burst. In *Goosley v Adams* (1971) RTR 465 under English Regulations it was held that where double wheels were fitted, the two tyres are not to be treated as one under the regulation. The 'tread' does not include the outer walls (*Coote v Parkin* (1977) RTR 61). See para 1.5.2.2 as to special provisions for trailers.

Tyres must be maintained properly, i.e. proper pressure. Again EEC Controls are evident—see European Communities (Tyre Pressure Gauges) Regulations SI 175/1988 regulating Tyre pressure gauges for motor vehicles.

As to 'contact with the road', this would not seem to include that part which only comes in contact on skidding or turning (*Sandford v Butcher* (1978) RTR 132). The compliance with the Regulation is a matter of fact and the Garda need not have special training (*Phillips v Thomas* (1974) RTR 28).

1.5.5.3 *Construction use and equipment*

There is a general ministerial control on the quality of types under the European Communities (Surveillance of certain motor car type imports) Regulations 1988 (SI 39/1988). Also European Communities (Agricultural or Forestry Tractors SI 162/1988 Tyre Approval) Regulations complement Council Directive 86/298/EEC in regard to these type of Tractors tyres.

Special permits allowing contravention of part II can be allowed by local authorities on specified conditions (R 17) This lengthy regulation is operational under section 13 of the 1961 Act. It deals with application for and processing and granting of permits. These can be granted on conditions and limitations and are normally valid for one year. See para 1.5.3 also for special permits.

Under the Local Government (Roads and Motorways) Act 1974 (Proscribed Traffic) General Regulations 1977 (SI 396/1977) Art 4, a special permit can also be issued for a mechanically propelled vehicle under Art 17 to use a motorway.

(c) Part III deals with equipment generally, except brakes. All mechanically propelled vehicles must have the following equipment while used in a public place. All such equipment must be maintained properly under R 34.

R 20 *Steering Mechanism*—which must be strong and efficient.

R 21 *Reversing Gear*—i.e. vehicles must be capable of backing, if over 8 cwt unladen.

R 22 *Wings*—are required to catch mud and water, except in tractors and certain similar vehicles.

R 23 *View of road*—the Construction of the vehicle must allow visibility to the front and sides.

R 24 *Safety glass*—necessary on windscreens. Amended by SI 158 to provide for laminated safety glass on new vehicles from 1 January 1986.

R 25 *Windscreen wipers*—must be efficient and automatic. Bikes and slow vehicles (up to 12 mph) excepted.

R 26 *Rear view mirror*—to enable driver to see road to rear from driver's seat. Two mirrors are necessary in a vehicle constructed to carry more than eight passengers. Mirrors must be properly fixed and adjusted and efficient.

R 27 *Speedometer*—must be efficient and easily visible to driver. Vehicles incapable of exceeding 30 mph (or 20 mph if a large tractor), defence forces and works vehicles are excepted. A revolution counter does not comply with this regulation (*Sellwood v Batt* [1962] Crim LR 841). See also EEC Regulation 443/1975.

R 28 *Horn*—This must be capable of giving efficient warning and not be a gong, siren, strident toned device or bell, with exceptions. Referred to in the regulations as 'an audible warning device'. See R 86 as to use of the horn. It must be maintained.

R 29 *Silencer*—Must be sufficient to reduce noise to a reasonable level and must be maintained. See R 85 as to noise level permitted.

R 30 *Exhaust*—Construction must reasonably prevent emission of smoke, vapour, gasses and odour. See also R 90. See also R 85 as to noise level permitted.

R 31 *Locks*—to doors and other devices must be fitted to prevent unauthorised driving. A detachable key must be fitted for the ignition. Large public service vehicles are exempted in certain circumstances.

R 32 Inessential *projections* are prohibited.

R 33 *Closets*—such as urinals, etc. are prohibited, with certain exceptions which still prohibit their discharge on roads, etc. (see R 89).

R 34 *Condition and maintenance*—all the above equipment must be in proper condition and properly maintained. In *Smith v Nugent* (1955) ILT 60 it was held that a missing handbrake rachet could be a defect of construction as well as of maintenance. Furthermore under R 34:

(a) *the body and floor* of all vehicles must be secure and strong; and
(b) *all electrical leads* must be insulated and placed so as not to cause danger; and
(c) *the fuel tanks* must be properly and safely placed; and
(d) *any vibrating parts* must be properly bolted or studded, etc.

R 25 *Loud Speakers*—these are prohibited from being placed on, or attached to the vehicle if capable of being heard outside the vehicle, unless:

(a) a police, ambulance or fire brigade vehicle;
(b) a system to address passengers in a large public service vehicle;
(c) a vehicle used during elections; or
(d) used under permit from a local authority. This can be applied for and granted under such conditions, limitations, and restrictions as the Local Authority considers necessary or desirable.

R 36 *Defence*—If the defendant shows the equipment defect arose on the day of the alleged offence and during the journey in question and he took immediate steps to repair the defect, this is a good defence. If the defect made the driving of the vehicle dangerous, he must show it was parked in the nearest safe place.

R 37 *Owner*—Liable for use of the vehicle in public place unless use unauthorised.

(d) Part IV is a complicated series of provisions which deals with the various types of *brakes* required on MPVs and trailers. The Part has special definitions of which an outline only is given here. The EEC approximation of laws on brakes is continuing under Directives 71/320/EEC and 88/194/EEC.

R 39 Allows various *combinations* of braking devices, subject to exceptions. These can be a service brake (normally foot brake), parking brake, emergency brake, etc.

R 40 *All mechanically propelled vehicles* (other than motor cycles) must have (a) *a service brake*, (b) *an emergency brake*, and (c) *a parking brake*, on the terms (e.g. foot worked) and conditions of the regulation and with the exceptions therein specified (and see R 45 below).

A serious absolutist view of similar provisions in England has been taken by the Courts there. In *Jones & Sons v Barnett* [1955] 1 QB 78 it was held if the brakes are not efficient both driver and owner can be charged with using the vehicle and that no 'mens rea' is required. In *Hawkins v Holmes* (1974) RTR 436 it was held that it was not a defence for a driver to show a regular system of maintenance. In *Smith v Nugent* (1955) LT 60 a missing handbrake rachet was held to be defect of construction as well as of maintenance.

R 41 *Brakes on trailers*—a trailer must be provided with scotches or chocks to hold it stationary, or brakes if it has more than two wheels or exceeds 15 cwt laden weight. Some must have service brakes.

R 42 *Combinations*—every combination of vehicles must have adequate brakes on both drawing vehicles and combinations.

R 43 *Service brake*—the regulation sets out specification of service brakes and how they should work.

R 44 *Parking brake*—must be operable from the driving seat and, in the case of a trailer when not attached, by persons standing outside trailer. Under the 2nd Schedule this should be sufficient to hold a vehicle or trailer stationary on a gradient of 16%, or a combination of vehicles on a gradient of 8%.

R 45 *Miscellaneous requirements*—all brakes to act together, be easily adjustable and accessible to maintenance and inspection, with a warning visible in relation to pressures, e.g. a red light on the dashboard.

Maintenance (para 8 of R 45)—'Every braking device shall be maintained in good and efficient working order and shall be properly adjusted'. This duty of maintenance of brakes is absolute (*Green v Burnett* [1954] 3 All ER 273), but a defence is provided by R 47 and 48 when an emergency occurs (and see above under R 40).

R 46 *Standard of performance of brakes*—various standards of stopping distances at specified speeds are set out in the 2nd Schedule to the 1963 Regulations for various types of vehicles for both service and emergency brakes, with the specification of the maximum pressure to be applied on the device, e.g. a non-passenger vehicle weighing over 2 tons unladen should have a service brake capable of stopping it within 66 feet and an emergency brake capable of stopping it within 132 feet at 25 mph with 150 lbs pressure on the brake. Time limits of working performance are laid down in detail. Reference should be made to the regulations for any problem that arises in those fields. The Rules of the Road guidelines are based on these regulations. (See Chapter 3 for speed and stopping distances).

In *Kennett v British Airport Authority* [1975] Crim LR 106 the fact that the disc brake on one wheel was badly worn made it mandatory to convict of maintaining a non-efficient braking system. In *R v Chadwick* [1975] Crim LR 105 the distances in the Rules of the Road were considered inadmissible hearsay evidence. An informal test (policeman could push the vehicle when the handbrake was on) will suffice (*Stoneby v Richardson* (1973) RTR 229).

R 47 *Defence*—it is a good defence to show that contravention of above regulations arose on the day and in the course of the journey in question, and that the vehicle was parked immediately and the defect remedied.

R 48 *Owner's liability*—the owner is also liable for breaches of this Part unless he shows that use of his vehicle was unauthorised.

(e) Parts V and **VI** concern additional requirements for small and large public service vehicles These provisions of the regulations are dealt with at Part 2 of Chapter 1 below.

(f) Part VII specifies drivers' duties:

R 85 *Noise*—driver must not use a vehicle causing excessive noise because of a defect in the vehicle or a faulty load. It is a defence to show that the noise was due to a temporary accidental cause to a defective design, or to default by person whose duty it was to maintain the vehicle. See R 29 as to the fitting of a silencer and R 30 as to exhausts.

R 86 *Horn*—must be used for warning only, and then only where reasonably necessary for safety or to give alarm of theft. It can only be used between 11.30 pm and 7 am within a 30 or 40 mph speed limit area when necessary to avoid immediate danger or to give alarm as to theft. Exceptions also exist for police and emergency services. See R 28 as to the fitting of a horn.

R 87 *Stationary vehicle*—shall not be left unattended unless (a) the engine is stopped, (b) the engine is closed off, if so capable, (c) the door is locked, (d) the ignition key or similar device is removed, and (e) the parking brake is on—unless Garda or parking attendant requires otherwise. 'Attendant' means there must be a person able to keep the vehicle under observation and prevent interference (*Starfire Diamond Rings Ltd v Angel* 1962 106 Sol Jo 854). See para 1.10 below and para 1.24.

R 88 *Races*—racing is prohibited on roads unless a closed portion of the road is allowed under s 35 of the Local Government Act 1955, or it takes place in a reliability test at reasonable speeds. (see para 5.10). This Regulation is now obsolete in reality.

R 89 It is not permitted to *discharge from closets*, urinals, etc. on to a road. See also R 33 above.

R 90 *Emission* of fumes, smoke, etc. is restricted. See also R 30 as to exhausts.

R 91 *Passengers on motor cycles*—limited to one, sitting behind the driver on a proper seat. The passenger must wear a helmet, as must the driver under the 1978 Regulations.

1.5.5.3 *Construction use and equipment*

R 92 *General duties* of drivers and others include:

(a) the driver, must not drive if his view of the road or control of the vehicle is seriously diminished. See also Rs 23, 25 and 26;
(b) passengers must not wilfully obstruct, impede, interfere with or distract the driver;
(c) the door should not be opened or allowed to remain open unnecessarily. Cases on this regulation and its breach are *Watson v Lowe* [1950] 1 All ER 100 and *Baldwin v Rearson* (1958) 122 JP 321;
(d) passengers should not alight where this causes danger or obstruction;
(e) fuel cap should not be removed while the vehicle is running.

(g) Part VIII contains miscellaneous provisions:

R 93 *Pedal cycles*—must have (a) a *bell* capable of being heard at a reasonable distance, and (b) an efficient *braking* device.

R 94 *Pedestrial controlled vehicles*—must be capable of being efficiently braked.

R 95 *Track laying vehicles*—must have efficient braking systems.

R 96 *Maintenance*—all vehicles must be maintained so as not be a danger. In *O'Neill v Browne* [1961] 1 QB 420 it was held that the vehicle, accessories and parts should not only be in good repair but also working efficiently, e.g. coupling properly done. See also *Reeve v Webb* (1973) RTR 130.

The obligation is absolute—*Austin Ltd v East* [1961] Crim LR 119 where the defect was latent (trailer locking equipment) and the trailer came loose during a journey. In *Hawkins v Bepey* (1980) RTR 392 the manufacturer's instructions were admitted to show the suitability of the vehicle or trailer for a particular use. In *Hollis v Bailey* [1968] 1 WLR 663 a badly stacked vehicle which caused danger was held not to be within the regulation which has to do with maintenance.

Wheels must be such as not to damage the road.

The Load must be adjusted so as not to interfere with the vehicle and must be consistent with the carrying capacity of the vehicle.

R 97 *Experimental vehicles*—the Minister for the Environment can allow by special permit experimental vehicles to be used, on such conditions as he specifies, which would otherwise be in contravention of the regulations.

Regulation 97 is amended by R 6 of SI 158/1985, which allows the Minister to issue permits for special vehicles, including one-person-operated buses, subject to conditions.

1.5.5.4 *Amending regulations*. The following is a list of amending Road Traffic, etc. regulations:

Road Traffic (Construction, Equipment and Use of Vehicles) (Amendment) Regulations 1965 (SI 79/1965). These effect 12 minor amendments to the

1963 Regulations. They also provide for:

(a) safety anchorages for seat belts, which must be fitted for front seats in all new cars;

(b) chassis marks. The name of the manufacturer must be marked indelibly on all trailers or semi-trailers over $3\frac{1}{2}$ tons laden weight and on every goods trailer with a weight unladen over 1 ton; they also have to be marked with the date of construction or assembly and a special serial number.

Road Traffic (Construction, Equipment and Use of Vehicles) (Amendment) Regulations 1967 (SI 293/1967). Defence forces equipment on certain vehicles is exempt from regulations as to suspension, tyres and brakes, by this regulation. Under the 1965 Regulations they were exempt from requirements as to wings, view of the road, rear view mirrors and speedometer provisions.

Road Traffic (Construction, Equipment and Use of Vehicles) (Amendment) Regulations 1969 (SI 138/1969). Tractors not exceeding $7\frac{1}{4}$ tons must have safety frames. There are exemptions, i.e. the driving components of an articulated vehicle and a mechanically propelled harvester. Certain auto types of frame are allowable, i.e. ones which comply with either the Optional Test (15) for Safety Cabs and Frames in The Standard Code for the Official Testing of Agricultural Tractors from the OECD (Organisation for Economic Co-operation and Development) Document C (66) 1935 (Final) of 30 January 1967 annexed to No. 79/1966 series in Agriculture & Food; or a frame marked with a manufacturer's test mark or number granted by the OECD.

Road Traffic (Construction, Equipment and Use of Vehicles) (Amendment) Regulations 1970 (SI 211/1970). These regulations allowed public service vehicles to have an overall length of 12 metres. They revoked R 62 of the 1963 Regulations dealing with the steering requirements of such vehicles.

Road Traffic (Construction, Equipment and Use of Vehicles) (Amendment) Regulations 1971 (SI 96/1971). These regulations made it obligatory to fit safety belts and anchorage points of specified standards for the front seats of all cars, station wagons and light goods vehicles first registered after 1 June 1971. Anchorage points alone were provided for by the 1965 Regulations. Safety belts must meet the prescribed standard, i.e. in accordance with the Regulation as per the EEC Directive of 28 June 1977, No 77/541/EEC. It was the 1978 Regulations (see below) that made the use of safety belts compulsory, stipulated that both the user and owner commit an offence, and applied the general penalty (see para 7.1).

Road Traffic (Construction, Equipment and Use of Vehicles) (Amendment) Regulations 1974 (SI 297/1974). These regulations provide for three children under 15 years of age to be treated as two adults in calculating the passenger accommodation of large public service vehicles used for school transport. (See also Part 2).

Road Traffic (Construction, Equipment and Use) (Amendment) Regulations (No 2) 1978 (SI 360/1978). The 1978 Regulations made the use of *seat belts* compulsory, except for—

(i) a Small Public Service Vehicles Licence holder under Part IV of SI 191 of 1963;
(ii) a driving instructor;
(iii) a driving tester conducting a competency test under Road Traffic Acts;
(iv) a Garda or defence forces member on duty;
(v) a person with a special substantial reason for not wearing a seat belt;
(vi) a person with a physical or mental disability, or medical or psychological considerations making it undesirable or inadvisable for him to wear a seat belt. He must produce a medical certificate to that effect within a month;
(vii) a person who, because of inconvenience or risk to person or property, finds it unreasonable for him to wear a seat belt, having regard to the nature of the use of the vehicle at the time;
(viii) in an exempt vehicle, e.g. electrically propelled goods vehicles capable of doing less than 24 miles per hour.

The burden of Proof of an exemption is on the defence on the balance of probabilities (*R v Carr-Briant* [1943] 2 All ER 150).

The driver is prohibited from allowing the front passenger seat to be occupied by—

(a) a person under 17 years who is over 150 cm in height, unless the person is wearing a seat belt; or
(b) A Child under 12 years and under 150 cm in height unless a means of restraint for the safety of that person is used;

unless in each such case no reasonable alternative seating accommodation is available for the person. It should be noted that non-compliance with the regulations has civil law consequences. Non use of a seat belt is normally considered contributory negligence if such non use contributed to the severity of the injuries (*Hamill v Oliver* [1977] IR 73.)

The 1978 Regulations make it mandatory for the driver and passenger of a motor cycle to wear *crash helmets* of prescribed standards. It is an additional offence for the driver to allow his passenger to travel without a crash helmet. The general penalty applies (para 7.1). In *Crank v Brooks* (1980) RTR 441 it was held that the need to wear a crash helmet does not arise while the driver is propelling the bike on foot. See also R 91 of the 1963 Regulations.

Road Traffic (Construction, Equipment and Use of Vehicles) (Amendment) Regulations 1983 (SI 119/1983). These have been largely replaced by the 1986 Regulations and dealt with *weight*. They substituted Art 5(2) of the 1963 Regulations.

Road Traffic (Construction, Equipment and Use of Vehicles) (Amendment) Regulations 1985 (SI 158/1985). These prescribe additional vehicle safety requirements by the fitting on new vehicles from 1 January 1986 of—

(a) laminated glass windscreens;
(b) rear under rim protective devices and side guards to goods vehicles and trailers of over 1524 kg (1½ tons), with certain exceptions. These regulations also allow the Minister for the Environment to issue permits for special vehicles, including one-man-operated buses, subject to conditions.

Road Traffic (Construction, Equipment and Use of Vehicles) (Amendment) Regulations 1986 (SI 278/1986). These basically substituted new R 7 and 11 in the 1963 Regulations. (see para 1.5.5.3 **(b)**. These new provisions increase permitted maximum *weights* and *lengths* of vehicles, which are expressed in metric form.

1.5.5.5 *Visitors.* Under the Mechanically Propelled Vehicles (International Circulation) Order 1961 (SI 193 of 1963 as amended), visitors are non-residents making a temporary stay in the State. This regulation exempts in a rather complicated way certain vehicles brought in temporarily by non-residents from the 1963 Regulations and certain amending regulations.

The extent of the exemption depends on whether the vehicle is registered in a State which is party to the Paris Convention of 1926 and/or the Geneva Convention of 1949. If the Paris Convention applies, then only the provisions dealing with weight, width, length, height of vehicles and trailers and the number of trailers apply. If the Geneva Convention applies, there is a wider exemption—only the regulations as to trailers apply.

1.6 Control of lighting

1.6.1 Need for lighting

The importance of vehicle lighting is self evident. It enables the driver to see and the vehicle to be seen. Therefore, stringent controls are in force. There are in existence a number of regulations under s 11 of the 1961 Act, even though the section does not specifically refer to lighting. Lights and reflectors are included, however, in the definition of 'vehicle equipment' in s 11(6) of the 1961 Act.

It will be noted later that the absence of lighting is an offence under s 55 of the 1961 Act as amended (see also Dangerous Parking at para 4.7), which increases that offence's penalty substantially.

Under s 11 of the 1961 Act, therefore, regulations can and have been made specifically regulating lighting. The regulations are long and complicated. The basic set of 1963 comprise 84 pages. These have been amended and added to and need to be consolidated. Modern amendments reflect the approximation of the law of Member States of the EEC.

1.6.1 *Control of lighting*

1.6.2 Lighting of vehicles regulations

The following regulations are in force controlling the use of vehicles in public places in respect of lights:

(1) Road Traffic (Lighting of Vehicles) Regulations 1963 (SI 189/1963).
(2) Road Traffic (Lighting of Vehicles) (Amendment) Regulations 1967 (SI 32/1967).
(3) Road Traffic (Lighting of Vehicles) (Amendment) Regulations 1970 (SI 128/1970).
(4) Road Traffic (Lighting of Vehicles) (Amendment) Regulations 1979 (SI 382/1979).
(5) Road Traffic (Lighting of Vehicles) (Amendment) Regulations 1985 (SI 157/1985).

An outline only of the main provisions is given below. In relation to any particular regulation the Statutory Instrument should be consulted to obtain the specific wording of the provisions.

1963 Regulations (SI 189/1963)

Part I

R 3 *Definitions*. There are a large number of these.
The most important is 'Lighting up hours', which means the period commencing half an hour after sunset on any day and expiring half an hour before sunrise on the next day. 'Sunset' means sunset according to local (not Greenwich) time (*Gardan v Cann* (1899) 63 JP 324).

In many of the regulations the term 'visible for a reasonable distance' is used—see *Silke v Whelan* 73 ILTR 248 as to its meaning, i.e. that another road user could see at a distance that there was another vehicle ahead. It is not necessary that he be able to identify the vehicle.

R 5 *Owner's liability* attaches to certain regulations unless the owner shows that the vehicle's use was unauthorised. These regulations are specified in the regulation. As to defences, see R 54 on Damaged Equipment.

R 6 *Maintenance* is necessary for all lights once fitted, e.g. kept clean. As to defences, see R 54 (Damaged Equipment).

R 7 An effective *combination* of lights is acceptable, i.e. a number of lamps, such as a head lamp and side lamp, in one unit.

Part II Obligatory Lighting

R 8 This Part applies to all vehicles (including trailers) and combinations, except cycles and invalid carriages.
(See Part III of these regulations as to these excepted types. Part IV deals with pedal cycles etc.)

R 9 Sets out *obligatory lighting—(a)* Every vehicle, other than a trailer, must have side, head, rear and stop lamps and identification mark lighting, according to the specifications on the regulations. *(b)* Trailers require side, rear and stop lights and identification lighting. *(c)* Marker lamps, etc. are provided for. *(d)* There are special provisions for different combinations of vehicles. *(e)* Rear and lateral projecting lamps are to be fitted to certain vehicles as well as marker lamps. *(f)* Direction indicators must be fitted. Exemption for racing vehicles is provided for under R. 53.

R 10 *Side lamps* must be visible 500 feet away at night in clear weather and not more than 5 feet from the ground; otherwise as per regulations. They must show diffused light, etc.

R 11 *Head lamps* must comprise 2 or 4 lamps, with white or yellow light, showing 325 feet in front etc.

R 12 *Rear lamps* must be visible from 500 feet and be of certain sizes, etc.

R 13 *Stop lamps* must show red, be of a certain size, etc. and be activated by the foot brake.

R 14/15 *Rear and lateral projecting lamps* must meet certain specifications.

R 16 *Marker lamps* must not exceed 7 watts, and must not be more than 5 feet from the ground.

R 17 *Internal lights* must be fitted in certain places in large and small public service vehicles.

R 18 *Direction indicators* are dealt with in detail as to type, colour, etc. on vehicles, trailers, combinations, etc.

R 19 *Identification mark lighting* should be placed over the number plate and be visible 65 feet away.

R 20 *Use of lighting obligatory*. Subject to exemptions in Part VII, all lights (side, rear, etc.) must be duly lit.

Note: Ambulances, Gardai and defence forces vehicles have conditional exemption from this Part under R 52.

Part III Obligatory Lighting of Mechanical cycles and Invalid carriages

R 22 Every cycle and invalid carriage must have position lamps, rear, lamps, identification mark lighting, a head lamp, and, in some cases, stop lamps as per the regulations. Owner liable. There is an exemption for racing vehicles under R 53.

R 23 *Position lamps* must be visible 500 feet ahead and comply with other details set out in the regulation.

R 24 *Rear lamps* must be visible 500 feet away and comply with other details set out in R 24.

R 25 *Indentification mark lighting* means a white light enabling the number plate to be seen 65 feet away.

R 26 *The head lamp* must illuminate the road 325 feet ahead and as per the specifications set out.

R 27 *The stop lamp* must come on when the service (foot) brake is operated. Details are set out in the regulation.

R 28 *Use of lighting* is mandatory in lighting up time, except for a reasonable period before and after if there is adequate lighting, or when the vehicle is stopped, or in a public lighting area.

Part IV Other Vehicles

R 29 *Pedal cycles* must have a front lamp, rear lamp, and reflector (see R 33 below).

R 30 *Animal drawn vehicles* must carry a right front lamp and a right rear lamp, showing white in front and red to the rear. The owner is liable.

R 31 *Hand propelled vehicles* require a right front lamp and a right rear lamp, showing white in front and red to the rear.

R 32 *Detached Trailers* must have side lamps and rear lamps as set out.

Part V Reflectors and Advance Warning Signs

R 33 *Obligatory rear reflectors* are required for almost every vehicle. Owner liable. Certain exemptions apply.

R 34 Their appearance and size is dealt with in this regulation.

R 35 Their position is set out, i.e. not more than 3 feet from the ground.

R 36 *Projecting loads must have reflectors*. Details are set out in the regulation. Owner liable.

R 37 Restriction on the use of non-specified reflectors, i.e. owners can only use a specified type, size, colour, etc. Owner liable. An exemption applies to racing vehicles under R 53.

R 38 *An advance warning device* must be kept in goods vehicles exceeding $1\frac{1}{2}$ tons unladen. The design, etc. is specified. It must be produced to the Gardai on request.

R 39 *Reflectorized material* is prohibited with certain exceptions. Owner liable.

See also SI 129/1970 below.
Note: Ambulances, Gardai and defence forces vehicles have conditional exemption from this Part under R 52 (see also paras 7.2. and 7.8).

Part VI General Requirements

R 40 All mechanically propelled vehicles and trailers *must comply* with all of Part IV. Other vehicles must comply with RS 41, 42, 45 and 48 only.

R 41 *Restrictions on colours*. White or yellow to front, red to rear only. Exception specified.

R 42 *Flashing lights* are prohibited. Exception for direction indicators.

R 43 *Lighting movement* is prohibited. No movable lamps are allowed, except as per regulations, i.e. normally the driver is not allowed to have lamps the beam of which can be altered. Other regulations require dipping devices. SI 32/1967 allows hazard lights and other exceptions.

R 44 *Height of lamps* is normally restricted to between 1 foot 8 inches and 4 feet above ground.

R 45 *Optional direction indicators and stop lamps* are provided for.

R 46 *Electrical arrangements* should be such as not to effect other lights.

R 47 *Dipping devices* must be fitted to front lights. As to their use, see R 49.

R 48 *Misleading and dazzling* lamps are prohibited.

R 49 *Use of lighting—(a)* Parked vehicles must show only side lamps, head lamps, or direction indicators. *(b)* Head lamps must be dipped in good time against oncoming traffic and in speed limit areas (except where street lights are not on) and in fog or snow (amended by SI 32/1967). *(c)* Indicators must be used to indicate direction, except where they are used as hazard lights. *(d)* Reversing lamps only for reversing. *(e)* Ploughing lamps, movable lamps, fog lamps are limited in their use.

Many regulations specify lights must be 'visible from a reasonable distance', and in *Silke v Whelan* 73 ILTR p 248 the High Court held this to be no more than that other road users can perceive at a reasonable distance that there are lights.

Part VII Exemptions

R 50 *Lawfully parked vehicles*, where street lighting is on, are exempt from lighting requirements if they are clearly visible and not a danger. If the vehicle is a street service vehicle or horse hackney it must be at its lawful stand. Small public service vehicles, station wagons and small goods vehicles are exempt if they have one outside front and one rear light. See para 4.7 as to Dangerous Parking.

Parked bicycles are also generally exempt.

R 51 *Private parking*. Vehicles parked on provided ground, even, if a public place, are exempt provided they do not cause a danger. The owner of the place has to give permission for such parking. However, the provision of s 55 of the 1961 Act as to Dangerous Parking (see para 4.7) should be borne in mind in respect of dangerously unlit parked vehicles. Each case will largely depend on its own facts, but the position on the road, the amount of vehicle traffic around, street lighting, etc. are all relevant factors in considering if an offence is created under the section or under these regulations.

R 52 Exemptions and modifications of certain vehicles—

(a) *land vehicles*, factory, or building site vehicles are generally exempt during day-time use from the requirements;

(b) *public service vehicles* (large) have certain special provisions as to positions of lamps. They are exempt from the precise terms of R 19 on identification mark lighting;

(c) *electrical vehicles* enjoy certain exemptions;

(d) *ambulances, blood delivery vehicles, breakdown vehicles, refuse vehicles, telephone, gas, ESB vehicles*;
(e) *Gardai, defence force and airport vehicles* enjoy certain exemptions from parts of the general regulation (amended by SI 328/1979) and can have a blue flashing light on the roof and be used in certain circumstances.

R 53 *Racing vehicles* are exempt from RS 9, 22, 29 and 33.
R 54 Defence in case of damaged equipment—

(a) *During day-time.* If charged with contravention of the regulations during day-time, it is a defence to show that the defect occurred during the journey or that it was due to a defect in respect of which steps had been taken to remedy it with all reasonable expedition. These defences are not available in respect of stop lamps or indicators (except in the case of parked vehicles).
(b) *During lighting up time.* The only defence available is if the vehicle is parked off the road in a safe position, and that the defect arose while or immediately before parking, and that steps to remedy the defect were taken at the earliest opportunity.
(c) *Breakdown or accident.* It is a defence to show that the vehicle was parked as result of either a breakdown or an accident, and that the lighting defect was a result of either such breakdown or accident, and that all practical warnings were given and an effort made to remove the vehicle to safety. It is no defence, however, that the lamp had blown unknown to the driver (*Howman v Russell* (1923) SLT 336 where a stone broke the glass of a rear lamp). Presumably this is still good law as the regulations seem to exclude *mens rea* by allowing only special defences. See also the case of *Maitland v Raisheck* [1944] All ER 272.
(d) *Towed away.* If a defect in lighting is detected and the vehicle is towed away as soon as practicable to have the lighting defect repaired, this is a good defence. It must be towed to a safe place as soon as practical so as to avoid danger to other traffic.

Road Traffic (Lighting of Vehicles) (Amendment) Regulations 1967 (SI 32/1967)

These regulations make minor amendments to the 1963 Regulations noted above. They also permit the fitting and use of *obstruction lamps* and *search lights* on ambulances, fire fighting, rescue, and radio service vehicles, and on the property of the Minister for Transport and Power in airports, etc.

Road Traffic (Lighting of Vehicles) (Amendment) Regulations 1970 (SI 128/1970)

These regulations require reflex reflecting and fluorescent markings to be displayed on the rear and sides of—

(a) goods vehicles exceeding 2 tons unladen, except dumpers;

(b) articulated goods vehicles exceeding 2 tons unladen and drawing components of the same; and
(c) tractors other than land tractors.

Definitions of these types of vehicles are given in the regulations. Exemption is granted to defence force vehicles, Fire Brigades and vehicles in the course of assembly. The same reflectors and markings must be affixed to the sides of trailers in a combination of vehicles where the overall length of the combination exceeds 11 metres, e.g. boat trailers, caravans, etc. These markings must be as specified in the schedules to the regulations and must be displayed at all times while the vehicle is in use in a public place. A partial exemption is given during loading or unloading which is likely to cause damage to the markings.

Road Traffic (Lighting of Vehicles) (Amendment) Regulations 1979 (SI 326/1979)

These regulations inserted a new sub-Art 52(18) in SI 189/1963 to allow the fitting of amber flashing lamps to certain categories of stationary or slow moving vehicles.

Road Traffic (Lighting of Vehicles) (Amendment) Regulations 1985 (SI 157/1985)

These regulations amend the 1963 Lighting Regulations so as to require the display of a 'Long Vehicle' sign or signs on the rear of goods vehicles exceeding 13 metres (42·8″) in length. Exceptions are provided for defence force vehicles, Fire Brigades, certain vehicles in the course of assembly and broken-down vehicles on tow. The regulations specify the configuration format, material, design, manner of affixing the sign(s), etc. They require such sign(s) to be kept clean and unobstructed.

1.6.3 Visitors

The Mechanically Propelled Vehicles (International Circulation) Order 1961 (SI 193/1963), as amended, exempts visitors' vehicles if they comply with the lighting requirements of The Geneva Convention 1949 or Paris Convention 1926 and are efficient and duly lit.

1.7 Control of weight

1.7.1 General

The weight of a vehicle has many implications. This applies to both its laden and unladen weight. Weight affects matters such as its safety, impact on to road surfaces, the taxation paid on the vehicle, drivers licences, etc. The Acts have a series of controls which are therefore applicable to weight. These are contained mainly in Part II of the 1961 Act, as amended by the Schedule of the 1968 Act, with further minor amendments in the 1984 Act.

1.7.1 *Control of weight*

These controls are in summary as follows:

(a) The Minister of the Environment is given power to make regulations controlling the maximum weight of mechanically propelled vehicles, trailers and combinations and the weight transmitted to axle or wheel—s 12 of the 1961 Act, as amended.
(b) The Minister is empowered to make regulations exempting by permit specific vehicles—s 13 of the 1961 Act, as amended.
(c) Road Authorities (e.g. County Councils) can permit vehicles to take exceptional loads for particular journeys, subject to safeguards—s 13 of the 1961 Act, as amended.
(d) Unladen weight is defined—s 14 of the 1961 Act, as amended.
(e) Road Authorities are enabled to appoint official weighbridges for the purpose of weighing vehicles—s 15 of the 1961 Act, as amended.
(f) Road Authority Officers and Gardai can require a vehicle to be weighed in certain circumstances—s 16 of the 1961 Act, as amended.
(g) Compensation damage done to public roads by vehicles can be recovered—s 17 of the 1961 Act.

The consequences which may follow from breach of the weight provisions are:

(i) criminal law sanctions. There are general penalties for normal breaches and also a series of special penalties for special excess weight in addition to the normal penalty. More than one prosecution can arise from excess weight—see *Theobald v Stacy* (1979) RTR 411 where the defendant was convicted for exceeding the overall gross weight and the weight of each two axles on three summonses;
(ii) compensation in the civil courts for the damage done to roads or bridges.

1.7.2 Maximum weight

1.7.2.1 *Statutory provisions.* Modern transport conditions and the exigencies of EEC membership require flexible standards to be available in dealing with weight standards applicable to vehicles. It is through the medium of regulations by the Minister for the Environment that the Acts seek to deal with this problem of weight, and thus a certain flexibility in regulation is achieved.

By s 11 of the 1961 Act (amended by Sch, 1968 Act and by s 3(2) of the 1984 Act), the Minister is empowered to fix maximum laden and unladen weights for vehicles or trailers or combinations of vehicles, plus the manner of calculating that weight and also the maximum weight to be transmitted to the ground by any part of a vehicle. These regulations can specify different standards for different classes of vehicles or combinations of vehicles, or in different circumstances.

A new concept was introduced in relation to weight calculation for the classification of vehicles in drivers licences applications. This is from the EEC Directive 80/1263/EEC. It provides for categories of vehicles to be defined by 'permissible maximum weight'. This subject is dealt with at para 2.3.3.

1.7.2.2 *Liability.* Use of a vehicle contravening these weight regulations on a public road is prohibited, whether the contravention is based on the weight of the vehicle, the combination of vehicles, or a fault indicated by a plate or certificate for the vehicle (see paras 1.7.4 and 1.7.5 below). The owner (if he is not the user) is also guilty of an offence unless he can show the user was unauthorised. The general penalty applied until s 3(2) of the 1984 Act substituted a fine not exceeding £350 and/or three months' imprisonment or both. There are extra penalties for excess weight beyond certain limits (see para 1.7.11).

1.7.2.3 *1963 Regulations.* These regulations should be looked at closely when dealing with a particular problem. There follows here only a summary of SI 190/1963 (Road Traffic (Construction Equipment and Use of Vehicles) Regulations 1963) Part II, as amended, which deals with the problem of maximum weight.

Regulation 5 deals with the interpretation of the Part.

Regulation 6 provides that the owner is liable for contravention of the regulations. See also para 1.7.1. above.

The current R 7 was substituted by Amending Regulations SI 442 of 1986. It provides as follows:

(a) The weight transmitted to the road by any wheel of a vehicle or trailer shall not exceed 5,250 kg, if the wheel has a pneumatic tyre.
(b) The limit is 16 kg per each millimetre width of cross contact surface if a soft tyre.
(c) Otherwise the limit is 10 kg for each millimetre of contact with the ground width.
(d) Furthermore, the total weight transmitted to the road by a vehicle or trailer with a single axle shall not exceed 10,170 kgs. For such vehicles with axles less than 1 metre apart the limit is 11,180 kg; for two single axles of between 1 metre and 1.2 metres (m) apart it is not to exceed 17,230 kg; Axles 1.2m to 3.5m—18,300 kg; axles 1.3m to 1.5m—18,800 kg; axles 1.5m to 1.8m—19,320 kg; axles 1.8m to 1.85m—20,000 kg; axles over 1.85m—20,340 kg. For three or more axles in a semi-trailer the maximum weight permissible is 22,890 kg, and there is a detailed scale set out in a Table in the Regulations as to the weight on any one axle in such vehicles, depending on their distance apart.
(e) In addition, vehicles, not being articulated, or a trailer attached have the following laden weight limits—

   (i) where there are two axles on the vehicle—17,000 kg,

   (ii) for a trailer with two axles, if the axles are less than 3m apart—16,260 kg,

(iii) where a vehicle or trailer has three axles and the distance between the extreme front and rear axles is less than 4.6m - 22,360 kg.; distance of 4.6m or more—24,390 kg,

(iv) where there are four or more axles and the distance between the extreme front and rear axles is less than 5.6m—25,410 kg; between 5.6m and 5.9m—26,420 kg; between 5.9m and 6.3m—28,450 kg; for 6.3m or more—30,490 kg.

(f) For articulated vehicles the maximum laden weight is—

(i) for two axles where the distance between front and rear is less than 2.7m—16,260 kg; if more than 2.7m—1,700 kg,

(ii) if there are three or more axles the weights totally and per axles are set out in detail and in various tables. These should be consulted in each individual case.

(g) Track laying vehicles are limited in their laden weight to 7,400 kg normally, but there is no limit if they are being loaded or unloaded on to a conveying vehicle, or while travelling up to 100m to such conveying vehicle.

(h) There is a general limit set on combinations of vehicles. Their laden weight must not exceed, for a vehicle and one trailer, 35,000 kg; or where there are five or more axles and the distance between the front and rear axles exceeds 3.7m, 38,000 kgs.

These standards are mostly international EEC standards and operate from 1 January 1987. See EEC Directive 85/3/EEC (OJ No L2/14 of 3 January 1985). There are certain short-term derogations in relation to EEC standards. For conversion purposes, it is to be remembered that 1 metre = 1.063 yards; 1 yard = 36 inches = 0.9144m; 1 kilogram (KG) = 2.2046 lbs; 1000 kg (1 tonne) = 0.9842 ton.

Regulation 8 of the 1963 Regulations deals with *marking* of weight (see para 1.8.5). As to *distribution* of weight, R 9 provides that weight should be distributed (or compensated for) so that each wheel will remain in contact with the road and not be subject to abnormal variations in adverse conditions. The regulation does not apply to any steerable wheel of a vehicle which does not transmit more than 2½ tons to the road surface.

1.7.2.4 *Special permits.* By virtue of s 13 of the 1961 Act the Minister has power to make regulations specifying that particular vehicles or combinations of vehicle may contravene the general (s 12) weight limits without legal penalty, on such conditions as are fixed. These special permits can contain safeguards by way of limitations, restrictions and conditions. Any such conditions can deal with compensation and deposits therefor for likely road damage. The regulations can specify by whom these special permits are to be granted and how they may be applied for.

Regulation 17 of the Road Traffic Construction Equipment and Use Regulations 1963 (SI 190 of 1963) (as amended by SI 79/1965, Schedule) deals with these permits at some length. Application is to be made to the appropriate local authority for special permits—County Councils, County Boroughs, and Corporations. Notice of the application has to be given seven days in advance to the Garda Commissioner, although this can be waived in urgent cases. The application must give specified details of the vehicle (including its weight, load, journey) and give an undertaking to compensate for road damage within 12 months of the last load. If the permit is granted and the vehicle is to travel an urban road, then the local Urban District Council must be notified.

In granting the permit the authority must be satisfied the compensation provisions are enforceable, and may demand deposits or security. The permit must describe the vehicle, (including its weight, load, journey) and set out whatever restrictions it considers appropriate, e.g. on weight, number of trailers, dimensions, speed, suspension, tyres, and wheels. A permit may on certain conditions allow the vehicle to travel on roads in other local authority areas, provided notice is given to those other authorities. The permit may run for up to a year but can be cancelled on seven days' notice. The permit must be carried on the vehicle.

1.7.3 Calculation of weight (unladen)

The following provisions are contained in s 14 of the 1961 Act, although the unladen weight of the vehicle is of no great significance for the Road Traffic Acts themselves. The real significance lies in taxation (see para 1.11).

Section 14 provides for the ascertaining of the unladen weight of a vehicle or combination of vehicles as follows:

(a) *Unladen weight* is the weight of the vehicle or combination *inclusive* of all additions (see (b) below) but *exclusive* of the weight of water, fuel or accumulators (other than boilers) used for the purpose of propulsion, and of loose tools or loose equipment. Similar provision is to be found in The Finance (Excise Duty) (Vehicles) (Amendment) Act 1960, where unladen weight is important for calculating tax payments (see para 1.11).

Loose equipment includes movable shelves (*Durling v Burton* (1928) SC (J) 11) but not loose boards fitted to the side of a lorry to enable it to carry a heavier load of coal (*Lowe v Stone* [1948] All ER 1076). In *LCC v Hayes Wharf Cartage Co* [1953] 2 All ER 34 ballast was held to be loose equipment.

(b) *Additions* are included in the calculation of the unladen weight. They are (i) a body, (ii) a part, (iii) a fitting, (iv) a receptacle (see (c) below), and any one or more of them is or are to be taken into the calculation. If there are a number of additions and only one is used at a time, then there is added the weight of the heaviest addition; if more than one is used, the weight of the heaviest combination is taken into account.

(c) *Receptacles* are one of the additions referred to above. It means anything placed on a vehicle or combination of vehicles for the purpose of the conveyance of goods or a burden of any other description, *unless* in relation to every journey such goods or such burdens are both loaded into and unloaded from it without its being removed from the vehicle or combination (i.e. container traffic). The defendant, however, carries the burden of proof of showing that he comes within the exception.

In *A.G (De Burca) v Murtagh* 95 ILTR 36 the High Court held (under the Finance (Excise Duties) (Vehicles) Act 1952 dealing with weight calculation) that a fitted container must be taken into account in calculating the unladen weight of a lorry. The container was a box-like arrangement with its own floor and sides but no roof. It was placed on the lorry and secured to it by claws when in use.

1.7.4 Weight plate—Certificate

For the purpose of facilitating ready and easy checking by the Gardai and others, provision is made by s 11 of the 1968 Act for the Minister for the Environment to specify that certain vehicles must exhibit a plate showing their maximum permissible weight. There must also be in force for the vehicle a certificate indicating the maximum weights which are not to be exceeded in the case of the vehicle, or any combination of vehicles of which it forms part. To use a vehicle in a public place without such a plate or certificate is an offence. The owner (if he is not the user) is also guilty of an offence, unless he shows the user was unauthorised. The general penalty applied until the 1968 Act, and under s 40 of the 1984 Act the penalty is increased to £350 maximum fine and/or three months' imprisonment.

To get a plate and certificate the owner applies to a prescribed Issuing Authority in the regulated manner. The Authority, on being satisfied that the application is properly made and the vehicle's weight does not exceed its proper maximum, must issue the plate and certificate.

Under s 115 of the 1961 Act it is an offence to give false particulars in order to obtain the plate or certificate; or to fraudulently alter, use, or allow to be used a false plate or certificate (see para 7.4).

The Minister has his usual broadly based power of making regulations to give effect to the above provisions, e.g. as to classes of vehicles affected, the mode of application and to whom the fees are payable, the forms of certificates and records to be kept, periods of validity, etc., with the power to make different provisions for the different classes of cases. If the regulation is penal its breach is an offence (which attracted the general penalty until s 4 of the 1984 Act increased the penalties to £350 maximum fine and/or three months' imprisonment).

It is also an offence under the section to destroy, damage, or deface a plate or certificate, again with maximum fine of £350, or imprisonment of up to three months or both penalties under s 4 of the 1984 Act.

1.7.5 Weight marking

Marking of weight generally is provided by R 8 of the Construction, Equipment and Use Regulations of 1963 (SI 190 see para 1.5.5.3). The unladen weight must be marked clearly on the rear or left side of all vehicles exceeding 2 tons unladen, on the drawing component of an articulated vehicle where the component exceeds 2 tons unladen, and on a trailer or semi-trailer exceeding 1 ton unladen. As to special provisions for trailers and semi-trailers see SI 35/1980 and para 1.3.6 *supra*.

1.7.6 Weighbridges

To ensure that the weighing of vehicles can be conveniently carried out by Gardai, Ministerial Inspectors and others so empowered, a legal framework for maintaining weighbridges is set up by s 15 of the 1961 Act (and Sch of the 1968 Act). The intention of the section is clear, even if the wording is confused by reference to 'appointed weighbridges' and the 'road traffic weighbridge' when both are apparently intended for the same purpose. The distinction appears to be that a road traffic weighbridge is provided by a Road Authority, whereas 'appointed weighbridges' are provided by others and appointed as official weighbridges under the Acts by the Road Authority appropriate. A local authority can 'appoint' a weighbridge in another local authority's area and may contribute to its cost. Again, many of the powers are similar to those under the Motor Tax Acts (para 1.11). A Road Authority can declare an existing weighbridge to be a road traffic weighbridge, or construct a weighbridge suitable to weigh road traffic vehicles and their loads at all reasonable times. The Minister can if he so wishes require a Road Authority to do so.

Road Authorities are County Councils, Corporations of County or other Boroughs and Urban District Councils (s 3 of the 1961 Act). (See para 7.8.) They can revoke any declaration of appointment. They can charge fees for the use of weighbridges, except where the weighing is requisitioned by its own officer, the Gardai or the Ministers Officer. There are in fact about 55 weighbridges available, most of them on or near national primary roads. It has been said that the number is to be increased (1987).

As we have seen above, Road Authorities can contribute to the maintenance or operation of weighbridges which do not belong to them for the purposes of the section. They can also provide mobile weighbridges and make them available to Gardai. The purpose of spelling out the powers to Road Authorities is to prevent them acting *ultra vires* by assisting in the operation of the Acts in these matters. It would appear to be intended, by inference from the terms of s 16 of the 1961 Act (see para 1.7.7), that these weighbridges would be situated only ten miles apart. When a Road Authority declares a weighbridge to be an 'appointed weighbridge' they must publish in at least two newspapers circulating in their functional area, a notice that such weighbridge has been so declared (Road Traffic (Weighbridge) Regulations 1963—SI 192/1963).

There is no authority in the Acts for stating how the accuracy of the weighbridge is to be determined, so presumably evidence of its accuracy from an expert would be necessary (contrast the Scottish case of *Grierson v Clarke* (1958) SLT 112 and the English case of *Nicholas v Penny* [1950] 1 All ER 89).

1.7.7 Request to weigh

To enforce the weight provisions of the Act certain persons called 'authorised officers' are empowered to require vehicles to be, *inter alia*, weighed (s 16 of the 1961 Act and Sch of the 1968 Act, and s 16 of the 1968 Act and s 3(3) of the 1984 Act).

These authorised officers are (a) Gardai, (b) officers or servants so designated by Road Authorities for the roads within their area, and (c) an officer by the Minister so authorised. These officers must produce their authorisation to so act, if requested by the person in charge of a vehicle. This does not apply to Gardai as they are *ex officio* entitled to act as an authorised officer. It should be noted that under s 111 of the 1961 Act the Garda would have to produce official identification unless in uniform (see para 7.2). It should also be noted that the powers of a Road Authority authorised officer only operate when the vehicle is observed in that Authority's area.

Before an authorised officer can act he must (i) observe a vehicle or combination of vehicles on a public road (and this road must be in 'his area', if a road authority officer), (ii) suspect that there is a contravention of the weight requirements for the vehicle, and (iii) if the suspected contravention relates to unladen weight, that there is no load or that it is one which can be unloaded without undue inconvenience. If these conditions are satisfied, then he can require the person in charge of the vehicle:

(a) forthwith to bring the vehicle as it is to a named appointed weighbridge within five miles by the shortest available route (see *Lovett v Payne* (1980) RTR 103—shortest route by Road is meant); *and*

(b) to carry the officer in the vehicle to the weighbridge; *and*

(c) to cause the vehicle to be weighed—or any part of it as the combination—with or without the load or additions, as appropriate, in the presence of the officer. 'Additions' has the meaning referred to above (para 1.7.3 (b)), except that no exception applies in this section as it does in the definition of 'receptacle' for anything placed on a vehicle or combination for the purpose of carrying goods in a receptacle; *and*

(d) if the unladen weight is that in question, to unload the vehicle or combination; *and*

(e) to allow inspection of any part of the vehicle to see if it complies with s 11 regulations regarding construction and use and s 12 (weight) regulations; *and*

(f) not to proceed further in the vehicle if and so long as either its weight, having been weighed, is in the officer's opinion in breach of the Acts, or it is in the opinion of the officer not complying with the regulations under ss 11 (construction) or 12 (weight) of the 1961 Act so as to be likely to cause damage to a public road. In this latter event a Garda can arrest without warrant a person who fails to comply with that request.

A person who contravenes a requirement under the section is guilty of an offence. The general penalty under s 102 of the 1961 Act applies (para 7.1). There is a provision for recompensation of the fee for weighing paid to a weighbridge not maintained by a Road Authority, back to the person paying it by the appropriate Road Authority.

1.7.8 Extraordinary traffic

To protect roads from heavy trucks, or rather to compensate Road Authorities, it is provided by s 17 of the 1961 Act (as amended by Sch, 1968 Act) that such authorities can claim compensation for extraordinary expenses incurred in public road repairs necessitated by excessive weight or other extraordinary traffic. However, it is not clear what 'other extraordinary traffic' means, although some guidance may be found in the old sections on this matter (see, for example s 1 of the Public Road Act 1911 (Vanstons Local Government Supplement, Vol 11, p; 196–207) and *Hill v Thomas* [1893] 2 QB 333). Section 17 itself does not appear to have come up for judicial interpretation as yet, and it is worded somewhat differently from the old Acts. *Hill v Thomas* (*supra*) indicates that 'extraordinary traffic' can connote more than a single vehicle and can include continuous and repeated user, which is out of the ordinary. Obviously heavy use for large building sites, etc. is envisaged by the section. See also para 5.14 for similar controls regarding construction sites and roadworks.

The section is not penal and traffic need not necessarily contravene legal limitations.

The following additional points are provided for in the section:

(1) The compensation is collectable as a simple contract debt in the High Court or at the election of the Road Authority in the Circuit or District Courts in the area where the damage was done or where the defendant resides or carries on business. While it is not stated, presumably the jurisdictions of the Circuit and District Courts are confined to their normal statutory jurisdictions of £15,000 or £2,500 respectively (1988 Jurisdictions). A person required to pay extraordinary expenses may agree on an amount with the Road Authority and pay it without judicial determination.

(2) Proceedings must be entered upon with the proper time limit which is—

(a) six months after completion of any contract or work where the damage is in consequence of any particular building contract or work extending over a long period; or

(b) otherwise, 12 months after the damage was done.

'Building contract or work' means operations carried out and 'work' means something *ejusdem generis* with a building contract (*Bromley RAC v Croydon Corp* [1908] 1 KB 353). 'Completion' was accepted by *Lancaster UDC v Fisher* [1907] 2 KB 516 and *Carlisle RDF v Carlisle Corp* [1909] 1 KB 471 as meaning completion of the constructional work comprised in the contract. It was held in *Norfolk CC v Green* 2 LGR 652 that 'particular' ruled out a series of contracts being treated together.

(3) The amount awarded is that which the Court is satisfied has been or is likely to be incurred by the Road Authority by reason of the damage from the extraordinary traffic. This is the equivalent of civil damages in tort on a restitution basis, but not allowing consequential loss, and there is no other sanction (fine, etc.) attached to the section. As to elements in calculation see *Aveland v Lucas* (1879) 5 CPD 211, at p 351.

(4) Exemptions are given to three groups—

(a) CIE Road Passenger Service (now Irish Bus and Dublin Bus under Act 31 of 1986);
(b) persons carrying on a passenger road service under a licence granted under the Road Transport Act 1932 (No. 2 of 1932) as amended (see para 1.35);
(c) a person carrying on a business authorised by a merchandise licence ('plate') under the Road Transport Act 1933 (No. 8/1933) (see para 1.35).

(5) The compensation is collectable from the person by whom or in consequence of whose order the weighted traffic was conducted. 'By whose order' is not confined to a person giving orders to a servant, but may include a person by whose determination and direction the traffic is taken along the road (*Kent CC v Gerard* [1897] AC 633).

'In consequence of' was considered in *Egham RDC v Gardon* [1909] 2 KB 120 where it was held that what happened is a consequence of the order if it naturally, though not inevitably, followed from the order.

The Road Authority can sue either the person giving the order or the person in consequence of whose order the damage was done (*Kent CC v Folkstone Corp* [1905] 1 KB 620).

1.7.9 Weight of international vehicles

It became necessary to implement EEC Council Directive 85/3/EEC (OJ No 12/14 dated 3 January 1985) on maximum weights, maximum dimensions and certain other technical characteristics of goods vehicles engaged in international traffic. This was done by The Road Traffic (Construction, Equipment and Use of Vehicles) (Amendment) Regulations 1986 (SI 442/K1986). In summary these provide as follows:

R 3 Introduces a number of definitions. 'International journey' is defined simply as a journey involving the crossing of one or more national frontiers. 'Refrigerated vehicles' are those constructed to carry goods at below ambient temperatures. Types of axles are also defined.

R 7 A vehicle or a combination of a vehicle and one trailer is deemed to comply with the general legal weight provisions (see para 1.72.) when undertaking an international journey if it complies with the following weights laden—

(a) *trailers* with two axles—not more than 18,000 kg; three axles—24,000 kg;
(b) *combinations* of a two axle vehicle with a three-axle trailer—maximum 38,000 kg; three-axle vehicles with a two- or three-axle trailer—maximum 38,000 kg;
(c) *articulated vehicles* of two axles with a three-axle semi-trailer—maximum 38,000 kg; a three-axle vehicle with a two- or three-axle semi-trailer—maximum 38,000 kg;
(d) *transmitted weight* by axles to road surface—maximum permitted is:
  (i) *single axles* of all vehicles—if sole driving axles, 10,500 kg; each other single axle, 10,000 kg,
  (ii) *tandem axles* of trailers or semi-trailers—the sum of the axle weights of a tandem axle shall not exceed 11,000 kg where the distance between the axles is less than 1m; 1m to 1.3m distance—16,000 kg; if 1.3m to 1.8m—18,000 kg; over 1.8m—20,000 kg,
  (iii) *The sum of axle weights* of a tri-axle shall not exceed, where the distance between adjacent axles is 1.3m—21,000 kg; where the distance is more than 1.3m—22,500 kg;
(e) *Driving axles* must bear at least 25% of the total laden weight of vehicle and trailer;
(f) *In combinations* the rear axle of the vehicle must not be less than 3m from the front axle of the trailer.

1.7.10 Weight on bridges

It is obvious that bridges can be more easily damaged than roads by exceptionally heavy traffic. Therefore, to protect bridges provision is made for regulating the weight and speed of vehicles on them, with criminal and civil sanctions. The placing of notices on bridges is provided for by s 93 of the 1961 Act, as amended by s 61 of the 1968 Act.

1.7.10.1 *Notices.* The body (e.g. County Council) liable to maintain bridges can, if it is reasonably necessary to ensure the protection of a bridge from excessive burdens, erect notices indicating restrictions of weight of vehicles that can pass over them. The restriction can be a total prohibition of vehicles over a specified weight or travelling at less than a specified speed, or passage may be allowed only on compliance with specified conditions. The notices have to be in the prescribed manner (as referred to below) and must be posted on the approaches to the bridge. There is a presumption of a notice being valid. Any person has a right to appeal to the Minister for the Environment against the placing of these notices. The Minister can give such directions as he thinks proper for the maintenance, removal or alteration of the notices, which directions must be complied within three days of their communication to the erector of the notices.

The general penalty (s 102 of the 1961 Act) (para 7.1) applies for failure to comply with the directions.

The Commissioner of the Garda Siochana can require additional signs to be erected to give advance warning of the prohibition notice.

The form of the bridge notice and the statement to be presented to the Minister on an appeal under this section are prescribed by the Road Traffic (Bridge Notice) Order 1933 (SI 108/1933) which is still in force under s 10 of the 1961 Act. The form of notice is as given in the Schedule to the Order and must be positioned so as to be reasonably legible to drivers. The statement must set out the location and identity of the erector of the notice, and contain a copy of the notice. Any objection must state what the objector wishes to be done, i.e. removal or alteration, and the grounds of appeal. A copy of this statement and of notice of the appeal must be sent to the erector by registered post.

1.7.10.2 *Weight*. The relevant weight stated on a bridge notice is that which is transmitted from the vehicle to the road. This is the weight of the vehicle or combination and of its load when stationary. It is not necessary to show that the forbidden weight is transmitted by all the wheels (*Martin v Robertson* (1949) SC (J) 19).

1.7.10.3 *Offence*. It is an offence to drive a vehicle or combination in prohibition of the notice. This is so even if it is subsequently found that the notice was not reasonably necessary. The general penalty (s 102 of the 1961 Act—para 7.1) applies.

1.7.10.4 *Damages*. Where a vehicle is involved in an offence as described in para 1.7.10.3 above and causes damage to a bridge, the authority responsible can sue for the damage done in civil action in a court of competent jurisdiction, i.e. District Court to £2,500; Circuit Court to £15,000; and the High Court has unlimited jurisdiction in this regard.

1.7.11 Penalties and special excess weight penalties

The general penalty applies for excess weight as outlined above, plus, in the case of damage to roads or bridges, the provision of compensation as stated at para 1.7.8 and 1.7.10.4 above.

However, s 15 of the 1968 Act lays down a scale of increasing additional fines for vehicles (or combinations of vehicles) exceeding this weight. The scale has been increased by s 4 of the 1984 Act. The weights not to be exceeded are 10,000 kg to 17,000 kg laden weight maximum, depending on the vehicles, as above. The owner of a vehicle exceeding the permitted weights is liable to the following fixed penalty (additional to the general penalty under s 12 of the 1961 Act) where the excess weight is not less than:

1,000 kg but is less than 2,000 kg—£50 extra
2,000 kg but is less than 3,000 kg—£100 "
3,000 kg but is less than 4,000 kg—£250 "
4,000 kg but is less than 5,000 kg—£350 "
Where excess weight is 5,000 kg or more—£650 "

In assessing these penalties, however, credit must be given for any payments made or compensation awarded under the extraordinary traffic provision (para 1.7.8 *supra*) and the bridge damage (para 7.10.4) provisions. Subsection (2) of s 15 of the 1968 Act provides that the penalty is payable to the Road Authority responsible for the maintenance of the road in which the offence was committed. In using the term 'committed' it is possible that the subsection could be taken to mean that an admission for conviction for driving the load through several Road Authorities' areas could result in several penalties. Normally, however, it will mean that the Road Authority in whose area where the offence is detected collects the penalty.

'*Excessive weight*' has complicated definition under s 15(5) of the 1968 Act, which states, in brief, that in single vehicles the excess weight is the excess over the maximum regulated laden weight; in combinations it means a similar excess in the combination, with excess weight in each individual vehicle involved (i.e. over each regulated specified laden weight—that is in reality the excess of weight over the weight specified for that type of vehicle in the regulations set out in this Chapter).

1.8 Tests of vehicles

1.8.1 Tests generally

A system of controls on vehicles required a system of checks and test to be enforced. There are two types under the Road Traffic Acts: (i) a test which leads to the issue of a certificate; and (ii) occasional tests—see para 1.8.5 *infra*. There are also EEC-based tests—see para 1.8.6 *infra*.

The basic power of testing vehicles for efficiency, construction and safety is found in s 18 of the 1961 Act (as amended by Sch, 1968 Act). It provides:

(a) *Minister specifies vehicles*. The type or classes of vehicles to be tested are to be specified in regulations made by the Minister for the Environment. He can exempt specific cases. He also nominates the authorities who issue test certificates (see (d) below) and how these are applied for, what tests are to be done, fees paid, etc. The regulations therefore specify all the details to enable the test to be carried out and certificates issued. Some provisions are declared penal regulations and when so declared carry the general penalty (see para 7.1).

(b) *Prohibition and offence*. It is prohibited to use a vehicle specified as requiring a test certificate without such certificate in a public place (s 18 of the 1961 Act). The person using the vehicle and the owner are both liable in breach to a fine of up to £350 and/or three months imprisonment (s 3 of the 1984 Act, Table, Item 10). It is presumed in a prosecution of this offence that the vehicle was being used in contravention of the section when there is evidence that a proper demand for the certificate was made (see para 1.9.2 below) and it was not produced or, if produced, the Garda was not permitted to read and examine it. As to what is a 'public place' and 'vehicle', see para 7.9.

In *Hewer v Cutter* (1974) RTR 155 a car with a disconnected gear box did not require a certificate. In *Davey v Towle* (1973) RTR 328 it was held to be no defence to say that the user was unable to obtain a certificate from the owner.

The existence of a certificate does not affect any prosecution for an offence under the rest of the Act's provisions, e.g. defective vehicle (see para 4.6).

(c) *Defences.*

- (i) The owner has a good defence if he shows that the vehicle was used without his consent *and* either that he had taken all reasonable precautions to prevent its use or, if used by a servant, that its use was in contravention of his instructions.
- (ii) It is a good defence for a servant to show that he was using the vehicle in obedience to the express orders of the owner.

(d) *Obtaining certificate.* The Minister specifies under s 18(6) of the 1961 Act the issuing authorities to whom persons wishing to have a certificate should apply to in the prescribed manner. The owner applies and pays the required fee. The vehicle is tested in accordance with the regulations. If the result is satisfactory, a test certificate is issued. If the authority is not satisfied that the vehicle complies with the regulated requirements, then it issues a statement of refusal with its reasons. An appeal lies to the appropriate District Justice, being the Justice for the District Court area where the vehicle is ordinarily kept. The Justice has only two courses open to him, i.e. to refuse the appeal or to direct a new test of the vehicle.

A precedent application should be in the form of that found at para 1.13 below referring to the appeal being against the refusal of a test certificate under s 18 of the Road Traffic Act 1961, as amended, and regulations thereunder. It should be addressed to the District Court Clerk and to the relevant test authority.

It should be noted that it is an offence punishable with the general penalty (see para 7.1) to make a false declaration by giving false particulars when applying for a certificate under this section (s 115 of the 1961 Act—see para 7.4). This covers particulars given under the regulations. The material date for deciding if a certificate is false contrary to s 115 of the 1961 Act is the date of the issue of the certificate, even though test itself took place earlier (*R v Evans* [1964] 3 All ER 666). An example of misleading particulars is found in *Murphy v Griffiths* [1967] 1 All ER 424, where a test certificate was back dated. Section 115 of the 1961 Act also deals with forging, fraudulently altering, using, lending or allowing the use of a false certificate under the Acts or regulations, which are criminal offences subject to a fine of £350 and/or six months imprisonment. The penalty was increased to that level by s 3 of the 1984 Act (Table, Item 18). It should be noted that summary proceedings under s 115 must be instituted within one year, instead of the usual six months under the Petty Sessions (Ireland) Act 1851.

(e) *Licensing/Taxation*. Section 17 of the 1968 Act extends the power in s 12 of Roads Act 1920 to make regulations to include a power to make regulations on taxation (or more correctly the licensing registration process) to require production of a test certificate in prescribed cases. See also para 1.11.

1.8.2 Production of certificate—demand

Power is given to the Gardai under s 19 of the 1961 Act (as amended by Sch of 1968 Act) to require the user and/or owner of the vehicle (being a vehicle he believes requires a test certificate) to produce a test certificate for it in certain circumstances. These circumstances are where a member of the Gardai has reasonable grounds for believing that the vehicle, being one which he believes requires a certificate, was used in a particular public place, not more than one month prior to the demand.

What are reasonable grounds are not specified, except that it is indicated that if the Garda observed or believed that the use took place in a public place, then that appears sufficient, unless the Garda was acting unreasonably, e.g. mala fides.

The requirement to produce can be met within ten days of the demand by production of the test certificate at any named Garda Station. It is presumed, until the contrary is shown, that a person did not produce it within the ten days. (See para 2.7 as to similar provisions; see also para 6.10.)

1.8.3 Offences

Failure to produce a test certificate is an offence under s 19 of the 1961, as is failure to allow the Garda to read and examine the certificate. Both offences carry the general penalty (para 7.1). If a person fails to allow the certificate to be read and examined the Garda can demand his name and address, and if he fails to give it or gives one which is believed to be false or misleading he is guilty of a similar offence. The Garda can arrest without warrant a person who fails to allow a certificate to be read or examined, or a person who refuses to give his name or gives a false or misleading name.

1.8.4 Defences

A servant has two defences: Either (i) that he did not use the vehicle, or (ii) that he did so on the express orders of his master.

The vehicle's owner also has two defences: Either (i) that the vehicle was not used, or (ii) that it was used without his consent, and either he had taken reasonable precautions to prevent its use, or that his servant had used it in contravention of his orders.

1.8.5 Occasional tests and examinations

These can be carried out by Gardai (1961 Act) or by Ministerial officers (1968 Act), as set out below.

1.8.5.1 *Garda powers.*

(i) Vehicles generally. Section 20 (1) of the 1961 Act provides as follows: 'Where a member of the Garda Siochana observes a mechanically propelled vehicle or combination of vehicles in a public place and he suspects that there is a defect affecting the vehicle or combination which is such that it is, when in use, a danger to the public, or in the case of a public service vehicle there is a defect affecting it which is such that either it is a danger to the public or it is rendered unfit for the carriage of passengers, he may inspect and examine the vehicle or combination and, for the purpose of carrying out the inspection and examination may do all such requirements in relation to it as are reasonably necessary.'

As to 'mechanically propelled vehicles', 'public place' and 'public service vehicle', see para 7.9.

Presumably the Garda must have reasonable grounds for believing in the existence of a defect based on his observations of the vehicle. He cannot do a spot check without such a basis, i.e. his suspicions must be aroused by, say, noticing a wobbling wheel. When the check is valid he is given wide powers to all things reasonably necessary. In particular he is given specific powers as follows:

(a) to require the person in charge to take it to a convenient place within five miles for inspection;
(b) to drive the vehicle for a reasonable time and distance; or
(c) to request the person in charge to do so and to carry the Garda during the journey; and
(d) to carry out or cause to be carried out such tests as the Garda considers reasonable.

Failure to comply with the Garda request is an offence attracting the general penalty (para 7.1). However, prosecution for breach of Construction, Equipment and Use Regulations is not dependant on such a test (*Phillips v Thomas* (1974) RTR 28).

(ii) Pedal cycles. Wide powers for testing pedal cycles and dealing with them are given to Gardai by s 20(6) and (7) of the 1961 Act. A Garda has power to test and drive away any such cycle to do all things reasonably necessary to test it, with specific powers to drive it or require it to be driven. Failure to co-operate with the Garda requirement is an offence attracting the general penalty (para 7.1). If the Garda finds a dangerous defect he can require the cycle not to be driven until the defect is remedied, and then to have it submitted for re-examination. It is a defence to show the defect did not exist or was not dangerous to the public. Similarly,

it is a good defence to a charge of disobeying an instruction from the Garda to show that at that time the cycle did not have the dangerous defect. By s 3 of the 1961 Act a 'pedal cycle' means a vehicle which is a pedal bicycle or pedal tricycle. The term 'pedal tricycle' is defined as a tricycle intended or adapted for propulsion solely by the physical exertions by a person or persons seated thereon. Ministerial officers referred to in the next sub-paragraph do not have the powers under these subsections.

1.8.5.2 *Ministerial officers' powers.*

(i) Vehicles generally. The Minister for the Environment is empowered by s 12 of the 1968 Act to appoint authorised officers, whose powers are to include the carrying out of tests on any mechanically propelled vehicle or combination observed in a public place. The officer can require the owner of a vehicle to submit it for examination, including testing or loading, as specified by regulations. Contravention of an officer's proper requirement is an offence, carrying the general penalty (para 7.1).

The Minister is given wide powers of regulation to enable the section to be carried out, which regulations are to govern the circumstances, notice, manner and type of inspections, who are officers, the records to be kept, etc. Contravention of a stated penal regulation is deemed an offence by s 4 of the 1968 Act. The penalty is a maximum fine of £350 and/or three months imprisonment. The owner will be liable in addition to any person using the vehicle, if the regulation so states.

The regulations can differentiate between different classes of vehicles and different circumstances. No regulations have been made to date.

In *Warzal v Reader Bros Ltd* (1974) RTR 383 it was held that production of a traffic examiner's authority is not a prerequisite to a conviction.

It will be noted that the officer's powers are wider in operation than a Garda's power, as he is not required to suspect that a defect exists. This probably is because of his specialised training in the detection of defects. Neither is there a restriction on proving use in a public place in the case of these offences, as is necessary under s 19 of the 1961 Act.

No officers have been appointed to date.

(ii) Fleets—Inspection and examination. Section 13 of the 1968 Act (as amended by s 4 of the 1984 Act) proposes that every person who owns or operates not less than the prescribed number of mechanically propelled vehicles, exceeding in unladen weight 2,000 kg, for use in public places should be subject to a special regime of inspection and examination.

The Minister for the Environment is given special power to make regulations requiring owners of large fleets of vehicles to arrange a scheme of inspection of prescribed vehicles and to keep records of the inspections. The records are to be available to the Minister's officers.

The owners involved will be specified in regulations by virtue of the fact that they operate more than a prescribed number of vehicles. No regulations have been made to date.

Contravention of a regulation stated to be a penal is an offence, with the general penalty applying (para 7.1).

1.8.5.3 *Discovery of defect.* By virtue of s 20(3) and (5) of the 1961 Act, as amended by Sch 1968 Act and s 12 of the 1968 Act, if the Garda or Ministerial officer has, consequent to an inspection or examination reasonable grounds for believing the vehicle (or a vehicle drawn by another vehicle) has a defect making it a danger to the public, he may instruct the person in charge of it not to allow it to be driven until the defect is remedied and it is submitted to be re-examined and retested at a specified time and place.

In the case of public service vehicles, where the Garda considers that the defect does not render it dangerous *per se* but does make it unfit to carry passengers, he can give similar instructions, i.e. to remedy and retest. This power, on the reading of the sections, is not given to the Ministerial officer in this instance, which may be a drafting omission in the section.

The contravention of a requirement by a Garda or officer is an offence attracting the general penalty (para 7.1). However, to drive before the alleged defect is remedied (unless in fact it does not exist) involves a penalty of up to £350 and/or three months imprisonment (s 3 of the 1984 Act). The defence of non-existence of the alleged defect is open in all these offences of failing to obey a requisition or instruction. It is sufficient to show that, even if the defect did exist, it was not a danger to the public. These offences and defences are set out in s 20(10)-(15) of the 1961 Act.

1.8.5.4 *Presence at examination.* Where a person is required to allow an examination or test to be made on his vehicle, he has a right to be present with a person (e.g. a motor assessor or mechanic) at the examination and he must be allowed to observe the examination. If the person does not wish to be present himself, he can still have a representative present to observe the examination (s 20(15) of the 1961 Act).

1.8.6 European communities tests

Pursuant to the policy of EEC members under the Treaty of Rome to approximate their transport law, a Directive requiring various types of vehicles to be tested and to conform with certain standards has been issued by the EEC. Under s 3 of the European Communities Act 1972, regulations have been made in Ireland bringing this Directive into force. The Directive is 77/143/EEC.

The following are the current regulations (Irish):

European Communities (Vehicle Testing) Regulations 1981 (SI 193/1981, as amended). These regulations provide that certain commercial vehicles must be tested annually. The vehicles are—

(a) goods vehicles, trailers and semi-trailers over 1½ tons unladen weight—the regulation expression is 'maximum permissible weight of over 3,500 kg'.
(b) buses with more than eight seats, excluding the driver;

(c) taxis in a taximeter area (see 1982 Regulations below); and
(d) ambulances.

A Certificate of Roadworthiness valid for a year is granted if the test is passed. The test is carried out by an authorised tester who is appointed by an Issuing Authority. Issuing Authorities are County Councils or Corporations. The test covers brakes, steering, visibility, lights, axles, wheels, tyres, suspension, chassis, nuisance, safety equipment, and vehicle identification. The tester issues a certificate of the positive result if he is satisfied as to the roadworthiness and the Issuing Authority then issues a Certificate of Roadworthiness.

The Regulations make it an offence to use in a public place a vehicle which requires a Certificate of Roadworthiness but which does not possess one. A Garda can demand production of a certificate within one month of the vehicle's use. If it is not produced within ten days of the demand, or if the Garda is not allowed to read it, then the person is guilty of an offence, as is a person who gives a wrong name and address. Such a person can be arrested without warrant (see paras 7.2 and 7.9). The penalty under R 14 for an offence is up to £500 fine and/or six months imprisonment. As to similar demands, see para 2.7.

The EEC Commission has before it at present proposals for the extension of compulsory annual roadworthiness testing to private cars and light goods vehicles over three years old. There are 600,000 such vehicles in the Republic. In a survey made in early 1988, in Dublin 53% of vehicles had defective brakes or tyres (see Dail Debates, 24 February 1988).

Amending regulations. The 1981 Regulations were amended by SI 331/1982; SI 33/1983; SI 68/1984; SI 214/1985. In brief, the amendments were:

(i) 1982 Amendment (SI 331/1982). Allows a PSV Licence from a Garda Commissioner to be a substitute for a Certificate of Roadworthiness.
(ii) 1983 Amendment (SI 31/1983). Requires, on 'taxing' vehicles governed by the 1981 Regulations, that the Certificate of Roadworthiness be produced to the Licensing Authority (see para 1.11 as to 'taxation' or licensing and registration).
(iii) 1984 Amendment (SI 68/1984). Increased fees. Allows ten days for production of a Certificate of Roadworthiness on demand by a Garda. Allows for replacement of faded or illegible certificates.
(iv) 1986 Amendment (SI 214/1986). Confines tests to trained personnel employed by vehicle testers and named on a register established by the local authority. Allows Garda to stop, inspect, demand production of certificates and test vehicle for which a roadworthiness certificate is issued.

If vehicle is used without a certificate, both the owner and the driver is liable. Imported vehicles of the types set out in the 1981 List, which are over one year old, must be tested and obtain a certificate. Increased fees for tests to £60 or, in certain cases, £40 allow for replacement of lost certificate.

1.9 Driving defective vehicles

This matter is dealt with fully at para 4.6 *infra*.

1.9.1 Owner's knowledge

Breach of the 1963 Regulations (see para 1.5.5.3) with regard to, for example, brakes can give rise to a serious condition in a vehicle. The condition of the vehicle, or the presence of a serious defect in it, can make it a dangerously defective vehicle. It is a specific offence under s 54 of the 1961 Act (amended by Sch, 1968 Act) if an owner knows of a defect affecting the vehicle which is such that, when the vehicle is in motion, it is a danger to the public. See para 4.6 generally with regard to this section.

It is sufficient to enable a conviction to be obtained that, even if the owner did not know directly of the defect, he could have ascertained its existence by the exercise of ordinary care. It is a defence for the owner to show that the driving by another person was unauthorised. The penalty is increased by s 3 of the 1984 Act to up to £350 or three months imprisonment.

In addition, by virtue of s 26 of the 1961 Act and the 2nd Schedule thereto, a second or subsequent conviction within three years leads to a consequential disqualification order automatically.

General or special tests can be carried out as in para 1.8.

1.9.2 Dangerous driving

One of the items specified to be taken into consideration on a dangerous driving charge is the condition of the vehicle. Indeed, in practice many convictions of dangerous driving under s 53 of the 1961 Act are founded on the defective condition of the vehicle, e.g. bad steering, bad brakes. It has been this author's experience that Justices are particularly reluctant to reduce the charge under s 53 of the 1961 Act in such cases to careless driving under s 52 of the 1961 Act, especially where the defect is of long standing or of a serious nature.

The position of dangerous driving is dealt with extensively in para 4.2. There are heavy penalties, including ancillary or consequential disqualification.

1.10 Unattended vehicles

Unattended vehicles are dealt with under Parking, etc., as relevant. See also para 1.24. As to Stationary Vehicles, see para 1.5.5.3 **(f)** above (R 87 of the 1963 Regulations) and as to Obstruction, see para 4.8.

For a vehicle to be attended there must be a person able to keep it under observation, see any attempt to interfere with it and to have reasonable prospects of preventing the interference (*Starfire v Angel* (1962) 106 Sol Jo 854). In *Attridge v Attwood* [1964] Crim LR 45 a taxi driver left his cab taking the ignition key—he, however, was convicted under a similar regulation.

1.11 Registration of vehicles

1.11.1 Control/Taxation

An important method of control of vehicles is by their individual identification. This is done by a registration system which enables the vehicles and their registered owners to be traced.

The registration system does not come under the Road Traffic Acts (except s 123 of the 1961 Act and s 17 of the 1968 Act) but under various Road Acts, Finance Acts and regulations. The subject is only sketched briefly in this paragraph. The main Acts are the Roads Acts 1920, the Finance (Excise Duties) (Vehicles) Act 1952, and the Finance Acts, 1958, 1960 and 1976, all of which have been, and continue to be, amended regularly, particularly through adjusting the amount of the 'tax' on vehicles. This is an excise duty, which is commonly called Road Tax or Motor Tax.

1.11.2 Registration

A new vehicle, under the Roads Act 1920 (as amended), must be registered, and its owner must obtain a licence disc and exhibit it. The vehicle must also have a registration number, which must be exhibited both in the front and rear in an easily distinguishable, regulated form. A registration or 'tax' book is issued, and the person last entered as the owner is the registered owner (see para 7.9). A transfer of vehicle, change of user, loss of the book or disc, change of owner's address, the destruction or export of the vehicle, or the alteration of the vehicle must be notified to the licensing authority (normally the local authority) under the regulations.

Section 17 of the 1968 Act extended the power to make regulations under s 12 of the Roads Act 1920, enabling regulations to be made requiring test certificates (see para 1.8 *supra*) to be produced in the prescribed cases on the registration/taxation of vehicles.

1.11.3 Regulations

The regulations covering the registration and licensing of vehicles are the Road Vehicles (Registration and Licensing) Regulations 1982 (SI 311/1982, as amended) (see para 1.11.5).

These regulations replace the old 1958 to 1981 Regulations (except in relation to trade licences and Post Office vehicles) as discussed below, and set out in detail the procedures as to registration.

Many of the duties are put on the owner. However, if in fact a person has ceased to be the owner, he may not be liable (*Spain v Jolus* (1950) 48 LGR 532), although he would normally have committed the offence of failing to report the change of ownership (*C McLennon v MacMillan* (1962) SLT 2).

These regulations in general deal with procedures to be followed in applying for licences and registration, the issue of licence and registration numbers, the display of licences and numbers, changes to be notified, the issue of registration books (tax books), calculations for taxation purposes, the exhibition of the licence disc, registration plates, defacement of licences, the registration book, visiting vehicles, exempt vehicles, change of use, alterations to the vehicle, surrender of the licence, refunds, register of vehicles, etc.

The 1958 Regulations (SI 13/1958), as amended by SI 13/1958 and SI 198/1958, deal with special types of licences, e.g. trade licences and other Post Office (An Post) vehicles, but are otherwise repealed, as are 17 other old regulations. A trade licence is a general licence issued under s 9 of the Roads Act 1920 and s 15 of the Finance Act 1922.

Reference is made to 'Hire or Reward' in the 1958 Regulations. The leading English case is *Albert v MIB* [1971] 2 All ER 1345 where it was held that this means a monetary reward legally recoverable under an express or implied contract, i.e. beyond social kindness. In *A-G v Brogan* (1953) 82 ILTR 181 a horse trainer took horses to a race meeting in an unlicensed vehicle. He was not guilty as it was at the owner's discretion whether he paid, and in the incident involved he had not done so. See para 7.9 also.

As to goods vehicles, in *A-G v O'Sullivan* (1958) 92 ILTR 21 it was held that a tractor adapted to carry sacks by fitting a detachable wooden platform was hauling goods and was taxable as a goods vehicle. See also *A-G v East* 100 3 LTR 4 at para 6.4.10.

1.11.4 Supply of particulars

Under the 1982 Regulations a licensing authority must give to other licensing authorities, Gardai, the Custom & Excise Collectors, or other authorised State offices or local authority officers, free of charge, full particulars of any vehicle registered with them.

They must supply similar information as to the name and address of the registered owner and particulars of any vehicle registered with that licensing authority on receipt of a prescribed fee, to a person 'showing reasonable cause' for requiring same, e.g. a solicitor investigating an accident in which a person or vehicle was involved.

SI 441/1986 provides that the address of the registered owner be included in such a certificate.

1.11.5 Amending regulations

The Road Vehicles (Registration and Licensing) (Amendment) Regulations 1985 (SI 293/1985) amend the 1982 Regulations to allow for reference to 'cubic centimeters' instead of 'horsepower' as a measurement of engine capacity. This was necessary under EEC Directive 76/770. This means that 'cc' rather than 'hp' is the base for calculation of duty to be paid.

From 1987 a new system of identification numbers was introduced by the Road Vehicles (Registration and Licensing) (Amendment) Regulation 1986 (SI 441/1986). Under the new system the registration number commences with a number indicating the year of first registration, e.g. 89 for the year 1989, then letters indicating the county of registration, e.g. KY (Kerry), and then the number of the vehicle, e.g. 89 KY 999. They also introduced a uniform system of identification/registration plates, i.e. black characters on a white background. Provision was also made for refunds of tax to be made to the registered owners.

The 1987 Regulation (SI 320/1987) amends the provision for identification marks to be used on imported vehicles not previously registered abroad. The registration marks assigned to those vehicles will include the 'year numerals' of the year of manufacture of the vehicle in 1988 and onwards. Thus, a vehicle manufactured in 1985 would read 85 KY 999.

1.11.6 Fixed penalty

By virtue of s 103 of the 1961 Act, the fixed penalty procedure applies to non-display of a tax disc (see para 5.11.2 below). The disc is issued on Registration or Renewal. It is normally displayed in the front windscreen of a vehicle.

1.11.7 Certificates of Roadworthiness

By the European Communities (Vehicle Testing) (Amendment) Regulations 1983 (SI 31 of 1983), an application for an annual or other licence under SI 311 of the 1982 (see para 1.11.3) must be supported by a Certificate of Roadworthiness in the case of (a) goods vehicles, trailers and semi-trailers over 1½ tons unladen weight, (b) buses with more than eight passenger seats, (c) taxis in a taximeter area, (d) ambulance. See para 1.8.6 above.

PART 2 PUBLIC SERVICE VEHICLES

1.12 General

In addition to the normal controls outlined in Part 1 of this chapter, certain further controls on public service vehicles (PSVs) are imposed, mainly by Parts VII of both the 1961 and 1968 Acts. This is basically because of the increased danger to a larger number of passengers and the size of these vehicles. The control in this country is not as elaborate as in Britain. Most large public service vehicles which provide passenger road services are operated by CIE (Coras Iompar Eireann), a statutory body which is indirectly Government controlled (i.e. is governed by the Transport Acts 1950 to 1987. The Road Transport Acts 1932 to 1986 are the legislative base for road transport in Ireland (see para 1.35 below).

The Transport Act 1932 is the legislative base for the licensing of schedule coach and bus services within the State. Under s 7 of the Act no person is permitted to carry on a 'passenger road service' unless he is the holder of a passenger licence granted by the Minister for Tourism and Transport. A 'passenger road service' is (s 2 of the 1982 Act):

> 'A service of one or more mechanically propelled vehicles travelling wholly or mainly on public roads and carrying passengers (whether passengers luggage, merchandise and mails or any of them are or not so carried) between specified terminal points or along a specified route or otherwise for separate charges in respect of each passenger'.

An 'omnibus service' is a passenger road service taking up and setting down passengers along its route on request or at fixed stopping places. Private hire, i.e. where a bus is hired by an individual or organisation in respect of a single block payment, is outside the scope of the 1932 Act.

Since 1986 CIE has operated its road service through two companies, called Irish Bus and Dublin Bus. These bodies are now governed by their own Statute of 1986 and the Transport Acts 1950-1987, with some similar provisions to the Road Traffic Acts control system. However, EEC transport policy is likely to cause continuous breaches of this hitherto virtual monopoly situation, with increasing private enterprise participation in the provision of public transport in the coming years (see para 1.35 below).

1.12.1 What are public service vehicles?

Section 3 of the 1961 Act states that a public service vehicle is a mechanically propelled vehicle used for the carriage of persons for reward. As to 'mechanically propelled vehicle' and 'use', see para 7.9.

The Act divides public service vehicles into two types:

(1) *Large public service vehicles* means a public service vehicle having seating accommodation for more than eight persons, exclusive of the driver (s 3 of the 1961 Act). A type that requires special mention is an omnibus.

An *omnibus* is a large public service vehicle which is, for the time being, used on a definite route for the carriage of passengers who are carried at separate fares and are picked up and set down along such route, whether on request or at fixed stopping places (s 3 of the 1961 Act).

(2) *Small public service vehicles* are those other than are mentioned in (1), i.e. accommodation of eight or less passengers. Section 3 of the 1961 Act says they are public service vehicles which are not large public service vehicles. They are divided by the regulations into—

(a) private hire vehicles ('hackney') and street service vehicles, which means a small public service vehicle, the driver of which offers in a public place himself and the vehicle for hire, and for that purpose stands or drives the vehicle in a public place (s 3 of the 1961 Act). By SI 273 of 1968, licensed public hire vehicles became small public service vehicles; and

(b) public hire vehicles, known as 'taxis'. Their fares are controlled by meter and they may be driven around for hire.

1.12.2 Calculation of passenger accommodation

Power is given to the Minister for the Environment by s 121 of the 1961 Act to make regulations setting out how the passenger accommodation of mechanically propelled vehicles is to be calculated for the purpose of the Act. These regulations may distinguish between seating and standing accommodation.

The Road Traffic (Passenger Accommodation of Mechanically Propelled Vehicles) Regulations 1962 (SI 143/1962) state that the total seating accommodation is calculated by excluding the driver's seat and allowing 16 inches seat width for each passenger.

1.12.3 Control of public service vehicles—Power to make regulations

In common with most other enabling sections in this chapter, the control and operation of PSVs is to be by Ministerial Regulation. These regulations made under s 82 of the 1961 Act (As amended by s 57 and Sch, 1968 Act and s 7 of the Dublin Transport Authority (Dissolution) Act 1987) give power to control public service vehicles in their operation, and special powers are given for regulating the licensing of vehicles, drivers and conductors of vehicles, the payment of fees for licences, badges and plates, the conduct and duties of such personnel and passengers, the conditions of operation of PSVs, the issue of certificates, records to be kept and the fixing of maximum fares. There is an additional power to make varying regulations for different classes of vehicles and different areas. The Minister for the Environment is the relevant Minister.

As to the current regulations, see para 1.13 below; as to regulations generally, e.g. their validity, proof, etc., see para 7.5.

1.12.4 Validity of certificates

Various types of certificates are provided for in the Acts and regulations. The 1961 Act provides (s 82) that a certificate purporting to be issued under the regulations:

(a) showing that on a specified day a specified maximum fare was fixed for street service vehicles in a specified area;
(b) showing a specified person was a licence holder or a licence exists for a vehicle;

is prima facie evidence of its validity without proof of the validity of the signature thereto.

The contents of s 115 of the 1961 Act (as amended by Sch, 1968

Act and s 3 of the 1984 Act) should be noted. It provides penalties of up to £350 and/or six months' imprisonment for furnishing false particulars and declarations; and for forging, fraudulently altering, using, or lending certificates (see para 7.4).

In *Donnelly v Glasgow Corp* (1953) SLT 161 it was held that a certificate of fitness is not *per se* a defence in an action for damages in negligence.

1.12.5 Offence

By virtue of s 82(6) of the 1961 Act, contravention of any declared penal regulation is an offence with the general penalty under s 102 applying (para 7.1). The regulations can and do contain individual regulations where both the owner and the user are liable, e.g. RS 5, 6 and 7 (see para 1.13 below).

1.12.6 Onus of proof—Licences

There are various types of licence for different types of vehicles and their drivers, as set out below. All PSVs must have the appropriate licence.

In a prosecution involving proof of a licence it is presumed, until the defence proves otherwise, that the licence was not held (s 82(7) of the 1961 Act). As to the effect of this presumption in somewhat similar provisions, see *A-G v Byrne and Another* 85 ILTR 93, where it was held the presumption did not arise as there was no evidence that the passengers were not employees.

This decision itself is overcome partly by s 82(8) of the 1961 Act, which creates a presumption that a person carrying eight or more persons, who are not his employees, is carrying them for reward and thus needs a licence. The position still is probably that the State, to benefit from the provisions of s 82(8), has to prove some (if not eight) of the passengers are not employees. This point, as to the number, was left undecided in *Byrnes* case.

As to certificates, see para 1.12.4.

1.12.7 Fare collection and arrest

Under a new subs (9), inserted as an addition to section 82 of the 1961 Act by s 57 of the 1968 Act, certain powers of arrest were given to a Garda of a person not paying his fare. This subsection has been re-enacted and extended by s 7 of the Dublin Transport Authority (Dissolution) Act 1987. This new subsection gives a number of powers:

(1) *Powers to the owner, driver or conductor*. If a person refuses or omits to pay to the owner, driver or conductor of a public service vehicle his fare, then that person must give his name and address to such a person if so required. If he does not, or gives a false or misleading one (i.e. one that the owner, driver or conductor reasonably believes it to be false, etc.), then he may be detained by that person until the arrival of the Garda Siochana.

(2) *Powers of Garda.* Where the Garda is called as aforesaid, he can request of the non-fare paying person his name and address and, if refused, or if the Garda believes reasonably that he is given a false or misleading one, the Garda can arrest such person without warrant.

A person who has refused to give his name and address, or has given a name or address that is false or misleading, is guilty of an offence. The general penalty applies (see para 7.1).

1.12.8 Visitors

Visitors are non-residents on a temporary stay in the State. Under the Mechanically Propelled Vehicles (International Circulation) Order 1961 (SI 269/1961), VI(1) (as substituted by SI 193/1963), the requirement that all public service vehicles have a licence is removed, provided the visitor's vehicle is licensed in the State where it is registered under similar licensing requirements.

1.13 Present regulations

The present main regulations under the above provisions are the Road Traffic (Public Service Vehicles) Regulations 1963 (SI 191/1963).

The Amending Regulations of the 1963 Regulations are as follows:

1964 – SI 106	1978 – SI s 15, 292
1967 – SI 274	1979 – SI 242
1968 – SI 273	1980 – SI 54
1970 – SI 200	1981 – SI 66
1973 – SI 225	1983 – SI 273
1974 – SI 296	1986 – SI 300
1976 – SI 24	1987 – SI 139
1977 – SI s 111, 177, 268, 284	1987 – SI 184

Those that are penal are so indicated by word 'penal', and where both owner and user are liable this is indicated by the words 'owner also liable'. As to the owner, see para 7.9. Only a summary of the regulations is given below. It must be stated that they are, by virtue of constant amendment, difficult to follow. A consolidating regulation is required. Reference to the actual regulation should be made in relation to any particular problem.

1963 Regulations (SI 191/1963). The main provisions of these regulations are:

R 3 *Definitions*—12 in all for the regulations, e.g. of Dublin Cork and Galway Taximeter Area, etc. These have been enlarged and amended. The important definitions are:

(a) a 'public hire vehicle' ('taxi') is a small PSV (eight passengers or less) used by a person by starting at an appointed stand for hire for reward, or using it on drives about for the hire or being contacted for hire by radio in a taximeter area. These areas are Dublin, Cork, Galway, Limerick, Waterford, Killarney, Sligo, Kilkenny, Carlow, Naas and Longford, as defined (see amending regulations below);

(b) 'private hire vehicle' ('hackney') is a small PSV (eight passengers or less) used for hire and reward otherwise than as a public hire vehicle. In 1983, by SI 273 of 1983, there was a new provision inserted in the 1963 Regulations. It placed a limitation on hackneys being hired in the main taximeter areas (e.g. Dublin, Cork and Galway and Limerick). This is to the effect that, except in connection with funerals, hiring may not be indicated or facilitated by telephone or radio communication with the vehicle while it is in a public place. This facility is granted to taxis only in taximeter areas.

Part II Operation of Public Service Vehicles
See presumption of carriage for reward in s 82(8) of the 1961 Act (para 1.12.6).

R 5 All vehicles used for the carriage of a person or persons for reward in a public place must have a public service vehicle *licence*. CIE exempt. Penal. Owners also liable. See SI 139/1987 below as to information about licences.

R 6 A public hire vehicle (i.e. one operating from a stand as in Dublin, Cork, etc.) must be a licensed public hire vehicle. Penal. Owner also liable, i.e. if not duly licensed.

R 7 As substituted by R 2 of SI 111/1977 and amended by SI 292/1978. In taximeter areas (e.g. Cork and Dublin, etc.) a public hire vehicle must have a taximeter. Penal. Owner also liable. There is an exemption where the contract for hire is made outside the taximeter area.

R 8 *Taximeters* must meet the specifications set out. Penal. The specifications are that it must be accurate, secure, visible and properly connected and maintained (as substituted by SI 35/1975).

R 9 *Maximum fares* can be fixed for their areas by Dublin, Cork, Galway Corporations, etc. and can be so certified. A statement of maximum fares can be purchased from Dublin, Cork, Galway Corporations, etc. See SI 242 of 1979. If the Corporation so certifies fares, then that certificate is proof in court, until the contrary is shown, and of the signature of a duly authorised officer who made it (S 82(4) of the 1961 Act).

The Road Traffic (PSV) (Amendment) Regulations 1979 (SI 242/1979) provide that the issuing of a certificate that on a specified day a specified fare was the maximum fare fixed for such vehicles is the responsibility of the Minister for Industry and Commerce.

He is also given the responsiblity of fixing the maximum fares for the Dublin, Cork and Galway and Limerick taximeter areas.

This regulation was amended by SI 242/1979—extended to Galway.

R 10 Revoked by SI 35/1975 (see below).

R 11 *Notice* of fees must be exhibited in taxis (amended by R 3 of 1970 and R 139 of 1987). A photo of the driver must also be exhibited. Penal.

R 12 (i) the word 'taxi' can only be used in a licensed public hire vehicle fitted with a taximeter.
(ii) Under R 2 of the 1968 Regulations only licensed public hire vehicles can advertise a telephone number etc. Penal.

R 13 A properly secured, etc. *vehicle plate* must be exhibited. Penal. Owner also liable. The provision of s 115 of the 1961 Act as to misuse also applies (see para 7.4). See SI 139/1987 as to the issue of plates.

R 14 Deals with large public service vehicles with more than 14 passengers:

(a) Conductors are to be used on certain large public service vehicles. This is now gradually being done away with in favour of one-person-operated buses.

(b) Properly controlled *exits* should exist.
Penal. Owner also liable. This regulation has been the subject of industrial controversy. The regulation has been amended by the 1967 and 1974 Regulations (below) in relation to school buses.

R 15 *Rest* periods of 24 hours a week must be given to drivers and conductors. Penal.

R 16 The use of a *defective* PSV is prohibited. Penal. Includes dilapidation and lack of cleanliness. See also para 4.6 also.

R 17 *Damage* to a PSV is prohibited. This regulation is probably largely superseded by s 56 of the 1968 Act (see para 1.19 below). Penal.

R 18 *Dangerous substances*—carriage generally prohibited (see para 1.33 also). Does not apply to the carriage of fuel for the vehicle; nor to securely packaged substances unlikely to cause damage if there is an accident; nor to firearms carried by defence forces or Gardai.

Part III

This was revoked by SI 292/1978, R 2(1). Its provisions, which dealt with the licensing of public service vehicles, have been replaced by a new Code in the Road Traffic (Public Service Vehicles) (Licensing) Regulations 1978 (SI 292/1978). See para 1.14 below.

Part IV Licensing of drivers of public hire vehices

By SI 273 of 1968 licensed public hire vehicles become small public service vehicles.

Note that s 82(7) of the 1961 Act raises a rebuttable presumption in a prosecution under these regulations that a licence is not held. This applies to drivers from stands and in Dublin and Cork, etc.—see Definitions.

R 34 (Substituted by R 9/1970 No 2, i.e. SI 200/1970, and amended by SI 252/1970 and replaced by SI 111/1977). Garda Commissioner grants licence, procedure with regard to certificates, etc. set out.

R 35 *Form* of licence set out; *duration* normally one year (R 12/1977 No 2) (SI 111/1977).

R 36 (Substituted by R 10 of SI 200/1970 (No 2), *revocation of licences* in certain circumstances.)

R 37 *Appeal* against refusal or revocation is to the District Court.

PSV Regulations 1963, Rg. 37: Precedent
The following is a precedent Notice for such an application:

[The District Court]

District Court Area   District No

Between

[AB]

Appellant

[CD]

Respondent

NOTICE OF APPEAL

TAKE NOTICE that AB of   in the County of   HEREBY APPEALS to the District Court sitting at   on the   day of   19   at 11 am or the next opportunity thereafter against the Refusal (Revocation) of a Licence to drive a small Public Service Vehicle to the Appellant by the Respondent pursuant to Article 37 of the Road Traffic (Public Service Vehicles) Regulations 1963 (SI 191/1963) as amended.

[Dated]

Signed: ______________________________
Solicitor for Appellant

To/The District Court Clerk, at
AND TO/CD Garda Siochana Officer, at

Notes:

(1) The Court Area in which the Appellant resides is the area in which to bring the application.

(2) The Respondent is a Garda Officer authorised by the Commissioner to perform the functions of the Commission.

(3) Ten-day service applies. The original must be stamped and a Declaration of Service given to the District Court Clerk at least four days before the Court sits.

R 38/39 *A badge* is given with the licence. It can be replaced. It must be returned if the licence is revoked. R 39 is penal.

R 40 *Change of address* must be notified. Penal.

R 41 (Amended by R 11/1970 (No 2) (SI 200/1970) and SI 252/1970 (No 3 and SI 111/1977). *Fees* payable.

R 42 A *register* of licence holders is set up. It is available for inspection.

R 43 Prohibits the driving of a small PSV without a licence (substituted by R 5 SI 273/1968). The 1968 Regulations substituted a new R 47 in fact, and added to the need of having the licence and the requirement that the driver must satisfy the Garda authority that he has an adequate knowledge of the taximeter area in which he operates. Penal.

Part V Duties of drivers, Conductors, Passengers

R 44 *A driver and conductor* must be in constant attendance, ensure the safety of passengers, give assistance and give information to Gardai or other persons having authority to examine the vehicle. Penal. In *Reid v MacNicol* (1958) SLT 42) the driver did not stop and a person stumbled getting on the bus. Held, the person was not entitled to get on a moving bus and the driver was acquitted. In *Police v Okaukno* [1954] Crim LR 869 it was held than an intending passenger may at his own risk get on a bus stationary at a traffic light. See *Amos v DPP* (1988) (Rim LR 248 a bus driver was charged with failing to behave in a civil and orderly manner and to take reasonable precautions for the safety of his passengers under two subparagraphs of the English Regulations. Held: The conviction was bad for Duplicity. The commentary in the Criminal Law Review is of interest on the Duplicity point.

R 45 *Conductor* must signal driver to start, stop, collect fares, and wear badge. He must not allow more than the permitted number of passengers. He should not deceive passengers. He must put away goods safely, and extinguish any fire. Penal. However, he is under a duty to prevent the vehicle remaining stationary unnecessarily. In *Nicholson v Goddard* [1954] Crim LR 474 it was held that a conductor should not open the door for passengers until bus stopped. See also R 49 below.

A conductor is entitled to assume that his driver will stop at a compulsory stop and that a passenger will not get off before the vehicle comes to a stop; and the conductor does not negligently endanger the safety of passengers if, being upstairs in the bus collecting fares, he does not prevent a passenger from alighting and suffering injury while the bus is passing a compulsory stop (*Askew v Bawtell* [1947] 1 All ER 883).

If the conductor allows more than the regulated number of passengers on the bus, he can be guilty of aiding and abetting a breach of the regulations (*Spires v Smith* [1956] 2 All ER 277.

In an earlier decision under somewhat differently worded regulations, an owner who was not present was liable when he had appointed an inexperienced unsupervised conductor who allowed overcrowding (*Gough v Rees* (1929) 94 JP 53).

R 46 *Driver* must stop and start in response to the signals and at appointed places. He should not allow himself to be distracted and should not converse. Penal.

R 47 *Employees* in large PSVs must be civil and orderly and must not smoke. Penal.

R 48 *Passengers* must not obstruct or impede the driver or conductor. They may enter only at stops and must comply with directions from the conductor or driver. Furthermore, they must not smoke in a non-smoking area, not use bad language, not spit, not distribute leaflets, not annoy others, not interfere with other passengers' comfort with radios, not litter the vehicle and not throw out anything, not interfere with equipment, and not give improper signals. They must deliver up lost property, pay the proper fare (see para 1.12.7) and produce their tickets on request, alight properly, not taking anything not belonging to them off the bus, and not carry awkward or unusual luggage, except with the conductor's consent.

R 49 *Powers of conductors* of large PSVs include the ability to exclude an offensive person or persons or if the bus is full. This regulation has proved difficult to enforce, and at times bus crews have refused to travel certain routes, particularly at night.

R 51 Deals with the commencement of hire of a public hire vehicle, i.e. when a driver accepts the hire, then he is under a duty not to hire to another.

R 52 *Public hire drivers* (amended by R 7/2968) must obey reasonable directions, drive at a reasonable speed and follow a reasonable route (SI 273/1968), as directed by the hirer. Normally they must accept a hirer unless he cannot or will not pay the fare or for some other reasonable excuse. The driver must wear a badge. If paid in advance, the driver must perform the service immediately. The driver must be in constant attendance, be civil and clean. Penal.

In *Levison v Powell* [1967] 3 All ER 796 it was held that a taxi driver was not bound to obey illegal directions, e.g. illegal parking. In *G Newton Ltd v Smith* [1962] 2 All ER 19 it was held that if an employee disobeyed the term of his employer's Road Service Licence, e.g. by diverting from the authorised route, his employer could be liable in certain circumstances.

R 53 (As amended by R 8 of SI 273/1968 and 300/1986). If a vehicle is fitted with a taximeter the driver must use it and charge the correct fare. Penal under SI 24/1976 (below). Allows charge in the case of phone or radio hiring.

R 54 *Passengers* in a taxi must not interfere with the vehicle, spit, throw things out of it, and must leave on lawful request. A passenger cannot carry on animal without the driver's permission. Penal.

R 55 *Powers of taxi drivers* include the ability to exclude any hirer not properly conducted, or with animals; or whose clothes would soil or damage the interior. The driver can demand the fare for a journey and any waiting period, and can terminate the hiring if the passenger refuses these lawful requests.

R 56 *Fares* must be paid by the passenger to the driver or conductor. Penal. The provisions of s 82(9) of the 1961 Act, as amended by s 7 of the Dublin Transport Authority (Dissolution Act), allow for the detention and arrest of person not paying the fare (see para 1.12.7) and so reinforces this duty to pay fares.

R 57 *Entry* except as a passenger is not allowed, unless the conductor, driver or person in charge consents.

R 58 Reasonable force may be used by the driver, conductor or Gardai to prevent improper entry. Penal.

R 59 The *name and address* of a person contravening this Part of the Regulations can be demanded by the driver, conductor or Gardai. Penal. See also para 1.12.7 above as to this power.

Part VI Miscellaneous

R 60 *School vehicle* licences can be granted by the Commissioner of the Gardai for safe vehicles for the carriage of children to school. The licence normally lasts three years and sets out the number of children to be carried. The Commissioner must be satisfied as to the character and previous conduct of the owner (inserted by R 2 of SI 15/1978). An appeal may be brought to the District Court. See also the 1967 Regulations (SI 274) and SI 296/1974 (below).

PSV Regulations 1963, Rg. 60: Precedent

[The District Court]

District Court Area District No

Between

[AB]

Appellant

[and]

[CD]

Respondent

NOTICE OF APPEAL

TAKE NOTICE that AB of in the County of HEREBY APPEALS to the District Court sitting at on the day of 19 at 11 am or the next opportunity thereafter against the refusal of the Respondent to grant him a School Vehicle Licence pursuant to Article 60 of the Road Traffic (Public Service Vehicles) Regulations 1963 (SI 191 of 1963) as amended.

[Dated]

Signed: ______________________
Solicitors for Appellant

To/The District Court Clerk, at
AND TO/CD Garda Siochana Officer, at

Notes: (1) The Court Area in which the Appellant resides is the area in which to bring the application.
(2) The Respondent is a Garda Officer exercising the function of the Commissioner.
(3) Ten-day service applies. Stamped original and a Declaration of Service to be given to the District Court Clerk at least four days before the Court sits.

Such school buses are normally run by or under the control of CIE. Since 1987 CIE operates by Irish Bus and Dublin Bus under the Transport (Reorganisation of Coras Iompair Eireann) Act 1986.

Irish Bus and Dublin Bus hire private buses also for this purpose, normally under a detailed contract.

R 61 These regulations amend Art 14 of the 1963 Regulations to allow *single deck large public service vehicles* without conductors for the transport exclusively of school children.

1967 Road Traffic (Public Service Vehicles) (Amendment) Regulations (SI 274/1967). Where a regulation specifies it is a penal regulation, the owner of the vehicle is also liable where the contravention or use is by the other person using it. This follows the provision of s 82(6) of the 1961 Act, and the general penalty applies (para 7.1).

1968 Road Traffic (Public Service Vehicles) (Amendment) Regulations (SI 273/1968). The amendment made to the 1963 Regulations by these regulations have been noted above. They amend 'Cork taximeter area'; prohibit the use of *advertisements* in hackneys, require drivers to have knowledge of the area in which they operate and effect other minor amendments.

1970 Road Traffic (Public Service Vehicles) (Amendment) (No 2) Regulations (SI 200/1970). Many of these regulations have been revoked by SI 292/1978. The amendments made to the 1963 and 1970 Regulations by these regulations have been noted above.

1970 Road Traffic (Public Service Vehicles) (Amendment) (No 3) Regulations (SI 252/1970). Amends the 1968 and 1970 (no 2) Regulations in minor respects as to licences for small public service vehicles. They also apply conditions for operators changing licences and for types of licences. Amended by SI 111/1977.

1973 Road Traffic (Public Service Vehicles) (Amendment) Regulations (SI 225/1973) (as amended by SI 24/2976; SI 292/1976). These regulations provide that application for the grant of a licence to drive a small public service vehicle must be made only, with exceptions, from 1 to 14 March, June, September, or December each year. The exceptions are where a person, who held a licence in the preceding year, and the application is for renewal of the licence or substitution of another vehicle by such person on such licence. Only Art 2(3) still applies (see SI 292/1978).

1974 Road Traffic (Public Service Vehicles) (Amendment) Regulations (SI 296/1974). These amend Rs 14 and 60 of the 1963 Regulations to extend the scope of the system of licensing school transport so as to include School-related physical activities and the carriage of a combination of school children and teachers.

1976 Road Traffic (Public Service Vehicles) (Amendment) Regulations 24/1976). These 1985 Road Traffic (Public Service Vehicles) (Amendment) Regulations (SI 35/1975). These allow for the purchase of a statement of the maximum permissible fares in Dublin and Cork. These amend the 1973 Regulations to make the only date normally specified for application for a licence for a small PSV used as a public hire vehicle (taxi) 1 to 14 September, with the same exception for a replacement vehicle, etc. (see below SI 268/1977, SI 247/1978, SI 259/1978 and SI 292/1978.)

These regulations also amend R 53 of the 1963 Regulations to enable a charge to be made where a taxi hiring is to be initiated by phone or radio. This is the main current relevant provision.

1976 Road Traffic (Public Service Vehicle) (Amendment) (No 2) Regulations (SI 160/1976). The amendment of R 9 of the 1963 Regulations effected by this instrument has been noted above. Replaced now by SI 242/1979.

1977 Road Traffic (Public Service Vehicle) (Amendment) Regulations SI 111/1977). Most of these regulations have been repealed by SI 292/1978, except Art 11–14. These amendments are noted above.

1977 Road Traffic (Public Service Vehicles) (Amendment) Regulations (SI 177/1977). These regulations prescribed that public hire vehicles in Cork taximeter areas had to have orange stripes painted on the front and rear of the roof. Now revoked by SI 292/1978.

1977 Road Traffic (Public Service Vehicles) (Amendment) (No 3) Regulations (SI 268/1977). Eliminated September 1977 as a licensing period for taxis—a temporary matter. Revoked by SI 247/1978.

1977 Road Traffic (Public Service Vehicles) (Amendment) (No 4) Regulations (SI 284/1977). Fixed dates 1–14 September for applications for licences for small public services vehicles, in non-taximeter areas. Prohibited use of such a vehicle in a taximeter area. Revoked by SI 247/1978.

1978 Road Traffic (Public Service Vehicles) (Amendment) Regulations (SI 15/1978). These have been noted above as amendments to R 60 of the 1963 Regulations and require that the owner of 'School Bus' type of transport must be a fit and proper person to get a relevant licence. If refused, the owner has a right of appeal to the District Court.

1978 Road Traffic (Public Service Vehicles) (Licensing) Regulations (SI 292/1978). See para 1.14 below.

1979 Road Traffic (Public Service Vehicles) (Amendment) Regulations (SI 242/1979). These empowered the Minister to fix different maximum fares in different taximeter areas and extended the taximeter area system to Galway City and an area of a three-mile radius

1980 Road Traffic (Public Service Vehicles) (Amendment) Regulations (SI 54/1980). Designate the Limerick taximeter area.

1981 Road Traffic (Public Service Vehicles) (Amendment) Regulations (SI 66/1981). Extends to Waterford and Killarney the provision of the 1963 Regulations as to the granting of licences for the use of vehicles as public hire vehicles.

1983 Road Traffic (Public Service Vehicles) (Amendment) Regulations (SI 273/1983). Substitute R 3(2) of the 1963 Regulations to effect that only taxis can be radio cabs in taximeter areas.

1986 Road Traffic (Public Service Vehicles) (Amendments) Regulations (SI 300/1986). Makes it an offence for the driver of a taxi to activate the taximeter while the vehicle is standing or not plying for hire in a taximeter area. Requires use of that taximeter when the taxi is hired and prevents the driver charging more than the fare shown by the taximeter or the maximum fare fixed for the service.

1987 Road Traffic Act (Public Service Vehicles) (Amendment) Regulations (SI 139/1987). Provide for the format and display of a roof sign (called a taxi sign) on all public hire vehicles operating in taximeter areas. This must be displayed when the vehicle is in use.

These regulations restate, with some amendments, the provisions for vehicle *plates* on PSVs and the information in PSV licences.

1987 Road Traffic Act (Public Service Vehicles) (Amendment) (No 2) Regulations (SI 184/1987). Add Sligo, Kilkenny, Carlow, Naas and Langford as Public Hire Areas. Each local authority determines from time to time the number of new public hire vehicle licences which may be granted for the area by the Garda Commissioner.

1.14 Licensing of public service vehicles

The original system under the 1961 Act was contained in the 1963 Regulations, Part III (see para 1.13). That Part has been revoked and replaced by the Road Traffic (Public Service Vehicles) (Licensing) Regulations 1978 (SI 292/1978). These 1978 Regulations have been amended by SI 184/1987, which are read with the 1963 Regulations and have a collective citation as The Road Traffic (Public Service Vehicles) Regulations 1963 to 1987 at present.

These regulations are in addition to the other requirements for vehicles generally, i.e. those mentioned elsewhere in this Chapter, e.g. para 1.11, etc.

The 1978 Regulations apply to all PSVs, except those in public service operated by statutory public transport, e.g. Irish Bus and Dublin Bus under the Transport (Reorganisation of Coras Iompair Eireann) Act 1986, and Lough Swilley Railway Company and County Donegal Railways Joint Committee (see Art 3(1) of SI 191 of 1963).

In summary, the 1978 Regulations provide that the appropriate local authority will determine the number of public hire vehicle licences to be granted by the Garda Commissioner. Such licences must specify the area in which the vehicle may operate.

Some regulations are penal, and in the following summary of each regulation are so indicated. Unfortunately, printing errors in the official copy of the regulations make them hard to follow:

R 5 As amended by SI 66 of 1981, restricts the *number of licences* (public hire licences) that the Garda Commissioner may grant in Dublin, Cork, Killarney, Limerick, Galway, Drogheda, Dundalk, Tralee, Ennis and Waterford, Donegal Town to the number of licences decided by the local authority to be appropriate to the area.

The Amending Regulation (SI 184/1987) adds Sligo, Kilkenny, Carlow and Longford boroughs or towns to this list.

R 6 The Garda Commissioner in granting the licence must be satisfied as to the applicant's character and previous conduct; that the vehicle is safe; that the vehicle is insured; and that it complies with Construction, Equipment and Use Regulations, Lighting Regulations, etc. made under s 11 of the 1961 Act (see Part 1 of this Chapter at para 1.5, etc.).

R 7 The public service vehicle licence must have a serial number and specify the type of vehicle (e.g. small PSV). Normally a large PSV licence is granted for three years; a small PSV licence is for one year. A licence is normally valid unless revoked or the owner dies, whichever is the case.

R 8 Allows licences to be surrendered to the Commissioner at any time.

R 9 Deals with *change of ownership*—particulars must be given to the Commissioner.

R 10 If the holder of a PSV licence *dies*, the licence goes to his personal representative. This recognises the value of these licences.

R 11 *Allows a committee* or guardian or trustee to hold a licence for a person under a disability (e.g. unsound mind).

R 12 (1) Allows for revocation of a licence by the Commissioner. Grounds are (a) vehicle condition, or (b) the character or conduct of the holder. Notice is served on the licence holder.
(2) Allows the court to revoke a licence on conviction of a crime which renders the holder unfit to hold a licence.

R 13 Enables a Commissioner to *suspend* a licence.

R 14 *Appeal* lies to the District Court for refusal, revocation or suspension of a licence on the grounds that the owner of the vehicle is not a fit and proper person. In any other case the appeal is to the Minister for the Environment.

PSV Regulations 1978, Rg 14: Precedent

[The District Court]

District Court Area District No

Between

[AB]

Appellant

[and]

[CD]

Respondent

NOTICE OF APPEAL

TAKE NOTICE that AB of in the County of HEREBY APPEALS to the District Court sitting at on the day of 19 at 11 am or the next opportunity thereafter against the decision of Respondent refusing a Public Service Vehicle Licence to the appellant in respect of vehicle No (or Revoking/Suspending) pursuant to Article 14 of the Road Traffic (Public Service Vehicle) (Licensing) Regulations 1978 (SI No 292/1978) as amended.

[Dated]

Signed: ______________________________

Solicitors for Appellant

To/The District Court Clerk, of
AND TO/CD Garda Siochana Officer, of

Notes: (1) The Court Area is where the Appellant resides.
(2) Respondent is a Garda Officer exercising the function of the Commissioner.
(3) Ten-day service applies. Stamped original and a Declaration of Service to be given to the District Court Clerk at least four days before the Court sits.

R 15 Commissioner on granting a licence must issue a *vehicle plate*. It must contain the words 'Feithicle Seirbhise Poibli' and the serial number of the licence. It can be replaced if lost. Amended by SI 139/1987.

R 16 The plate must be given back to the Commissioner on the licence ceasing, being annulled or suspended. Penal. Amended by SI 139/1987.

R 17 If the licence holder *changes address*, the Commissioner must be notified within three days. Penal.

R 18 Sets out the fees payable in various applications, inspections, and grants.

R 19 Commissioner must keep a *register* of PSV licences, which must be available for public inspection.

R 20 Enables the Commissioner to have a PSV examined and/or inspected. The owner must co-operate and produce the vehicle. Penal.

Notes: (1) Section 82(7) of the 1961 Act provides a presumption, until the contrary is proved, that a licence under the Regulations is not held.
(2) Section 115 of the 1961 Act sets out penalties for false declarations, certificates, licences, plates, their wrongful use, etc. (para 7.4).

1.15 Control of taximeters

Section 83 of the 1961 Act is a very technical section and must be read together with the Weights and Measures Acts (1889–1961). These are beyond the scope of this book. The Acts and sections in question, however, appear to be s 35 of the Weights and Measures Act, 1889 as extended by s 10 of the Weights and Measures Act 1928, and s 5 of the Weights and Measures Act 1904.

Section 83 of the 1961 Act deals with the verification of taximeters, and for that purpose it extends the definition of measuring instruments in the Weights and Measures Acts to include taximeters. The Commissioner of the Garda can appoint inspectors, called special inspectors, subject to sanction by the Minister for Finance, for the inspection, verification and stamping of taximeters, with the powers of Weights and Measures Inspectors. The section allows fees to be charged for these verifications, etc. Any such special inspector can be suspended or removed by the Commissioner. He must have a certificate under s 8 of the Weights and Measures Act 1904 or a special certificate under s 83 of the 1961 Act, granted by the Minister for Trade, Commerce and Tourism.

The special inspector has, in addition to his powers under s 83 of the 1961 Act, all the powers of an Inspector under the Weights and Measures Acts. The Commissioner must provide him with standards to be set and equipment to enable him to perform his duties. The powers of Weights and Measures Inspectors of Dublin and Dunlaoghaire are restricted in dealing with taximeters, i.e. their powers under these Acts do not apply to taximeters since 1964. This leaves control in the hands of the Garda Commissioner for the Country, i.e. of those areas which are the taximeter areas as defined in the Regulations of 1963 as amended (listed above—para 1.13).

The Minister for Trade, Commerce and Tourism, after consulting with the Minister for the Environment (or the Minister for Finance in respect of certain matters), can make regulations in relation to certain matters, e.g. the provision and maintenance of standards and equipment.

No specific regulations have been made under s 83 itself, but the following regulations made under the Road Traffic Act 1933 are deemed under s 10 of the 1961 Act to be made under the section (having been made under an identical s 136 of the 1933 Act)

Taximeters (Fees on verification and stamping by Special Inspectors) Regulations 1938 (SI 284/1938). These provide for payments by a person who submits the taximeter for verification and stamping to the special inspector of a fee of $12\frac{1}{2}$ pence.

Special Inspectors (Taximeter)(Grant of Certificate) Regulations 1937 (SI 285/1938). These regulations provide that a Garda who wishes to become a special inspector must go through an examination (in accordance with a syllabus on the lines specified by the Minister for Industry and Commerce) conducted by a person appointed by such Minister. The examiner reports on satisfactory candidates to the Minister. The Minister can grant any candidate mentioned in the report a Special Inspectors Certificate.

Weights and Measures (Taximeter: Section 136 of the Road Traffic Act 1933) Regulations 1938 (SI 286 of 1938). These state that the Garda Commissioner must provide equipment for special Inspectors which has to be verified annually. Records must be kept by special inspectors. The regulations set out the marks to be used in the verification of taximeters and the taximeter specification on slots, flags, etc.

Inspection must be annual. The regulations provide for secrecy by special inspectors. Inspectors are not to be bribed. The regulations also set out other guidelines for inspectors e.g. that a taxi has a 'For Hire' flag.

The regulations are somewhat quaint, viewed 50 years later, with references to shillings and pence, etc. also remaining in force.

Weights and Measures (Taximeter: Section 136 of the Road Traffic Act 1933) (Amendment) Regulations, 1958 (SI 139 of 1958). These regulations effect minor amendments to SI 286/1938, setting out a new design for the verification stamps.

1.16 Control of taxi stands

The control of taxi stands is dealt with by s 84/1961 Act (as amended by Sch, 1968 Act).

1.16.1 Bye-laws

The Commissioner of the Gardai can with the consent of the Minister, make bye-laws for a specified area designating 'Appointed stands' as the places where street service vehicles may stand for hire.

A specified power under this section can by order of the Minister under s 62 of the 1968 Act, be transferred for a specified area to a specified Road Authority.

Section 3 of the 1961 Act defines 'street service vehicle' as a small public service vehicle, the driver of which offers in a public place himself and the vehicle for hire, and for that purpose stands or drives the vehicle in a public place.

The bye-laws can and do normally fix the appointed stands; the maximum number of taxis at the stand; prohibit taxis from standing elsewhere than at appointed stands; and generally regulate and control the use of the appointed stands. They normally prohibit the vehicles from 'standing' elsewhere. Also, the stand can only be used as such. Thus, in *Rodgers v Raylor*, *The Times*, 28 October 1986 it was an offence to leave the taxi unattended for an hour when the driver was not plying for hire, i.e. just parking.

Before making such bye-laws the Commissioner must consult with the local authority (County Council, Urban District Council, etc.) for the area and must also get the consent of the Minister for the Environment. Different bye-laws can be made in respect of different circumstances.

In order to get the Minister's permission and to publish Notice of the bye-laws, the provisions of the Road Traffic (Bye-laws and Temporary Rules) Regulations 1961 (SI 219/1961) must be complied with. These require the Commissioner to send two copies of the bye-laws to the Minister with proof that the local authority was consulted as required in s 6 of the 1961 Act (see para 7.6). When the Minister approves, a Notice of making the bye-laws has to be published in at least three newspapers (one at least being a daily) circulating in the effected area. The Notice must specify the section under which the bye-law is made, the area of operation, and where a copy can be purchased and at what price.

Note: The fixed penalty procedure for 'on the spot' fines for parking on these stands by non-taxis applies (see para 5.11.2).

Normally the provisions of bye-laws are largely repetitions of the Act, with additional details such as the location of the stand, the number of vehicles that can stand there and the conditions of standing. The following bye-laws are in operation:

Carlow	SI No 283 of 1988
Cork	SI No 179 of 1965
Donegal	SI No 243 of 1986
Drogheda	SI No 77 of 1988
Dublin	SI No 104 of 1986
Dundalk	SI No 171 of 1965
Ennis	SI No 162 of 1965
Galway	SI No 303 of 1986
Kilkenny	SI No 200 of 1988
Killarney	SI No 71 of 1981
Limerick	SI No 102 of 1981
Longford	SI No 185 of 1987
Naas	SI No 201 of 1988
Tralee	SI No 203 of 1965
Waterford	SI No 288 of 1982

1.16.2 Temporary rules

The Commissioner is given power to make, with the consent of the Minister for the Environment, temporary rules as to taxi stands as in para 1.16.1. Again, under s 62 of the 1968 Act this can be transferred to a local Road Authority. This power is intended for experimental rules and particular events, e.g. public festivals, etc. They have normally operated for one year and Notice of their making must be given. They come into operation one week after they are made and will, during the period of their operation, overrule bye-laws under the previous paragraph. Different rules can be made for different circumstances.

The procedure for making the rules and for giving Notice of them is set out in SI 219/61 and I 60/1962. It is referred to in para 7.6 in more detail, but is briefly that Notice of the rules must be given in three newspapers (one at least of which is a daily) circulating in the effected area. The Notice must state the section under which rules are made, the date and the area effected, and where and for how much copies can be bought.

1.16.3 Offence

A taxi driver contravening a bye-law or rule is guilty of an offence, to which the general penalty under s 102 of the 1961 Act (para 7.1) applies. The owner, if not the driver, is also liable, unless he shows that the use at the time was not authorised by him.

1.17 Control of omnibus stops and stands

1.17.1 Directions

This control is dealt with in s 85 of the 1961 Act. In the Act a bus is referred to as an 'omnibus', and this is defined in s 3 of the 1961 Act as a large public service vehicle which is for the time being used on a definite route for the carriage of passengers who are carried at separate fares and are picked up and set down along such route, whether on request or at fixed stops.

The Commissioner of the Garda Siochana can issue written directions as to the routes, stopping places (for picking up and for setting down of passengers) and the stands of omnibuses, which directions he can amend or revoke. His powers include directing that these stops shall have a notice indicating they are such, i.e. the normal bus stop signs we see in cities. The directing notice must be addressed to the operator of the 'Bus Service', signed by the Commissioner or other authorised officer, and be served on the operator by registered post. It operates from the date stated in the directing notice or date of service, whichever is the later. Calculation of the service time is governed by s 18 of the Interpretation Act 1937 which provides that such service is deemed, unless the contrary is proved, to have been affected as that which such letter would normally be delivered in the ordinary course of post. A Garda's certificate as to a notice having effect for a specified day or period is prima facie proof of its validity without proof of the signature.

Under the Transport (Reorganisation of Coras Iompair Eireann) Act 1986 bus services are now run by Irish Bus Company and Dublin Bus Company as subsidiary companies of Coras Iompair Eireann.

Specified powers of the Commissioner for specified areas can be transferred by Order of the Minister to a Road Authority specified under s 62 of the 1968 Act.

1.17.2 Regulations

Under the provisions of s 86(2) of the 1961 Act and s 58 of the 1968 Act, the Minister for the Environment can make regulations in respect of stopping places and stands for omnibuses. These regulations would be supplemental to and more general than the Commissioner's directing notices under para 1.17.1 above.

They can provide for the controlling of the stopping of buses on routes, the uses of stops and stands by buses, the prohibiting of other vehicles from using or being near stops, and the regulating of the order and queuing of passengers at stops and stands. The regulations can be varied for different classes of vehicles or different circumstances. Contravention of the regulations is an offence (general penalty para 7.1 applies). The owner of an omnibus involved is liable in addition to the person using it, unless he shows the use was unauthorised. If a vehicle other than an omnibus is involved in the improper use, then the user, the registered owner, or (if the vehicle is on hire drive) the hirer is liable. In this latter case the registered owner has two defences—either (a) that the use was unauthorised, or (b) that the vehicle was on a hire drive. The hirer of a vehicle on hire drive has the defence of unauthorised use available to him only if he establishes that the use in question was both unauthorised and by another person.

Under s 6(7) of the 1961 Act every bye-law under s 86 is required to be laid before each House of the Oireachtas and may be amended by resolution of either within 21 sitting days of such laying, but without prejudice to the validity of anything done thereunder. It should be noted that under the 1961 Act it was the Garda Commissioner who made the Regulations. The 1968 Act transferred the power to the Minister for the Environment. The present regulation is the Omnibus (Stopping Places and Stands) General Bye-laws 1961 (SI 122 of 1962). Its main provisions briefly are:

R 3 Bus drivers can only stop at designated stops if there are such on his route. If stops are on position of route, only they must use them.

R 4 If the stop is designated to let persons down only, the driver cannot take up passengers there; and if only for picking up, then he cannot set down passengers there.

R 5 Driver cannot, without reasonable cause, park at a stop. A reasonable cause is a circumstance beyond his control, e.g. breakdown.

R 6 When a driver stops at a designated stop he can remain there only for the period necessary to discharge his function. See s 85(4) of the 1961 Act. If an omnibus bears a notice indicating that it will stop only at designated stopping places, the driver must stop only at those places.

R 7 If markings are provided on the road at stopping places, he (driver) must stop within them, unless prevented by road conditions, etc. If no markings are provided, then he must stop as near to the left edge as possible (i.e. not more than 1½ feet out).

R 8 When stopping the driver must have regard to the queue on the roadway and other circumstances.

R 9 The bus can only be parked at designated stands, or for taking up or setting down passengers in accordance with regulations, or because of accident or breakdown. If markings are provided he must park within them if possible, unless prevented by road conditions, operations, obstruction or other sufficient cause.

R 10 No one else can park a vehicle within the markings, except during any period of taking or of setting down passengers or while unloading goods to adjacent premises, or on the occurrence of an accident, breakdown or other circumstances beyond his control.

R 11 A Garda or official of the bus operator (e.g. Dublin Bus/Irish Bus) can give persons at stands directions to maintain order and for queuing. If no orders are given and more than six persons are at the stop, they should queue. All persons waiting must be orderly and obey signs at the stop, and queue as per the signs, e.g. not more than two abreast. The queue must be facing the direction indicated in the sign on the footpath and in their order of entering the queue, and enter the bus in that order. Persons waiting must wait for disembarking passengers to alight before entering themselves.

Parking at stops—Fines
By virtue of s 103 of the 1961 Act, as amended, and the regulations thereunder the fixed penalty or 'on the spot' fine procedure applies to parking at bus stops and stands (see para 5.11.2).

1.17.3 Markings and shelters and lanes

Signs and markings
Mention has been made in para 1.17.1 of the Garda Commissioner's power under s 85 of the 1961 Act to direct by notice that bus stops be indicated. Section 86(9) of the 1961 Act allows the Commissioner to enjoin the operator of the service (who can do it voluntarily also) to provide at stops and stands signs and markings on the road showing where other vehicles may not stop or park, and the regulations discussed in para 1.17.2 adopt and enforce these. These markings must be of a type approved by the Minister for the Environment. The consent of the relevant Road Authority (e.g. Corporation) is not necessary for these markings. In a prosecution relating to the marked area, the markings are presumed valid until the contrary is shown. The existing regulations are the Road Traffic (Signs) Regulations 1962 (SI 171/1962, Part III) (as amended by SI 233/1966, R 7) which specify the type and size of bus stop signs, form and colour of markings, the white lines' distance from kerbs and longitudinal broken white lines, etc.

Shelters
The operator of a bus service can provide and maintain, or contribute to the provision of, shelters at stops or stands. If the shelter is on a public road (see definition, para 7.9), the Road authority's consent must be obtained.

It is an offence attracting the general penalty (para 7.1) for a person without lawful authority to remove, deface or damage a sign or shelter.

Controls under the Local Government (Planning and Development) Act 1963 as amended, apply to the erection of 'bus shelters, etc.', as these would be 'development' within the meaning of that Act.

Lanes
There is a special provision for markings of roads to allow special bus lanes and to erect signs therefor. These are in the Road Traffic (Signs) (Bus Lanes) Regulations 1980 (SI 358/1980 and SI 333/1981 (amending). These regulations allow for not only special lanes for buses only, but also for contra flow bus lanes, i.e. so that buses can proceed along lanes in the direction opposite the normal flow of traffic. They allow markings, signs and plates to be in Irish or English.

1.18 Control of lost property

1.18.1 Bye-laws

A variety of articles may be left inadvertently or otherwise in a public service vehicle. The Garda Commissioner is empowered to make bye-laws to deal with this matter under s 87 of the 1961 Act (as amended by Sch, 1968 Act). These bye-laws can provide for depositing by the owner, driver or conductor of the articles at a specified place within a specified time; the redelivery to owners of deposited articles; and their custody in the interim and fees therefore. Disposal of unclaimed articles, live animals, perishable or offensive articles, etc. can also be regulated. Before making such bye-laws, however, the Commissioner must be satisfied that satisfactory provision has not been made for the safe custody, redelivery and disposal of such property. It is therefore rather curious that after over 28 years of operation only one set of bye-laws has been made under the section, and that is only in relation to the Dublin taximeter area. The section says that bye-laws can be made only for areas and vehicles where satisfactory provisions have not been made for the safe custody, delivery and disposal of the lost property.

Present bye-laws

These are Street Service Vehicles (Dublin) (Lost Property) Bye-laws 1983 (SI 365/1983). These repealed earlier 1963 and 1968 bye-laws which also dealt with the Dublin situation.

The 1983 bye-laws provide that if a passenger leaves property in a street service vehicle, the driver must within 24 hours (excluding night time 6 pm–9 am) return it to the passenger or lodge it in 'The Carriage Office', which is The Garda Siochana Carriage Office, Harcourt Street, Dublin. The driver gets a receipt. The owner can claim it there. If not so claimed within 31 days, the depositor is notified, and if he claims it within a further 31 days it is returned to the depositor. If not claimed by the owner or driver within these periods, it is forwarded to the Dublin Metropolitan Garda Division Stores at Kevin Street Garda Station and it can be disposed of by public sale. The periods mentioned above can be extended by The Carriage Office because of the nature or value of the property.

If the property lost is a live animal, or is perishable or offensive in character, The Carriage Office can take any necessary steps for the safe custody or disposal of the property.

1.18.2 Offence

Contravention of a bye-law is an offence carrying the general penalty (para 7.1). In any proceedings under the bye-laws an extract from the register of lost articles is prima facie evidence of its contents without providing the validity of the signature of the signing Garda Officer. The register itself is absolute proof of its validity on production by a Garda Officer.

1.18.3 Register

The Commissioner is obliged to have set up a Register of Lost Property where there are bye-laws in operation, in such form and manner as he directs. The register must be available for public inspection at all reasonable times on payment of the prescribed fee, and certified extracts must likewise be made available on payment of a like fee.

1.18.4 Larceny Act 1916

This Act provides for larceny by finding, i.e. if one finds a lost article one must take reasonable steps to find the owner otherwise one is guilty of larceny. Normally articles are taken to Garda Stations.

1.19 Control of damage

An unfortunate type of hooliganism which has been particularly manifest in recent years is damage to public or semi-public property. In addition to the normal criminal sanctions under the Malicious Damages Acts, etc., a special provision is found in s 56 of the 1968 Act in relation to damage to Public Service Vehicles. This provides a further criminal sanction for such damage with the general penalty as under s 102 of the 1961 Act (para 7.1) and a power to award compensation against the convicted persons to the owner for damage or injury, plus compensation for time lost by the owner, driver or conductor in attending Court. The last provision is in part superfluous as Courts have the power to award witness expenses, but it may cover consequential loss apart from the damage. These and the compensation provision may be unconstitutional having regard to the decision concerning a somewhat similar provision under s 57 of the 1961 Act (see para 6.3.3) on compensation for breach of insurance requirements (*Cullen v A-G* [1979] IR 394).

Before the sanctions come into force the persons must be found guilty of wilfully or maliciously committing any damage or injury to a public service vehicle. No definition of 'maliciously' is set out, so presumably it covers intentional or reckless disregard for the consequences of the action in line with the general criminal Law. Also ancillary (discretionary) disqualification and endorsement may apply. A Garda has power to arrest without warrant a person he reasonably suspects of having committed such an offence and who refuses to give his name and address, or gives one which the Garda believes to be misleading.

1.20 Control by tests and examinations

1.20.1 Introduction

See para 1.8, and in particular para 1.8.5, as to special additional provisions re public service vehicles and fleet inspections; and para 1.8.6 as to EEC requirements on tests.

There is a special mention of public service vehicles in s 20 of the 1961 Act (as amended by Sch, 1968 Act) in relation to powers of Gardai to carry out occasional examinations and tests on vehicles.

1.20.2 Control of weight

As to weight of vehicles generally, see para 1.7 *supra*.

Regulations 7(6) of Road Traffic (Construction Equipment and Use of Vehicles) Regulations 1963 (SI 190/1963) states that in calculating the weight (laden) of a large public service vehicle, or the weight transmitted by an axle or wheel thereof, the vehicle shall be deemed to be carrying its full complement of standing and sitting passengers, and weights of 140 lbs each shall be placed in the correct relative positions for the driver, conductor and each passenger.

1.20.3 Control of driving periods

There are special limitations on continuous driving of large public service vehicles. These are dealt with at para 4.12.

1.20.4 Driving licences and test

The separate classification of large public service vehicles for the purpose of driving licences and driving tests is mentioned at para 2.3

1.21 Control of construction

Parts V and VI of Road Traffic (Construction, Equipment and Use of Vehicles) Regulations 1963 (SI 190/1963) deals with application of the provisions (those specified at para 1.5 (*supra*) of this chapter) to small and large public service vehicles. An outline of these provisions is set out below.

Part V Small Public Service Vehicles

R 49 *Equipment* which must be carried—spare wheel, jack and tool kit.
R 50 *Limits* passenger accommodation to that specified under the public service vehicles regulations 1963, but allows three children under 15 to be counted as two adults for the purpose of the regulations.
R 51 *Licensed Public Hire Vehicles* must have four doors, a permanent top and proper seats. This Regulation was amended by SI 291/1978 to the effect that seats must be properly upholstered and kept clean.
R 52 *School vehicles* under licence exempt.

PART VI Large Public Service Vehicles

R 53 Has *definitions* of vehicles, entrance, exit, double or single decker vehicles.
R 54 All large PSVs must *comply* with the provisions of Art 55 to 79 (below) while in a public place.
R 55 *Maximum height*—15 feet.
R 56 *Stability*—standards set out.
R 57 *Suspension* must prevent excessive sway.
R 58 *Turning* circle not to exceed 82 feet.
R 59 *Side overhang* not to exceed 6 inches.
R 60 Revoked by SI 194/1969.
R 61 *Guard rails* between wheels more than 2 feet apart.
R 62 Revoked by SI 211/1970.
R 63 *Hub projection* not to be more than 3½ inches outside tyre.
R 64 *Fuel tanks* must be safe and per specifications.
R 65 *Exhaust pipes* must be safe to prevent fire and from fumes point of view.
R 66 *Electrical* equipment must be safe from going on fire.
R 67 *General construction* must be proper—i.e. body upholstery, good, fittings, floors, roof ventilation, signals to driver, etc. in order.
R 68 *Steps, platforms and stairs* must be safe and adequate.
R 69/74 *Exits* must be proper, including emergency exits, with proper access as specified in detail.
R 74 *Seats* must be of adequate dimension, comfort, etc.
R 76 *Driver's* accommodation must be adequate and safe.
R 77 *Accommodation* must be *marked* on vehicle.
R 78 *Maintenance* of outside and inside and parts must be proper.
R 80 *Passenger limited*—method of calculation as to children's seating amended by SI 297/1974 to extend the under-usage of School Transport, allowing large PSVs to calculate passenger load on basis of three children being equal to two adults.
R 81 *Equipment* must include fire extinguisher, jack, first-aid kit.
R 82 *Number of passengers* must not exceed specified capacity.
R 83 *No obstruction* of exits and gangways should be allowed.
R 84 *Exemption* was granted to certain pre-1961 vehicles and school vehicles.
R 85 *Owners* liable for breach of Regulations as well as users.

1.22 Visiting vehicles

Regulations with regard to visiting vehicles are important, as Ireland receives a great deal of tourist traffic each year. Paragraph 4 above deals with the general dispensing and regulating power of the Minister for the Environment and relation to vehicle requirements generally under s 38 of the Local Government Act 1955.

1.22 *Visiting vehicles*

A vehicle brought into the State temporarily by a visitor does not require a public service vehicle licence if it is licensed in the State in which it is registered under provisions corresponding to those here (Art 3 of the Mechanically Propelled Vehicles (International Circulation) (Amendment) Order 1963 (SI 193/1963). The 1963 Regulations have been amended by a series of amending regulations up to SI 140/1987.

Drivers of visiting vehicles are also exempted from the special controls that apply to drivers of these types of vehicles.

1.23 Horse-drawn vehicle permits

The Towns Improvement Act 1854, and some local Acts of like effect, provide for the control of horse-drawn hackney carriages. The 1854 Act provides for the licensing of such hackneys and their drivers and for bye-laws for fixing stands and fares.

PART – 3 OTHER CONTROL OF VEHICLES

In this Part we look at odds and ends of controls on vehicles. They are of general application.

1.24 Control of unattended vehicles

Unattended vehicles can be left so for short or long periods. See para 1.10 for the short-term offence. The removal, storage and disposal of abandoned or unlawfully parked vehicles is provided for by s 97 of the 1961 Act (as substituted by s 63 of the 1968). This is done by regulations made by the Minister for the Environment. The regulations can apply to vehicles which:

(a) have been, or appear to have been, abandoned on a public road; and
(b) have been parked in contravention of s 101 (para 5.5); and
(c) have been parked in contravention of the Acts or of a regulation, bye-law or Rule made thereunder.

'Vehicle' includes a part of a vehicle, a load on or in a vehicle, or a non-functioning vehicle. The regulations can specify who does the removal, etc. and how the owners can get the vehicles back and at what cost. They can also arrange for the disposal of unclaimed vehicles (with different regulations able to be made for different circumstances where appropriate). Disposal can be effected six weeks after removal or two weeks after giving the prescribed notice, whichever is the longer. An indemnity against liability for acts done in good faith, without negligence, is given to persons acting under the section in removal, storage or disposal. Any person obstructing the removal of a vehicle shall be guilty of an offence, with the general penalty apply (para 7.1).

This matter of removal, etc. of vehicles is dealt with in para 5.12 more fully.

1.25 Control of approval marks

Vehicles and their parts are becoming standardised internationally, so it is important that external and internal marks be standardised and be given legal recognition. The Merchandise Marks Acts 1887-1931 normally gave the validity of markings as a trade description. Section 14 of the 1968 Act allows the Minister for the Environment to designate markings of vehicles (or parts) approved under any international agreement to which the State is a party to be approved markings amounting to a trade description under the Merchandise Marks Acts. Before use of such a mark it will be necessary to get permission from the Minister and the competent authority of the country of origin. The Minister is given power to make regulations to give effect to the section. Unauthorised application of an approved mark or one closely resembling it is an offence to which the general penalty applies (para 7.1).

This section enables the State to accede to the 1958 European Agreement concerning Uniform Conditions of Approval and reciprocal Recognition of Approval for Motor Vehicle Equipment Parts.

1.26 Holding on, etc. to vehicles

This is dealt with at para 4.11.

1.27 Taking vehicles without authority

This is dealt with at para 4.10.

1.28 Interference with vehicles

This is dealt with at para 4.11.

1.29 Control of nuisance by vehicles

1.29.1 Saver

It is relevant to mention here that nothing in the Act (e.g. possession of certificates, re-construction, etc.) prevents the bringing of an action for a private nuisance created by a vehicle or an indictment, as the case may be (s 125 of the 1961 Act). This means that recourse to the Common Law remedies and other statutory provisions are unaffected by these Road Traffic Acts.

1.29.2 Rights of way

The obstruction of a right of way over a public road is normally a nuisance if the obstruction is unreasonable. As to obstruction see para 4.8. It can be a public nuisance actionable at the suit of the Attorney-General or a private nuisance actionable by an injured individual. The immunity of the State in tort has been abolished in Ireland generally. See McMahon & Binchy on 'Torts' and their casebook in relation to this matter.

1.29.3 Criminal nuisance

There are also criminal sanctions, albeit slender ones, for such nuisances in some of the provisions of the Summary Jurisdiction Act 1851:

s 13(3)—Obstructing free passage of a person—Fine £1
s 10(2)—Playing games to danger of passengers—Fine 50p
s 10(3)—Leaving carts unharnessed on road, unless accidentally broken down—Fine 50p
s 10(4)—Leaving dead beast on road or within 30 yards of centre—Fine 50p
s 10(8)—Making bonfires on roads or within 60 feet of its centre—Fine 50p
s 10(9)—Carrying loads projecting over 2 feet beyond wheels—Fine 50p
s 12(14)—Leaving unattended/uncontrolled carts on road—Fine 50p

By s 14 Gardai can remove the nuisance to a safe place as security for the fine or get a warrant from a District Justice so to do. A Road Authority can get a similar warrant. A Garda can arrest without warrant an offender unknown to him, i.e. whom he does not know.

The Towns Improvement Act 1854 and the Town Police Clauses Act 1847 have somewhat similar provisions which, because of their tiny penalties, are largely of historic interest, i.e. offences done to the obstruction, annoyance, or danger of residents or passengers on streets by:

Holding shows or repairing carts	Fine 50p
Drawing timber or iron beams unsecured	Fine £1
Placing merchandise and awnings	Fine £1
Rolling casks, wheelbarrows, except for loading	Fine £1
Making bonfires, or snow slides	Fine 50p
Unfenced cellar entrances	Fine 50p

The Dublin Police Act 1842 has somewhat similar provisions.

1.29.4 Litter

The Local Government (Planning Development) Act 1963, s 52 imposes up to £10 fine on any person (including a vehicle user) who throws down, places or leaves on a public place food remnants, rubble or rubbish except in litter bins, etc. Planning authorities would prosecute.

The Litter Act 1982 deals with the problem of litter. It creates liabilities and severely punishes the offences of the creation of litter, and allows for the appointment of Litter Wardens. The provisions of particular relevance to vehicles are;

(1) Section 3 creates a fairly wide prohibition on the creation of litter in a public place or litter that is visible from a public place. It further prohibits the loading, transport, or unloading of material that creates or tends to create litter. Where a mechanically propelled vehicle is involved by use in the commission, then the registered owner, or, if on hire drive, the hirer or user is liable if the vehicle is not a public service vehicle. The registered owner has a defence if he shows the vehicle was used by an unauthorised person or was on hire drive. A hirer under a hire drive agreement has a good defence if he shows unauthorised use by another person. 'Hire drive agreement' is widely defined in s 1—more widely than in the Road Traffic Acts (see para 7.9). In the Litter Act 1982 it means all agreements under which the vehicle is hired, except a hire-purchase agreement, an agreement merely for the carriage of goods or persons, or an agreement under which the registered owner of the vehicle drives, or provides a driver for, the vehicle. 'Public place' is also more widely defined than that under the Road Traffic Act, as is 'vehicle'. 'Public place' includes the places referred to in the Road Traffic Acts but with the addition of the seashore; 'vehicle' is stated to include part of a vehicle, an article designed as a vehicle, a skip designed or used for carriage in a vehicle and a load on a vehicle. 'Registered owner', 'mechanically propelled vehicle', and 'public service vehicle' have the same meanings as under the Road Traffic Acts—see para 7.9.

The maximum fine for an offence is £800 (s 1(5)).

(2) Under s 9-13 duties are created for local authorities to provide places for abandoning vehicles. Prohibitions are created on the abandonment of vehicles on other people's land unless authorised (fine £800). Such a vehicle may be removed by a local authority, on service of Notice to the occupier of the land, and subject to certain conditions. The local authority can then dispose of the vehicle. Any money accruing on such disposal is to be disposed of as the Minister for the Environment directs.

1.29.5 Other nuisances

Vehicles can create nuisances which may be public or private in their legal classification, e.g. an excessive or dangerous load, or a load which is a nuisance.

An information of alleged danger or nuisance, if the regulation so specifies, may be bad for duplicity (*St Albans v Minnis* (1981) RTR 231).

1.29.6 EEC standards

Under para 1.5 above many standards for vehicles are set out. The EEC by Directives and Regulations lay down many standards of reference. It is not possible to discuss all these, but some examples are given here:

(a) Council Directive 88/76/EEC, amending 70/220/EEC relating to measures to be taken against air pollution by gases from the engines of motor vehicles.
88/77/EEC has similar provisions for diesel engines.
88/195/EEC deals with laws on engine power.
(b) Directive 88/194/EEC approximate laws on breaking devices and their trailers (see para 1.5.5.3).

1.30 Control of driving and parking of vehicles

The control of the misuse of vehicles is also referred to and substantial penalties imposed by:

(a) Section 53 of the 1961 Act (*dangerous driving*) which has consideration of the condition of the vehicle—see para 4.2.
(b) Section 54 of the 1961 Act (*driving a dangerously defective vehicle*)—see para 4.6.
(c) Section 55 of the 1961 Act (*dangerous parking*)—see para 4.7.

1.31 Control of animal traffic

While animals are not vehicles they form part of road traffic. Traffic is not defined in the Acts, but obviously animals are traffic. In modern times the law takes a less indulgent view of the conduct of this type of traffic.

1.31.1 Old controls

The Dublin Police Act 1842 imposes penalties of £2 for various offences, such as turning animals loose on the street, causing mischief by negligently driving cattle on the street and leading or riding animals on the footpath.

The Town Police Clauses Act 1847 and the Towns Improvement Act 1854 have somewhat similar provisions—exposing animals for sale except at a market fair; turning loose animals; letting unmuzzled ferocious dogs loose—fine 50p. You can be fined £1 for leading or riding a horse on a footpath, or indeed driving a cart on the footpath. Beware of these unrepealed laws!

The Summary Jurisdiction Act 1851 penalises many types of conduct, including:

urging a dog to attack a person or animals in a public place—fine 50p (s 10(1));
turning animals loose on a street—fine 50p (s 10(1));
negligently driving cattle that cause mischief—fine 50p (s 10(1));
exposing animals for sale or hire except at fairs — fine £2
allowing swine and animals to wander on roads—fine 10p (s 10(11)).

Gardai and Road Authorities have abatement powers under s 14.

Other Acts controlling dogs were Dogs Act 1871, s 2 and Dogs Act 1906, s 1. More particulars of these offences can be found in O'Connor's '*Justice of the Peace*'. See para 1.31.3**(iv)** re Control of Dogs Act 1986.

1.31.2 Impounding animals

Under some of the above Acts and the Pounds (Provision and Maintenance) Act 1935 wandering animals can be impounded. This 1935 Act was substantially amended by the Animals Act 1985 giving wider powers of impoundage, increasing the cost of keeping these animals or obtaining their release, and allowing for the creation of private pounds (see below 5.17.5).

1.31.3 Modern controls

(i) Section 92 of the 1961 Act prevents obstruction of traffic by fairs and markets by allowing its regulation (see para 5.7).

(ii) The Road Traffic General Bye-laws 1964, Part V (as amended) deal with animals on the road.

BL2 Provides that 'animal' does not include a cat or dog; that a person riding or leading an animal is deemed to be the driver; and every driver is deemed to be in charge of the animals.

BL30 Requires a driver of a vehicle meeting or overtaking an animal to reduce speed or halt if requested to do so (by signal or otherwise) by a person in charge of the animal.

BL31 Provides that drivers on a road must take reasonable steps to ensure that the animal does not obstruct traffic; is not driven on cycle track or footpath; and that overtaking vehicles can do so in safety.

BL32 A person leading a horse along a road must do so on the right side of the road. It should be noted that under s 13(2) of the Summary Jurisdiction (Ir) Act 1851 a person riding or leading a horse shall lead the horse on the side farthest away from any carriage on passing him on the road—if he does not he is liable to a fine of 50p.

BL33 Drivers in lighting up hours—drovers must carry a lamp to warn other road users of the presence of animals. The lamp must show a white light to the front, and red to the rear and should be visible at a reasonable distance. The bye-law does not apply—

(1) Under BL5 circumstances (below); and

(2) where non-compliance does not, and is not likely to, endanger other traffic or a pedestrian.

Breach of bye-laws is subject to the general penalty (para 7.1).

Limitations

It should be noted under these general bye-laws that the above rules may be varied as to compliance by:

BL3 Directions by Garda Siochana can override them.
BL4 If conflict arises between Special Traffic Regulation (see Chapter 7), bye-laws and temporary rules, these latter will prevail.
BL5 The rules do not bind a driver where road works, building operations, or obstruction of traffic, or emergencies not reasonably anticipated arise (see also para 5.3—General Bye-law 1964 (SI 294/1964), Part V).

(iii) Animals Act 1985, s 2 removed the old rule under *Searle v Wallbank* [1947] AC 341, and now there is a duty of care to prevent animals straying on to the public road.

Sections 4, 5 and 6 extend substantially the powers of impounding animals.

(iv) Control of Dogs Act 1986 generally strengthened the law on the control of dogs. This licensing system of dogs was tightened and the powers of collection of and distribution of stray or unwanted dogs are extensive under the Act. Section 9 limits the right of leaving dogs in public places. The dog must be in the charge of a person who must control it. Section 10 states that a person shall not permit a greyhound in any public place, unless such greyhound is being held by means of a sufficiently strong chain or leash. A person shall not lead, or cause or permit to be led by any one person, more than four greyhounds at a time in any public place. As to 'public place', see para 7.9.

1.31.4 Control of vehicles for animal use

The Diseases of Animals Act 1966 enables the Minister for Agriculture and Fisheries to make orders:

(a) regarding the cleansing of vehicles used for the conveyance of animals, etc. to deal with disease;
(b) prescribing the construction, dimension and fitting of vehicles used for conveyance of animals, etc. to deal with disease and injury.

1.32 Control of visiting vehicles

The Local Government Act 1955, s 39 empowers the Minister for the Environment by order to modify the requirements of any Act in respect of vehicles in relation to visiting vehicles. Under this section the Mechanically Propelled Vehicles (International Circulation) Orders 1961-1966 (SI 269/1961, 12/1962, 193/1963, 59/1964, 99/1966, 346/1980, and 215/1983) have been made. The effect of these in so far as this chapter is concerned is that if the vehicle complies with International Conventions specified, it is deemed to comply with all regulations made under ss 11 and 12 of the 1961 Act (paras 5, 6 and 7 above), except those relating to weight, dimensions and the number of trailers drawn (see Art 12 of the 1961 Order as amended by Art 4 of the 1962 Order, which also inserts a new Part III to First Schedule of the 1961 Order).

The Conventions in question are the International Convention Relative to Road Traffic, adopted in Paris on 24 April 1926, and a similar one adopted at Geneva on 19 September 1949.

1.33 Control of vehicle fuel and movement of dangerous substances

1.33.1 Keeping vehicle fuel

The 1961 Act, s 122 allowed the Minister for the Environment to make regulations to control the owners of vehicles in relation to the keeping and using of petrol and other inflammable liquid or fuel. This was repealed by the Dangerous Substances Act 1972.

1.33.2 Petroleum storage licences

The Dangerous Substances Act 1972 enables local authorities to grant licences for the storage of petroleum spirit.

Lengthy regulations called the Dangerous Substances (Conveyance Petroleums by Road) Regulations 1979 (SI 314/1979) have been made under the Act. These require in relation to vehicles (tankers and trailers) conveying, loading or unloading petroleum that, *inter alia*:

(1) competent persons be employees;
(2) they be instructed and supervised;
(3) drivers get safety booklets;
(4) drivers have periodic medical examinations;
(5) employees have proper first-aid, protective clothing, etc.;
(6) vehicles be properly designed;
(7) sources of ignition, explosion, etc. be prevented;
(8) spillages, leakages, escapes be prevented;
(9) documentation, signs, markings are provided for;
(10) firefighting appliances are to be carried on vehicles;
(11) arrangements to be made governing parking and attendance on tanks—vehicles are specified;
(12) safe operation practices by carriers and drivers to be regulated. SI 128/1988 Dangerous Substances Regulations deal with the method and apparatus for testing Petrol and Petrol Flash Point. They give effect to EEC Directive 84/449 etc.

1.33.3 Vehicle tank filling

It is an offence in a public place to cause or permit the filling of the fuel tank, or indeed remove the tank's filler cap, while the engine is running. The general penalty (para 7.1) applies for breach. This is under R 92(4) of The Road Traffic (Construction, etc.) Regulations 1963 (SI 190/1963).

For general control of the supply of fuel, especially in the times of emergency, see Fuel (Control of Supplies) Act 1971. This allows, *inter alia*, the Minister for Energy to regulate and control supply of fuels such as motor fuels.

1.33.4 Hydrocarbonated oil

For finance and taxation purposes a licence is necessary for the sale or delivery of hydrocarbonated oil (as defined in the Finance Act 1935). It is chargeable with duty under the Imposition of Duties (No. 221) (Excise Duties) Order 1975.

This oil is divided into two types (a) marked gas oil—normally known as 'Red diesel'—used in agricultural tractors' and (b) unmarked gas oil.

Special tax exemptions apply to marked 'Red' gas oil. It is an offence to misuse marked gas oil under para 12(1) of the 1975 Order.

There are very complicated provisions in relation to this matter in the Finance Acts 1935 onwards and the Hydrocarbonated Oils Regulations 1941 (SI 490/1941) onwards, the Imposition of Duties Act Excise Duties Orders, and the Excise Acts. These provide severe penalties and wide powers of inspection and forfeiture of the vehicle and fuel in certain circumstances. Mitigation of penalty is by the Revenue Commissioners generally. The law in this area is untidy and complicated and is outside the general scope of the book. Problems in relation to same would require reference to the appropriate Acts and regulations, and general guidance can often be had from the appropriate Governmental Department, e.g. Finance, Transport and Power, etc.

'Motor vehicle' has a special meaning assigned to it for the purpose of these Acts (by the Finance Act 1935, s 21 as amended), being a mechanically propelled vehicle which is designed, constructed and suitable for use on roads but does not include a tractor which is designed and constructed for use for agricultural purposes or a road roller.

In *A-G v McGuinness* (HC, 20 December 1968, unreported, No 276 SS) it was held that to qualify for the agricultural exemption a vehicle had to be (a) a tractor, and (b) designed and constructed for use for an agricultural purpose. Thus, if redesigned or adapted it does not qualify (*A-G v Carroll* (HC, 8 November 1971, No 57 SS). In *A-G v Woods* (HC 15 May 1974, SS 27/1973) it was held that a vehicle which had been a truck and which had its cab area modified so that it was normally used only for hauling a trailer did not qualify for the exemptions; 'design' and 'constructed' were held to be words with separate meanings. 'Design' referred to mechanical and structural design; 'construction' referred to build and materials.

1.33.5 Gas

Motor vehicle gas has duty imposed on it by s 42 of the Finance Act 1976. There is a presumption of non-payment in the event of a prosecution. Again, heavy penalties apply with possible forfeiture of both fuel and vehicle in certain circumstances. Mitigation of penalty is by the Revenue Commissioners generally.

1.33.6 Court mitigation

It appears that a court has no discretion to mitigate generally any excise penalties unless specifically so empowered, or to take them into consideration with other penalties or similar offences and thus avoid the full rigour of the Acts. This emerged in *DPP v Gray* 1987 ILRM 4. The Excise (Management) Act 1827, as amended by s 70 of the Finance Act 1982, allowed Justices in excise cases, where no contrary provision obtained, to mitigate penalties to half the statutory provision. The defendant sought to avail himself of further mitigation in reality, by asking the Justice, when convicting of one of a number of similar offences, to take into consideration pursuant to s 8 of the Criminal Justice Act 1951 the other offence to which he was pleading guilty. The District Justice did so. On a case stated the Supreme Court held the Justice was wrong in so doing, i.e. that he has no such discretion or power.

1.33.7 Petrol pumps on public roads

It should be remembered that certain provisions of the Local Government (Planning and Development) Act 1963 relate to petrol pumps, etc. (see also the Local Government (Planning and Development) Act 1963 (Licensing) Regulations 1965 made thereunder). On submission of plans and information the appropriate Planning Authority may grant a person a licence to erect, construct, place and maintain petrol, oil pumps, etc. This licence can be withdrawn in certain circumstances.

1.33.8 Dangerous substances

In dealing with the control of fuel above (para 1.33.2), mention has been made of the Dangerous Substances Act 1972. This Act is the main legislation controlling dangerous substances and their conveyance by road. Under the Act effect is given to the European Agreement concerning the International Carriage of Dangerous Goods by Road (ADR), done in Geneva on 30 September 1957. This Agreement can be obtained from The Government Stationary Officer, Molesworth Street, Dublin 2, and comprises three volumes of about 600 pages. It is a United Nations publication and reflects its attempt to create worldwide standards.

The 1972 Act provides, among other things, that persons engaged in the conveyance of dangerous substances must take all practical steps to prevent risk of injury to persons or property. This is sought to be achieved by control of (a) persons so involved, (b) their vehicles, and (c) the substances. The personnel involved have different duties under the Act and Regulations (below):

(i) The consignor must package, label, and check for suitability the substances and issue a certificate to the carrier or driver. The certificate sets out details of the load, the substances, the dangers involved, how to treat them, who to contact, etc.

(ii) The carrier must check the load, ensure the vehicle is suitable and properly secure, provide safety equipment, arrange safe parking, appoint a properly instructed driver, etc.

(iii) A driver must follow safety procedures, get the consignor's certificate, carry no passengers other than crew, take appropriate steps in the event of an accident, and park the vehicle safely. Drivers must be trained in the manner prescribed. Organisations such as An Co run courses for drivers.

Vehicles are goods vehicles within the meaning of the Road Traffic (Construction Equipment and Use of Vehicles) Regulations 1963 (SI 190/1963—see para 1.5 above) and so are articulated vehicles, trailers and semi-trailers. A carrier cannot use a vehicle to carry a dangerous substance unless permitted under the ADR, and then only in a vehicle of the type and with the equipment and a trained driver as prescribed. The vehicles must be marked and plated indicating their cargo clearly.

Substances are divided into two categories by the ADR for carriage by road: (a) restrictive classes, being substances acceptable for carriage by road in restricted conditions, and(b) non-restrictive classes where the carriage is prohibited. Substances of class (a) are given an item number and substance identification number and a class number. The numbers are internationally recognised and there are class numbers indicating the hazard identification. There are several thousand classified substances. These are set out in the Dangerous Substances (Part IV Declaration) Order 1986 (SI 267/1986) in detail, with reference to each substance's class type, item number and substance identification number (UN number).

The main regulations made in relation to carriage by road are:

(i) SI 267/1968 referred to above;

(ii) Dangerous Substance (Conveyance of Scheduled Substances by Road) (Trade or Business) Regulations 1980 (SI 235/1980) and 1986 (SI 268/1986);

(iii) Dangerous Substances (European Agreement concerning the International Carriage of Dangerous Goods by Road (ADR) Regulations 1986 (SI 269/1986);

(iv) European Communities (Dangerous Substances) (Classification, Packaging and Labelling) Regulations 1979 (SI 383/1979) and 1988 (SI 47/1988).

These are detailed and need to be studied for any particular problem. Only a general outline is given above. The Department of Labour, Dublin 4, publishes very useful guides to these regulations, and their Inspectorate is involved in enforcement.

1.33.9 Other controls

The law of nuisance, which would extend to nuisance by fuels, is dealt with at para 1.29 above. There are various and numerous EEC Directives which directly or indirectly impinge on the subject, e.g. 88/76/EEC and

88/77/EEC on measures to be taken against air pollution by gases from petrol and diesel engines.

1.34 Control of natural impedence of vehicle

1.34.1 Trees and hedges

Vehicles may be impeded by trees or hedges, or the view of drivers may be so impeded. This problem is dealt with in general by two Local Government Acts, i.e. the Local Government Act 1925, s 34, as amended by the Local Government Act 1946, s 97. These declare hedges and trees to be prejudicial to a road if they:

(i) shade the road so as to make the maintenance of the road unduly difficult or expensive; or
(ii) cause an obstruction of the road; or
(iii) obstruct the view of the driver (user) in a dangerous way.

The owner/occupier can be served with a Notice to trim or cut down the hedge or tree. There is an appeal procedure and a procedure for getting a District Court Order to enforce the notice.

However, in modern times these sections are little used, as most Road Authorities now control hedges by large machines owned or hired by them. This is less troublesome than the procedures under these sections.

1.34.2 Obstruction

The wider issue of man-made obstructions is dealt with at para 4.8.

1.35 Road transport control

1.35.1 Irish position generally

A series of controls on road transport ran parallel to the road traffic controls. These were designed to favour rail transport by restricting road transport. As part of these former controls the Road Transport Acts 1932 and, more importantly, 1933 were passed. These have been amended by subsequent Road Transport Acts, i.e. Nos 17/1934; 23/1935; 21/1944; 2/1955; 13/1956; 19/1958; 40/1959; 8/71; 8/78; 16/1986.

The Acts divided the Road Transport Service into two groups—passenger services and merchandise transport.

(a) *Passenger services*—see para 1.12 above for an outline of its effect, i.e. public service vehicles. See para 1.35.2 below as to EEC position.

A virtual monopoly was created by the 1932 Act in favour of Coras Iompar Eireann (CIE) with power being given to the Minister to grant private licences. Private transport is now eroding that monopoly increasingly.

(b) *Merchandise transport.* A brief outline of this group is given here. The 1933 Act sought to give a virtual monopoly to State carriers (CIE eventually, who were the rail operators). Existing private hauliers were granted Merchandise (Existing Carriers) Licences, and in limited, certain circumstances a new Merchandise Licence could be granted. It rarely was. It was illegal to carry merchandise for hire or reward without a licence for a private haulier. Each such vehicle had to have a merchandise 'plate'. Exemptions for short distances were created around major urban areas. A business could carry only its own goods without a 'plate'.

Liberalisation of this rigid system began in 1955, 1958 and 1971 in relation to agricultural product haulage. The 1971 Act extended all haulage licences to allow them to operate throughout the State. Entry into the EEC in 1972 brought in the further freeing out of the system under the Communities' Common Transport Policy. Quality controls were introduced by the European Communities (Merchandise Road Transport) Regulations 1977 (SI 386/1977) to give effect to EEC Council Directive 561/74 (amended by SI 431/1981 and 77/796 EEC). Those Regulations have been amended and strengthened by SI 180/1988 the European Communities (Merchandise Road Transport) Regulations 1988. All these regulations require hauliers to hold a Road Freight Certificate as proof of goods repute, being financially sound, and competent at haulage before being issued with a merchandise licence.

Restrictions on carriage of goods for reward in vehicles of 2.5 metric tonnes or less were removed by the 1978 Act. The 1986 Act removes the idea of quantity controls. It abolishes exempt areas, and operators therein are free to go about the whole country from 30 September 1988. However, the system of quality control will remain, i.e. control of the good standing of the operator or/and his business.

By s 2 of the 1986 Act, substituting a new s 11(1) in the 1933 Act, merchandise licence applications are put on a new footing. Application is made either for:

(a) a national road freight carriers licence, which is to be granted to existing merchandise licence holders or holder (from 1975) who so qualify. The holder has to be of good repute, sound financial standing and have professional competence—see para 1.35.2 on these; or
(b) an international road freight carriers licence, which is to be granted to existing holders of a road freight certificate under EEC regulations (1977 Regulations) and to current holders of a merchandise licence in exempt areas in substitution therefore.

The national licence entitles the holder to carry on a merchandise road transport business in the State with such vehicles as may be specified in the licence. An international road freight licence allows the holder to operate vehicles inside and outside the State.

The requirement of licencees under a road freight carriers licence having a vehicle 'plate' on each vehicle continues. These are issued through the 90 Garda Siochana vehicle plate issuing stations in the country. They are now displayed on the windscreen. There is a fine of £500 for misuse. SI 180/1988 introduces severe penalties for giving false or misleading information. The 1986 Act therefore puts the system firmly on a quality control basis, i.e. the Minister for Transport and Tourism must be satisfied as to the credentials and qualifications of the haulier. An appeal against certain Ministerial decisions lies to the District Court (s 6 of the 1986 Act and Art 10 of SI 386/1977 as amended by SI 432/1981) and therefrom on a question of law only to the High Court.

The 1986 Act provides for transport officers with wide powers (s 16) to be appointed to ensure the act is enforced. See a useful commentary on the 1986 Act in '*Irish Current Law Statutes*', as annotated, published by Sweet & Maxwell.

The business must be carried on under an old licence owned, not rented or substituted, by the applicant - *Twomey v Min. for Transport and Tourism* 1989/73 JR 1988 ILL 276.

1.35.2 EEC position

Passenger transport operators generally

EEC Directive 74/562 required Member States to ensure that from 1 January 1978 persons or firms carrying on road passenger transport business are of (a) good repute, (b) sound financial standing, (c) professionally competent. To give effect to this Directive the European Communities (Road Passenger Transport) Regulations 1977 (SI 388/1977) and 1981 (SI 432/1981) were passed. They require persons carrying on a business in road transport of passengers for reward in vehicles carrying ten or more persons (i.e. buses, minibuses or coaches) to hold a Road Passenger Certificate, unless exempt.

Exempt persons are:

(1) persons holding school vehicles licences;
(2) persons driving school-owned vehicles in relation to school travelling;
(3) employers carrying workers as passengers to and from work;
(4) voluntary organisations carrying non-commercial passengers in their own vehicles;
(5) an operator carrying passengers, having a main occupation other than a road passenger transport operator in a vehicle constructed or equipped to carry not more than 17 persons, including the driver.

There are two types of certificates—National and International—requiring somewhat different qualifications. Certificates must be renewed annually by new entrants, but not so for persons in business on 1 January 1975. Where a person fails on the qualification criteria, the licence can be revoked. As to 'good repute', convictions under the Road Traffic Act 1961 (as set out in the 2nd Schedule), and certain Road Transport Act 1932 and Roads Act 1920 convictions, these are taken into consideration, as are breaches of the EEC Regulations and breaches of other Member States' laws.

'Financial standing' is judged by the person's capability of establishing and running the business properly, the vehicles being taxed and insured, bank references and capital being sufficient, and the person not being an undischarged bankrupt.

As to 'professional competence', there is a system of issuing a Certificate of Competency by the Minister for Tourism and Transport. This is issued on the result, for new entrants (operator or manager), of an exam conducted by the Chartered Institute of Transport. They are also given to persons who operated a lawful road transport business prior to and since 1975, and to the holders of certain diplomas. Subjects for the exam include law, business administration, technical standards, road safety and access to markets. The certificates are of two types: (i) a National Certificate of Competence for Ireland only, or (ii) an International Certificate of Competence covering both national and international operations.

International coach and bus traffic

EEC Council Regulations 117/66, 516/72 and 517/72 as amended, which set out the rules for the carriage of passengers by coach or bus between EEC Member States, were incorporated into Irish Law by the European Communities (International Carriage of Passengers) Regulations 1974 (SI 133/1974) and 1985 (SI 396/1985). They apply to vehicles carrying more than nine persons. The services are divided into:

(a) regular—require authorisation from the Department of Tourism and Transport;
(b) shuttle—also require authorisation; and
(c) occasional;

each requiring somewhat different documentation.

Under the said 1985 Regulations, the procedures for operating occasional services (e.g. holiday buses) were extended to Norway, Sweden, Finland, Austria, Switzerland and Turkey under what is known as the ASOR Agreement under EEC Council Decisions 82/505/EEC. Breach of the regulations causes a fine of up to £400 and £20 a day, the total not exceeding £1,000.

The effect of the regulations is that there is a system developing to allow free movement of coach and bus trips within the EEC countries and the six other countries above. Thus, the provisions of the Road Transport Acts, i.e. s 7 of the 1932 Act, s 6 of the 1935 Act, and s 8(8) of the 1958 Act do not apply in relation to authorisation, certificates, waybills, etc. issued in accordance with these EEC Regulations. Those provisions of the Transport Acts deal with unlicensed passenger road services, importation licences, and CIE's right to refuse any particular traffic offered to it. The 1981 Regulations also prohibit the transfer of certain business based on regular service, except with the Minister's consent. The Minister in this context is the Minister for Communications.

Chapter 2

Control of driver—Drivers licences

'We must not allow ourselves to be warped by any prejudice against motor cars and so to strain the law against them.'
Lord Alverstone CJ (1907) – in 'Bastible v Little'

2.1.1 Introduction

There is an obvious need to control the persons who drive vehicles. The Road Traffic Acts therefore seek to achieve this control in many ways, including saying a person cannot lawfully drive in a public place without a drivers licence.

There is set up a system of screening whereby persons are prohibited from driving unless they hold a lawful licence. Application for this licence is to the local authority, based on a specified form and information. The licence must be granted, except in special circumstances. There are different classes of licences required for different classes of drivers and vehicles. The person must have a licence for the type of class of vehicle he is driving. The licences run for a period of one year or three years. They can be cancelled by court order, i.e. disqualification, or in the events of other statutory circumstances. A record of serious offences is kept on licences by court order of endorsement of the particulars on the licence.

2.1.2 Statute law

The statute law on this matter now is contained in Part III of the 1961 Road Traffic Act; Part III of the 1968 Act; and certain minor amendments were made by the 1984 Act.

EEC law, particularly Directive 80/1263/EEC, required a new form of licence. This is being introduced in Ireland in 1989, expected date of commencement to be 1st July.

2.1.3 Regulations

The regulations applicable in this area are the Road Traffic (Licensing of Drivers) Regulations 1964 (SI 29/1964) and Road Traffic Licensing of Drivers (Amendment) Regulations 1966 (SI 47/1966) and the further amending regulations SI 24/1967; SI 113/1967; 140/1969; SI 120/1973; SI 295/1974; SI 277/1975; SI 337/1979; SI 342/1979; SI 225/1980; SI 334/1980; SI 198/1981; SI 276/1981; SI 27/1982; SI 49/1983; SI 18/1984; SI 233/1984; SI 234/1984; SI 20/1985; SI 254/1985; SI 23/1986; SI 340/1986; 236/1987. It is intended to introduce New Consolidated (with some amendments) Regulations in 1989.

The regulations are only set out briefly in the text of this chapter, and reference to the actual texts of the regulations should be made for a full statement of the position applying to the circumstances of any particular case.

There is wide power given to the Minister for the Environment to make regulations under s 42 of the 1961 Act, as amended by the Schedule of the 1968 Act. The section is a very long one, enabling the regulations to specify the manner of application for licences (including provisional licences); the issue, surrender, duplicates of, information as to, and fees for licences; requiring certificates of competency and of fitness; tests and forms; production of licences in Court; and the endorsement of licences. Different provisions in regulations can be made for different classes of cases coming within the same matter.

Contravention of a regulation stated to be penal attracts the general penalty (see para 7.1).

Section 5 of the 1961 Act also contains a general power to make regulations.

2.1.4 Division of chapter

This chapter is divided for convenience into two parts, viz:

Part 1 — Licences generally (paras 2.2 to 2.8).
This Part deals with prohibitions; applying for and granting of licences; types; need for certificates; provisional licences; enforcement; visitors.

Part 2 — Disqualification and endorsements (paras 2.9 and 2.10).

PART 1 LICENCES GENERALLY

2.2 Prohibition

2.2.1 Offences

Under the provisions of s 38 of the 1961 Act a person cannot lawfully drive or allow another to drive his vehicle in a public place without an effective drivers licence. In case of breach of these provisions, both can be liable to the general penalty (para 7.1), and there applies ancillary disqualification (para 2.9.4) and optional endorsement (para 2.10). It is also an offence to employ an unlicensed person to drive a vehicle—s 38(3) of the 1961 Act.

The onus of proof is on the driver and/or owner to show he had the licence, as he is presumed in certain circumstances under s 38(2)(b) of the 1961 Act not to have it. This overcomes the decision under the 1933 Act of *A-G (McGowan) v Carville* 95 ILTR 41, which held there must be more evidence than the mere driving of a vehicle in a public place.

In the event of the unlicensed driver being a disqualified driver or a person who must produce a certificate of competence or fitness (see under paras 2.5 and 2.6 below) before obtaining a licence, an offence by an unlicensed disqualified driver attracts, instead of the general penalty, the maximum fine of £1,000 or maximum imprisonment of six months or both. This penalty of £1,000 was set at this level by s 3 of the 1984 Act.

In a prosecution under s 38 it is a good defence to show that the driver had an effective provisional licence for that vehicle (s 35(3)(a) of the 1961 Act).

In fact proof is normally given in court of demand and non-production (see para 2.7 below).

English decisions on similar arrangements tend to show that the liability of the owner is absolute and that lack of knowledge is irrelevant. See *Griffiths v Studebabers* [1924] 1 KB 102.

In *Ferrymasters Ltd v Adams* [1980] Crim LR 187 the employer was convicted as he had no system of checking renewal of licences, which seems to be taking the criminal law a bit too far. However, under s 35(3)(b) of the 1961 Act, if an owner is summonsed under s 38 of the 1961 Act for employing a person without a licence, it is a defence to show that the employee had an effective provisional licence. As the section refers to employment, unauthorised use also seems to be a defence presumably.

2.2.2 Exemptions

Exemptions exist to the need for driving licences. The following are so exempt:

(a) Members of the Gardai driving in the course of their duty (s 38(6) of the 1961 Act) (see para 7.2 and 7.8).
(b) Persons using such specified pedestrian controlled vehicles as are exempted by Ministerial regulations, as empowered by s 38(7) of the 1961 Act. These vehicles, by Art 7 of SI 29/1964, are those neither constructed nor adapted for use for carrying a driver or passenger and which do not exceed 8 cwt unladen weight.
(c) Person undergoing a driving test (s 33(7) of the 1961 Act) (but such person must hold a provisional licence). Article 18 of SI 29/1964 does not extend this exemption to provisional licences.

(d) Members of the defence forces, driving State owned or controlled mechanically propelled vehicles during a period of duty or emergency (Defence Forces Act 1954, s 113) (see para 7.8).

2.3 Applying for a driving licence

2.3.1 Procedure

Application for a licence to drive a mechanically propelled vehicle is made to the Licensing Authority for the area in which the applicant ordinarily resides. Residence is a question of fact. The County Councils of each county and the Corporation of each County Borough are the Licensing Authorities (s 21 of the 1961 Act).

The procedure to be followed on an application is outlined in s 22 of the 1961 Act and SI 29/1964, Art 15 (as Amended by SI 198/1981, R 5 and SI 340/1986, R 5). At a date not earlier than one month before his/her old licence expires a person must lodge the following with the Licensing Authority:

(a) An appropriate complete form (D 305). See para 7.4 as to false and misleading declarations under s 115 of the 1961 Act. The forms are set out in the First Schedule of SI 29/1964, as amended by SI 340/1986.
(b) Fee or excise duty—£4 for annual ordinary or provisional licence; £12 for three years licence (1987 level of fees).
(c) A certificate of competency or fitness, if applicable (see paras 2.5 and 2.6 *infra*). In the case of an application for a Class H Licence, a certificate of fitness is essential in relation to certain cases, as we will see at para 2.6. Certificates of competency are dealt with at para 2.5. If a certificate of fitness is not required, there must be a specific declaration that the applicant is not suffering from the diseases and disabilities specified in the Fifth and Sixth Schedule of SI 29/1964, as inserted by SI 340/1986. See para 2.3.4.
(d) The old licence unless lost or destroyed. In fact, licences are issued in a handy book form and each renewal is by slip of paper inserted into the book.

2.3.2 Disqualified persons forbidden

Persons disqualified from holding a licence or a licence for a class or classes are forbidden from making an application accordingly, i.e. for a licence or a class(es) (s 22 of the 1961 Act). If such a person does so wrongfully apply, under s 39 of the 1961 Act (as amended by s 3 of the 1984 Act) he is liable on conviction to up to £1,000 fine and/or six months' imprisonment. However, where a disqualification relates only to certain classes or a specific class, then he is forbidden only from applying for those classes (s 22(3) of the 1961 Act) and during the appropriate period of disqualification.

This does not apply to visitors under SI 269/1961, as amended by SI 59/1964.

2.3.3 Classes of vehicle

The application may be for a specified class or classes of vehicle. At present the classifications are (SI 29/1964 R 6, as inserted by R 3 of SI 198/1981):

CLASS A	Motor bicycles, with or without side car (see G below)	*minimum age* 18
CLASS B	Tractors used in connection with agriculture and work vehicles	17
CLASS C	Vehicles (other than Classes A and B and the drawing components of articulated vehicles) not exceeding 2 tons unladen and having passenger accommodation for not more than eight passengers	17
CLASS D	Vehicles (other than Vehicles of Class B, Class E and Class H) exceeding 2 tons in weight unladen, the drawing components of articulated vehicles and vehicles having passenger accommodation for more than eight persons	18
CLASS E	Vehicles having passenger accommodation for more than eight persons in use for the carriage of passengers for reward	21
CLASS F	Vehicles of classes A, B and C specially constructed or adapted for use and used by persons suffering from a physical disability	17
CLASS G	Class A vehicles used by persons under 18 years of age, the engines of which do not exceed 150 cc in cylinder capacity	16
CLASS H	Articulated vehicles	18

One can apply for certain combinations of classes, e.g. classes A, B, C and D. A person must hold a licence for the class of vehicle which he is driving.

Article 15 of SI 29/1964 specifies in detail the contents of the forms of application and declaration (D 305 at present), plus what must accompany the application, i.e. as in para 2.3.1.

Definitions

Article 4 of SI 29/1964, as amended by SI 140/1969, gives the following definitions:

(i) '*Tractor used for agriculture*' means one which is taxed thus (para 1.11). See *A-G v East* (1964) 98 ILTR 33 where turf held to be capable of being an agricultural product.

(ii) '*Works vehicle*' means a vehicle incapable of exceeding 24 mph which is constructed primarily for any work other than conveyance by road of goods or a burden of any other description, and which when used on a public road for the conveyance of a load in connection with a loading, unloading, lifting or dumping operation is so used only at the site at which it is being worked or within a radius of half a mile from the site.

(iii) '*Minibus*' means a class D or class E vehicle primarily constructed for the carriage of passengers and having passenger accommodation for not more than 18 persons. See Chapter 1, Part 2 re Public Service Vehicles.

Licensing authorities normally send reminders of the impending expiry of a licence. It is no excuse, however, for a person to show no reminder was sent to him (*Calwell v Hague* (1914) 79 JP 152). Nor is it sufficient to take out a licence on the same day but after driving without a licence (or to have money sent to the Authority but the licence not issued) (*Campbell v Strangeways* (1877) 42 JP 39). These matters may, of course, be used in mitigation of penalty.

There are no 'days of grace' in relation to renewal of driving licences. This is so even if documents have been posted to the Licensing Authority (*Nattgross v Gibbons* (1968) 112 AJ 866).

The proposed 'Classification for the new EEC form' of licence is that the eight driving licence classes set out above will be replaced by six new categories of licence. These will be uniform classifications among Member States. Some of these categories will be divided into sub-categories. Details are as follows:

Category	*Vehicles in category*	*Minimum Age*
A	Motor cycles (with or without a side car).	16 years
	A(1) 'Mopeds'—motorcycles with an engine capacity not exceeding 50cc or design speed not exceeding 50 kmh (31 mph).	
	A(2) Motor cycles not in sub-category A(1) which have an engine capacity not exceeding 150 cc.	17 years
	A(3) Motor cycles exceeding 150 cc.	18 years
B	Passenger and light goods vehicles not exceeding 3,500 kg permissible maximum weight and having not more than 8 passenger seats. (This category includes private cars.)	17 years
C	Rigid goods vehicles exceeding 3,500 kg permissible maximum weight and passenger vehicles exceeding this weight with not more than 8 passenger seats.	

	C(1) Vehicles in this category with a permissible maximum weight of 3,501 kg to 7,500 kg.	18 years
	C(2) Vehicles in this category exceeding 7,500 kg.	18 years
D	Passenger vehicles with more than 8 passenger seats (buses and minibuses).	
	D(1) Minibuses—up to 18 passenger seats.	21 years
	D(2) All other buses.	21 years
E	Combinations of vehicles (vehicle plus drawbar trailer(s) or articulated vehicle).	18 years
F	1. Agricultural tractors.	16 years
	2. Work vehicles.	17 years
G	Schoolbuses	
	1. Minibuses limited to schoolbuses.	21 years
	2. All other buses limited to schoolbus.	21 years

Unfortunately it is stated that, while there will be a Community-wide licence eventually, these steps are the only ones to have been taken in that direction at present. These new forms will operate in 1989 onwards. The 1989 Regulations will cover these EEC licences.

Notes

(1) *Combinations of vehicles (Category E)*
Subject to certain exemptions referred to below, this category of licence will be necessary to drive either a vehicle with a drawbar trailer or an articulated vehicle. The existing Irish separate licence (Class H) for an articulated vehicle will, therefore, disappear.

A person who has passed a category E Irish driving test in an articulated vehicle will qualify for a licence covering categories C and E.

A category E licence will not be required where:

(a) the permissible maximum weight of the trailer does not exceed 750 kg; or

(b) the towing vehicle is in category B (private cars, etc.), and

  (i) the permissible maximum weight of the trailer, while exceeding 750 kg, does not exceed the unladen weight of the towing vehicle, and

  (ii) the total permissible maximum weight of the combination of vehicles (towing vehicle plus trailer) does not exceed 3,500 kg.

(2) *Licences for persons suffering from a physical disability*
A person suffering from a physical disability will be issued with the appropriate category of licence on which particulars of the required adaptations to the vehicle will be recorded. The existing Irish special licence (Class F) for driving vehicles specially constructed or adapted for use by such persons will no longer apply.

(3) *Transitional arrangement*
When the new licence becomes operational, existing licence holders will, on renewal of their driving licence, be granted a licence for the approximate equivalent category(ies) based on the existing class(es) of the licence held.
(4) *Weight*
To comply with the Directive it should be noted that the question of its weight is generally its 'permissible maximum weight' and not its unladen weight, which has been the basic Irish criterion heretofore (see paras 1.7 and 1.11). Thus, the new standard would deem a vehicle with an:

(a) unladen weight of not more than 1½ tons (1,524 kg) = 3,500 kg maximum permissible weight;
(b) unladen weight of not more than 3½ tons (3,556 kg) = 7,500 kg maximum permissible weight.

2.3.4 Granting licences

It is mandatory for licensing authorities, under s 23 of the 1961 Act, to grant a driving licence, except in special circumstances. Entitlement to a licence was recognised as a 'statutory right' in *A-G v Conroy* [1965] IR 411. This is also recognised by Directive 80/1263/EEC, which provides that a person who is granted a driving licence in one Member State may, on taking up residence in another Member State, exchange his licence for one in the State he has moved to, with the exceptions of classes A(1) and F.

The exceptions to this mandatory granting in Ireland are:

(a) Where an application is not properly made, e.g. form wrongly filled or not accompanied by appropriate certificates, fees, etc.
(b) Where the applicant is disqualified from applying (para 2.3 above)—see s 22(4); s 23(1)(a); s 39—i.e. where under a Court Order an applicant is disqualified from driving or from holding a licence. (see para 2.10.)
(c) Where the applicant has not a satisfactory knowledge of The Rules of the Road, having regard to the particulars on his application. The Rules of the Road are stated under s 3(4) of the 1961 Act to be the latest edition of a so entitled publication issued by the Minister for the Environment. The standards prescribed in this pamphlet do not have statutory force, in so far as they are not contained in a statutory instrument or in a statute.
(d) Where the applicant is under age. The ages applicable to the various classes are specified in the regulations made under s 31 of the 1961 Act, i.e. SI 29/1964, R 8 as inserted by R 4 of SI 198/1981 and R 4 of SI 340/1986.

The ages are:

Class G—16 years minimum
Classes B, C & F—17 years minimum
Classes A, D & H—18 years minimum
Class E—21 years minimum.

A person reaches 16 years on the day preceding the sixteenth anniversary of his birth. By s 31 of the 1961 Act, under no circumstances can a person under 16 years apply for a licence. In *Kinsley v Hertfordshire CC* (1972) RTR 498 the applicant was under age when applying for a provisional licence. It was held by the court that he therefore did not 'hold' the licence which had been issued to him.

Section 31 of the 1961 Act gives power to make the above regulations as to age qualification for the different classes. The Minister has power to fix limits (subject to the overall lower limit of 16 years), below which a person shall be disqualified from holding a licence for a specified class. There is no upper age limit as such, but a person may be disqualified under disability provisions (see next paragraph) or have special requirements imposed, e.g. Certificate of Fitness (para 2.6). Thus, a person aged 70 years or over has to get a Certificate of Fitness annually. In *R v Saddleworth Sol Jo* [1968] 1 All ER 189 it was held that a person driving under age can be convicted under a similar English section and also under a section as to driving while disqualified.

(e) Where the applicant is disqualified because of ill health (s 32 of the 1961 Act). This section prohibits a person who is suffering from any disease, physical or mental, specified by the Minister from holding a drivers licence for the period of such disability.

By virtue of Art 8 of SI 29/1964, as amended by Art 4 of SI 340/1986 and the Fifth Schedule thereto (as inserted by latter regulations), the following are the diseases or disabilities that disqualify a person from holding a licence:

(i) Diplopia;
(ii) Defective binocular vision (i.e. seriously deficient eye condition);
(iii) Epilepsy;
(iv) Chronic alcoholism;
(v) Dependence on psycho-active drugs;
(vi) Severe renal deficiency (kidney failure).

A person so suffering is not completely excluded from getting a licence. He must declare the disease and get a Certificate of Fitness, as set out later in this chapter (para 2.6), under s 33 or 34 of the 1961 Act. See paras 2.5 and 2.6 below.

In *Devon CC v Hawkins* [1967] 2 KB 26 it was held that a person who had controlled his epileptic fits fully for two years by drugs was still suffering from epilepsy and should disclose this. See also *Secretary of State v Adams* [1982] Crim LR 530. In *Balmer v Hayes* (1950) SC 497, a case where a bus driver failed to disclose epilepsy, lost consciousness and caused injury, it was held that *per se* failure of the driver to disclose the malady does not give a third party a right of action for damages.

If a person does disclose a malady such as arthritis, he should be given a test to see the degree of disability (*Guest v Kingsworth, The Times*, 5 February 1972). A person who is subject to periodic attacks of unconsciousness is not fit to hold a driving licence (*Swift v Norfolk CC* [1955] Crim LR 785).

2.3.5 Forms of licence

The authority must issue the licence in book form, stating particulars of the applicant, including his name and address and the classes of vehicles for which he is licensed. This form of licence is detailed in R 16 of the 1964 Regulations (SI 29/1964 as amended by R 6 of SI 140/1969).

This licence is on a specified form which shows the name and address of the applicant and the classes of vehicles, as set out in the First Schedule of the 1964 Regulations.

2.3.6 Period of licence

The licence normally commences to run from the day it is granted, or, if granted during the currency of a previous licence, on the expiration of such licence (s 23 of the 1961 Act). Under the section a driving licence is normally granted for 12 months, but by Art 14 of SI 29/1964 it may be granted for 36 months where:

(a) an application is made for that period; and
(b) the applicant is not or will not be 70 years or more on the commencement day; and
(c) the period of validity of any Certificate of Fitness which is required to accompany the application is not less than three years (see para 2.6).

2.3.7 Signing of licence

Normal licences are stated to take effect only from the date of signing by their holder. In this event it is the duty of the licence holder to sign it forthwith, otherwise it is not effective except as proof that the licence was granted (s 24 of the 1961 Act). This provision as to signing ties in with s 41 of the 1961 Act, which enables a Garda to require a driver to furnish a specimen signature (see para 2.7.2). However, even if the grantee does not sign it, he is still deemed the holder of the licence. Thus, the licence can be endorsed even if not signed.

This ineffectiveness of an unsigned licence is repeated by Art 14 of SI 29/1964, which deals with the form of the licence, i.e. book form, and the Article states the licence 'shall be expressed not to have effect until it is signed by the Grantee'.

2.3.8 Improper licences

Article 13 of the Road Traffic (Licensing of Drivers) Regulations 1964 (SI 29/1964) makes it an offence attracting the general penalty (para 7.1) for an officer of a Licensing Authority or a Licensing Authority to grant a licence or duplicate licence, or for an officer so empowered to issue a certificate which is not in accordance with the Act or Regulations.

2.3.9 Particulars

Certain persons are entitled to information about drivers licences from Licensing Authorities. By Art 10 of SI 29/1964 (amended by SI 12/1973), the Authority must give:

(a) to a Garda, another Licensing Authority, or the Minister's Authorised officer, free of charge, such information as they request about a licence or notification received about the licence, e.g. of endorsement;
(b) to any person, on paying the prescribed fee, similar information in relation to a licence granted to a specified person;
(c) admission to a Garda or an authorised officer of the Minister to their offices to inspect and make copies of records.

2.3.10 Visitors

A visitor holding a driving permit (i.e. a national or domestic driving licence or international driving permit) can drive in a public place a vehicle of the class the permit allows, unless disqualified. This is a modification of s 38 of the 1961 Act and is allowed by the Mechanically Propelled Vehicles (International Circulation) Order 1961 (SI 269/1961, as amended by SI 59/1964 and other regulations) (see para 2.8 below).

A visitor is a person temporarily resident in the country. In *Flores v Scott* [1984] 1 WLR 690 a student at Oxford for five years was held to be not so resident; 'temporary' was contrasted with regular habits of life.

2.4 Provisional licences and driving instruction

2.4.1 Learner drivers

Special provision obviously has to be made for learner drivers. This is done by s 35 of the 1961 Act, s 18 of the Act and Part III of SI 29/1964 as amended by SI 47/1966; SI 198/1981, and SI 254/1985. These regulate the issue of provisional licences and driving instruction. Their purpose is to allow the learner driver to drive under supervision until he can obtain a certificate of competency. This requirement was suspended at one stage. The need for a supervisor was reintroduced by SI 254/1985.

Applications for provisional licences are made to the same Licensing Authorities and in a similar manner (Form D 311) as that described above in relation to an ordinary licence, i.e. in accordance with Regulations and with the prescribed fees, etc. (see para 2.3.1). Generally all the law on full licences applies to provisional licences, unless a special rule applies.

In *Longman v Valentine* [1952] 2 All ER 803 it was held that when a learner driver is found guilty of driving without a licence the supervisor cannot be found guilty of aiding and abetting unless evidence is given that he knew that the learner had no licence (see para 2.4.4 below).

2.4.2 Regulations

Part III of the Road Traffic (Licensing of Drivers) Regulations 1964 (SI 29/1964), as amended, deals with provisional licences. It applies nearly all of the provisions of the Acts to provisional licences. These provide that a provisional licence must:

(a) be in five-page book form;
(b) be signed by the Grantee; and
(c) be for the appropriate classes—see SI 198/1981, Art 6 and para 2.3.3 above.

Furthermore:

(a) The applicant must not be disqualified—Art 18.
(b) The application must be accompanied by the appropriate fee—Art 20.
(c) The applicant must declare that he understands the Rules of the Road.
(d) The old licence, if in existence, must be surrendered/produced.
(e) A certificate of fitness must accompany the application in the appropriate cases—see para 2.6 below.
(f) Proof is required that a driving test has been applied for in the appropriate cases, i.e. an application for a third such licence.
(g) The term of the provisional licence is, however, only 12 months (previously six months), and normally a second one is granted for a further year without any special requirements. However, under SI 254/1985 a holder of a provisional licence must apply for a certificate of competency (see 2.5 below).
(h) Under Art 19 of SI 29/1964, as re-enacted in Art 3 of SI 254/1985, a provisional licence entitles the holder to drive on the following conditions the following types of vehicles—
   (i) Class A, B and G vehicles, on condition that no passenger is carried other than a qualified driver,
   (ii) Class C, D, F or H on condition of:
      (1) being accompanied by a qualified driver, i.e. full licence holder; and
      (2) an 'L' plate being displayed on the front and rear of the vehicle. This does not apply, however, to a pedestrian controlled vehicle;
   (iii) Class C, D or F, on condition that the vehicle does not draw a trailer,
   (iv) in all cases there is a prohibition on the use of a vehicle for carriage for reward. Therefore, one cannot get a Class E provisional licence as it relates to carriage for reward of more than eight persons.

These conditions in relation to the various classes do not apply, however, where the licence holder is driving a vehicle of a class for which he holds a certificate of competency (see para 2.5) or such certificate has a statement limiting it to that class type which he is driving (see amendments of the original portion of Art 19 inserted by Art 7 of SI 198/1981).

(i) Article 20—prescribed fee is £8 (1987). Amended by Art 7 of SI 49/1983.

(j) Article 21 of the 1964 Regulations (as substituted by Art 4 of SI 254/1985) limits the right to third and subsequent provisional licences to applicants who have applied for a certificate of competency, i.e. test, or who are excused because of illness or other unavoidable circumstances.

(k) Article 22 (as amended) governs forms to be used on applying. The current form is D 311.

(l) The applicant must declare (and the form sets this out) that he understands the Rules of the Road. Also see SI 340/1986, Art 7. He must make a declaration that he is not suffering from certain disabilities or diseases, epilepsy, alcoholism or taking any drugs which will affect his driving so as to render him a source of danger to the public—similar to the requirement in para 2.3 above.

(m) Classes and ages are similar to those set out at para 2.3.3, except that a provisional licence for Class E cannot be applied for.

2.4.3 Defence

Provided the Act and regulations are complied with, the production of a provisional licence has the same effect, i.e. being a good defence for prosecutions for 'no driving licence' (s 38 of the 1961 Act offences), as production of a full driving licence (s 40 of the 1961 Act). It is sufficient to comply with the requirement of a policy of insurance that the driver holds a drivers licence. It has been held that a holder of a provisional licence unaccompanied complies with this condition in an insurance policy (*A-G (Wren) v O'Brien* (High Court, 16 July 1965) and *A-G (McDonagh) v Reilly* (Supreme Court, 17 November 1966).

2.4.4 Instructors/Supervisors

The duties of those instructing a learner driver are not set out in the Act, save in so far as s 18 of the 1968 Act relates to such instructors operating for hire and reward. This section gives the Minister for the Environment wide powers to regulate such commercial activities—licensing them, qualifications, fees, duties, records, etc. So far no regulations have been made under that section.

While no regulations have been made to date, the general duties of supervisors are inherent in their obviously intended function—*Rubie v Faulkner* [1940] 1 All ER 285—i.e. to do what is reasonably possible to prevent the driver from acting unskilfully, carelessly or dangerously. Failure to exercise proper supervision could lead to a charge of aiding and abetting.

In *Smith v Jenner* [1968] Crim LR 99 it was held that where a learner driver drives without a valid provisional licence, his instructor is not guilty of aiding and abetting the offence unless he knew (or turned a blind eye to the fact) of the lack of that licence. In this case the supervisor had warned the learner to keep his licence renewed which he did not.

In *Bentley v Muller* (1968) RTR 7 a learner driver was convicted of failing to stop and the instructor of aiding and abetting.

In *BSM Ltd v Simms* (1971) RTR 190 it was held that an examiner was not a driving instructor or passenger supervising a learner driver. His duty was not to intervene but to examine and see if the learner passed the test.

2.4.5 Grant and duplicates of licences

There is a duty on the Licensing Authority to grant the provisional licence where the application is duly made with the above conditions being met; and to issue a duplicate if the original is lost, destroyed or mutilated, if application is duly made for a replacement licence (Arts 23 and 24 of SI 29/1964 as amended).

Limitation of application

Article 21 of SI 29/1964 (as amended by Art 5 of SI 47/1966) places certain limitations on persons applying for a series of provisional licences. This is intended to make tests mandatory. Under these Articles you cannot get a third provisional licence unless you have applied for a certificate of competency. As to certificates of competency and tests, see para 2.5.

2.4.6 Improper licences

Art 13 of SI 29/1964, which prevents the issue of improper licences, applies to provisional licences as it does to full licences (see para 2.3.8).

2.4.7 Particulars

The same position applies to provisional licences as applies to full licences (see para 2.3.9).

2.4.8 Visitors

The same position applies to provisional licences as applies to full licences (see para 2.3.10). See also para 2.8 below.

2.5 Certificates of competency

2.5.1 Driving tests

Competent skill at driving is both a personal asset and a social safeguard.

Section 33 of the 1961 Act (as amended by s 21 of the 1968 Act) and Part IV of SI 29/1964 (as amended) set up the legal background to ensure that certain persons must have a certificate of competency, arising from certain tests, before getting a drivers licence.

2.5.2 Who must obtain a certificate

The persons who must now obtain such a certificate of competency are:

(1) persons who are disqualified by a Court until they produce such a certificate (s 33(2) of the 1961 Act). In *R v Donnelly* [1975] 1 WLR 390 it was stated the court should not order this unless driver's competence in issue. In that case drink alone was in issue;

(2) those persons whose licence application must be accompanied by such a certificate by virtue of s 33(2) of the 1961 Act, specified in Art 29 of SI 29/1964, as replaced by Art 9 of SI 198/1981, and amended by Art 2 of SI 276/1981, Art 5 of SI 233/1984 and Art 6 of SI 254/1985. These persons are in two categories—

(a) When the licence application relates to a class or classes without limitation or to a type of vehicle for which the applicant has not held a licence within the previous five years, i.e. 'new drivers', unless:

(i) the applicant is a new resident who comes from another EEC country and who holds a valid national licence which he surrenders. This application must be made within one year of taking up normal residence in the State and must relate to a class or classes without limitation, or to a specified type of vehicle belonging to a class, in respect of which the applicant holds a national licence. The application must be accompanied by a statement that such licence is valid at the date of application. This exception gives effect to Art 8 of the EEC Council Directive 80/1263/EEC to allow free movement of persons within the EEC. There is an extremely detailed and complicated explanation of a driving licence in respect of a class without limitation in Art 29(2) of the 1964 Regulations. Study it if necessary.

(ii) certain defence force officers can gain exemption.

(iii) the application relates to Class H (articulated vehicles) licences and the applicant held a Class D licence on 30 June 1981 and had used and driven articulated vehicles for at least 65 days. This is to be certified on a form set out in Part 2 of the Third Schedule of the Regulations.

The Certificate of competency must be related to the class applied for in the drivers licence application.

(b) Where a decision on an application for a Certificate of fitness to accompany an application for a driving licence was deferred pending the production of a certificate of competency, then such an application must be accompanied by a certificate of competency

2.5.2 *Certificates of competency*

(Art 29 of the 1964 Regulations, as amended by Art 9 of SI 198/1981).

2.5.3 Application procedure

The procedure for applying for a certificate of competency is set out in Art 30 of SI 29/1964 (as substituted by Art 8 of SI 340/1986). The application is made:

(a) on the scheduled form, which is normally obtained from the issuing authority (Form D 401 at present). It must be completed properly and give the appropriate information and declaration;

(b) by sending the appropriate fee (£19 in 1987). By an amendment made by SI 236/1987 this fee is forfeited if the applicant does not submit to the test, unless—

(i) he notifies the issuing Authority at least seven days in advance that he will not be attending, or

(ii) he shows to such Authority an adequate reason for not undergoing the test.

If (i) or (ii) does not apply he must also resubmit a fresh application form, etc. and reapply fully for the test for the certificate of competency.

(c) If the application is for Classes A, B, C or G it must be accompanied by an eyesight report (see para 2.5.6. below), unless either:

(i) a valid certificate of fitness has been issued to the applicant (see para 2.6); or

(ii) the applicant has within two years before that date made a previous application which contained an eyesight report.

Eyesight report

The Articles prescribe the standards of an eyesight report to be presented with an application for a certificate of competency. Such a report (Art 8) must be in a prescribed form and be from an opthalmic optician or a registered medical practitioner. This report must be such that it satisfies the issuing Authority that the applicant's eyesight complies with (or can be corrected to comply with) the standards set out in the regulations.

The Seventh Schedule of the 1964 Regulations, as inserted by the 1986 Regulations, details these standards as:

(i) Visual acuity of not less than 0.4 (6/15) in one eye or 0.5 (6/12) in both eyes together, and at least 0.2 (6/30) in the worse eye.

(ii) The applicant shall not suffer from diplopia or defective binocular vision.

(iii) The person shall not suffer from a loss of more than 20 degrees in the temporal part of his field of vision.

(iv) A person with the sight of one eye only shall have a visual acuity of at least 0.8 (6/7.5), an unrestricted field of vision in his eye, and monocular vision must have existed for sufficient time to allow adaptation.

By virtue of Part VII of SI 29/1964 (inserted by Art 15 of SI 340/1986), if the Certificate states the applicant should wear contact lenses, the licence sets out that requirement in red ink. Similarly, if in a Class F application adaptations to the vehicles are necessary to take account of the person's incapacity, the licence must have this set out in red on the licence.

2.5.4 Disqualified applicant

A person disqualified from holding a licence under s 32 of the 1961 Act (ill health) cannot apply for a test. This extends to a person who is suffering from any disease or physical or mental disability declared by Ministerial Regulation to disqualify applicants from holding a driving licence. See as to diseases paras 2.3.4, 2.4.2 and 2.6.

2.5.5 The test

The test is conducted under the direction of the Minister for the Environment by the issuing Authority who issues the certificate (s 33 of the 1981 Act). Application is made on the special form (D 401) outlined above with the correct fee, the present fee being £19. Tests are carried out at local centres. They consist of:

(a) an oral or written test to ascertain the applicant's knowledge of the Rules of the Road;
(b) a practical driving test, normally conducted around an urban area in a type of vehicle of one of the classes being applied for.

The official tester must be satisfied that applicant knows and can comply with the Rules of the Road and is generally competent to drive the vehicle, and in particular is competent in starting, stopping, moving off, dealing with traffic, turning, parking, using equipment, reversing, signalling and obeying signals and signs.

The applicant must provide the vehicle for the test, which must be representative of the class he is applying for and must be roadworthy.

2.5.6 Eyesight

Section 21 of the 1968 Act requires that before the test may be conducted the Minister must be satisfied in the prescribed manner that an applicant's eyesight reaches the prescribed standard. The regulations prescribing the manner of so satisfying the Minister on the standard of sight are set out in SI 340/1986. See para 2.5.3 where those standards are set out.

2.5.7 The result

Any one of three results can be obtained on a test:

(a) refusal of the application for the certificate of competency; or

(b) deferral of a decision until a certificate of fitness is produced. If there is such a deferral, then under Art 31 of SI 29/1964 the applicant must submit a valid certificate of fitness for all relevant classes. This certificate is then referred to the driver tester concerned who shall, subject to the provisions of s 33(4) of the 1966 Act, either refuse the application or grant the certificate of competency (see para 2.6.1 (vii)); or

(c) grant of a certificate of competency as applied for, which can be either for any class or for a specified class or classes (s 33 of the 1961 Act). If the latter type of certificate is granted, then the subsequent licence is limited by s 22 of the 1968 Act to those specified classes (see para 2.5.8 below) and extends for a period of 18 months (R 26 of the Regulations and R 8 of the 1969 Regulations).

2.5.8 Limited certificates

Section 22 of the 1968 Act allows an issuing Authority on an application to grant a limited Certificate of Competency. This certificate can be limited to a specified type of vehicle belonging to a specified class. The licence issued on such a certificate must contain a statement that in relation to that class it is limited to a vehicle of the type specified in the certificate.

2.5.9 Appeal

An appeal against these decisions on a test lies to the District Court where applicant ordinarily resides (s 33(6) of the 1961 Act). The Court can:

(i) where the decision is to defer (see para 2.5.7(b)), refuse the appeal or direct that the application be dealt with without a certificate of fitness;

(ii) on any other decision, refuse the appeal; or

(iii) if satisfied the test is not properly conducted, direct a further test.

The District Justice's decision is final and not appealable (s 33 of the 1961 Act). The tester should be respondent on the summons. The Court cannot enquire into the examiner's findings. It can only determine whether he conducted the test with malice or unfair conduct (*Geraghty v Morris* [1939] 2 All ER 269 and *Corrigan v Fox* (1966) SLT 79).

In *R v Cumberland JJ* (1931) 95 JP 206 it was held that a person could not appeal where his form had disclosed serious defective eyesight; but in *R v Cardiff JJ* [1962] 1 All ER 751 it was held that an appeal was possible where the refusal was based on enquiries made by the Licensing Authority.

Under Art 32(1) of SI 29/1964, if the Justice directs that an application (for a certificate of competency) be dealt with without a certificate of fitness, then the issuing Authority must refer the application back to the tester, who must without further test either refuse the application for valid reasons or issue a certificate of competency under Art 32(2) of SI 29/1964. If the Justice directs another test to be carried out, the issuing Authority must arrange to have it conducted by another tester.

Precedent

The District Court

District Court Area of District No

Between

AB

Appellant

and

XY

(Issuing Authority) Respondent

Notice of Appeal

Take Notice that the above AB of
in the County of *Hereby Appeals* to the District Court sitting at on the date of 19 at 11 am or the next opportunity thereafter pursuant to s 33 of the Road Traffic Act 1961 as Amended against the refusal of the Respondent to issue to him a Certificate of Competency (or to carry out test/Defer a Decision pending a Certificate of Fitness).

Dated this
Signed: . . . .
Solicitors for Appellant
of
County

To: The District Court Clerk
of
and TO/ Issuing Authority
of
and TO/ Tester

Notes

(1) The Court is that of the area in which the Appellant resides, or if a visitor holding a driving permit, any Justice.
(2) The Respondents are 'the Issuing Authority', e.g. the Minister for the Environment and the Tester. The functions of the issuing Authority are delegated to the driver tester (Art 25(2) of SI 29/1964).
(3) At least ten days' Notice must be given.
(4) The Original Notice should be stamped and lodged with the Court Clerk with a Declaration of Service at least four days before the return date.

2.5.10 Exemption

A person undergoing an official test is not in breach of the law requiring a drivers licence to be held, even though he has no licence (s 33(7) of the 1961 Act). This does not exempt him from the requirement to hold a provisional licence.

2.5.11 Period of validity

A certificate of competency ceases to be valid:

(a) on the expiration of a period of 18 months after the date of issue, unless within that period the person to whom it is issued—
  (i) produces it to a Licensing Authority in pursuance of a disqualification order under s 26, 27 or 28 of the 1961 Act, or
  (ii) submits it to the issuing Authority where a decision on his certificate of fitness application has been deferred pending production of a certificate of competency, or
  (iii) submits it to a Licensing Authority with an application for a driving licence;

(b) where a court order made after the date of issue of the certificate of competency disqualifies the person under s 26, 27 ot 28 of the 1961 Act he produces a certificate of competency to the appropriate Licensing Authority.

See Art 26 of SI 29/1964 as amended by SI 140/1969.

2.5.12 Substitute/Impersonation

When a person undergoes or attempts to undergo a driving test in the name of another person, any certificate or licence granted as a result is void. Such person is liable to a fine of up to £350 or six months' imprisonment or both (s 23 of the 1968 Act as amended by s 4(6) of the 1984 Act).

2.5.13 Duplicate certificates

If the certificate of competency is lost or destroyed the issuing Authority can issue a duplicate, provided it is satisfied the applicant has adequate reasons for requiring the duplicate (Art 33 of SI 29/1964).

2.6 Certificates of fitness

2.6.1 When necessary

Reference has been made above to a need to produce, in certain circumstances, with a driving application a certificate of fitness, e.g. see paras 2.3.4; 2.5.3. The circumstances of such need can be summarisd as follows in three groups:

(1) Where the person is disqualified from holding a drivers licence until he produces such a certificate (s 34(a) of the 1961 Act).
(2) Those persons specified in Art 39 of SI 29/1964, as amended by Art 12 of SI 340/1986. These are persons who have a medical fitness problem(s). This group includes seven sub-groups relating to applicants' health or condition—

(i) Where the application form for the licence does not contain the required declaration that the applicant is not suffering from any disease or physical or mental disability, epilepsy, alcoholism, or that he is not taking, on a regular basis, drugs or medicaments which would be likely to cause his driving to be a source of public danger.
(ii) Where the applicant on a previous application produced a certificate of fitness but does not make a declaration that he is not suffering from any new or further disease or incapacity.
(iii) Applicants for provisional licences in circumstances similar to (i) and (ii) (see para 2.4.2).
(iv) Certain persons with medical conditions or ailments. There are three broad categories:
  (a) applicants suffering from the diseases set out in the Sixth Schedule of SI 29/1964. There are 14 listed categories which are parallel to those listed at para 2.6.3 *infra*. The above regulations specify—
    (1) physical disablement which is likely to affect ability to drive;
    (2) cardiovascular diseases;
    (3) diabetes;
    (4) encephalitis, multiple sclerosis, myasthenia gravis or hereditary diseases of the nervous system associated with progressive muscular atrophy and congenital myotonic disorders;
    (5) diseases of the peripheral nervous system,
    (6) trauma of the central or peripheral nervous system,
    (7) cerebrovascular diseases,
    (8) lesion with damage to spinal cord and resultant paraplegia,
    (9) mental disturbance due to disease or trauma of, or operation upon, the central nervous system,
    (10) severe mental retardation,
    (11) psychosis,
    (12) psycho neurosis or personality disorders,
    (13) serious blood disease,
    (14) any disease of the genito-urinary system which is likely to affect ability to drive safely;
  (b) applicants who suffered in the past from epilepsy or chronic alcoholism; or
  (c) applicants who take on a regular basis drugs/medicaments likely to affect driving ability.
(v) Any applicant who will be 70 years of age on the commencement date of the licence and no certificate of fitness has been produced by him on an application within six months before the commencement date. This certificate has to be produced annually.

(vi) applicant is aged 40 or more and has subnormal vision after correction with corrective lenses, unless he held a licence within the five years before 1 January 1983.

(vii) Where a decision on a certificate of competency is deferred pending production of a certificate of fitness. A driver tester who, in the course of a driving test, forms the opinion that the applicant may be suffering from some disability which may affect his ability to drive safely may defer his decision on the application for a certificate of competency until that person produces a certificate of fitness (see 2.5.7(b)).

(3) According to the type of licence:

(i) Where the application is for a Class D or Class H provisional licence, unless the applicant has an already valid certificate for either class.

(ii) Where the application is for a Class E licence, unless there was a certificate of fitness for Classes D or H valid in existence.

Persons disqualified under s 32 of the 1961 Act (specified diseases, etc.) cannot apply.

2.6.2 Application

The application for a certificate of fitness is made to the Minister on a specified form (D 502), with a medical report on Form D 501 (see para 2.6.3). The form is sent to The Drivers Fitness Section, Department of the Environment, O'Connell Bridge House, Dublin 2. The Minister is the issuing authority under s 34 of the 1961 Act and Art 34 of SI 29/1964. He has power to delegate these functions. If refused the certificate an applicant cannot apply again within the following six months. The Minister notifies the licensing Authority of all decisions relevant to its area. The fee with the application was 25p, but under SI 113/1969 no fee is payable now.

2.6.3 Examination

The applicant must within the prescribed time be examined by a registered medical practitioner and send with his application a written signed report by the doctor certifying on a prescribed form (D 501) that, within one month prior to the application, he has examined the applicant as to the relevant aspects of his physical and mental condition (s 34(3) of the 1961 Act).

The Report should specify the classes of licence being applied for. It is necessary that doctors know these classifications. The medical aspects are detailed in Art 35 of SI 29/1964 (as inserted by Art 9 of SI 340/1986). Those that are relevant are:

(a) eyesight;

(b) ear conditions (vertigo and labyrinthine conditions);
(c) general physique and physical disabilities;
(d) the condition of the cardio-vascular, haemopoietic, endocrine, respiratory, gastro-intestinal, genito-urinary, nervous and mental systems, in so far as they or any abnormality would affect the applicant's fitness to drive safely vehicles of the class or classes concerned, having regard to—
  (i) His ability, physically and mentally, to operate the controls efficiently and safely for a reasonable period,
  (ii) his susceptibility to sudden incapacity, such as loss of consciousness, fainting or giddyness, which might affect his ability to operate the controls so as to stop safely, and
  (iii) his susceptibility to fatigue, such that his ability to operate the controls of the vehicle might be seriously impaired.

Details of many of these disorders and standards of test are set out in the seven pages of the Eighth Schedule of SI 29/1964 which is inserted by SI 340/1986. This Schedule goes into detail on each aspect of the person's physical and mental conditions and sets up minimum standards of physical or mental fitness. A very comprehensive examination is envisaged, and reference to the regularity detail would be necessary by the doctor. An explanatory leaflet called 'Guide for Registered Medical Practitioners', which details these, was issued to doctors in 1986 by the Department of the Environment.

In addition to dealing with the specific details of each of the above aspects, the Eighth Schedule requires some general matters to be looked into by the doctor during his examination:

(1) *Alcohol.* The Doctor cannot give a certificate if the applicant suffers from chronic alcoholism, with special reference to the risks arising in respect of Classes D, E and H.
(2) *Drugs/medication.* Fitness shall not be certified if the applicant is dependent on psycho-active drugs. In the case of other drugs/medication which are taken on a regular basis, due account must be taken of the potential effects on safe driving ability, with special attention again being accorded to Classes D, E and H.
(3) *Blood diseases.* Doctors are directed to pay special attention to any serious disease of the blood.

These regulations indirectly provide tougher sanctions on the users of intoxicants (drink or drugs) and widen the powers of District Justices to require certificates of fitness for repeated offenders.

Rather unusually, however, no specific criminal sanction is provided for improper reports (Forms D 501) being issued by doctors, nor indeed is there specific provision for any system of independent checking by the Minister. However, s 115 of the 1961 Act (see para 7.4) is probably wide enough to catch false certificates and the general penalty would apply (para 7.1). It is also undecided to what extent, if any, an injured third party might claim successfully from a doctor for a negligently issued certificate.

The form of the certificate of fitness was set out in the 1964 Regulations originally, but SI 340/1986 amended these to provide that a certificate of fitness shall be in a Schedule form. A list of Scheduled forms is contained in the Fourth Schedule to the 1964 Regulations, as inserted by Art 15 of SI 340/1986.

2.6.4 Signature and period of certificates

The person to whom the certificate of fitness is issued must sign it. It can be valid for an unlimited period or for a limited period of not less than a year, if so specified thereon. However, it ceases to be valid:

(a) within six months of the application being lodged with the issuing authority; or
(b) if the applicant is disqualified; or
(c) if a further certificate is required.

See Art 36 of SI 29/1964.

2.6.5 Decision

Any one of three results can flow from the application:

(i) refusal, in which event unless successfully appealed (see para 2.6.7) no application can be for a further six months (Art 40 of SI 29/1964); or
(ii) decision deferred pending production of a certificate of competency (which can be appealed—see para 2.6.7); or
(iii) grant of the certificate as applied for or limited to a specified class of classes.

2.6.6 Class validity

The certificate of fitness must be valid on the commencement day of the licence and must be issued for the class or classes to which the application relates (Art 39 of SI 29/1964). Under the same Article certain classes have cross or dual validity. The classes listed in Column I of the Table below are deemed valid for the classes listed in Column 2 of the Table:

Column 1	*Column 2*
Class G	Classes A and G
Class E	Classes A, B, C, D and E
Class D	Classes A, B, C and D
Class C	Classes A, B and C
Class B	Classes A and B

2.6.7 Appeal

An appeal lies to the District Court against any of the decisions set out at para 2.6.5 above (s 34(5) of the 1961 Act). The court can either:

(a) refuse the appeal; or
(b) give such direction to the Minister as the Justice considers just. The Minister must comply with the direction.

The District Justice's decision is final and unappealable.

In *Devon County Council v Hawkins* [1967] 1 All ER 235 the applicant had suffered from periodic epileptic fits for some time. The last fit was two years prior to his application and he claimed that the chance of another attack was practically eliminated so long as he continued to take the necessary drugs. *Held*: The licence refusal was upheld as the disease remained and the drugs only prevented its manifestations.

However, in *Re Leddingtons Application* [1958] Crim LR 550 the magistrates allowed an appeal in similar circumstances.

Precedent
In an application under s 34 of the 1961 Act, use the Precedent and Notes at para 2.5.9 *supra*, inserting s 34 instead of s 33 and either 'Refusal to issue a Certificate of Fitness' or 'Deferring decision pending production of Certificate of Competency'.

2.6.8 Duplicate

The issuing authority can issue a duplicate certificate of fitness if the original is lost or destroyed and there is good reason for its reissue (Art 43 of SI 29/1964).

2.7 Enforcement generally

There are certain specific enforcement provisions for these parts of the Acts which should be noted. These are additional to the other offences and procedures referred to in this chapter. They are two in number and relate to:

(1) production of licences to Gardai; and
(2) furnishing a specimen signature to Gardai.

2.7.1 Production

The specific provisions dealing with this power of the Gardai are contained in s 40 of the 1961. It provides as follows:

(i) Any Garda can require any person driving or accompanying a driver (e.g. with a learner driver) of a vehicle in a public place pursuant to regulations (see para 2.4.4 *supra*) to produce a proper current licence allowing him to drive the vehicle.
(ii) If produced immediately, then the Garda must be permitted to read it or the relevant parts of it containing his name and address, signature, photograph (if any), operational dating, Licensing

Authority and classes of vehicles (s 40(5) of the 1961 Act and Sched, 1968 Act).

(iii) If the person does not have the licence with him for inspection on demand, then he can produce it within ten days at a Garda Station of his own choosing.

(iv) In the latter two events above he must give his correct name and address.

(v) The section also creates a rebuttable presumption against the defendant i.e. that the defendant who does not produce a licence properly as above has not got one (s 40(6) of the 1961 Act). This was to get over a decision under the 1933 Act—*A-G v Carville* [1960] IR 330; 95 ILTR 41—to the effect that demand and non-production was not sufficient proof of the non-existence of a licence.

Breach of any of these requirements is an offence attracting the general penalty under s 102 of the 1961 Act (see para 7.1), optional endorsement, and optional ancillary disqualification. The request or demand is to be made of a person driving—it cannot be made of a person who has ceased driving (*Boyce v Absalom* (1974) RTR 248). As to 'driving', see para 7.9.

Defences
Two special defences are provided:

(i) by s 35(3)(c) of the 1961 Act, production of a current proper provisional licence is sufficient once it is effective and the Garda allowed to read it;

(ii) by s 38(7) of the 1961 Act, certain pedestrian controlled vehicles are to be excepted from the need for a licence by regulation. Article 7 of SI 29/1964 provides exemption for those vehicles of this type which are neither constructed nor adapted for use for carrying a driver or a passenger and which do not exceed 8 cwt unladen.

Impossibility of producing the licence is not a defence—*Sparkes v Worthington* (1986) RTR 64—but would be a vital mitigating factor.

Inspection time
In the event of production, whether on a roadside 'hold up' or at a Garda Station, a reasonable time to allow examination must be given (*Tremelling v Martin* (1971) RTR 90).

Powers of arrest
A Garda may arrest without warrant:

(a) any person who produces a licence on demand but refuses or fails to permit the Garda to read it; or

(b) any person who on lawful demand fails or refuses to give his name and address or gives a name and address which the Garda has reasonable grounds for believing to be false (s 40(4) of the 1961 Act).

2.7.2 Specimen signature

Under s 41 of the 1961 Act any Garda may request either:

(a) a driver (or/and a person accompanying a driver with a provisional licence) of a mechanically propelled vehicle in a public place; or
(b) a person producing a licence at the Garda Station under s 40 to sign his name in a book with a pen or pencil provided by the Garda. The section states this can only be requested in relation to licences which contain on that day an express condition that the licence is inoperative until signed by its holder. In fact this condition is included in all licences presently issued. Therefore, the only exemption possible is under s 38(7) of the 1961 Act, which exempts from the section pedestrian controlled vehicles which do not carry a driver or passengers and weigh less than 8 cwt unladen (Art 7 of SI 29/1964). The intention of the section is to provide comparative signatures to confirm that a person is not using another person's licence.

To refuse to give the signature is an offence attracting the general penalty under s 102 of the 1961 Act (see para 7.1), optional endorsement and ancillary (optional) disqualification. It seems there is no power of arrest without warrant in s 41.

It should be remembered that under s 24 of the 1961 Act and Art 19 of SI 29/1964 a licencee must sign his licence or provisional licence to make it effective (see paras 2.3 and 2.4 above).

2.8 Visiting drivers

2.8.1 Statute

In a tourist country such as Ireland, which is also a member of the EEC, the position of visiting motorists requires mention. The Local Government Act 1955, s 38 allows the Minister for the Environment to modify by order, in relation to visiting non-residents, the provisions of any enactment dealing with drivers licences.

2.8.2 Regulations

Under the above section and Part III of the 1961 Act as amended, the Mechanically Propelled Vehicle (International Circulation) Orders 1961–1987 (being SI 267/1961; 12/1962; 193/1963; 59/1964; 96/1966; 71/1976; 346/1980; 215/1983; 140/1987) are made.

These briefly provide:

(a) A visitor wishing to drive in Ireland can either use an international driving permit or his own national licence, provided he does not become a resident. The visitor may, if he so wishes, apply for an Irish licence (full or provisional) on the same basis as any Irish resident. However, such a licence is stamped 'Visitors Driving Licence' or 'Visitors Provisional Licence', as the case may be.
(b) Generally the law applying to driving licences (e.g. age, disqualification, court orders, etc.) applies equally to the visitors permit. If the visitor is disqualified here, his permit is sent to Dublin

Corporation who endorse it and return it to him on his leaving the State.

(c) An international driving permit may be issued to the holder of an Irish driving licence (except a visitor) wishing to drive abroad.

(d) New licences issued from 1989 onwards under EEC Directive 80/1263/EEC may be easily surrendered and exchanged for licences in host Member countries. This applies only to people who take up residence in another Member State. Under SI 234/1984—European Communities (Licensing of Drivers) Regulations 1984, giving effect to Art 8 of Council Directive 80/1263/EEC—a person who holds a valid national driving licence issued by another EEC Member State may for one year after taking up residence in Ireland drive any vehicle which he is licensed to drive by such licence. Under SI 233/1984 he can apply for an equivalent Irish licence and be granted it on surrender of his national licence.

2.9 Disqualification

2.9.1 Powers

A disqualification order is a court order removing and/or preventing a person from holding a legal drivers licence. Wide powers of disqualification from holding or terminating a driving licence are given to various courts, as will be seen below. The Court must have a valid reason and act judicially to hold a person is unfit to hold a driving licence and so should be disqualified. The valid reason can be mandatory or discretionary.

A valid reason

(i) In *Conroy v A-G* [1965] IR 411, at p. 440 the Supreme Court stated that:

> 'In all these cases the Act clearly indicates that the making of any such disqualification order is a judicial act and it follows, therefore, that before any such order is made the court concerned must act judicially in respect of the disqualification order in addition to hearing and determining the charge which leads to the conviction.'

This passage was cited with approval in the Court of Criminal Appeal *in toto* in *The People (Attorney-General) v Poyning* [1972] IR 402, the headnote of which reads in respect of this matter (though the actual text of the judgment does not clearly set this out):

> 'That the question of a disqualification under s 27 of the Act of 1961 involved a finding that a person was unfit to hold a driving licence and it should be judicially determined upon the appropriate evidence as a separate matter; and that it should not be treated as the imposition of an additional punishment for an offence under the Act of 1961.'

The Court, after citing from the *Conroy* case, added by way of a practice note 'for the guidance of all trial Judges, whether they be Judge of the District Court, Circuit Court or High Court this Court (Court of Criminal Appeal) thinks it desirable and necessary to direct attention to the effect of the decision in *Conroy v The Attorney-General*'.

(ii) In *The People v Michael Hogan* (unreported—see Frawen, 'Judgement of the Court of Appeal', Vol 1,360) the same approach was taken. The charge was a larceny charge. The Court of Criminal Appeal stated 'a car was undoubtedly used in the crime but *People v Payning* shows that this is not the type of case in which a disqualification should be imposed'. See para 2.9.4 also.

(iii) The same approach was adopted in *Joyce v Circuit Court Judge for the Western Circuit* (1987) ILRM 316. Judicial review of the Circuit Court Judge's order of disqualification was sought on the grounds that he did not act judicially in imposing the disqualification for failure by driver to observe his duties under s 106 of the 1961 Act. It was contended that after conviction of the offence there ought to be an additional investigation into the matter of whether or not disqualification should be imposed. In the High Court it was held that the evidence necessary for the Judge to make the judicial determination was already before him, and it was not necessary to reconsider that evidence in making the judicial determination to disqualify. In the instant case the defendant had an opportunity himself to present evidence by witnesses as to why he should not be disqualified. The case is, however, under appeal and a decision is expected in early 1989. *R v Money* (1988) Crim LR 626 reasserts the principle that where a disqualification is not mandatory and an indication given that disqualification will be imposed before it is imposed, some will be quashed unless the Court gave Counsel for the defence an opportunity to address the Court in the matter. The case involved using a vehicle in the course of committing crime.

(iv) In England, in *R v Bignell* (1968) 52 Cr App R, it was held that a disqualification order can be made without any other sentence. This view would probably be held to be correct in Ireland as the sections refer to 'conviction' only, and the Courts do not regard disqualification as a penalty. A contrary view was stated in *R v Surrey QS* [1963] 1 QB 990.

It is permissible to take into consideration another offence of a similar kind when disqualifying, per *R v Jones* [1970] 3 All ER 815.

(v) Where there is no reason to question the driver's competence, a disqualification order subject to a certificate of competence should not be ordered (*R v Donnelly* [1975] 1 WLR 390—defendant had 229 mg/100 blood alcohol).

(vi) In *R v Guilfoyle* (1973) RTR 272 such an order was allowed to stand on appeal where a 19-year-old was guilty of dangerous driving causing death.

2.9.1 *Disqualification*

An order requiring production of a certificate of fitness should be made where there is reason for it, e.g. age or infirmity (*R v Banks* (1978) RTR 535).

2.9.2 Types of disqualification

One of the severest sanctions that can be imposed on a motorist now is disqualification from driving. This disqualification may be:

(a) mandatory on conviction of certain offences or repeated convictions of certain offences (consequential disqualification); or
(b) an optional extra punishment in all road traffic offences (ancillary disqualification); or
(c) there is a third type of disqualification order which can be made where no offence has been committed (special disqualification).

In *Conroy v A-G* [1965] IR 41 the right of a citizen to trial by jury was refused in cases where disqualification was mandatory on the basis (largely) that the Supreme Court took the view that disqualification was not a punishment in the strict sense. Few citizens would agree, even though in *R v McNulty* [1965] 1 QB 437 it was held that an order of disqualification is not a 'sentence', and in *R v Arundel JJ* [1959] 2 QB 89 it was held that where a period in excess of jurisidiction was applied it was severable from the remainder of the order which remained good.

To maintain a record of serious offences a system of endorsing a record of convictions on licences, known as endorsements, is provided for in the Acts (see para 2.10).

General summary
There are therefore three types of disqualification orders:

(1) consequential—which means mandatory (see para 2.9.3); and
(2) ancillary—which means discretional (see para 2.9.4); and
(3) special (see para 2.9.5).

The provisions of the Acts are elaborate so that a summary of each provision only can be given below.

A disqualification order is an order made by a Court with proper jurisdiction to do so, preventing a person from validly holding a drivers licence or applying for one for a stated period. There is no power to limit disqualification to certain classes of licence.

Disqualified means (in insurance cases) disqualified by Order of the Court and does not include a person refused a licence because of mental deficiency (*Edwards v Griffiths* [1953] 2 All ER 874).

It should be noted that under s 124 of the 1961 Act the Minister for Justice cannot remit a disqualification order under s 23 of the Criminal Justice Act 1951 (No 2).

2.9.3 Consequential orders

2.9.3.1 *Mandatory nature*. A Court must make such an order on convicting a person of the following 17 offences set out in the Table (only one in the previous 1933 Act) on the occasion and within the time specified (per Second Schedule of 1961 Act, as amended by Sch, 1968 Act and s 24 and 25 of 1978 Act).

The Table specifies minimum periods. Imposing additional periods is a matter of discretion, but it must not be too harsh or oppressive, or be outside the normal discretionary limits; if it is it would involve an error in law reversible by judicial review (*certiorari*) (*R v St Albans Crown Court* (1981) RTR 139). In *R v Cunningham* (1979) RTR 465 three years' disqualification for intoxicated driving was reduced to one year where the defendant was imprisoned for other matters, as the disqualification would impede rehabilitation. See the principles in the cases set out at para 2.9.4.1 below.

2.9.3.2 *Effect.* The effect of the consequential order is twofold:

(a) first, the convicted person is declared by the Court to be disqualified from holding a licence and cannot hold any driving licence during the period declared, or during a period until a certificate of competency or fitness (or both) is produced if the Court so orders—s 26 of the 1961 Act; and
(b) secondly, under s 39 of the 1961 Act the convicted person cannot apply for any licence during the period of disqualification.

2.9.3.3 *Period.* **(a)** The period of disqualification cannot be less than six months in all cases.

(b) In the case of offences Nos 4, 4A, 5, 5A, 5C, 5D, 6A and 9 (see Table), it must be not less than one year in the case of a first offence and not less than three years in the case of a second or subsequent offence. In regard to these offences, 26 of the 1961 Act (as amended by s 25 of the 1978 Act) provides that a conviction under No 4 (s 49 intoxication offences) stands as a previous conviction under the other previous Acts and vice versa, except in relation to the charge of dangerous driving (where these previous convictions do not count in that way). In relation to these two offences, it is further provided by s 26(5) of the 1961 Act that on conviction for a second or subsequent offence the court can treat it as a first offence if more than four years has elapsed since the end of the previous disqualification period.

(c) Disqualification may be until a certificate of competency (para 2.5) or fitness (para 2.6) is produced. See para 2.9.1 as to reasons for these. This should not be done unless competence or fitness is in question (*R v Donnelly* [1975] 1 WLR 316).

(d) In Insurance cases under s 26(3A) of the 1961 Act (as inserted by s 3(4) of the 1984 Act) the period of disqualification is to be one year on a second or subsequent conviction within three years.

These periods are minimum periods. The court can impose longer periods.

Consequential disqualifications

No	*Offence*	*Section*	*Occasion*	*Time limit*	*Minimum period*
1	Using vehicle without test certificate	s 18(2)/1961	Second or subsequent offence	Within any period of 3 years	6 months
2	Driving before remedying dangerous defect	s 20(10)/1961	Ditto	Ditto	6 months
3	Driving while unfit	s 48/1961	Ditto	Ditto	6 months
4	Intoxication Driving or attempt	s 49/1961	Each offence	None each offence	12 months — 1st offence 3 years — 2nd or subsequent
4A	Failure to provide specimen at Garda Station	s 13/1978	Ditto	Ditto	1 year — 1st offence 3 years — 2nd or subsequent
5	Intoxication Drunk/drugged in charge	s 50/1961	Second or subsequent offence (but taking into account previous offence — s 49/1961 Act, s 30(3) and 33(3)/1968 Act offences) or s 13/1978 Act and s 14/1978 Act	Within any period or 3 years	6 months
5A	Failure to provide specimen at Station on s 50/1961 offence	s 14/1978	Second or subsequent offence (but taking into account previous offence s 49/1961 Act and s 30(3) and 33(3) 1968 Act offences) or s 13/1978 Act and s 14/1978 Act	Ditto	6 months
5B	Careless driving of mechanically propelled vehicle	s 52/1961 (vide s 50/1968)	Third or subsequent offence	Ditto	6 months

No	*Offence*	*Section*	*Occasion*	*Time limit*	*Minimum period*
5C	Obligation to provide breath specimen	s 15/1978	Each offence	Within 3 years	1 year — 1st offence 3 years — 2nd or subsequent
5D	Breath specimen procedure breach under s 15/1978 Act	s 16/1978	Each offence	Ditto	Ditto
5E	Obligation to provide urine in drug offences	s 17/1978	Each offence	Ditto	6 months
6	Dangerous driving of mechanically propelled vehicle	s 53/1961	*(a)* causing death or serious bodily harm to another	None each offence	1 year — 1st offence 3 years — 2nd or subsequent
			(b) otherwise second offence where at least one offence involved mechanically propelled vehicle	Within any period of 3 years	6 months
			(c) Subsequent offence where at least one offence involved mechanically propelled vehicle	Ditto	6 months
7	Driving dangerously defective vehicle	s 54/1961	Second or subsequent offence	Ditto	6 months
8	Dangerous parking at night	s 55/1961	Ditto	Ditto	6 months
9	Using uninsured vehicle	s 56/1961		Ditto	1 year
10	Driver's failure to fulfil duties on the occurrence of accident	s 106/1961	Ditto (Provided injury to person involved)	Ditto	6 months
11	Taking without authority	s 112(2)/1961	Second or subsequent offence	Ditto	6 months

2.9.3.3 *Disqualification*

See para 2.9.1 as to valid reasons and also para 2.9.4.1 for some general cases.

In *R v Phillips* (1955) 119 JP 499 it was held that if a court imposes a disqualification with a prison sentence, the former should be sufficiently long to ensure the greater part of it is unexpired when the defendant is released from gaol. Contrast that decision with *R* v *Parhley* (1973) RTR 149, which is more in line with modern penal thinking, i.e. where a three-year disqualification with one year's imprisonment was reduced to one year's disqualification as the defendant would face financial difficulties when leaving gaol, strengthening the temptation to drive while disqualified. See also cases and commentary at (1988) Crim LR 348–351.

As this question of disqualification frequently arises in connection with dangerous driving, some further cases are mentioned at para 4.2.9 on that subject but with general interest.

2.9.3.4 *Appeal.* In an appeal against a conviction involving a consequential disqualification order, the appeal court can annul (but only if it reverses the conviction), confirm, or vary (within the limits of the Act as *supra*) the order of consequential disqualification (s 26(7) and (8) of the 1961 Act). It can also vary the period of disqualification.

The order on appeal has the same consequences as the primary order (unless it contains an annulment or variations) and all the provisions referred to above apply to it.

The appeal is normally a full rehearing by the Circuit Court. The only exception to that is in the case of charges of manslaughter or dangerous driving causing death or serious bodily harm when that charge is indictable, so the appeal would normally be to the Court of Criminal Appeal. (See paras 4.1 and 4.2 below.)

2.9.3.5 *Endorsement.* Particulars of all consequential orders must be endorsed on the licences of convicted persons—see endorsements at para 2.9.6.

2.9.3.6 *Operation generally.* See para 2.9.5 below.

2.9.4 Ancillary orders

2.9.4.1 *When imposed.* Consequential orders, as their name indicates, are mandatory impositions by courts as seen above. Unlike them, ancillary orders are optional additions to any other lawful penalty. They can be imposed in two circumstances:

(i) On conviction of any offence in relation to a mechanically propelled vehicle or its driving (not being an offence which attracts a consequential order) under the Road Traffic Acts or otherwise. In respect of the phrase 'or otherwise' in s 27(1)(a), it is not clear what it means. Presumably it is intended to catch offences created by regulations and other statutes, e.g. use of a car in an illegal fishing under the Fisheries Consolidation Act 1959 as amended.

The point has received no judicial pronunciation yet, but applying the *ejusdem generis* rule of construction it would seem that the words will not be so construed and probably they are superfluous. Alternatively, one might wonder about the constitutionality of the section if there are a multitude of penalties—it may well cease to be a 'minor offence'. 'Or otherwise' may refer to bad driving of such a type that a Justice in the District Court considers that the disqualified person must be subjected to tests before he is allowed to drive again, i.e. certificates of competency (para 2.5) or fitness (para 2.6).

(ii) On conviction of any crime or offence in the commission of which a mechanically propelled vehicle was used, e.g. a getaway car in a crime such as a bank raid. Thus, in *R v Matthews* (1975) RTR 32 where motor vehicle was used to go to ten banks so as to draw £30 from each on stolen cheques, the defendant, a passenger accomplice, was disqualified. In *R v Parrington* (1985) Crim LR 452 it was held that onus is on prosecution to show vehicle used in connection with the actual offence charged. See para 2.9.1 also as to valid reasons.

Period

An ancillary disqualification should not be for an indefinite period (*R v Fowler* [1937] 2 All ER 380). Excessive periods can be harmful (*R v Bond* [1968] 1 WLR 188). In the absence of special circumstances it is wrong to disqualify the defendant for life (*R v North* (1971) 115 Sol Jo 389). In *Sopwith v Chucksbank* (1959) SLT 50 an order disqualifying for six months reduced to one month as being harsh and oppressive—a case involving inefficient steering gear in a car.

A previous good or bad record is important (*R v Mackle* (1964) Crim LR 329—where there were 16 previous serious offences then 20 years' disqualification upheld). In *R v Rous* (1965) Crim LR 378, five years was reduced to three because of the chauffeur's good record in a case of overtaking in bad visibility causing death.

See para 2.9.1 as to valid reasons and para 2.9.3.3 for other cases on length of disqualification.

2.9.4.2 *Effect*. The effect of the ancillary order is to disqualify the convicted person from holding any licence or specified class(es) of licence(s) for a specified period by the Court, or until he produces to the Licensing Authority a certificate of competency (i.e. passed driving test—see para 2.5), or a certificate of fitness (medical test—see para 2.6) or both such certificates—s 27 of the 1961 Act (see para 2.9.1 above as to reasons). Note that no minimum or maximum periods are prescribed as to disqualification of this type.

2.9.4.3 *Appeal*. An appeal can be brought against the conviction plus the ancillary order, or against the ancillary order alone (s 27 of the 1961 Act). The appeal court can make, confirm, annul or vary (increase/decrease/

different classes, etc.) the order with the same consequences as the lower Court (s 30 of the 1961 Act as inserted by s 20 of the 1968 Act).

On appeal the Court can impose an ancillary order or vary a one imposed by the lower Court. Such order has a like effect as the original one save as varied.

An ancillary order, like any other disqualification order, cannot be remitted by the Minister for Justice under s 23 of the Criminal Justice Act 1951 by virtue of the provisions of s 124 of the 1961 Act.

2.9.4.4 *Endorsement.* Particulars of all ancillary orders must be endorsed (see endorsements at para 2.10) on a person's licence on conviction (s 36 of the 1961 Act). In *State (Carthew) v DJ Dunleavy* (HC 1965, unreported) it was stated that failure to order that disqualification be endorsed may invalidate the disqualification.

In *A-G (Slavin) v Halpin* [1952] IR 196 it was held that the word 'months' in an ancillary disqualification order means calendar months. As to endorsements, see para 2.10 below.

2.9.4.5 *Operation generally.* See para 2.9.6 below.

2.9.5 Special disqualification orders

2.9.5.1 *When made.* The first two classes of disqualification orders above require conviction of an offence before they can be imposed. Special orders do not require this.

They arise under s 28 of the 1961 Act. By virtue of that section, when an officer of the Garda Siochana has reasonable grounds for believing a licensed driver is either:

(i) unfit to drive by reason of physical disease; or
(ii) unfit to drive because of physical or mental disability; or
(iii) incompetent to drive any vehicle or any class of vehicle;

he (the Garda Officer) can apply to the District Court for a special order. The procedure is that the application is made in the Court area in which the driver ordinarily resides after at least ten days' written notice has been given to him. If the District Justice is satisfied that the allegation of unfitness or incompetency is proved, he declares the person is disqualified until:

(a) in case of (i) and (ii) above (unfitness), he produces a certificate of fitness (see para 2.6); or
(b) in case of (iii) (incompetency), he produces a certificate of competency (see para 2.5).

The disqualification may be general or relate to a class or classes. This provision as to incompetency was new in the 1961 Act. In practice this section is little used.

Who is 'an officer of the Garda Siochana' and what are 'reasonable grounds' are matters of evidence. It is not clear whether, say, a prosecuting Superintendent or officer must act on his own knowledge or, say, information from an ordinary (non-officer) member of the Garda, or on information from the general public.

One must relate the section also to the general bar imposed by s 32 of the 1961 Act, allowing the Minister to specify types of disease or disability which will disqualify a person from holding a drivers licence. These are referred to above at paras 2.6 and 2.7, and these and other appropriate regulations presumably will be a guide to the Court.

2.9.5.2 *Appeal.* An appeal against the special order can be taken to the Circuit Court. While the Act does not say so directly in s 28 of the Act 1961, it is by way of full rehearing and the Court may annul, vary or confirm the order.

2.9.5.3 *Endorsement.* Special orders must be recorded on the licence under s 36(4) of the 1961 Act. (See endorsements at para 2.10.)

2.9.5.4 *Remission.* By virtue of s 124 of the 1961 Act, a special disqualification order cannot be remitted by the Minister for Justice exercising his powers under s 23 of the Criminal Justice Act 1951.

2.9.5.5 *Operation generally.* See para 2.9.6 below.

2.9.6 Operation of disqualification orders

Section 30 of the 1961 Act (as substituted by s 20 of the 1968 Act) specifies the provisions regarding the operation of all three types of disqualification orders.

2.9.6.1 *Consequences of disqualification.* The consequences of the order are three-fold, viz:

(1) to disqualify the person from holding a licence; and
(2) to suspend his existing licence during the period of the order. The period would be (i) a specified period, or (ii) until the required certificate of fitness or competency is produced (or both), or (iii) a removal of disqualification order (para 2.9) is made. Consequential orders extend to all vehicles' classes but ancillary or special orders may be confined to a class or classes;
(3) to prevent application for a drivers licence—see para 2.9.6.2 and para 2.3 above.

2.9.6.2 *Bar on licence.* A disqualified person cannot apply for a licence while so disqualified. If he does he is liable to £1,000 fine and/or six months' imprisonment (s 39 of the 1961 Act (amended by s 3 of the 1984 Act)).

2.9.6.3 *Commencement.* By virtue of s 30 of the 1961 Act (inserted by s 20 of the 1968 Act) the time of commencement of disqualification orders is as follows:

2.9.6.3 *Disqualification*

(a) special orders—immediately, unless suspended by order of the Court making the order pending the outcome of an appeal if brought. Its operation cannot be postponed.
(b) consequential or ancillary orders—on the fifteenth day after it is made, unless suspended by a Notice of Appeal. In *R v Meese* (1973) RTR 400 it was held a disqualification order cannot be ordered to be run consecutively to any other order of disqualification or imprisonment. The Notice of Appeal if served within 14 days of the making of the order automatically suspends the order in question pending the outcome of the appeal. Their operation can be postponed (see below).

2.9.6.4 *Postponement of consequential or ancillary orders.* The Court making either a consequential or an ancillary order (but not a special order) has a discretion to postpone the operation of the order for a period of not more than six months from the date of the conviction (see s 30 of the 1961 Act, as inserted by s 20 of the 1968 Act). This would mean a six months period at a maximum from the fifteenth day of the making of the order by the Court. It is mandatory, however, that before exercising its discretion the Court has evidence from the convicted person that a special reason exists relating to his personal circumstances which justifies the postponment. It is necessary for the Court to specify (in the order itself presumably) the special reason. What is a special reason is not clear, but the Act includes one specific reason, i.e. the nature of the convicted person's employment. However, family, health problems and any reasonable reason special to the person seems to receive favourable consideration from courts.

2.9.6.5 *Appeal.* As we have seen above, the operation of all three types of order can be affected by an appeal, i.e. order suspended. Two possibilities follow (s 30 of the 1961 Act, as inserted by s 20 of the 1968 Act), viz:

(a) An appeal withdrawn—If an appeal is withdrawn in writing, the suspension of operation of the disqualification order ends and the period if disqualification begins on the day of the notification of withdrawal. Therefore, the suspension is regarded as terminating on the day immediately preceding the day on which the notification is made.
(b) Appeal dealt with—If the appeal is not prosecuted (and therefore the lower Court's order stands) or the Appeal Court confirms or varies the order, the disqualification stands from the date of the making of the Appeal Court's order, unless a postponement of the order is obtained from the appeal court as above, i.e. of up to six months for a special reason.

2.9.6.6 *Certificates required.* In any case where the operation of any disqualification order is made conditional on the production of either a certificate of competency or certificate of fitness, a Licensing Authority must make a note of such production on the driving licence itself (s 30 of the 1961 Act, as inserted by s 20 of the 1968 Act).

2.9.6.7 *Procedure.* When any type of disqualification order is made then the procedure set out in Part VI of the Road Traffic (Licensing of Drivers) Regulations 1964 (SI 29/1964 as amended by SI 140/1969) is followed. The main regulations are Rs 45 and 46, and these have been replaced by Rs 12 and 13 of SI 140/1969 (Amending Licensing Regulations).

In summary the present provisions are as follows:

Consequential orders

The convicted person must give, within five days of the coming into operation of the disqualification order, his licence to the District Court Clerk or Registrar of the Courts, unless the order is suspended pending an appeal or postponed. The Court officer retains it until the fifth day after the coming into operation of the order, then endorses it and sends it to the Licensing Authority which granted it, if no appeal is lodged. If an appeal is lodged, then he sends it to the Registrar of the appellate Court. If the order has been postponed it is not forwarded to a Licensing Authority until disqualification is operative. It is returned to licensee during the intervening period. He must hand it in to the Court again within five days of the disqualification becoming operational.

If he does not hand in his licence, then, under Art 53 of SI 29/1964 (as inserted by Art 17 of SI 140/1969), he is guilty of an offence which carries the general penalty (para 7.1). Also, courts, on an application for removal of a disqualification, normally will take the failure to hand in the licence as a 'black mark' against the applicant and be slow to remove the disqualification.

Ancillary orders

Under Art 46 of SI 29/1964 (as inserted by Art 13 of SI 140/1969), again, the licence must be handed in by the disqualified person within five days of the operation of the order to the relevant court officers. If this is the District Court Clerk, he sends it to the County Registrar if there is an appeal; if not he sends it duly endorsed with particulars of the conviction to the Licensing Authority.

If a postponement has been ordered, the five days apply from the end of the period of postponement. If, on appeal, the order is confirmed, the County Registrar forwards it to the Licensing Authority duly endorsed. This also applies where the ancillary order is made *de nova* by the appellate court, with similar provisions if the appellate court postpones the order.

As in case of consequential orders, failure to hand up the licence is an offence (Art 53 of SI 294/1964) carrying the general penalty (para 7.1).

Special orders

Under Art 47 of SI 29/1964 (as amended by Art 14 of SI 140/1969), similar provision exists for the delivery of the licence within five days to the District Court Clerk by the disqualified person, unless the order is suspended pending an appeal. The District Court Clerk, if there is no appeal, endorses the licence and sends it to the Licensing Authority. If there is an appeal he sends it to the County Registrar.

If the special disqualification order is suspended because of an appeal and the appeal is withdrawn, then the licence must be sent to the Licensing

Authority by the County Registrar. If on appeal the order is annulled, then the County Registrar cancels any endorsement and returns the licence to the licensee. If the appellate court cancels the old order and makes a new one, then the procedure of endorsement and forwarding to the Licensing Authority applies.

As in the case of the other orders, failure to give up the licence is an offence (Art 53 of SI 29/1964) carrying the general penalty (para 7.1).

2.9.6.8 *Lost licence.* If the licence which should have been produced and endorsed is lost or destroyed, or the person held no licence, then those persons must within five days of obtaining a new licence give it to the officer of the Court for endorsement (Art 50 of SI 29/1964, as amended by Art 15 of SI 140/1969). The Court officer then:

(i) endorses it and, if the consequential or ancillary order is not then in operation, returns it to the licensee; or
(ii) if such an order is in operation, sends it to the Licensing Authority.

2.9.6.9 *Different classes.* If the disqualification order does not relate to all the classes in a person's licence, then on surrender of the licence he obtains from the Licensing Authority a duplicate licence for the remaining permitted classes. He must surrender this duplicate if he gets his full licence back. If he does not surrender the duplicate he is guilty of an offence to which the general penalty applies (see para 7.1).

These provisions are contained in Art 54 of SI 29/1964. They are peculiar, as the wording of the Act refers to disqualification being on the *total licence* and not classes—see ss 26, 27, 28 and 30 of the 1961 Act. However, an ancillary or special disqualification may only apply to certain class(es).

2.9.6.10 *Retention of licence: Return.* The Licensing Authority retains the licence until the disqualification order expires or is removed. Then they return it to the licensee, unless it has been already returned to him by the Court (Art 52 of SI 29/1964).

2.9.6.11 *Notice by Court officers.* The Court officer must notify the Minister and the appropriate Licensing Authority of all disqualification orders, postponements or suspensions of orders to be endorsed on licences by Court Order (Art 51 of SI 29/1964, as amended by Art 16 of SI 140/1967). The appropriate Licensing Authority is the one which granted the licence or, if there was no drivers licence, the Authority for the area in which the convicted person ordinarily resides.

2.9.7 Removal of disqualification

2.9.7.1 *When and how.* A consequential order can be removed at the end of six months or later by virtue of s 29 of the 1961 Act, as amended by s 19 of the 1968 Act. An ancillary order of over three months duration can be removed at the end of three months or later by the Court imposing it. To obtain such a removal the disqualified person can apply after three months in the case of a consequential order and after two months in the case of ancillary orders of the commencement of their operation. The applicant must give 14 days' notice in writing to the Garda Superintendent of the District in which that person ordinarily resides. The original of the notice must be lodged with the Court. A precedent is set out at para 2.9.6.7 below. More than one application can be made, e.g. if the earlier applications are refused and there are changed circumstances. However, a fresh application cannot be made within three months of the previous refusal.

The removal order cannot operate earlier than six months from the coming into operation of a consequential order or three months from the beginning of an ancillary order.

The Court can order the applicant to pay the whole or any part of the costs of the application as the court deems appropriate.

R v Cottrell [1956] 1 WLR 280 decided on similar English legislation that a court can allow the application or dismiss it but cannot put conditions on part of the disqualification.

2.9.7.2 *Considerations.* The Court before it makes the removal order must consider that circumstances exist which justify its taking this course (s 19 of the 1968 Act). No exact reasons for such justification are specified, but the Court must have regard to all matters that appear relevant. The section does state, however, that the Court should, in particular, have regard to the character of the applicant, his conduct after conviction and the nature of his offence. As noted above, the fact that the applicant did not give in his licence for endorsement or did not pay his fine will also be likely factors to be considered. Again, employment prospects, family illness, or any hardship caused wil be considered.

In *Damer v Davidson* (1976) RTR 44 it was held that there is no distinction between discretionary and mandatory disqualification, except that the Court may be somewhat less ready to remove the latter even if the minimum period has expired.

2.9.7.3 *Proper court.* Where no appeal was brought against the disqualification order imposed, or such original order was upheld by an appeal, then any application for removal of the disqualification must be made to the Court which originally imposed such disqualification. Otherwise it is to the Court making the order or varying it that one applies, i.e. to the Circuit Court, or Central Criminal Court or Court of Criminal Appeal.

2.9.7.4 *Appeal.* An appeal against refusal to remove the disqualification or the date ordered for removal can be brought to the Circuit Court from the District Court, or to the Court of Criminal Appeal from all other inferior Courts (s 29(6) of the 1961 Act).

The court can order the applicant to pay the whole or such part of the costs of the appeal as it deems appropriate.

2.9.7.5 *Disqualification*

2.9.7.5 *Procedure*. Under R 49 of SI 29/1964, the Court Officer endorses the removal of the disqualification and returns the licence to the holder if the period of disqualification has expired. If the date has not passed, he sends it to the Licensing Authority which granted the licence. Similar provisions apply to the County Registrar or other such officer in the event of a successful appeal for removal of a disqualification order.

Under s 36(5) of the 1961 Act, the Court must order that particulars of the removal of the disqualification be endorsed on the licence or, if no such licence exists at the time, on any subsequent licence granted to the applicant.

Under the Courts Fees Orders, the application must be stamped with the appropriate Court stamp.

2.9.7.6 *Specimen application*. A specimen Notice of Application for removal of a disqualification order follows:

Precedent

An Chuirt Duiche
(The District Court)

District No District Court Area of

In the matter of the Road Traffic Acts 1961–84
And in the matter of the Application of AB
TAKE NOTICE that at the sittings of the District Court at in the County of at 11 a.m. on the day of 198 or the next opportunity thereafter application will be made by and on behalf of AB of in the County of for the removal of a disqualification Order imposed on him by this Court on the day of 19 pursuant to section 29 of the Road Traffic Act 1961 (As amended). The said Order came into operaton on the day of 19

Dated this day of 19

Signed: ....
Solicitor for Applicant
County

To/
The Superintendent
Garda Siochana,
at
And to/
The District Court Clerk
of

Notes

(1) Application must be stamped.
(2) Application must be served at least 14 days before the Court.
(3) Stamped original with Declaration of service should be lodged with Court Official at least 4 days before Court.

2.9.8 Remission

Section 124 of the 1961 Act states that a disqualification made under the Act is not capable of being remitted under s 23 of the Criminal Justice Act 1951. Section 23 allows broadly the operation of the prerogative of mercy to the Minister for Justice, which would normally be applied for on Petition.

2.9.9 Driving while disqualified

A disqualification order has as one of its results that a disqualified person is no longer licensed to drive while such order is in force. If a person drives while so disqualified, he is driving without a licence and is guilty of an offence under s 38 of the 1961 Act (as amended by s 3 of the 1984 Act). See para 2.2 above. The fine is £1,000 or/and six months' imprisonment (maximum).

It is not a defence that defendant did not know he was disqualified (*Taylor v Kenyon* [1952] 2 All ER 726). Imprisonment may be appropriate, especially if there were previous convictions (*Davidson Houston v Lanning* [1958] 2 All ER 73). Proof of disqualification is by certified copy of the order, which should refer to that conviction only (*Stone v Bastick* [1965] 3 WLR 1233) or by endorsement on the licence (*ibid*). Allowing a person who is disqualified to drive can amount to aiding and abetting (*Pope v Minton* (1954) Crim LR 711), but not if, after making reasonable enquiries, the defendant was ignorant of the disqualification (*Bateman v Evans* (1964) 108 Sol Jo 522).

The offence can be committed even though subsequently the conviction imposing disqualification was quashed on appeal (*R v Lynn* (1971) RTR 369).

Oddly, in Ireland, a power to arrest without warrant is not given by s 39 of the 1961 Act.

R v Pomeroy (1035) 24 Cr App R 147 it was held that such a charge should not normally be tried with other charges. This is to prevent prejudice. Attempting to drive while disqualified is also an offence (*Shaw v Knill* (1974) RTR 142).

2.9.10 Applying for a licence while disqualfied

Section 39 of the 1961 Act creates a special offence of applying for a licence while disqualified. Ths fine was increased to £1,000 by s 3 of the 1984 Act, and a six-month sentence can be imposed or both such fine and imprisonment.

This is an absolute offence and the driver's belief in the absence of disqualification is irrelevant (*R v Muller* (1975) RTR 479).

2.9.11 Visitors

As seen at para 2.8 above, disqualification applies to a driving permit held by a visitor under SI 26/1961, and the appropriate Licensing Authority to be notified is the Dublin Corporation. As to endorsements not applying to visitors, see para 2.10.7 *infra*.

2.10 Endorsements

An endorsement on a driving licence is a record of a conviction of the licence holder of an offence pursuant to a Court Order. The powers to order endorsements are mandatory in two classes of cases, and in other cases are optional under a general power.

2.10.1 Power to endorse licences

Section 36(1) of the 1961 Act (as amended by Sch, 1968 Act) reads as follows:

> 'Where a person is convicted of an offence under this Act or otherwise in relation to a mechanically propelled vehicle or the driving of any such vehicle or of a crime of offence in the commission of which a mechanically propelled vehicle was used, the Court, if it does not make a consequential or ancillary disqualification order, may (and, in the case of an offence which would be an offence such as is specified in paragraphs 1, 2, 3, 5, 5A, 5B, 7, 8, 9, 10 or 11 or sub-paragraph (b) of paragraph 6 of the second schedule to this Act if it were a second or any subsequent offence within any period of three years, shall) by order direct particulars of the conviction to be endorsed on the driving licence held by such person or, if he is not the holder of a driving licence but subsequently a driving licence is granted to him on that driving licence.'

A court, under s 36 of the 1961 Act, can endorse a licence:

(a) mandatorily in the types of cases mentioned (see para 2.9.3 for details of these) (s 36(1)); and
(b) mandatorily on a special disqualification order being made (s 36(4)); and
(c) optionally in all other cases where endorsement is possible (s 36(1)).

The use of the phrase 'if it were a second or any subsequent offence within any period of three years' within parentheses in s 36(1) has caused problems of interpretation. *The State (Carthew) v D J Dunleavey* (1965, High Court, unreported) casts doubt on the validity of a disqualification order which is not ordered to be endorsed by the court, having regard to the mandatory word 'shall' being used in s 36(3) of the 1961 Act. However, normally the court pronounces such endorsement and the order so contains it. In *A-G (McConville) v Brannigan* [1962] IR 370 it was held 'second' or 'subsequent' meant second or subsequent similar offence(s).

In *A-G v Maguire* (1973, High Court, unreported) it was held that an (see Table, para 2.9.3.1). This point will be decided by the Supreme Court in a case stated—*DPP v O'Brien*—in early 1989 i.e. whether or not it is mandatory pursuant to s 36(1) of 1961 Act to endorse a conviction under s 52/1961 Act as amended.

In *A-G v Keane* 106 ILTR 5 it was held that, in respect of the offences within the parentheses, endorsement is mandatory on a first offence. The High Court Judgment is disappointingly short and unreasoned. It related to a conviction under s 56 of the 1961 Act, i.e. no insurance.

In *R v Newcastle-upon-Tyne JJ* (1972) RTR 5 it was held that an omission to endorse can be repaired in certain circumstances; or if not done the prosecution can get a judicial review order in the nature of mandamus.

In *R v Bignell* (1967) 111 S.J. 773, dealing with disqualification, it was held that there need be no penalty to make an order; the same principle would appear to operate under the Irish section which refers to 'conviction' if Probation Act applied.

In *Bell v Ingham* [1969] 1 QB 563 it was held not proper to endorse for an offence of attempting to take a vehicle without authority.

In 1989 there is likely to be a decision in the Supreme Court in a case of *DPP v O'Brien* about s 36(1) in relation to a conviction for careless driving under s 52/1961 Act.

2.10.2 Procedure

Under Art 48 of SI 29/1964 (Licensing of Drivers Regulations), on the making of an endorsement order the licence must be given in to the Court Officer within five days and the officer must return it duly endorsed to the holder. This is a penal regulation and attracts the general penalty (para 7.1) for breach (Art 53). If the order is annulled on appeal the Court Officer of the Appeal Court notes the annulment and delivers the licence to the licensee. If the licence is lost or destroyed, then the next licence granted is the appropriate one (Art 50).

Under Art 51 the Court Officer is bound to notify the Minister and the appropriate Licensing Authority of all endorsements and any order annulling, or varying such endorsement (see para 2.9.6.11).

Where the defendant was disqualified but was driving before producing his licence to be endorsed, then he produced his licence as being a valid licence, he was held guilty of an offence (*R v Bogdal* (1982) RTR 395). See also *Taylor v Keynon* [1952] 2 All ER 726.

2.10.3 Other crimes

It should be noted that the power of endorsement extends to all crimes involving use of a mechanically propelled vehicle, e.g. bank robbery car driver on conviction. See para 2.9 above.

2.10.4 Appeal

If an appeal is brought against the conviction in relation to which the endorsement was made, the appellate court can make, confirm or annul the order. If it sets aside the conviction it is bound to annul the endorsement. If it confirms the conviction unvaried as to sentence it must confirm the endorsement also. If the Court varies the sentence only it must make a new endorsement order in those cases where the offence requires a mandatory order under the section. Otherwise than in those cases specified in s 36 as amended, it has the same optional authority as the lower Court.

2.10.5 Mandatory endorsement on a disqualfication

In all three types of disqualification orders (consequential, ancillary and special) the court must endorse both the conviction and the disqualification on the person's licence or, if he has not got one at the time, on any subsequent licence he may obtain (s 36(3)(a) of the 1961 Act).

If an appeal is brought and withdrawn but the disqualification order (and automatically the endorsement order) was suspended pending the appeal, then the suspension of the endorsement order comes to an end on the day before the date of notification of withdrawal is given, i.e. endorsement then takes effect (s 36(3) of the 1961 Act).

Where an appeal is taken in cases involving consequential or ancillary orders (and endorsement), the appellate court must, where it annuls the disqualification order, also annul the endorsement; or, alternatively, may make new variation orders annulling the old ones which were made in the lower court or confirm both orders. That means generally that it removes the endorsement if it annuls the disqualification order; otherwise it confirms or varies it (s 36(3) of the 1961 Act).

In cases involving special disqualification orders the Court must order the endorsement of the particulars on the licence. If the order is suspended pending an appeal, the endorsement is suspended. The Appeal Court can confirm or annul the endorsement, or annul it and make a new one, depending on the success or otherwise of the appeal. If the appeal is withdrawn endorsement comes into operation immediately (s 36(4) of the 1961 Act).

Where removal of a disqualification is ordered, particulars of the removal must also be ordered under s 36(5) of the 1961 Act, and such removal is endorsed on the licence or, if no licence is held, on any subsequent licence.

2.10.6 Transfers of endorsements: Lapse

If a person's driving licence has been endorsed under the 1961–68 Acts (or the 1933 Act), then all new licences given to him must show this endorsement unless either:

(i) the endorsement order was annulled on appeal; or
(ii) he shows that for not less than three years continuously he has held a licence not endorsed.

If he has not held a driving licence continuously, then he must have held one without any new endorsement for a series of discontinuous periods totalling not less than five years (s 37 of the 1961 Act). Thus, if even a lapse of one day occurs the period is not continuous and the five-year period applies.

This section therefore allows licences to be issued as 'clean' licences, provided either:

(a) an endorsement is annulled on appeal; or
(b) sufficient time (three years continuous licence holding or five years discontinuous holding) has elapsed without any new endorsement on the licence.

2.10.7 Visitors

As seen above at para 2.8, generally the law relating to drivers licences applies to driving permits, i.e. the national or domestic drivers licences useable in Ireland or international permits. However, by SI 269/1961 (as amended by SI 59/1964) the provisions of s 36 of the 1961 Act as to endorsements do not apply to these documents, and a court should therefore not order endorsement. Instead, on conviction with disqualification the licence or permit is sent to Dublin Corporation to be retained there until the visitor leaves or the period of disqualification expires. The Corporation notes on it that the right to use the permit in the State was withdrawn for the period involved.

Chapter 3

Control of speed

'A motor enthusiast gave a Chinese Sage a lift from Cork to Dublin. They arrived at the GPO and the motorist said to the Sage "Isn't it great we broke the record for the journey by two minutes". "Well," said the Sage, "what do we do with the two minutes?"

3.1 Speed limits

3.1.1 Need for limits

The control of vehicular speed is an obvious social and traffic necessity. This control is implicit and explicit in many offences, e.g. dangerous driving, where speed is a factor to be taken into account. A more direct control is achieved by a scheme of speed limits. The 1865 Locomotive Act brought in a general speed limit of 4 mph, reduced to 2 mph in built up areas. This was known as the Red Flag Act, as it required that a locomotive should be preceded by a man carrying a red flag to warn horse-drawn vehicles of their approach.

The specific law on the control of speed and speed limits is set out in Part IV of the 1961 Act, s 105 of the 1961 Act and Part IV of the 1968 Act, and numerous regulations. The main speed control regulations are the Road Traffic (Speed Limits) Regulations 1963 (SI 18/1963) (referred to in this Chapter as 'the 1963 Regulations'). These have been substantially amended. They deal with ordinary speed limits. Local speed limits are indicated by signs. Limits affect types of vehicles and areas of road. The limits vary.

The regulations and speed limits must be reviewed under the Acts by the Minister. This is done normally at the request of the local authority and in consultation with the Gardai. Local authorities carry out a review of speed limits on a country wide basis every three or four years normally, and submit proposals to the Minister for amending regulations.

Summary limits:

55 mph—general limit, all roads and vehicles
50 mph—station wagons and certain PSVs
40 mph—certain PSVs, articulated vehicles and built up areas
35 mph—certain towing vehicles
30 mph—built up areas generally
20 mph—multiple towing vehicles.

3.1.2 Type of speed limits

There are four types of speed limits:

(1) ordinary speed limits;
(2) general speed limits;
(3) built up area limits;
(4) special speed limits.

These limits apply only on public roads (see para 7.9) and any summons must specify that the offence was committed on a 'public road'.

The effect of breaking a speed limit is not *ipso facto* evidence of civil negligence (*Barna v Hades* (1962) 106 S.J. 194). In *Hood v Lewis* (1976) RTR 99 it was decided that, on a charge of exceeding the speed limit in a built up area, it was not a defence that the driver's view of the sign was obstructed by bushes, posts and other traffic. This decision is a broad one and may not apply in full in different circumstances.

Where prescribed signs are not erected there should be no conviction—*Mackereth v Ridge* (1968) 112 S.J. 98 (absence of repeater signs)—although commentators have cast doubt on this decision as a general rule.

3.1.3 Ordinary speed limits

These limits can be imposed on all public roads, or all public roads with exceptions, or with exceptions also for any class of mechanically propelled vehicles (with such sub-class exceptions, if any, as are specified), as the Minister for the Environment specifies by Regulations (s 44 of the 1961 Act). Such limits are known as 'ordinary speed limits'.

The current regulations are the Road Traffic (Speed Limit) Regulations 1963 (SI 18/1963), as amended (see para 3.2.1 below).

Limits
The following ordinary speed limits are prescribed by Art 4 of the 1963 Regulations (save where a lower limit otherwise applies, e.g. built up limits when the lower limit automatically applies):

3.1.3 *Speed limits*

(a) 50 miles per hour (mph) on all roads for—

(i) station wagons. Station wagons are defined as including estate cars, and vehicles so constructed or adapted and vehicles with collapsible or detachable seats; and

(ii) single decked mechanically propelled vehicles intended or adapted primarily for the carriage of passengers, which have passenger accommodation for more than eight passengers.

'Adapted' was held to mean that some amount of alteration is effected to the original construction of the vehicle (*Taylor v Meade* [1961] All ER 426). A vehicle can be reconstructed to be in another class (*Keele v Miller* [1950] 1 All ER 261), but it must be a major reconstruction (*Fry v Bevan* (1937) 81 S.J. 60). See also para 7.9.

Passenger accommodation is dealt with in the Road Traffic (Passenger Accommodation of Mechanically Propelled Vehicles) Regulations 1962 (SI 143/1961). Article 2 of these regulations provide that such accommodation shall be the total seating accommodation calculated by allowing for a separate seat measuring 16 inches per person other than the driver.

(b) 40 mph on all roads for—

(i) vehicles intended or adapted primarily for the carriage of passengers and capable of accommodating more than eight persons and which is a double decker, e.g. bus;

(ii) non-passenger vehicles exceeding two tons in unladen weight.

(See para 1.7 as to unladen weight.)

In *Plume v Suckling* (1977) RTR 271 a coach adapted for six persons, kitchen equipment and a stock car was held to be a goods vehicle with a 40 mph limit.

(c) For vehicles drawing another vehicle (unless it is less than 5 cwt unladen) or vehicles the limits are—

(i) 40 mph where the drawn vehicle is attached to the vehicle by way of superimposition and no other vehicle is drawn, i.e. articulated vehicles;

(ii) 35 mph where not so attached and no other vehicle is drawn, e.g. car drawing a family caravan;

(iii) 20 mph where more than one vehicle is drawn.

A trailer and car amalgamated into one four-wheeled rigid unit is one trailer not two (*Baker v Esau* (1972) Crim LR 559).

A vehicle with a closely coupled trailer, not being an articulated vehicle, is not one vehicle (*Dixon v BRS (Pickford) Ltd* [1959] 1 All ER 449).

Signs

No traffic signs are required to indicate the existence of ordinary speed limits, as ordinary speed limits are in respect of specified classes of vehicles and apply to all times.

Lower limit

Under Art 4 of the 1963 Regulations, such vehicles, on entering an area which has a lower speed limit, must comply with that lower limit, e.g. built up area limit.

3.1.4 General speed limits

The Minister for the Environment has power under s 24 of the 1968 Act (which inserted a new s 44A into the 1961 Act) to make regulations prescribing a general speed limit on all public roads for mechanically propelled vehicles, with such exceptions as to roads or classes of vehicles as are specified. This is a somewhat wider power than that conferred in relation to ordinary speed limits. It is basically intended to extend to all vehicles on all roads.

The section allows the exception of certain roads or classes of vehicles. Also, the regulations may restrict the limit to a particular period(s).

As to 'public road' and 'mechanically propelled vehicles', see para 7.9.

By virtue of Road Traffic (General Speed Limit) Regulations 1979 (SI 176/1979), from 1979 a general speed limit of 55 mph applies on all public roads other than those to which a built up area speed limit or a special speed limit applies. The following vehicles are excepted:

(a) ambulances;
(b) fire brigades; and
(c) vehicles used by Gardai in performance of their duties.

In *Aitken v Yarwood* [1964] 2 All ER 537 exception (c) was extended, with hesitation, to a policeman going to court to give evidence. See also *Jones v CC of Bedfordshire* (1987) Crim LR 502, where it was stated that exceptions must be looked at carefully and limited to duty operations only, e.g. fire brigade going to a fire. In the earlier case of *Strathern v Gladstone* (1937) SC(J) 1 a motorist who trailed a police car to get evidence it was speeding was held not to be entitled to the exemption.

This general limit of 55 mph applies therefore to all public roads to which a built up speed limit or a special speed limit does not apply, and with the exception of ambulances, fire brigades and Gardai vehicles.

Signs

No signs are needed to indicate the general speed limit, as is also the case for ordinary speed limits, but general information signs are often erected to remind persons (especially visitors) of the position.

3.1.5 Built up area limits

The 1961 Act, by s 45, provides for built up area speed limits.

A built up area is either:

(a) a public road situate in a county or other borough, an urban district or town, except those roads specified by the Minister for the Environment not to be so; or

(b) a public road situate elsewhere declared by the Minister to be within a built up area.

There are five County Boroughs, six Boroughs, and forty-nine Urban Areas in the country, so these limits apply extensively. As to 'towns', there is no definition in the Act. However, the two legs of the definition of 'Powers' combined are wide enough to enable the Minister to deem any road a built up area once he is acting *intra vires* the section, i.e. there must be evidence of area being 'built up'. One therefore need normally only look at the Act and Regulations to find what roads are stated or deemed to be within built up areas.

The format of the regulations (see para 3.2.3. *infra*) generally is County orientated, and the regulations specify:

(i) what roads within a County or County Boroughs, Urban areas or towns are not 'public roads in a built up area' (i.e. roads not subject to the 30 mph limit); and
(ii) roads which are declared to be in a built up area, i.e. roads subject to the 30 mph limit within these areas, and these normally are all roads other than (i); and
(iii) roads to which a 40 mph or other limit applies (see para 3.1.6 as to special speed limits; and
(iv) vehicles excepted from the limits, i.e. ambulances, fire brigades and Gardai vehicles used in the course of their duties (see para 3.1.4 as to this exemption).

A list of current regulations is set out at para 3.2.3 below.

Art 5(1) and (2) of 1963 Regulations specified by reference to schedules what respectively were and were not public roads in a built up area for the purpose of s 45 of the 1961 Act. These have been superseded by those regulations specified in para 3.2.3, below which deal with the limits on a County basis.

The normal limit applying in a built up area is 30 mph for all mechanically propelled vehicles. Approaches to the 30 mph area sometimes have a limit of 40 mph (see para 3.1.6 below). The Minister for the Environment can reduce or increase the limit, or restrict it to particular periods of day and night, and he may also except any class of vehicle from the limit.

Signs

The erection of signs denoting built up speed areas is authorised by Road Traffic (Signs) Regulations 1962 (SI 171/1962). The appropriate sign is No 211 at present—a circular sign with '30' or '40' or '50', as appropriate, written on it. It normally has on its back or reverse side sign No 203, indicating the end of the speed limit area to a driver leaving the built up speed area. 'Repeater' or reminder signs half the size of the normal sign No 211 are also provided for in the regulations.

There are slight variations regarding the placing of signs in dual carriageways and motorways, i.e. on the appropriate direction of the carriageway.

As to road signs generally, see para 5.8.

3.1.6 Special speed limits

By virtue of s 46 of the 1961 Act (as amended by s 25 of the 1968 Act) the Minister for the Environment can prescribe by regulation special speed limits. The features of these limits are:

(a) they can apply to any specified public road or all public roads in any specified area;
(b) they may apply to all mechanically propelled vehicles, or any class of such vehicles (and any class or any subclass may be exempted from the limit applying to the class);
(c) they may be restricted to specified periods or occasions, e.g. race meetings, etc.

Article 6 of the 1963 Regulations specifies a special speed limit of 40 mph for all vehicles travelling on the roads specified in the Third Schedule of those regulations. There is a lengthy list of these roads in the Schedule. The regulation has been amended by a number of the regulations mentioned in this Chapter for various local roads, especially by a series of regulations specified at para 3.2.3 below.

The existence of such a limit is, of course, indicated by an authorised sign, as is the termination of such a limit. Ambulances, fire brigades and Gardai vehicles on duty are exempt from these limits. (See the limits of this exemption in para 3.1.4).

Signs
The sign used for special speed limits is the same as the sign for the built up area speed limit, i.e. sign No 211 at each side of the Road, showing '40' or '50' as appropriate. The reverse side can be sign No 203 (end of special speed limit) or a built up speed limit sign, as appropriate.

These signs are set out in the Road Traffic (Signs) Regulations 1962 (SI 171/1962), as amended (see para 5.8). Repeater signs at one-quarter mile intervals are also allowed—these are half the size of the main signs.

There are slight variations for the placing of signs in dual carriageways, i.e. they can be placed only on the appropriate direction of the carriageway.

3.2 Speed limit regulations

3.2.1 Main regulations

The main Regulations of 1963 (SI 18/1963) are dealt with above briefly. Many of their provisions have been repealed or amended. They deal with ordinary speed limits, as set out at para 3.1.3 above. They also deal with built up speed limits and special speed limits, specifying the roads in the different parts of the country to which they apply, but these are too detailed to be examined in this book. They have been replaced by the following regulations (paras 3.2.2 and 3.2.3) in relation to the areas mentioned on a county basis.

3.2.1 *Speed limit regulations*

Amending Orders cover wide areas of roads, although these in turn have been superseded by those in para 3.2.3 below for specified areas.

3.2.2 General limit regulations

Road Traffic (General Speed Limit) Regulations 1979 (SI 176/1979). See para 3.1.4 above.

3.2.3 Local speed limit regulations

These extend to 'built up' areas and 'special speed limits'. They prescribe local speed limits on a county-wide basis. They are set out alphabetically by County as follows:

Carlow	SI 398/1985	Limerick	SI 104/1984
Cavan	SI 63/1985		38/1986
Clare	SI 126/1987	Longford	SI 229/1984
Cork	SI 457/1986	Lough	SI 272/1987
Donegal	SI 103/1986	Mayo	SI 216/1980
Dublin	SI 358/1977	Meath	SI 318/1985
	325/1978	Monaghan	SI 119/1988
	169/1981	Naas by-pass	SI 298/1983
	330/1982	Offaly	SI 81/1983
	217/1983	Roscommon	SI 251/1988
Galway	SI 273/1987	Sligo	SI 162/1987
Kerry	SI 334/1983	Tipperary	SI 206/1986 (NR)
Kildare	SI 277/1983		SI 234/1982 (SR)
Kilkenny	SI 271/1988	Waterford	SI 8/1986
Laoighis	SI 72/1986	Westmeath	SI 365/1981
Leitrim	SI 278/1980	Wexford	SI 45/1983
		Wicklow	SI 141/1987

The normal format of each of these regulations is that it has citation, commencement and interpretation sections. Then the regulations specify with the aid of Schedules:

(i) what are and what are not public roads for 'built up area speed limits';
(ii) the roads 'special speed limits' affect, i.e. 40 mph;
(iii) the exemption of ambulances, fire brigades and Gardai vehicles (see para 3.1.3 as to limits of these).

In case of difficulty about a road the appropriate regulation should be studied

Normally roads are fully signed indicating the limit applying, but these signs are not absolute evidence. Signs raise a presumption of validity and the existence of the indicated limit under s 26 of the 1968 Act. See para 5.8 also.

3.3 Speed limit offences

3.3.1 Offences

If a person drives a mechanically propelled vehicle on a public road in excess of any speed limit applying in relation to the type of vehicle, he is guilty of an offence (s 47 of the 1961 Act). The general penalty under s 102 applies (see para 7.1). As to 'Mechanically propelled vehicles' and 'Public road', see para 7.9.

As to 'person', it was held in *Beresford v St Albans* JJ (1905) 22 TLRI that a Justice must find that an accused drove the whole distance (or speed trap measured distance), but that if a person is driving at the end of the distance this is prima facie evidence that he drove the whole distance.

Endorsement and disqualification are optional additional penalties under ss 27 and 36 of the 1961 Act respectively. Disqualification can only be made after a judicial determination on the appropriate evidence of the accused's unfitness to drive (*A-G v Ponying* [1972] IR 402) (see para 2.9).

3.3.2 Presumption

By s 26 of the 1968 Act a presumption is raised that where a traffic sign indicates that a built up area limit or special speed limit exists, such a limit in fact applies on that particular road, until the defendant shows the contrary.

Traffic signs indicating the speed areas are authorised under s 95 of the 1961 Act and the Road Traffic Act (Signs) Regulations 1962 (SI 171/1962) as amended. See para 5.8.

3.3.3 Notice of prosecution

Notice of intention to prosecute must be given or served under s 104 of the 1961 Act (see para 7.3).

3.3.4 Multiple offences

It may occur that a driver can break as many as three limits at one time, e.g. a heavy lorry can break the particular road limit, the general 55 mph limit and the particular vehicle limit.

In *Cross v Oliver* (1964) 108 Sol Jo 583 it was held, however, that an information alleging that the defendant drove in excess of two different speed limits at two different but adjoining parts of the same road was bad for duplicity.

3.3.5 Bar to prosecution

In an English case of *Welton v Taneborne* (1908) 72 JP 419 it was held that where the defendant had been convicted of dangerous driving and the Justice had taken speed into consideration, this barred proceedings for speed. See the decision on the same type of principle in *R v Beatie* (1946) Ir Jur R 62. This would probably be still accepted as good law in Ireland, even though the wording of the dangerous driving section (s 53 of the 1961 Act) has been altered somewhat. An acquittal on the dangerous driving would not be a bar to a speeding conviction. See para 4.2 as to dangerous driving.

3.4 Evidence of speed

3.4.1 Nature of evidence

Evidence of speed often presents practical difficulty, as it may be a matter of opinion or an estimate as to the speed a vehicle travels at. This difficulty is recognised by s 105 of the 1961 Act, which provides a negative and a positive evidential position in relation to proof of speed. Negatively, it states that the uncorroborated evidence of one witness stating his opinion as to speed shall not be accepted as proof of speed. This reflects the general prohibition on opinion evidence in courts. However, the inclusion of the word 'uncorroborated' is important. Thus, if an ordinary speedometer reading was available it would be considered corroboration, if shown that the speedometer was ordinarily in proper working order. In *Russell v Beesley* [1937] 1 All ER 527 the evidence of a police officer driving a police car following the defendant's car and recording that the speed limit was exceeded was sufficient. In *Blight v Pearson* [1938] 4 All ER 127 the opinion evidence of two officers was held not to be in corroboration of each other. In *Nicholas v Penny* [1950] 2 All ER 89, where a driver was accused of exceeding the limit by 10 mph, the Court said if the accusation was of excess by 2 mph over the limit, that might require evidence of the accuracy of the meter, i.e. a tolerance level allowed in practice. Thus, while opinion evidence on speed is admissible under the section, by itself it is not enough safely to base a conviction on without some material corroboration. See *Crossland v DPP* (1988) Crim LR 756. Car hit a pedestrian. A police officer, expert in accident reconstruction visited the scene, found skid mark and examined the car damage. He deduced the car was travelling at 41 mph. Held: this was not unsupported evidence of an opinion nature. It was evidence of facts (marks and damage and opinion). Conviction upheld.

Positively, s 105 states that speed can be prima facie established by tendering evidence of indications from which the speed can be inferred. These indications can be given by a watch or by an electronic apparatus. What is meant by 'indications'? The term seems so perilously vague, the Court may yet hold it lacks sufficient precision to merit a criminal conviction. This is particularly so in view of the section's further provision that it is not necessary to prove that the watch or electronic or other apparatus was accurate or in good working order. The whole provision seems to fall sadly short of normal standards of the rules of evidence. In practice however, the Gardai normally test the accuracy of the apparatus and give evidence of its accuracy.

In *Gillespie v McMillan* (1957) SLT 283 a stopwatch test by two policemen on a measured portion of road was upheld. The measurement of distance may be proved by a rotometer or ordnance sheet (*Morrison v McCowan* (1939) SLT 422). In *Farrell v Simpson* (1959) SLT 23 a radar speed meter reading by two constables was upheld on basis that the road was straight and level, and the car was the only vehicle on the road, and the device had been tested that day. In England there are not the presumptions referred to in these tests as set out above. The burden is more difficult for the defence in Ireland.

The need to maintain the 'evidence' of these electronic meters is only inferential because they can be interfered with by other traffic, electrical interference, etc. However, a Justice may not reject these devices if shown that they can provide evidence in principle capable of giving such corroboration (*Barton v Gilbert* (1984) RTR 162, a case which dealt with the 'Miniquip' meter). In another case involving a 'Travelo' meter—*Kent v Stamps* (1982) RTR 273—it was held that the Justices were entitled to use their local knowledge in evaluating the evidence; but it was stated that the basic principle must be that the reading on the machine is evidence, although we have not reached the stage when the reading on such a piece of apparatus as this has to be accepted as absolutely accurate and true no matter what.

Another common method of detection is by a Garda car or bike following the alleged offender. The accuracy of the pursuing vehicle's speedometer need not be proved now—see s 105 and *Russell v Beesley* (*supra*)—but normally it is. These official vehicles, as they are usually Garda cars or bikes, often have Special Speedometers in fact for this purpose. In *Swain v Gilbert* (1974) RTR 446 a speedometer reading was held to be capable of corroborating a policeman's opinion without a test of its accuracy. In *Houston v Leslie* (1958) Crim LR 477 a variaton between the evidence of two policemen as to their vehicle's position behind the other vehicle created a doubt sufficient to cause the charge to be dismissed by the Court.

3.4.2 Anti-electronic devices and vehicle parts

The provisions of s 9 of the 1968 Act should be noted here. The section is discussed at para 1.3 above—it deals generally with the control of the importation, supply and fitting of vehicle parts.

In defining a vehicle part, subs (5) states that it includes 'any device which is capable of being used to indicate the existence of, or frustrate the operation of, electronic or other apparatus being used to give indications from which the speed at which a person was driving can be inferred'. Regulations have yet to be made to implement the section. Breach of any such regulations will attract the general penalty (para 7.1).

In *Invicta Plastics Limited v Clare* (1976) RTR 251 a company advertising such devices was convicted of inciting the commission of an offence. This was under operative English legislation.

3.4.3 Warnings

It can amount to the offence of obstructing a Garda in the execution of his duty to give a warning of a 'speed trap' to another driver, but apparently only if before the warning the person so warned was doing an illegal speed (*Bastable v Little* [1907] 1 KB 59).

In *Newmon v Overnighton* (1929) 93 JP 46 the owners of motor coaches who advertised a time table which necessarily involved breaking speed limits were held guilty of counselling and procuring the breach of a speed order.

3.5 General duty on speed and distance covered

3.5.1 General duty

Under the Road Traffic General Bye-laws 1964 (SI 244/1964), bye-law 18 a driver shall not drive at a speed exceeding that which will enable him to halt the vehicle within the distance he can see to be clear. The general penalty applies (para 7.1). As to these bye-laws generally, see para 5.3. This bye-law is much quoted in particulars of negligence (including breach of statutory duty) in civil cases resulting from road accidents.

3.5.2 Distances covered

The following is a general guideline calculation for the distance covered per second at the given speed. According to Pamphlet RT 2 (part of Rules of Road—see para 7.9) issued by the Minister for the Environment, the average person with good reflexes, good vision, etc. will take about seven-tenths of a second to react to an emergency. The following table illustrates the position, presuming good brakes on a dry level road, of the average stopping performance (measurement shown in feet and metres);

Speed per hour	(km) (nearest)	32	48	64	80	97	113
	(miles)	20	30	40	50	60	70
Reaction distance	(metres)	6	9	12	15	18	21
	(feet)	21	30	42	51	60	70
Braking distance	(metres)	6	14	24	38	55	75
	(feet)	21	45	81	126	180	245
Overall stopping distance	(metres)	12	23	36	53	73	96
	(feet)	42	75	123	177	240	315

Slow-reacting drivers, heavy vehicles, wet conditions, slippery roads, poor brakes, bad tyres, tired drivers and other circumstances may increase these distances up to double or more. Looked at from the perspective of distance covered per second, a chart as follows results:

Miles (kms) per hour	*Feet per second (nearest foot)*	*Metres per second*
20 (32)	29	8.8
30 (48)	44	13.4
40 (64)	58	16.7
50 (80)	73	22.3
60 (97)	88	26.8
70 (113)	103	31.4

In *R v Chadwick* (1975) Crim LR 105 it was stated that these tables could be used for cross examination, i.e. with reference to similar English tables.

3.5.3 Space between vehicles

In the Rules of the Road the distance which is recommended as a rule of thumb in following a car, is that the following driver should allow at least 20 feet between his vehicle and the vehicle in front for each 10 mph of the speed.

In *Scott v Warren* (1974) RTR 104 the defendant driving in a line of traffic was unable to avoid a piece of metal which fell from a lorry. He was charged with careless driving on the basis that he did not leave a sufficient distance between him and the lorry. It was held that it was a question of fact, rather than the recommendations of the highway code, whether he had driven carelessly.

Chapter 4

Control of user—Main offences

'*In some people's views to kill someone with a motor car happens to be a respectable criminal offence.*'

Lord Hutchinson (1984)

4.1 Manslaughter

4.1 What is manslaughter?

The principles of this Common Law crime are to be found in standard works on Criminal Law, to which the reader is referred. It is, however, proper to touch briefly in this book on this particular crime. Indictments for manslaughter are rare nowadays in view of the 1961 Road Traffic Act, s 53 crime of dangerous driving causing death (sometimes called 'motor manslaughter'). See para 4.2.

Manslaughter is an unlawful homicide which is not murder, infanticide or abortion.

It is, of course, to be remembered that charges of murder, and various types of assault charges, can result from improper driving. Charges of such offences are rare.

4.1.2 Degree of negligence

In *The People (A-G) v Dunleavy* [1948] IR 95; 82 ILTR 70 the Court of Criminal Appeal held that on the trial of an accused person charged with manslaughter arising out of his alleged negligence in the control and management of a mechanically propelled vehicle on a public road, the Judge should see that the jury is given clearly to understand as follows:

(a) that negligence in this connection means failure to observe such a course of conduct as experience shows to be necessary if, in the circumstances, the risk of injury to others is to be avoided, i.e. failure to behave as a reasonable driver would;
(b) that the jury must be satisfied that negligence on the part of the accused was responsible for the death in question;
(c) that there are different degrees of negligence, fraught with different legal consequences; that ordinary carelessness, while sufficient to justify a verdict for a plaintiff for damages for person injuries, or a conviction on prosecution for careless or inconsiderate driving, falls far short of what is required in the case of manslaughter; and that the higher degree of negligence which would justify a conviction on prosecution for dangerous driving is not sufficient; and
(d) that manslaughter is a felony and a very serious crime, and that before convicting the accused of manslaughter the jury must be satisfied that the fatal negligence was of a very high degree, and was such as to involve, in a high degree, the risk or likelihood of substantial personal injury to others.

This decision has been followed regularly since, e.g. *A-G v O'Neill* (1964) Ir Jur R 1 where the Appeal Court agreed with a jury finding that evidence of driving at 50 mph on the incorrect side of a wide road approaching a curve was sufficient to establish that high degree of negligence.

Another example of the application of a series of wrongful acts amounting to manslaughter and other crimes is found in *The People (A-G) v Crosby* (unreported, CCA No 1 of 1961). Crosby was convicted by a jury of manslaughter, dangerous driving and driving a defective vehicle. He was sentenced to two years' imprisonment and disqualified for five years, as he had killed one person and injured others. He appealed to the Court of Criminal Appeal. There had been evidence at his trial that he had been drinking in a number of licensed premises, had approached a bridge at speed, and then collided with three pedestrians whilst driving on the wrong side of the road. The accused admitted he had hit these pedestrians, in a statement to the Gardai, but claimed it was in an effort to avoid a man in his path on his correct side. He had not given evidence in his trial. The Court of Criminal Appeal dismissed his appeal. (Its careful examination of the evidence is set out in G Frewens 'Judgments of the Court of Criminal Appeal', Vol 1, p. 231.) It, *inter alia*, said that the fact the brakes were defective was irrelevant in the manslaughter charge because, by the time the driver came to apply the brakes, the situation was hopeless.

4.1.3 Accessory

In *The People (Burke) v McArdle* (1940) Ir Jur R 22 it was held that where the owner of a motor vehicle knows that the brakes of the vehicle are in a dangerous condition, and with that knowledge he instructs his servant to drive the vehicle upon the highway, and where the servant, driving it with ordinary care, is involved in a fatal accident caused by the defective brakes, then the owner can rightly be convicted of being an accessory before the fact of manslaughter. See also *R v Millar* at 4.2.5 *infra*.

4.1.4 Death

As in all manslaughter cases, death must be proved to have occurred within a year and a day.

Presumably it must be shown that the criminal action or ommission was a cause in a real sense of the death—see *People v Gallagher* [1972] IR 366, where the jury acquitted the defendant on a manslaughter charge and the Court of Appeal held it was so entitled, given the view it took of the facts. (below also see para 4.2.7).

4.1.5 Autrefois acquit

This plea, in law, is not available to a person charged with driving a dangerously defective vehicle who has been acquitted on the same facts on a manslaughter charge. The test is not whether the evidence to support both is the same, but whether the same degree of negligence is necessary to constitute both offences (*A-G v Woods* 74 ILTR 80).

See para 4.6 as to dangerously defective vehicles.

In England since Seymore (1983) AC 493 an alternative count of causing death by reckless driving cannot be added. The 1988 North Report recommended reversal of this decision.

4.1.6 Alternative acts

The duty of a trial judge to direct a jury where both manslaughter and dangerous driving were alleged is dealt with in *The People (A-G) v Dixon* 86 ILTR 39. The Judge should clearly instruct on the different degrees of negligence involved and direct the jury's attention to the evidence in the light of this difference.

4.1.7 Coroners Act

By virtue of s 25 of the Coroners Act 1962, a coroner must adjourn any inquest when requested by an officer of the Gardai not below the rank of Inspector on the grounds that criminal proceedings are being considered or have been instituted. On termination of the Court proceedings, the Court Clerk informs the Coroner of the result of those proceedings and the inquest is resumed.

4.1.8 Penalties

The penalties which may be imposed for manslaughter are as follows:

(a) a fine at the discretion of the Court; and/or

(b) penal servitude for life or a term of not less than three years; or imprisonment not exceeding two years;
(c) discretionary disqualification (see para 2.9);
(d) discretionary endorsement (see para 2.10);
(e) binding over to keep peace (offences against the Person Act 1861, ss 5 and 71).

4.2 Dangerous driving

4.2.1 Background

This is a charge very much used in proceedings brought in respect of bad driving. This offence is created by s 53 of the 1961 Act. Four changes were made in the wording of s 53 by the 1968 Act, s 51, which have an effect on the nature of the offence. The penalties were substantially increased by the 1984 Act.

Section 51 of the Offences against the Person Act 1861 first dealt with this type of offence. It stated:

> 'Whosoever having charge of any carriage or vehicle shall by wanton or furious driving or racing or other wilful neglect, do or cause to be done any bodily harm to any person whatsoever shall be guilty of a misdemeanour.'

This section is still in force, even though its force is largely spent, having regard to the 1961-1984 Acts. It should be noted that s 53(5) of the 1961 Act now specifically provides that, in reference to the same occurrence, a person shall not be liable to be charged under s 51 of the 1861 Act and s 53 of the 1961 Act.

The 1903 Motor Car Act was the first Act passed to regulate solely the then still novel phenomenon of the motor car. Section 1 of this 1903 Act dealt with the offence of reckless or dangerous driving. The wording of this section was closely followed in drafting the 1961 offence. The Road Traffic Act, 1933 s 51 was on the same lines as the original section in the 1961 Act, with the less severe consequences, following as it did s 1 of the 1903 Act but omitting the offence of reckless driving. The 1968 Act changed the wording of the 1961 section but not its general nature. It joined together two branches of the 1961 Act offence and made it a one offence section. The 1988 English North Committee Report makes interesting reading on this subject of bad driving.

4.2.2 Present offence

Section 53(1) of the 1961 Act, as amended by s 51 of the 1968 Act, now provides that:

> 'A person shall not drive a vehicle in a public place in a manner (including speed) which having regard to all the circumstances of the case (including the

condition of the vehicle, the nature, condition and use of the place and the amount of traffic which then actually is or might reasonably be expected then to be therein) is dangerous to the Public'.

As to 'person', 'public place' and 'vehicle', see para 7.9.

The 1968 Act wording made two important changes in this subsection to the effect that:

(i) the section now contains only one offence. Previously there were two offences—(a) driving 'in a manner', or (b) driving 'at a speed' dangerous to the public. In *State (McLoughlin v Shannon* [1948] IR 439 and *People v Blogh* [1958] IR 91, it was held that the 1961 Act, s 53 created two offences and that a charge alleging a single offence under the terms of the old format section was bad for duplicity. This caused the amendment of the section in the 1968 Act. Now only the offence of driving 'in a manner' dangerous to the public remains, but the Court, in judging the manner of driving, can look at the speed.

(ii) The condition of the vehicle is now a specific consideration to be looked at by the Court. Therefore, the driving the Court looks at is the overall picture or manner of driving, with specific consideration of particular matters, i.e. speed, condition of vehicle, nature of place, condition of place, use of place, and actual or expected traffic, in order to form an overall judgment of whether the accused was driving in a manner dangerous to the public. What is not too clear in a legal sense is whether one such item on its own, e.g. speed, can amount to a dangerous manner *per se*—probably not, unless it results in a manner of driving which is dangerous, e.g. speed around a blind bend (see para 2.4.2 *infra*). This means other circumstances have to exist to bring merely excessive speed (or other single such circumstances) up to the standard of negligence and *mens rea* necessary for dangerous driving (see para 4.2.3.1).

It should be noted the offence covers all vehicles (see para 7.9) and is not confined to mechanically propelled vehicles. However, the penalties set out below (para 5.2.8) do make the consequences in the case of mechanically propelled vehicles more serious.

4.2.3 Manner

'In a manner which . . . is dangerous to the Public' is an overall criterion for this offence.

The evidence of damage to vehicles should be treated with caution in drawing inferences as to how the accident occurred (*Lord v Ball* (1981) RTR 21). It is for the prosecution to adduce evidence of the manner of driving. As to the factors involved, see (1959) Crim LR 491, at p. 715.

Where two persons are charged with dangerous driving in respect of a collision between two vehicles driven by both accused respectively, one is a competent and compellable witness in the prosecution of the other (*A-G v Egan* [1948] IR 433).

In *Hellet v Warren* (1929) JR 225 evidence of dangerous driving a few minutes before, but two miles from the scene of, the accident was held to be admissible. Momentary negligence is enough and the fact that the defendant's mistake was due to an error of judgment may not be a good defence.

Sleep or drowsiness may lead to prosecution, as a driver is under a duty to stop if he is falling asleep; but if he is made unconscious due to some unforeseen circumstances, this would be a defence (*Kay v Butterworth* (1945) 110 JP 75).

It was said in *R v Evans* [1963] 1 QB 412 that the manner of driving must be looked at objectively.

> 'It is quite clear from the reported cases that if in fact a driver adopts a manner of driving which the jury thinks was dangerous to other road users in all the circumstances, then on the issue of guilt it matters not whether he was deliberately reckless, careless, or momentarily inattentive, or even doing his incompetent best. Such considerations are highly relevant if it ever comes to sentence . . .'

This decision may not be accepted *in toto* here.

An interesting example of this English view is the case of *R v Ball & Loughlin* (1966) 50 Cr App R 266, where the accused was driving a scout car with restricted vision, taking direction from a commander in the turret. He obeyed a negligent direction to emerge into a major road and collided with a motor cycle. He was convicted of dangerous driving, even though the Court accepted that he was 'blameless'. This must have been poor consolation to a private obeying his commanding officer—and it was a far cry from our ordinary notions of Justice surely! This case has been disapproved of in *R v Gosney* (1971) RTR 321, where it was held that while proof of *mens rea* (meaning an intention to commit the offence) was excluded in the definition of the offences, evidence of fault has to be adduced. 'Fault' involves a failure, a falling below the standard of care or skill of a competent and experienced driver in relation to the manner of driving and to relevant circumstances of the case. See also *People (A-G) v Crosby* (No 1/1961 CCA) referred to at para 4.1.2 above for an analysis by the Court of Criminal Appeal of acts constituting wrongful driving.

A series of acts can amount to the crime, i.e. drink, speed, going to wrong side of the road. The court can ignore acts or omissions which do not contribute (e.g. absence of proper brakes in the *Crosby* case) where their use would not have corrected or avoided the situation. The *Dunleavy* case (para 4.1.2 above) seems to import negligence/fault in degrees that certainly, in dangerous driving, involves an element of *mens rea*.

The defence of automatism has succeeded in a number of cases and, indeed, various sudden, personal afflictions such as an epileptic fit, a blow on the head while driving, unconsciousness and an attack by a swarm of bees, all have provided good defences. See *Hill v Baxter* [1958] 1 QB 277, etc. in para 7.9 under 'Driving'.

A sudden mechanical defect, due to no fault of the driver, causing loss of control (*R V v Spurge* [1961] 2 QB 205) was a good defence, but if the defence does not put it forward the Court should not speculate on such a potential defence (*Bensly v Smith* (1972) RTR 221).

It is important to remember that skid marks alone are not evidence of dangerous driving or of an offence. While this may often be the only evidence of the Gardai, they are in themselves ambiguous signs (*Devane v Murphy* (1958) Ir Jur R 73; see also *Laurie v Raglon* [1941] 3 All ER 332) and they can equally be the result of an effort on the part of the driver to avert a sudden crisis.

Overtaking two lines of traffic at speed when traffic is approaching from the other direction can be dangerous driving (*Squire v Metropolitan Police Commissioner* (1957) Crim LR 817). In *Johnstone v Hawkins* (1959) Crim LR 854 it was held that going through a junction which has a 'slow' sign at 85 mph was prima facie dangerous driving.

Evidence of damage to the vehicles should be treated with caution in drawing inferences as to how the accident occurred (*Lord v Ball* (1981) RTR 211). The doctrine of *res ipsa loquitur* has no place in charge of criminal driving (*Wright v Wenlock* (1971) RTR 228) (and two cases in the same volume at pp. 232 and 234).

See also para 4.2.12 as to 'Nature of the offence'.

4.2.4 Speed

Speed was previously a separate offence amounting, in certain circumstances, to dangerous driving. The question of speed is now only a consideration in determining the manner of driving. The provision of subs (3) should be borne in mind, i.e. observance of the speed limit is not a defence *per se*.

Where the court takes into consideration the speed of the vehicle as an element of the dangerous driving, conviction of that dangerous driving is a bar to a subsequent conviction for speeding (*Welton v Taneborne* (1908) 108 LT 668).

As to high speed alone not being evidence of negligence—100 mph on a motorway—see *Hurlock v Inglis* (1963) 107 Sol Jo 436. Apparently, excessive speed, while not itself constituting the offence, can be decisive in determing the 'manner' of driving, and merely driving too fast in all the circumstances can be driving in a manner dangerous to the public (*Bracegirdle v Oxley* [1947] KB 349).

4.2.5 Circumstances

All circumstances are to be taken into consideration, although the word 'including' is used to specify that *certain* circumstances should be considered. It is not necessary to specify what circumstances were used in convictions in the Court order (*R v Dublin JJ* [1904] 2 IR 698).

Those circumstances specially mentioned (in addition to speed, above) are:

(i) 'condition of vehicle'. See *R v Spurge* [1961] 2 QB 205, where it was held that if the driver is deprived of control due to a mechanical defect which is not his fault, or which he could not reasonably have safeguarded against, this is a good defence. The burden of proof of this is not on the accused, though it is for him to put the defence forward. See also 95 ILT and Sol Jo 25. In *R v Millar and Co* [1970] 1 All ER 577 the driver and managing director of the owning Company were both convicted when a known dangerously worn tyre burst and the lorry hit a car and killed the occupants. See also *People v McArdle* at 4.1.3 above.

(ii) 'Nature of place', e.g. bends and dips in the road are relevant here.

(iii) 'Condition of place', e.g. presumably weather factors such as floods, or state of repair, etc.

(iv) 'Use of place', e.g. if construction work, near school, etc. Busy urban streets obviously differ from a clear dual carriageway in the consideration they require.

(v) 'Amount of traffic'. In *Person v Tompin* 120 JP 129 it was held that evidence by a policeman as to the amount of traffic which would pass the spot on a summer's day was allowable.

The section refers not only to the actual traffic but also that which might reasonably be expected there.

Other circumstances

(i) The personal circumstances of the ability of the driver cannot be taken into account. However, the consideration of the circumstances enumerated in the section and all other relevant circumstances places the determination of the offence on a flexible base. Possibly the Irish Courts will seek a less rigid basis than in England where, historically, crime is largely objective. The English offence is now replaced by an offence of reckless driving which seems to require a different standard. As to a Judge's charge to a jury where evidence is open to two constructions in all the circumstances, see *A-G v Dixon* 86 ILTR 39, dealing with manslaughter and dangerous driving. (see para 4.1.6 above.)

(ii) Drink is a circumstance which can be dealt with by the jury or Justice where it is admissible as being relevant. The principle of relevance of the driver's drinking has been dealt with in three cases:

(a) *R v McBride* [1962] 2 QB 167, where it was held that consumption of liquor should only be admitted as evidence when it tended to show that the accused was adversely effected thereby. In this case the result of blood analysis of 130 mg/100 ml was admitted as evidence.

(b) *People v Patrick O'Neill* (1964) Ir Jur R 1. Here the Court followed the *McBride* case and a new trial was ordered where the Judge had admitted evidence that the accused had taken a shandy and two glasses of ale an hour to two hours before the accident. There was evidence that the accused was sober on leaving the pub an hour before the accident.

(c) *A-G v Moore* (1964) Ir Jur R 6, the accused, aged 18, made two written statements about visits to pubs before the accident and having three pints of stout. These were admitted, but in directing (on recall) the jury the Judge told them to disregard them. *Held*: that statements were properly admitted, Davitt J saying—

> 'where a person has during a period of *time which is material* consumed a *significant quantity* of alcoholic drink it will, therefore, tend to render his driving unsafe. The evidence that he has consumed such a quantity during such a period is therefore in our opinion of probative value on a charge of dangerous driving and therefore relevant and admissible in law. To this extent I venture to differ from the principle enunciated in *O'Neill*'s case.'

He further stated that it was for the Judge to decide what was a significant quantity and that he should exercise his discretion to exclude the evidence where its prejudicial effect outweighs its probative value.

The importance of the *A-G v O'Neill* and *A-G v Moore* decisions cannot be overstressed, or the fact that there is some shifting of the ground shown in the latter decision. Though both are reported in the same volume, the *O'Neill* case was first in time and is stricter than *McBride* in refusing the admission of drink. In *Moore*'s case, the defendant did appeal to the Supreme Court but, like many other litigants, then fled from the country, as he had fled from the scene of the fatal accident in the first instance. The law as stated by the Court of Criminal Appeal in this case is generally accepted as being correct. The *Moore* case was expressly approved of in *People (A-G) v Regan* [1975] IR 367. The Court held the evidence that the accused consumed a significant quantity of intoxicating liquor within a material period prior to the time of the commission of the offence charged is relevant and admissible in a s 53 charge. The fact that the Judge, in the absence of the jury, has heard the evidence of only one of the available witnesses to the accused's state of intoxication does not necessarily preclude him from ruling on the admissibility of that class of evidence.

In *Regan*'s case a Garda was killed on a wide road while on duty holding up other traffic. A good deal of evidence on drink was given. The defendant has been convicted by a jury of dangerous driving and sentenced to six months' imprisonment and disqualification for five years. The Court of Appeal decided not to define 'a significant quantity of drink' while expressly following *Moore*'s case and its view there, but said:

> 'What is a significant quantity? The effect of drink upon a person's faculties will depend on his tolerance of alcohol and this in turn may depend upon his physical and psychological state. It will be a matter which the trial Judge will have to decide in each case.'

These Irish decisions were ones in which blood/urine content results were not available. Presumably a reading over the statutory limit will be 'a significant quantity'.—see *R v McBride* above where, in England, a reading of 130/000 ml was admitted.

(iii) Exculpating circumstances can arise also e.g. duress, necessity—see *R v Conway* 1989 Crim LR 74.

4.2.6 Dangerous to public

Judge Barra O'Briain's (then President of the Circuit Court) standard charge to a jury is a good guide to the nature or the kernel of the offence, i.e.:

> 'Driving in a manner (including speed) which a reasonable prudent man having knowledge of all the circumstances proved in court would clearly recognise as involving unjustifiably definite risk of harm to the public.' (*People v Quinlan* (1962) Circuit Court, noted at ILT and Sol Jo 1962, p. 123 and 1963, p. 219 and slightly amended by the Judge later.)

It seems to be as good an explanation of the position as one can evolve. It emphasises the objective standard of the reasonably prudent driver's actions in the circumstances proved and his realisation of a direct and serious risk. He must have knowledge (*mens rea*?) of all of the circumstances—this incorporates a subjective element.

4.2.7 'Death or serious bodily harm'

While the above proofs comprise those necessary for the offence itself, it is well to consider here another proof which is necessary when the charge is indictable, i.e. when death or serious bodily harm is caused to another person.

The creation of this 'second leg' of the offence was due to few convictions of manslaughter for deaths caused by dangerous driving (see para 4.1 above). This was because of the high degree of negligence required for manslaughter (*see A-G v Dunleavy* 82 ILTR 70). Presumably, the standard of negligence now required is lower than the pre-1961 one for manslaughter. It is only an element of the one offence of dangerous driving, and s 53 does not contain two offences *A-G v Fitzgerald, Power and Thornton* [1964] IR 458 where it was held 'What is dual—or more correctly what is alternative—is the mode of prosecution'.

Some points of this proof are as follows:

(i) 'Death'. Presumably there is no time limit as to when death should occur (unlike murder) and, as this 'leg' of the offence is indictable, there is no time limit on the bringing of a prosecution.

(ii) 'Serious bodily harm'. This is a question of fact to be decided in the light of the medical and other evidence in each case. An interesting equation of 'serious' with 'grievous' is found in *People v Messitt* [1974] IR 406. It is not necessary, per the Supreme Court in that case, that the injury be a permanent one.

(iii) The question of causation can be difficult. Under a similar English Act it was held that, where a bus driver overtook another vehicle, ignoring a signal not to do so, and a cyclist approaching fell into the centre of the road and was killed, the bus driver should be convicted (*Marson v Thompson* (1955) Crim LR 319).

The older authorities—*R v Swindall & Osborne* (1846) 2 Cox CC 230; *R v Dalloway* (1847) 3 Cox CC 273—established that in criminal cases, as distinct from civil cases, it is no defence that the victim contributed to his harm by his own negligence. This view has been narrowed in the case of *R v Gould* [1964] 1 WLR 145 where it was said: 'The Law in this matter is "a substantial cause" not "the substantial cause"'.

In *R v Hennigan* [1977] 3 All ER 133 it was held that if the driving was a cause, conviction could follow unless the causative nexus between the defendant's driving and the accident was *de minimis*.

The first Irish reported case was heard by Judge Deale in a Circuit Court case, *A-G v McGrath* (1965) Ir Jur R 57. He held that the dangerous driving of the accused must be the sole cause of the death or serious bodily harm. The Court of Criminal Appeal has now dealt with the matter and overruled Judge Deale. In the *People (A-G) v Matthew Gallagher* [1972] IR 365; 106 ILTR 61 it was held:

(1) Dangerous driving and not its consequences is the offence created by s 53. Accordingly, it is not necessary for the prosecution to prove that the dangerous driving of the defendant was the sole cause of the death or injury. It is sufficient if the dangerous driving is one of the causes.
(2) The correct construction of s 53 is that the jury must be told that they must be satisfied beyond a reasonable doubt that the dangerous driving was one of the causes which contributed in a real way to the death or serious bodily harm, and that they must decide this by applying principles of common sense.
(3) The fact that the negligence of the dead or injured person may have been one of the causes of the death or serious bodily harm, in the sense that it contributed in some way to the accident, is not a matter which should be put to the jury as being a ground on which they are entitled to acquit the accused.

There is one interesting passage in the judgment of Kenny J in *People v Gallagher* above at page 369 of the Irish Report which illustrates the nature of the charge:

> 'Problems of causation have been the subject of arguments in Universities and in Law Courts for centuries and it is important that the jury should not be confused by refined distinctions between material, effective, substantial or predominant cause. If they are told that they must be satisfied beyond reasonable doubt that the dangerous driving was one of the causes which contributed in a real way to the death or serious bodily harm and that they must decide this by applying principles of common sense, they will understand the issue which they have to try.'

(iv) 'To another person'. This includes a passenger (*R v Klein*, *The Times*, 13 April 1960) in the accused's car. (*Powley v Whardall* (1966) QB 373.)

4.2.8 Mode of trial

If the death or serious bodily harm is the result of the dangerous driving, then trial is by way of indictment—otherwise it is a summary trial. If trial is to be on indictment, there must be a preliminary investigation in the District Court.

The procedure of preliminary investigation is dealt with in the Criminal Procedure Act 1967 and the District Court (Criminal Procedure Act 1967) Rules 1967 (SI 181/1967). Under s 6 of the Criminal Justice Act 1951, if the accused is sent forward on indictment, the indictment may contain counts of summary offence (see *A-G v Francis Doyle* (1967) 101 ILTR 136). If so, the District Court looses seisin of the case (*The State v President of the Circuit Court*; *A-G v DJ Fitzpatrick* 87 ILTR 114). The 1961 Act marks a recession of the District Court jurisdiction. Prior to the Act, where accused's dangerous driving caused death the District Court could deal with it (*A-G v Woods* 74 ILTR 80).

In *A-G v Mary Wall* (unreported, High Court No 3 ss, 1969) it was held that once the Attorney-General has elected for summary trial, a District Justice has jurisdiction to hear the case, notwithstanding that he comes to the conclusion that serious bodily harm was caused. In practice this procedure of trial by indictment is rarely used. This has been because of the difficulty of getting convictions before a jury. It is possible, however, that the climate may be changing, and in 1986 there was a branch of the USA Organisation MADD set up in Ireland, as a criticism of the apparent leniency of the law and its application in the courts in road traffic cases.

Coroners Act

By s 25 of the Coroners Act 1962 a Coroner must (as in para 4.1.7) adjourn a fatal road traffic accident inquest on request of a senior Garda officer, pending disposal of criminal charges.

4.2.9 Penalties

(a) *Fines*

(i) Ordinarily £1,000 maximum (s 3 of the 1984 Act).
(ii) In death/serious bodily harm cases—£3,000 maximum.

This is based on punishment by result, gratifying public feeling, etc. and seems to be a distinction in punishment not based on the culpability of the accused which raises a question of equality before the law?

In *R v McLarew* (1984) RTR 126 (reckless driving causing death) a fine of £100 and five years' disqualification increased to £500 and disqualification. It was stated that such a figure was an absolute minimum.

(b) *Imprisonment*

(i) Ordinarily six months maximum.
(ii) Death or serious bodily harm cases—five years penal servitude.

There are no sentencing guidelines set out in a formalised way by the Irish Courts. In England there are guidelines set out in *R v Guilfoyle* (1973) RTR 272 to the effect, in broad terms:

(1) A distinction should be made between cases where the accident was due to momentary inattention or misjudgment, and those which exhibit recklessness or selfish disregard for other road users. In the latter cases the penalty would be more severe and, if death resulted, a custodial sentence with a long period of disqualification would be appropriate. See *R v Bibi* (1980) Crim LR 732 for general guidelines on the use of imprisonment.
    In *R v Marshall* (1976) RTR 483 disqualification for five years was upheld on an 18-year-old showing off and hitting an 80-year-old lady. He was doing 50 mph in a 30 mph area.
    In *R v Gisbourne* (1977) Crim LR 299, a case of 'simply inattention at the critical moment', three years' disqualification reduced to one year on an 18-year-old.
    In *R v Eadie* (1978) RTR 292 it was stated that a driver causing death or serious injury with too much drink must expect imprisonment, except in exceptional cases.
    In *R v Lobley* (1974) RTR 550 it was stated that a period of disqualification should be fixed without regard to the right of the defendant to apply to have it removed.
(2) A bad driving record would increase the imprisonment and the disqualification. However, in *R v Farrugia* (1979) RTR 422 the Court of Appeal stated that long disqualifications can be counter productive, especially with young people. See para 2.9 as to disqualification.
    In *R v Abraham* (1980) RTR 471 a policeman found guilty of non-deliberate driving which caused death was not imprisoned.
(3) The longer the disqualification, the more important it is to order that a driving test be undertaken before the driver obtains a licence again.

(c) *Disqualification*

(i) Optional in all cases under s 27 (the ancillary disqualification section).
(ii) Mandatory under s 26 and second Schedule of the 1961 Act where:

    (1) death or serious bodily harm results; or
    (2) it is a second offence where the first offence, or one of earlier offences, occurred in any period of three years and involved a mechanically propelled vehicle—must then be for not less than six months (s 26)4)).

    See cases under (b) above for guidelines and also para 2.9.

(d) *Endorsement*

Endorsement of a licence under s 36 is optional in all cases, except where a consequential order or an ancillary disqualification order is made, or it is a second offence within three years. There are no guidelines set out, but see para 2.10.

Mitigating factors would be in optional cases:

(i) one-off on momentary mistake;
(ii) plea of guilty;
(iii) effect on defendant—victim a friend, shock;
(iv) good character;
(v) good driving record;
(vi) remorse.

4.2.10 Arrest

Section 53(6), as amended by the 1968 Act, now reads 'where a member of the Garda Siochana is of opinion that a person has committed an offence under this section he may arrest the person without warrant'. The original subsection of the 1961 Act allowed arrest only when death or serious bodily harm resulted. It is hard to justify in principle (having regard to the already wide powers of the Gardai under the Act) the extension of this power in the 1968 Act.

In the interesting English decision of *R v Renouf* (1986) RTR 191 it was held on this power apparently confined to cases where the acts so alleged (as to reckless driving), could also amount to allowing the use of reasonable force for the purpose of assisting a lawful arrest; in such latter purpose then it may afford a defence. In that case the defendant 'edged the car off the road' containing persons who had committed offences in order to detain them for the police.

4.2.11 Effect of non-proof

(i) If a court feels that dangerous driving was not proved the charge can be dealt with under s 52 of the 1961 Act by virtue of s 53(4) of the 1961 Act, remembering that there is a new s 52 (careless driving) substituted by s 50 of the 1968 Act.

Query: Why not allow it to be dealt with under ss 51A or 52? See, however, the Criminal Justice (Verdicts) Act 1976 which would seem to allow this, and see also *McAdams v DUTC* [1929] IR 327 where it was held that a complaint of a lesser offence can always be made orally to the Justice if the defendant is in court. See para 4.4.5 below.

This reduction to an offence under s 52 of the 1961 Act can be done on either summary proceedings or on trial on indictment.

A-G v Clifford (1962-63) Ir Jur R 41. In this case it was held that if a direction is given by the Judge, the jury is not entitled to consider careless driving. See also Criminal Procedure Act 1967, s 8(4) for a somewhat similar provision.

4.2.11 *Dangerous driving*

A-G (O'Maonaigh) v Fitzgerald [1964] IR 458. Accused acquitted by direction of a Circuit Judge on a serious bodily harm charge on the basis that there was no evidence of serious bodily harm. A fresh summary dangerous driving charge was brought against him. The District Justice dismissed the case on the basis of the previous acquittal.
Held: District Justice was correct.

(ii) Plea in bar

A-G (McElwain) v Power [1964] IR 458. The defendant was charged with dangerous driving causing serious bodily harm and careless driving. The District Justice received information on the dangerous driving charge. At the Circuit Court the case of dangerous driving was dismissed, the Judge not addressing the jury on the right to convict of careless driving. When the matter came on for hearing in the District Court again, the District Justice dismissed the summary charge of careless driving.
Held: He was correct in so doing as there was a plea in bar.

A-G (Ward) v Thornton [1964] IR 458. Thornton was charged on both the indictable part and summary charge in s 53. In the District Court he pleaded guilty on the summary charge and asked the Court to deal with it. The State sought to have it adjourned until the indictable charge had been dealt with. The Supreme Court held that the summary proceedings having been brought and terminated in a conviction, it was not open to the State to return Thornton on indictment.

It is interesting to note that the Supreme Court and High Court decisions differed in all three last quoted cases. It is hard to get a clear principle running through these decisions

In *R v Maxom Tritsh* (1988) Crim LR 46 the defendant had pleaded guilty to careless and intoxicated driving. A subsequent attempt to charge her with a more serious charge was dismissed as an abuse of the court process.

(iii) The 1961 Act, unlike the old 1960 English Act, does not empower a special verdict of dangerous driving *simpliciter* where it is shown that the death or serious harm was not caused by the accused. However, the English 1960 Act did not allow a verdict of careless driving to be brought in. The English 1972 Act does allow the alternative of careless to reckless driving.

(iv) End of matter

In *A-G v Savage* (1959) ILTSJ 25 it was held that if an indictable charge and summary charges arising from same incident are brought and the State offers all its evidence at the preliminary hearing, then, if informations are refused, the Justice can also dismiss the summary charges on the merits.

4.2.12 Nature of offence

It is difficult to come to grips clearly with the nature of this offence. It is obviously a general offence intended to cover a multitude of driving sins. Some problems are:

(a) *Absolute offence or mental element?* In England generally *mens rea* appeared to be ruled out (*R v Scates* (1957) Crim LR 406; *Hill v Baxter* [1958] 1 QB 277). Glanville Williams in his general part of *Criminal Law* (Second Ed, p. 119) criticised this view. The idea of *mens rea* is inherent in the law of negligence. The exercise of care is a human mental faculty, surely?

The position of *mens rea* is restored somewhat by *R v Spurge* [1961] 2 QB 205, where it was held that a sudden emergency caused by an unforeseeable defect in a vehicle could afford a good defence to a charge of dangerous driving. Salmon J in that case pointed out that once this defence is put forward the onus of proof is on the State.

The direction of Judge Barra O'Briain referred to above (para 4.2.6) seems to advocate an objective type of judgment with elements of *mens rea* akin to the civil law principle of foreseeability and knowledge. The position has not been clarified by the Irish Courts. Since the *Dunleavy* case (para 4.1.2 above), which accepted varying degrees of negligence, it would seem elements or degrees of *mens rea* are involved. The position in England was clear (i.e. no *mens rea*) until the decisions in *Hill v Baxter* and *R v Spurge* (*supra*). In the Circuit Courts in Ireland, in practice juries seem to consider a mental element of disregard for the public necessary before convicting.

(b) *Question of fact and degree?* It appears that a higher degree of negligence is necessary in dangerous driving—*People (A-G) v Dunleavy* [1948] IR 95; 82 ILTR 70—than in careless driving. Momentary negligence is sufficient (*R v Parkes* (1957) 41 CAR 134, where driver went through red lights). In *R v Evans* [1962] WRL 1475 the English Court of Appeal held that the slightest negligence was sufficient to convict of dangerous driving. However, this decision has been severely criticised by many judges and in *R v Gosney* (1971) RTR 321, where the concept of fault was stated to be an essential ingredient, as the offence of dangerous driving was not an absolute one. This reason was hard to follow; the English position is that the English Act did not allow an alternative conviction of careless driving, and therefore the Courts seem, in practice, to have equated dangerous with careless driving.

It seems that the reality is that there is a concept of negligence involved, fitting into a graded scale of what is called criminal negligence (*Dunleavy* case). There should be three elements involved:

(i) Is there the appropriate degree of negligence which is 'dangerous to the public', i.e. below the degree in manslaughter and above the degree in careless driving? The answer in Irish law appears to be yes!

(ii) Is it of a criminal nature? This seems so if the offence involves an element of *mens rea*. Again, on balance it seems the answer in Ireland is yes!

(iii) Is it proved to the degree (i.e. beyond reasonable doubt) necessary to sustain a criminal conviction? This is answered in the affirmative always in a criminal trial. See para 5.3.5 for discussion of the relationship between dangerous driving and careless driving.

4.2.13 Notice of intention to prosecute

This is necessary in respect of the offence of dangerous driving. See para 7.3 in respect of same.

4.2.14 Words and phrases

As to 'person', 'drive', 'mechanically propelled vehicles', 'public place' and 'vehicle', see para 7.9

4.3 Careless driving

4.3.1 Offence

The Road Traffic Act 1968, s 50 replaces s 52 of the 1961 Act, and subs (1), which creates the text for the offence of careless driving, now reads: 'A person shall not drive a vehicle in a public place without due care and attention'. It is half the wording of the old s 52 of the 1961 Act. It is part of the general broad scheme of wide offences covered now by s 52; s 51A (inconsiderate driving) and s 53 (dangerous driving). The penalties which may be imposed were increased in the 1984 Act, s 3.

4.3.2 Proofs

(i) '*Person*'. See para 7.9

(ii) '*Drive*'. See para 7.9. In *Jones v Carter* (1955) Crim LR 275 a conviction was quashed as no evidence was given of the identity of the driver of the car allegedly carelessly driven.

(iii) '*Vehicle*'. See para 7.9. Note that any type of vehicle is sufficient.

(iv) '*Public place*'. See para 7.9.

(v) '*Due care and attention*'? It has been held in England that this is an objective standard, and a learner driver has the same obligation as to degree of skill as a rally driver (*McCrane v Riding* [1938] 1 All ER 157). The standard is that of 'the reasonably prudent man'. The 1964 General Bye-laws for Control of Traffic and The Rules of the Road presumably are a guide of how the reasonably prudent man should drive. Having regard to the comparative penalties, a serious breach of one or more of these principles based on a lack of care and attention would seem necessary to establish that an offence has been committed. The main obligations created by these regulations include the duties to obey signs and road marks; drive to left; drive at a speed such as to enable the driver to stop within the distance he can see to be clear; rules of overtaking; yield right of way; reversing and parking rules, etc., and these are set out as appropriate elsewhere in the text (e.g. see para 5.3). However, it does not necessarily follow that a driver committing a breach of the regulations is guilty of careless driving (*Gibson v Kuhl* [1956] 3 All ER 345, a case involving breach of pedestrian crossing regulations).

In *Pratt v Bloom* (1958) Crim LR 817 a driver who signalled right and then turned left without checking for traffic from behind was guilty of careless driving. In *Bensely v Smith* (1972) Crim LR 239 it was held that crossing a white line, in the absence of an explanation, may be evidence of carelessness. In *Webster v Wall* (1980) Crim LR 186 the English High Court refused to set aside an acquittal of a motor cyclist who at night collided with an unlit stationary vehicle on a wet road in poor visibility.

If two offences are charged, e.g. careless driving and failing to observe a traffic sign, conviction on the graver charge will be sufficient (*R v Parker* (1957) 41 Crim App R 134). The supervisor of a learner driver who does not supervise properly can be guilty of aiding and abetting careless driving (*Rubie v Faulkner* [1940] 1 All ER 285).

There is no exemption for police, fire engines, ambulances, etc. (*R v O'Toole* (1971) 55 Cr App R 206). In *Wood v Richards* (1977) RTR 201 it was held the defence of necessity was not justified in a similar type case, but a contrary view was accepted in *R v Miller*, *The Times*, 16 March 1986, where youths threatened to kill the driver and he mounted the pavement.

In *Broome v Perkins* (1987) Crim LR 271 the defence of automatism was rejected. The defendant was a diabetic. He could slip into a hypoglycaemic state without warning. He was, however, held not to be on 'automatic pilot' on the occasion and was convicted.

From the cases of *Taylor v Rodgers* (1960) Crim LR 260 and *McCrane v Riding* (*supra*) it is clear that the standard of care under the section is objective and is regulated by the needs of the public determined by general principles of safe driving for all traffic, and does not depend on the subjective experience or skill of the accused.

It seems that civil standards of negligence are not always relevant in the consideration of offences under this section (or indeed of ss 51A or 53 offences), since the burden of proof is higher. Too often the nature of criminal offences and their differences of mental element and onus of proof are forgotten in consideration of (more profitable) insurance claims. However, it should be noted that in the manslaughter cases of *People (A-G) v Dunleavy* [1948] IR 95; 82 ILTR 70 Davitt J seemed to equate the lack of care in civil negligence with that of criminal careless or inconsiderate driving (para 4.1.2. above) Judge Barra O'Briain did the same in *People v Quinlan* (para 4.2.6 *supra*). The only difference then would, if they are correct, be the standard of proof of beyond reasonable doubt as opposed to the balance of probabilities. The author feels this is not necessarily a correct view, with respect, on a general view of the authorities, especially as the *Dunleavy* Judgment referred to degrees of negligence and differentiates as to its meaning and degrees. The common practice of charging dangerous driving only by prosecution and leaving it to court to decide whether to convict under s 53 or s 52 emphasises this difficulty of degree of blame or fault or care.

The question of whether a person is driving carelessly is one of fact. If the accused was not exercising that degree of care (in the criminal sense?) and attention that a reasonable and prudent driver would exercise in a public place he should be convicted, but if the circumstances indicate that this conduct was not inconsistent with that of a reasonably prudent driver he should be acquitted—see Lord Chief Justice Goddard's remarks in *Simpson v Peat* [1952] 2 QB 24. He also said in that case that it is undesirable to complicate these cases by considering whether or not there had been an 'error of judgment', which he characterised as being 'a loose and vague expression'.

The authorities quoted above are mostly English. The later English case of *R v Gosney* (1971) RTR 321 seems to have emphasised a 'fault' principle in this branch of law. Whether those degrees of fault are equivalent to degrees of negligence as stated in the *Dunleavy* case, has yet to be seen. The nature of the offence should be judged in accordance with the facts and circumstances and the degree of lack of care and attention. If an emergency arises (e.g. sudden light failure in a properly maintained vehicle), then the test is did the driver act reasonably in the circumstances known to him—*Jones v CC of Avon and Somerset* (1986) RTR 259—and a court should not consider the matter with the benefit of hindsight.

There is no reported Irish decision as to what 'care and attention' combined means. It would seem that attention, being a condition of the mind, invokes the need to prove an element of *mens rea*. Thus, a claim of automatism, etc. in relation to driving (dealt with at paras 4.2 and 7.9 under the heading of 'Driver') could prove a defence if shown to exist.

Not obeying bye-laws or regulations can also amount to careless driving in the circumstances of the case, e.g. see para 5.5.3, BL 23 as to signals and cases referred to therein; para 5.8.5 as to disobedience of signs.

4.3.3 Punishment

(a) *Maximum fine £350.* Made more severe by the 1984 Act, s 3. This type of maximum would apply in a bad case, e.g. *R v Krawec* (1985) RTR 1, where the Court imposed £250 as death resulted, but reduced the lower court's fine of £350 as death was an unforeseen and unexpected result of the carelessness. In the earlier fatal case of *R v Simpson* (1981) Crim LR 650, the same Court of Appeal reduced to £100 and three months disqualification the sentence on a lorry driver who knew his brakes were defective but did not know what would happen on an emergency stop. His employers were fined £550 under Construction Use and Equipment Regulations in the same case.

(b) *Imprisonment.* Three months maximum and can be in addition to other penalties or on its own, except in (c)(ii) below.

(c) *Disqualification*

- (i) Optional ancillary disqualification orders under s 27 can be made at the discretion of the Court in all cases.
- (ii) Mandatory disqualification may be ordered under s 26 and the Schedule of the 1961 Act and the 1968 Act, which inserts in the Second Schedule of the 1961 Act a provision, 5B (which makes disqualification mandatory), which reads 'An offence under s 52 where the contravention involved the driving of a mechanically propelled vehicle, being the third or any subsequent such offence within the period of 3 years'. Note the limitation on the type of vehicle. 'Mechanically propelled vehicle' is defined in s 3 of the 1961 Act (see para 7.9). As to 'third or any subsequent such offences', see para 2.9, which deals with disqualification generally.

  As to the period of such consequential disqualification, and the position as to appeals, etc., see para 2.9 also.

(d) *Endorsement.* Under s 36 of the 1961 Act a person convicted of this offence for the second time in three years has his licence mandatorily endorsed. Otherwise endorsement is optional. See para 2.10 as to endorsement generally. In *DPP v O'Brien* in 1989 it is likely a definitive view on the endorsement question will be stated.

4.3.4 Notice of intention to prosecute

A notice of intention to prosecute is necessary in respect of the offence of careless driving under s 104 of the Road Traffic Act 1961. See para 7.3.

4.3.5 Careless and dangerous driving

What is the difference between these two offences?
This question is not easily answered. However, some differences are identifiable:

(a) Differences in penalties. The more minor transgressions obviously are those of a 'careless' nature as they attract lesser penalties. The more serious penalties are reserved for the poorer driving, i.e. dangerous driving.
(b) Differences in the possible consequence of the manner of driving. In the more serious offence of dangerous driving, the consequence of 'danger to the public' has to be established. In some cases death or serious bodily harm is a necessary ingredient also. This is not present in the lesser offence of careless driving.
(c) Differences in the question of degree of bad driving, it is suggested, must be looked at—*Dunleavy* case (*supra*). It is usually a matter of opinion on the type and weight of evidence.
(d) The Legislature seems to have intended a pyramid of offences—dangerous driving, then careless driving, driving without due consideration and, lastly, offences under the regulations. These must be based on different considerations. Manslaughter is a common law offence and would be outside the legislative pyramid but within a court's view of criminality and fault with its consequences.

Attorney-General v Madden [1967] IR 344 seems to support the view that different standards be applied in considering dangerous and careless driving. In that case the defendant was charged on both counts summarily. The District Justice convicted of dangerous driving and dismissed the careless driving summons. The defendant appealed to the Circuit Court and raised a preliminary point that the dismissal of the careless driving was a plea in bar to the further prosecution of the dangerous driving charge. *Held*, by the Supreme Court, in a case stated it was not such a bar.

It is obviously true that the offences are not mutually exclusive. Judge Davitt P, in *People (A-G) v Dunleavy* [1948] IR 95; 82 ILTR 70, stated that the negligence required to convict of dangerous driving was higher than that in careless criminal driving or careless civil driving. He seems to have accepted a pyramid of negligence degrees in driving offences. However, The English view, as expressed in *R v Evans* [1962] 3 All ER 1086, is that the slightest negligence is sufficient (in that case overlooking a dip in the road), once the actions are objectively dangerous. As stated above, this view is probably not accepted in Ireland. One of the difficulties in the use of the word 'negligence' is whether the concept admits degrees? If so, it is a very loose term. The concept of reckless driving has gained prominence in England but not in Ireland.

In these offences on bad driving there seems to be a hierarchy of offences as stated above. This hierarchy derives from their gravity or difference of consequences. But is there a hierarchy of *mens rea* as well as negligence (or 'fault')? This latter of offences seems to be as follows:

(a) At the top of the ladder stands *manslaughter* (para 4.1). Here, according to *People (A-G) v Dunleavy* (supra), a very high degree of negligence must be proved. This is probably because it is a common law offence and the Judges were less concerned with public gratification than the Legislature. It involves *mens rea*. This difference in culpability was recognised in the hierarchy approach stated in a leading modern English case on manslaughter/recklessness—*R v Lawrence* (1981) RTR 217.

(b) *Dangerous Driving* (para 4.2). The standard of driving is the same whatever the consequences. The English Courts adopted an objective standard, in so much as they have adopted any standard. In *R v Parker* (1957) 41 CAR 134 the court refused to define dangerous driving, saying it was a matter for the jury. In Ireland, in *A-G v Dunleavy*, Davitt P. seemed to accept the standard of a high degree of negligence and that this involved *mens rea*, presumably lower than (a) above and higher than that required for (c) below. *R v Evans* (*supra*) probably reduces the position in England to one low standard (the slightest) of negligence in all these cases. However, the case of *R v Gosney* (*supra*) seems to have raised it slightly. It is probably a simplification of tests for a jury in England, due to the fact that in England the Jury could not prior to 1972 bring in a verdict of careless driving. In 1972 reckless driving replaced dangerous driving and the alternative conviction for careless driving was allowed.

(c) *Careless driving* (para 4.3). The standard here seems to be generally accepted to be the objective one of the reasonably prudent man—*McCrone v Riding* (*supra*)—which is akin to civil negligence subject to the strict criminal burden of proof as being beyond reasonable doubt. It probably involves some *mens rea*, in Ireland, as the word 'attention' is included in the defining subsection. 'Attention' and, indeed, 'Care' seem to be very much human mental attributes.

(d) *Reasonable Consideration* (para 4.4). There is little authority on this offence, and it has always been linked in the same section as careless driving. The standard appears to be 'reasonable' joined to 'consideration to the public'. It possibly involves *mens rea* in Ireland, as consideration involves the human mind. It relates to 'nuisance' rather than bad driving.

(e) *Regulation offences*. These seem to be absolute and without negligence or *mens rea*, e.g. if you are on the wrong side of the road, then, unless you come within one of the stated exceptions, it does not matter how you got there. You break the law in the regulation automatically.

If there is no quantative *mens rea* approach to the classification of offences, then, logically, driving may be dangerous without being careless (e.g. deliberate bad driving), or grossly careless driving without being dangerous (e.g. driving on the wrong side when no other traffic).

Contributory negligence

The judgment of the Court of Criminal Appeal in *People v Gallager* [1972] IR 366 (see para 4.2.6) would lead one to believe that, one can describe as contributory negligence by a third party, will not prevent conviction. In that case some evidence that the dead third party was on the wrong side of the road did not prevent conviction by the jury of careless driving, and would not have prevented the Court of Criminal Appeal from convicting of manslaughter or dangerous driving causing death.

4.3.6 Case stated

In *Thompson v Wrigley* (1956) Crim LR 205 it was stated that only in the most exceptional of cases is it justifiable to state a case when the Justice dismisses a 'due care and attention' charge, as such cases usually raise only pure questions of fact.

4.4 Inconsiderate driving

4.4.1 Offence

Section 51A(1) of 1961 Act, as inserted by s 49 of the 1968 Act, states that a person shall not drive a vehicle in a public place without reasonable consideration for other persons using the place.

4.4.2 Proofs

(a) '*A person*'. See para 7.9.
(b) '*Drive*'. See para 7.9.
(c) '*Vehicle*'. See para 7.9.
(d) '*Public place*'. See para 7.9.
(e) '*Without reasonable consideration*'. The law of criminal negligence again comes in by virtue of the words 'reasonable' and 'consideration'. The standard of what is reasonable consideration is objective—*McCrone v Riding* [1938] 1 All ER 157—in England, but some element of *mens rea* appears necessary as reasonableness and consideration are mental matters.
(f) '*Other persons using the place*'. Includes passengers in a vehicle being driven by the accused (100 ILT & Sol Jo 138; *Powley v Whardall* (1966) QB 373. Similarly, in *Dilkes v Bowman Shaw* (1981) RTR 4 it was stated that an actual road user must be inconvenienced before a person may be convicted under the section. In the unusual case of *Downes v Kell* (1969) 113 Sol Jo 387, a motorist who kicked out at a pedal cyclist was not convicted as there was no evidence that his machine and leg came near enough to the cycle to constitute the offence. This is an element not required in careless driving charges, i.e. the necessity of other persons being affected.

This seems to be a lesser offence than careless driving—the penalties involved show this clearly. One could say that 51A is designed for 'nuisance' driving, whereas s 52 relates to bad driving and s 53 to dangerous driving. Presumably, this section covers things like a driver negligently splashing a person on the sidewalk—see 1966 ILT & Sol Jo 427, where a driver was fined £5 for such an offence.

The element of consideration for other persons using the place must be considered by the Court. The combination of reasonableness and consideration of others seems to import *mens rea*. The onus of proof would be beyond reasonable doubt, so it differs in many ways from civil negligence. Thus, in *Dilkes v Bowman Shaw* (1981) RTR 4 (*supra*) it was held that overtaking on the left on a motorway is not necessarily driving without reasonable consideration.

4.4.3 Penalties

(a) The *general penalties* set out in s 102 of the 1961 Act (see para 7.1) apply. These are:

- (i) 1st offence—£150 maximum;
- (ii) 2nd and subsequent offences—£350;
- (iii) 3rd and subsequent offences—if offences occur within 12 months of one another, £350 or/and three months' imprisonment.

(b) *No consequential disqualification* provisions apply to offences under this section. The Court would, of course, have the powers of ancillary disqualification under s 27 (see para 2.9).

(c) *Endorsement* under s 36(1) is optional (see para 2.10).

4.4.4 Notice of intention to prosecute

This is necessary under s 104 of the 1961 Act, as amended by s 6 and Sch of the 1968 Act. As to such notices, see para 7.3.

4.4.5 Alternative verdict

A little used subsection of s 1 of the Criminal Justice (Verdicts) Act 1976 seems to entitle a court to bring in an alternative verdict, where a court believes the offence is lower than careless driving and not endorseable and should have no disqualification implications normally. This subsection 1(2) reads:

> 'Where a person is lawfully before a court charged with an offence, the Court should have jurisdiction to convict a person, on a plea of guilty, of another offence of which he is not specifically charged and of which he could be convicted by that court after trial for the offence specifically charged.'

See also *McAdams v DUTC* (1929) IR 327 referred to at para 4.2.11. (i) above.

4.5 Driving while unfit

4.5.1 Offence

Section 48(1) of the 1961 Act says:

> 'A person shall not drive or attempt to drive a mechanically propelled vehicle in a public place when he is, to his knowledge, suffering from any disease or physical or mental disability which would be likely to cause the driving of the vehicle by him in a public place to be a source of danger to the public.'

Section 29 of the 1933 Act had similar provisions.

The main idea of the section is that these incapacities are not self-induced, but are known to driver, e.g. bad eyesight, deafness, etc. Section 48(2) of the 1961 Act, dealing with the penalties under the section, was re-enacted in s 3(5) of the 1984 Act (see penalties at para 4.5.3).

4.5.2 Proofs

(i) As to 'person', 'drive', 'public place' and 'mechanically propelled vehicle', see Definitions and Phrases at para 7.9 below.

(ii) '*To his knowledge*'. The need of knowledge brings in subjective *mens rea*. It is possible that the question of doctors' privilege would arise in the case of a prosecution. Also, it is difficult to imagine persons with certain types of incapacitating mental illness having this knowledge.

Where the infringement of this provision (under the 1933 Act) resulted in death and the offender was charged with manslaughter, his acquittal on the manslaughter charge would not be sufficient to bar a subsequent charge under this section, as the degree of negligence is not the same and evidence may be sufficient for a s 48 charge even though it might be insufficient to establish manslaughter (*A-G v Woods* 74 ILTR 80).

(iii) 'Suffering from any disease or physical or mental disability'. The types of diseases or disability may be mental or physical. The degree of incapacity is governed by an objective standard, i.e. danger to public (see para 4.2.6 as to this). It seems difficult to prove this offence in many cases. Medical evidence is probably always necessary, *per* Davitt P. in *A-G v Kenny* (1960) 94 ILTR 185. Little judicial interpretation is available outside of *obiter dicta* in that decision. In the Supreme Court Lavery J said, 'But where the physical or mental condition is the very fact in issue, to admit an expression of opinion involves the danger that the judgment of the Court may be seriously affected by the judgment of the witness'.

It seems possible that a prosecution might be sustained under this section where it would not be possible to prove the influence of a drug under the other provisions of the Road Traffic Acts 1961-84. See *Flahive v Lawless* (1953-54) Ir Jur R 37, where the accused was held by the Circuit Court not to be driving under the influence of a drug or drink, he being a diabetic and having taken insulin on his doctor's orders, even though he was subject to comas. Insulin was regarded as a drug in somewhat similar circumstances in *Armstrong v Clarke* (1957) 3 QB 391, a person in a coma due to insulin was held guilty of the offence charged under the drug/drink English provision.

Some guidance for a court or a doctor as to 'disease or physical or mental disability' which might be a source of danger can be found under the Drivers Licensing provision at para 2.3. above where health provisions when applying for a licence are discussed. Also see para 2.6 where certificate of fitness standards are set out.

(iv) An *attempt to drive* is covered as well as driving. See, as to 'attempts' para 7.9.

(v) '*Danger to the public*'. See paras 4.5.5, 4.6.2 below and para 4.2.6 above.

4.5.3 Penalties

Section 48(2) of the 1961 Act, as re-enacted by s 3(5) of the 1984 Act, deals with penalties applicable for an offence under s 48(1).

(a) *Fines/Imprisonment*. First offence, £150 maximum or/and one month's imprisonment; second or subsequent offence, £350 and/or three months' imprisonment.

(b) *Disqualification*

- (i) Mandatory under second Schedule, item 3 of the 1961 Act on a second or subsequent offence within three years;
- (ii) As with all other offences under the Acts, an ancillary disqualification order can be made under s 27 of the 1961 Act, i.e. optional disqualification at the discretion of the court. See para 2.9.

(c) *Endorsement*. This is mandatory on the licence under s 36 for a second offence under s 48 in three years. Otherwise optional. See para 2.10.

4.5.4 Notice of intention to prosecute

Not necessary.

4.5.5 'A source of danger to the public'

This is an important proof. It is only when this is shown, i.e. that it is likely that the public was endangered, that an offence is committed. See para 4.2.6 above regarding dangerous driving and what constitutes it, as there is a general similarity of wording here.

4.5.6 Arrest

There is no specific power of arrest given in the section. Neither is there a specific power to require a medical examination.

4.5.7 Related provisions

Under the 1961 Act, s 28, Gardai can apply to a District Justice for a special disqualification order if they have reasonable grounds to believe a person is unfit to drive by reason of disease or physical or mental disability. See para 2.9.5 above.

Under s 32 of the 1961 Act the Minister for the Environment may by regulation prescribe any disease or disability to be such as to disqualify one from holding a licence. See para 2.3 above.

Section 34 of the 1961 Act provides that the Minister may prescribe that certain persons must produce with their applications for a driving licence certificates of fitness in respect of such aspects of their physical and mental condition as may be prescribed. See para 2.6 above.

4.5.8 English cases

Two English decisions are of interest, in this context:

(a) *Devon CC v Hawkins* [1966] 2 WLR 285. A person who had suffered from epileptic fits, the last occurring more than two years before the application, and who was taking drugs which practically eliminated the possibility of a further attack, was held to be 'suffering from epilepsy' and should have disclosed it.

(b) *Balmer v Hayes* (1950) SC 477. A driver's failure to disclose a malady does not give a third party a right in damages *per se*.

4.6 Defective vehicle

4.6.1 Offence

Section 54 of the 1961 Act, as amended by s 6 and Sch of the 1968 Act, now comprises only one offence, i.e. the owner's liability for a dangerously defective vehicle. The 1968 Act deletes subsection (1) from 1961 section on the basis that the condition of the vehicle is a specifically enumerated circumstance under s 53, i.e. dangerous driving (see para 4.2 above). Such condition had been held in England to be such a 'circumstance' which it is relevant for the Court to consider.

Section 54(2) reads.

> 'Where a mechanically propelled vehicle is driven in a public place while there is a defect affecting the vehicle which the owner thereof knows of or could have discovered by the exercise of ordinary care and which is such that the vehicle is, when in motion, a danger to the public, such owner shall be guilty of an offence.'

The provision is similar to s 52 of the 1933 Act.

It is relevant here to mention the question of the owner's liability for defects generally under the Road Traffic (Construction, Equipment and

Use of Vehicles) Regulations 1963 (SI 190/1963), as amended. These regulations were made under s 11 of the 1961 Act and deal with:

(a) weight, dimensions, and construction of vehicles;
(b) Equipment other than brakes, e.g. steering, wipers, horn, silencers;
(c) Brakes, etc.

By Art 37 and 48 of the regulations the owner is made liable generally as well as the driver. See para 1.5 where these regulations are discussed.

4.6.2 Proofs

There is little judicial interpretation of s 54. There is no similar section in England, where the matter is dealt with under regulations.

The following matters must be proved:

(i) '*Mechanically propelled vehicle*', '*drive*', '*public place*'. See Definitions and Phrases at para 7.9.

(ii) '*Defect affecting the vehicle*'. This defect must be one which affects the vehicle when driven and in motion. Breach is usually proved by a public service vehicle inspector or other expert after examination. It obviously must be a serious defect to make the vehicle dangerous to the public.

(iii) '*Owner thereof knows of*'. The owner must have either actual or imputed knowledge of the defect. This can be imputed because of negligence in not exercising care to find the defect (see *Provincial Motor Cab Co v Dunning* (1909) 73 JP 387). The section refers to the owner, not the registered owner. The owner is the person by whom the vehicle is kept, and therefore includes the hirer under a hire-purchase agreement (see para 7.9).

Under this provision as to the knowledge, the concept or type of *mens rea* is defined. Presumably, delegated, regular, competent service is sufficient to amount to a defence as most owners have not the skills necessary to maintain the vehicle on their own.

(iv) '*Danger to the public*'. See 'Dangerous driving' at para 4.2.6. Reference was made earlier to the case of *R v Spurge* [1961] 2 All ER 688 under the heading of Dangerous Driving (noted in (1961) ILT & Sol Jo 250). There, the defendant became aware on a journey that his brakes were pulling to the right. He continued and later had to brake severely, and his car crossed a double white line and hit a scooter. He was fined £50 and disqualified for a year on a dangerous driving charge, mainly on the basis that he continued to drive a vehicle he knew to be defective.

4.6.3 Special defence

Under s 54(3) it is a defence for the owner to show that the vehicle was driven without his authority. However, in England, in *Richardson v Baker* (1976) RTR 56, the area of authority was widely construed as meaning any use in the employer's business, unless the employee went off on 'a frolic of his own'.

Under Arts 36 and 47 of the Construction, Equipment and Use regulations 1963 there are similar defences provided under many of the parts of the regulations, e.g. Part 3 dealing with equipment generally (R 36); Part 4 (brakes) (R 47). Also, s 11(5) of the 1961 Act provides that it is a good defence to all charges under the Regulations for the owner to show that the vehicle was used without his authority (see para 1.5 above). See also s 118 of the 1961 Act and para 6.4.7 re consent.

4.6.4 Penalties

The fine is increased by the 1984 Act, s 3. The penalties are now:

(a) *fine*, not exceeding £350 and/or;
(b) *imprisonment* of up to three months;
(c) *disqualification*—
  (i) in any case an ancillary disqualification order can be made under s 27 of the 1961 Act,
  (ii) mandatory under s 26 on a second or subsequent offence within three years. See para 2.9;
(d) *endorsement* of the defendant's licence is mandatory under s 36 on conviction for a second offence within three years; otherwise optional. See para 2.10.

4.6.5 Inspection

It is relevant to mention briefly the existence of the very detailed s 20 of the 1961 Act, which gives Gardai power to require examination, inspection and testing of vehicles. See para 1.8.

4.6.6 Notice of intention to prosecute

Not necessary.

4.7 Dangerous parking

4.7.1 Offence

The 1961 Act, s 55(1), as substituted by s 52 of the 1968 Act, reads: 'A person shall not park a vehicle in a public place, if, when so parked, the vehicle would be likely to cause danger to other persons using the place'.

This whole section was a new provision in Irish law in 1961. A number of bad accidents occurred at the time of the drafting of the bill (1959), and there was one particulary bad one at night. This led to the stringent terms. It is aimed at persons leaving vehicles around blind corners, etc. and especially the unlighted vehicle at night.

The offence is a close neighbour in law to the offence of obstruction discussed at para 4.8 below, and many cases referred to in para s 4.7 and 4.8 of this chapter relate to both. See para 4.7.5 for other related offences.

4.7.2 Proofs

(i) '*Person*'. The identify of the person is often difficult to prove, e.g. Gardai finds the car parked and do not know who parked it. See, however, para 7.2 as to Garda powers of obtaining information. Generally see Definitions and Phrases at para 7.9 as to 'person'.

A registered owner's duty to disclose information about user under s 107 should be noted, but he may not always know who did the parking. Defending solicitors should be careful in making admissions about persons parking—see para 7.2.

(ii) '*Park*'. Defined in s 3 as keeping or leaving a vehicle stationary (see para 7.9). Therefore, the original parking may be safe but later become dangerous, e.g. by nightfall coming. No duration is stated—day or night—but special penalties exist for unlawful night parking under s 55(2). Thus, in exercising one's common law right of leaving a car outside one's own house, one could be committing a criminal offence (see para 4.8.3, and *Police v O'Connor* (1957) LR, where parking a large vehicle outside the driver's house in a cul-de-sac was not unlawful.

The rules as to normal parking are found in the General Bye-laws 1964, bye-law 26 (see para 5.3). Presumably, if these are observed one could not come within the section. These rules state that one must not park a vehicle so as to:

(a) obstruct, inconvenience or endanger traffic;
(b) obstruct the view of another driver at or near a bend, road junction, corner, brow of hill or traffic sign;
(c) obstruct an entrance to any premises (unless the occupier consents), fire brigade or ambulance station;
(d) obstruct the free flow of traffic or pedestrians; and
(e) be where there is a continuous white line, zebra crossing, traffic lights or bus stop.

It should be noted in this respect that these General Bye-laws (bye-law 27) impose on a driver or person in charge the obligation to remove a vehicle in the event of a break-down or accident when parked in contravention of the above rules. A relevant provision of the Construction, Equipment and Use Regulations 1963 should also be borne in mind here—Art 87—which prohibits a driver leaving his vehicle on a public road unless it is locked and the parking brake is on (see para 1.5). As mentioned below, it can be dangerous to park a car on an incline without a brake.

'Lighting-up time' is defined in the Road Traffic (Lighting of Vehicles) Regulations 1963, Art 3 as the period commencing one-half hour after the sunset and lasting to one-half hour before sunrise on the following day (see para 1.6 as to Lighting).

(iii) '*Vehicles*'. All types of vehicles are covered by the section. See Definitions and Phrases at para 7.9

(iv) '*Public place*'. See Definitions and Phrases at para 7.9

(v) '*Likely to cause danger*'. *Parish v Judd* (95 ILT & SJ 38) gives an idea of what is meant by this phrase, even though it was a civil case. The facts were that the defendant's car lights broke down on a dark night. A lorry towed it to within six yards of street lights. The car was left unlighted but the lorry left its rear and front side lights on. A car crashed into the unlit vehicle and the plaintiff (a passenger) was injured. A civil action case on nuisance and negligence failed. The observations of Edmond Davis J can be summarised as follows: To establish a nuisance there must be three things shown—

(a) That the vehicle was an obstruction;

(b) that it was a danger (The Judge held that this element was not present due to the street lighting);

(c) that such a vehicle became unlighted by reason of some fault on the part of the driver (or owner) or, if not due to his fault initially, that he thereafter was guilty of such fault.

On the negligence issue, the presence of such unlit car was prima facie negligence—but the Judge stated that this applied only where there was no adequate street lighting. In this case the Judge held that, due to adequate street lighting and the efforts of the motorist, he had done all a reasonable man could do.

However, the Courts may yet hold that this offence is an absolute one, although this is unlikely. Normally, *mens rea* in the form of reckless neglect of the consequences of one's acts will be obvious and necessary where causation is in issue. It would seem unfair to the motorist who suffers a mishap to be bracketed with the driver who was too lazy to put his car off the road. Again, look at some of the defences allowed under the regulations at para 1.5, e.g. R 47 of the Construction, Equipment and Use Regulations 1963.

The Irish decision of *O'Reilly v Evans* (91 ILTR 161) should be noted, in which Kingsmill Moore J said that drivers on the highway at night must depend on the illumination they carry themselves unless there is adequate street lighting. See also the decision in *Ideal Poultry Farm Ltd v Freeman* (84 ILTR 85), where the driver did not see an unlighted tractor at night because of an oncoming car. It was held that he was not guilty of contributory negligence; and the decision in *A-G v Joyce* (90 ILTR 47), under s 35 of the Offences Against the Person Act 1861, that having an unlighted horse-drawn vehicle on the road at night was evidence on which the jury could find 'wilful neglect' within that section. The line between these decisions is very fine and each case largely stands on its own facts.

A note regarding the civil side of this matter—it was held in *Cloke v Brims* [1947] KB 497 that breach of requirements of lighting does not *per se* give a civil remedy. Nevertheless, the absence of lights is a very relevant consideration.

Parking a car without a brake can become dangerous parking, e.g. if the car runs down a hill unattended as a result (see *Maguire v Grouch* [1941] KB 108).

In *A-G v Hourigan* (1945) 79 ILTR 133 it was held that a summons was not bad for duplicity for charging the offence in the alternative. The order should be only in relation to one of the two bases set out. However, the 1968 wording is confined to 'likely to cause'.

(vi) '*To other persons using the place*'. Gentleman or lady passengers should note this—too often the offenders under this section are accompanied by a member of the opposite sex at night! Any other person, other than person who did the parking, using the place is sufficient.

4.7.3 Penalties

(a) If it is a first offence (except during lighting up hours) there is a *fine* of £50 maximum and/or one month's *imprisonment*.

(b) Where it is a first offence of dangerous parking during lighting up hours, or a second or subsequent offences a *fine* is imposed of up to £350 and/or three months' *imprisonment*. The regulations covering lighting of vehicles are the Road Traffic (Lighting of Vehicles) Regulations 1963 (SI 189/1963). These regulations run to 84 pages and deal with lights on mechanically propelled vehicles, tractors, cycles, invalid carriages with reflectors, early warning devices, etc. See para 1.6.

(c) *Disqualification*:

  (i) first offence—optional under s 27 of the 1961 Act;
  (ii) second or subsequent offence within three years under section 26 and Second Schedule of the 1961 Act disqualification is mandatory, if the offence occurs during lighting up time. See para 2.9.

(d) *Endorsement of the licence* is mandatory under s 36 if it is a second offence within three years, otherwise it is optional. See para 2.10.

4.7.4 Arrest

Section 52 of the 1968 Act inserted a new s 52(4) to enable a Garda to arrest without warrant anyone he believes has commited an offence under this section. Presumably, this was inserted to overcome to some extent the difficulty of proof of identity of a person parking illegally. It is supplemented by the powers of enquiry (see para 7.2).

4.7.5 Related offences

Obstruction—see para 4.8 *infra*.

Parking control at large assemblies—see para 5.6.
Parking control at fairs and markets—s 92 of the 1961 Act (see para 5.7).
Parking under general bye-laws—see para 5.3 and *supra*.
Local parking bye-laws and temporary rules—s 90 of the 1961 Act (see para 5.5).
Parking an omnibus—see para 1.17.
Taxi stands—see para 1.16.
Removal of vehicles abandoned, etc.—s 97 of the 1961 Act (see para 5.12).

4.8 Obstruction

4.8.1 Offence

Section 98(1) of the 1961 Act states that 'A person shall not do any act (whether commission or omission) which causes or is likely to cause traffic through any public place to be obstructed.'. As to 'person', 'traffic', 'public place', see para 7.9. As to 'cause or is likely to cause' see 4.7.2(v).

See also s 55 of the Road Traffic Act 1961 as to dangerous parking, especially at night (para 4.7 above), the provision of the General Bye-laws 1964, bye-law 26(1)(f) as to obstructing access (para 5.3), para 5.8 as to the erection of private signs and para 4.7.5 as to other related offences.

4.8.2 Special defence

Section 98(3) provides that it is a good defence to a charge under subs (1) to show that either (a) there was lawful authority for the act complained of, or (b) that it was due to an unavoidable accident.

4.8.3 What is obstruction?

Every article and vehicle on the highway is an obstruction to some degree, especially if it is stationary. However, the law in this regard has to have a 'live and let live' element.

At common law it was provided that there was a public right to pass and repass, as the highway was considered dedicated to the public. It (the right of way) was to the space between the fences—*A-G v Mayo Co Co* [1902] 1 IR 13—and included the grass verges.

The right of passage included the right to stop for a reasonable time and in a reasonable place, e.g. a stage coach could set down and take up passengers (*R v Cross* (1812) 3 Compb 224 NP). That case held it was an indictable misdemeanour to stand for public hire in the public street, and this became an obstruction. Hence, as seen in Chapter 1, Part 2, public service vehicles have to have special legislative permission for stands (para 1.16). See also para 5.14 as to legalised obstructions (ramps, bollards, etc.)

A reasonably modern Irish case illustrates the point of what is obstruction. In *O'Connor v Leonard* 103 ILTR 43 it was held that s 98 of the 1961 Act was not an absolute and unqualified prohibition, and the test of reasonableness had to be applied. The defendant driver stopped his vehicle in Tralee to unload near a shop. The road was about 20 feet wide and the defendant's van about 6 feet wide. Parking was permitted on the other side of this street for one hour. The fact there was one free lane was central to the decision. *Held*: there was not an obstruction. See a similar decision in *Absalm v Martin* (1974) RTR 145.

Unreasonable use of the roadside by one's own vehicles—e.g. constant loading outside one's own premises—can amount to obstruction (*A-G v Brighton* [1900] 1 Ch, see para 2.7.6), but this would not extend to unloading for a reasonable period in a reasonable way, especially if traffic can move. It also would not apply to an adjoining owner's right of reasonable access to his premises, or where the road is unusually wide, thus causing no interference (*A-G v Smith* (1910) 103 LJ 96). This right to load and unload is recognised often in parking bye-laws (see para 5.5).

The principle of reasonableness as used in relation to vehicles applies outside private houses (*Original Hartlepool Colleries Co v Gibbs* (1871) 5 Ch D 713). At common Law an obstruction on a road due to an unavoidable accident is not actionable *Maitland v Raisbeck* [1944] 1 KB 689. This whole element of give and take was emphasised in *Harper v Hadden & Sons Ltd* [1933] Ch 298.

Legislative summary penalties were introduced for obstruction on public roads as towns developed, e.g. s 13(3) of the Summary Jurisdiction (Ireland) Act 1851 for interrupting free passage—fine £1. In *Lowdens v Keavney* 36 ILTR 21; [1903] IR 82 it was said by Gibson J. at page 91 of Volume 2 of the Irish Reports:

> 'Is the obstruction contemplated such an obstruction as would be in the nature of Common Law nuisance or does the statute extend to every physical obstruction apart from the question of reasonableness? I think the former view is the correct one.'

See para 1.29 as to nuisances. See also *Yeldham v Carpenter* (1912) 46 ILTR 186, construing a similar provision in the Summary Jurisdiction (Ireland) Act 1857 as meaning 'unreasonable obstruction'.

Straying animals were subject to a special position of non-liability under *Searle v Wallbank* [1947] AC 341. This was not changed by s 98 of the 1961 Act (see note on *O'Brien v McNamara* (1966) ILT & Sol Jo 421) but was changed in relation to negligence in s 2 of the Animal Act 1985.

Some more modern examples of unreasonable use of the highway are found in:

(a) *Mounsey v Campbell* (1983) RTR 36—van parked against front bumper of car which could be moved backwards at the time. However, it was later penned in from behind by another car. Defendant refused to move the van. Convicted.

(b) *Browne v Cardle* (1983) SLT 218—parking in a bus bay for five minutes was not an obstruction in the absence of evidence that a bus was trying to park there.

(c) *Waltham Forest LBC v Mill* (1980) RTR 201—selling refreshments from a mobile snack bar was not an obstruction in itself.

(d) *Waite v Taylor* (1985) 149 JP 551—a juggler obstructed a pedestrian precinct, even though people were free to move along the street. He sought donations by putting his cap on the ground.

See also s 98 of the 1961 Act (para 4.13 *infra*).

4.8.4 Penalty

The general penalty applies for obstruction (see para 7.1). Disqualification and endorsement are optional (paras 2.9 and 2.10).

4.8.5 Related offences

See para 4.7.5 above.

4.9 Intoxicated driving

4.9.1 Introduction

Few subjects have produced such heated controversy in law as the intoxicated driver problem (being normally alcohol based, with the related offences of drugs). Most of this part of the chapter refers to 'drink', but the law equally applies to drugs. The heat of controversy stems basically from the different levels of tolerance to alcohol experienced by different persons (see para 4.2.5—*A-G v Regan* [1975] IR 367). Because of scientific advances the issue is less difficult today than it was in 1961. The 1961 Act itself had, what is called, the 'incapacity test' approach, i.e. the court had to conclude the defendant was under the influence of an intoxicant to such an extent as to be incapable of having proper control of the vehicle.

Harsh legislative provisions have not eradicated the problem, as society does not still fully accept as a 'real criminal' the intoxicated driver. This may be due to the difference in law between the 'drunken' driver and what is regarded as a socially drunk person—or, indeed, what is regarded as drunkeness in other branches of the law.

The current provisions are generally those introduced under the amending Acts in a rather untidy way, though they were pulled together somewhat in the Road Traffic (Amendment) Act 1978, with increased penalties under the 1984 Act. The 1978 Act (replacing the earlier, similar 1968 Act) specifies the additional 'analysis test'. A sample of the defendant's blood or urine is taken and analysed. If he is found to have more than 100 mgs of alcohol in his blood (or 135 mg in urine) per 100 ml of blood (urine), then he is guilty of an offence. There are detailed procedural provisions, many of which have been tested in court, and some of which were enacted to overcome earlier court decisions.

4.9.2 Historically

Section 12 of the Licensing Act 1872 provided, *inter alia*, that any person who was drunk while in charge of any carriage, horse, cattle or steam engine on any highway or other public place, or (in the same category presumably) of loaded firearms, was liable to a fine not exceeding £2 or one month's imprisonment.

In the present century the rapid growth of motor transport produced comprehensive legislation, which contained a range of offences to deal with the 'drunken driver'. These were contained in ss 29 and 30 of the 1933 Road Traffic Act. Their concept of an incapacity to drive test (as opposed to the normal concept of drunkenness) and the penalty of automatic disqualification are to be found in the present law. The 1933 provisions were re-enacted with some modifications in the Road Traffic Act 1961.

On the world scene, the advance of science sought to make more precise the tests whereby a judgment could be made on the capacity to drive. This continues and many detection systems now exist.

In the Republic of Ireland in 1961 a Commission was appointed by the Government on the problem of 'Driving whilst under the influence of drink or a drug'. This Commission (generally referred to as the Davitt Commission) made many recommendations, the main one being the introduction of a scientific alcohol analysis test. Substantially, the recommendations are incorporated in Part V of the 1968 Act. This Act has been largely replaced, first by the 1974 Act and later by the 1978 Act, and amended in relation to penalties by the 1984 Act. Nevertheless, the extent to which these tough laws have affected the problem is a matter of conjecture. In a survey result published at the end of 1987 by the National Road Safety Association, only 8% of drivers were aware of a possible prison sentence and 13% that the maximum fine was £1,000 for intoxicated driving.

4.9.3 Main criminal provisions

The law on drink and driving is statutory almost in its entirety. The main criminal provisions cover:

- (a) driving or attempting to drive a mechanically propelled vehicle while intoxicated, i.e. 'drunk' or drugged on the basis of being incapable of driving properly or having excess urine in blood or alcohol—s 49 of the 1961 Act (three offences);
- (b) intoxication (drunk or drugged) while in charge on the basis of incapacity or of concentration—s 50 of the 1961 Act (three offences);
- (c) driving animal-drawn vehicles and pedal cycles under the influence of intoxicating liquor or drugs—s 51 of the 1961 Act (two offences);
- (d) being found in a public place under the influence of liquor or drugs—s 59 of the 1961 Act (two offences);
- (e) refusal in relation to breath tests under ss 12, 13, 14 and 15 of the 1978 Act (four offences);

(f) refusal in relation to specimens under ss 13(3)(a), s 13(3)(b), 14(3), 14(3)(b) and 17(4) (five offences);
(g) drugs (not accompanying Garda to station, etc.)—s 17(2) of the 1978 Act; and
(h) taking steps to frustrate a prosecution—s 18(3)(a) of the 1978 Act.

When studying the law on intoxicated driving it should be borne in mind that this law generally deals with drugs also, and with a combination of drink and drugs. Drugs are specifically discussed at the end of this Chapter, i.e. para 4.9.8 *infra*, but, generally speaking, the law covering both drink and drugs is the same.

As there have been a number of fairly considerable amendments to the law in this area, it is as well to set out the main offence sections as amended in full:

(a) *Driving or attempting to drive*
Prohibition on driving a mechanically propelled vehicle while under the influence of an intoxicant—s 49 of the 1961 Act (as re-enacted by s 10 of the 1978 Act and amended by s 3 of the 1984 Act).
Section 49 now reads—

(1)(a) A person shall not drive or attempt to drive a mechanically propelled vehicle in a public place while he is under the influence of an intoxicant to such an extent as to be incapable of having proper control of the vehicle.
(b) In this subsection 'intoxicant' includes alcohol and drugs and any combination of drugs or of drugs and alcohol.
(2) A person shall not drive or attempt to drive a mechanically propelled vehicle in a public place while there is present in his body a quantity of alcohol such that, within three hours after so driving or attempting to drive, the concentration of alcohol in his blood will exceed a concentration of 100 milligrammes of alcohol per 100 millilitres of blood.
(3) A person shall not drive or attempt to drive a mechanically propelled vehicle in a public place while there is present in his body a quantity of alcohol such that, within three hours after so driving or attempting to drive, the concentration of alcohol in his urine will exceed a concentration of 135 milligrammes of alcohol per 100 millilitres of urine.
(4)(a) A person who contravenes subsection (1), (2) or (3) of this section shall be guilty of an offence and liable on summary conviction to imprisonment for a term not exceeding six months or, at the discretion of the court, to a fine not exceeding £1,000 or to both.
(b) A person charged with an offence under this section may be found guilty of an offence under section 50 of this Act.
(5) Section 1(1) of the Probation of Offenders Act, 1907, shall not apply to an offence under this section.
(6) A member of the Garda Siochana may arrest without warrant a person who in the member's opinion is committing or has committed an offence under this section.

(b) *In charge*
Prohibition on being in charge of mechanically propelled vehicle while

under the influence of an intoxicant—s 50 of the 1961 Act (as re-enacted by s 11 of the 1978 Act and amended by s 3 of the 1984 Act).

Section 50 now reads—

(1)(a) A person shall be guilty of an offence who, when in charge of a mechanically propelled vehicle in a public place with intent to drive or attempt to drive the vehicle (but not driving or attempting to drive it), is under the influence of an intoxicant to such an extent as to be incapable of having proper control of the vehicle.

(b) In this subsection 'intoxicant' includes alcohol and drugs and any combination of drugs or of drugs and alcohol.

(2) A person shall be guilty of an offence who is in charge of a mechanically propelled vehicle in a public place with intent to drive or attempt to drive the vehicle (but not driving or attempting to drive it) and in whose body there is present a quantity of alcohol such that, within three hours after having been so in charge of the vehicle, the concentration of alcohol in his blood will exceed a concentration of 100 milligrammes of alcohol per 100 millilitres of blood.

(3) A person shall be guilty of an offence who is in charge of a mechanically propelled vehicle in a public place with intent to drive or attempt to drive the vehicle (but not driving or attempting to drive it) and in whose body there is present a quantity of alcohol such that, within three hours after having been so in charge of the vehicle, the concentration of alcohol in his urine will exceed a concentration of 135 milligrammes of alcohol per 100 millilitres of urine.

(4)(a) A person who is guilty of an offence under this section shall be liable on summary conviction—

(i) in the case of a first offence, to a fine not exceeding £100 or, at the discretion of the court, to imprisonment for any term not exceeding three months, or to both, and

(ii) in the case of a second or any subsequent offence to a fine not exceeding £1,000 or, at the discretion of the court, to imprisonment for any term not exceeding six months, or to both.

(b) A person charged with an offence under this section may be found guilty of an offence under section 49 of this Act.

(5) In a prosecution for an offence under this section it shall be presumed that the defendant intended to drive or attempt to drive the vehicle until he shows the contrary.

(6) A person liable to be charged with an offence under this section shall not, by reference to the same occurrence, be liable to be charged under section 12 of the Licencing Act, 1872, with the offence of being drunk while in charge, on a highway or other public place, of a carriage.

(7) Where a person convicted of an offence under this section has been previously convicted of an offence under section 49 of this Act (inserted by the Road Traffic (Amendment) Act, 1978), or section 30(3) or 33(3) of the Road Traffic Act, 1968, he shall be treated for the purposes of this section as having been previously convicted of an offence under this section.

(8) A member of the Garda Siochana may arrest without warrant a person

who in the member's opinion is committing or has committed an offence under this section.

(c) *Driving animal-drawn vehicle or pedal cycle*

Prohibition on driving such a vehicle while drunk or under the influence of drugs—s 51 of the 1961 Act (as amended by s 3(6) of the 1978 Act).

Section 51 now reads:

(1) A person shall not in a public place—

(a) Drive or attempt to drive or be in charge of an animal-drawn vehicle; or

(b) Drive or attempt to drive a pedal cycle, while he is under the influence of intoxicating liquor or a drug to such an extent as to be incapable of having proper control of the vehicle or cycle.

(2) A person who contravenes subsection (1) of this section shall be guilty of an offence and—

(a) If the offence relates to an animal-drawn vehicle he shall be liable on summary conviction in the case of a first offence to a fine not exceeding £150 or, at the discretion of the court to imprisonment for any term not exceeding one month or to both such fine and such imprisonment and in the case of a second or any subsequent offence, to a fine not exceeding £350 or, at the discretion of the court, to an imprisonment for any term not exceeding three months or to both such fine and such imprisonment, and

(b) If the offence relates to a pedal cycle, he shall be liable on a summary conviction to a fine not exceeding £350 or, at the discretion of the court to imprisonment for any term not exceeding three months or both such fine and such imprisonment.

(3) A person liable to be charged with an offence under this section shall not by reference to the same occurrence be liable to be charged under section 12 of the Licensing Act 1872, with an offence of being drunk while in charge, on the highway or other public place, of a carriage.

(4) Where a Member of the Garda Siochana is of the opinion that a person is committing or has committed an offence under this section he may arrest the person without warrant.

(d) *Being found in a public place under the influence of liquor or drugs*

Prohibition on being found drunk or drugged in a public place—s 59 of the 1968 Act.

Section 59 reads:

(1) A person who is found in a public place in such a condition, because he is under the influence of intoxicating liquor or a drug, as to be a source of danger to the traffic or himself shall be guilty of an offence.

(2) A person charged with an offence under this section shall not in respect of the facts alleged to constitute such offence be charged under section 12 of the Licensing Act 1836, section 12 of the Licensing Act 1872, section 25 of the Licensing (Ireland) Act 1874 or section 9 of the Summary Jurisdiction Act 1908.

(3) Where a Member of the Garda Siochana is of the opinion that a person is committing an offence under this section he may arrest the person without warrant.

4.9.4 Present law: Approaches to the problem

As to the modes of proving guilt, the law now has two standards for judging the right to drive of a person who has taken alcohol/drugs. For convenience these are called.

(i) the incapacity test, i.e. that the person charged must not be under the influence of an intoxicant 'to such an extent as to be incapable of having proper control of the vehicle'; and
(ii) the intoxicant concentration test, i.e. that a person has not in his body a quantity of alcohol such that, within three hours after the alleged act or situation, the concentration of alcohol in his blood will exceed a concentration of 100 milligrammes of alcohol per 100 millilitres of blood (or 135/100 in the case of a urine test).

As to offenders, the law covers:

(1) drivers of mechanically propelled vehicles;
(2) persons attempting to drive mechanically propelled vehicles;
(3) persons in charge of a mechanically propelled vehicle with intent to drive or attempting to drive;
(4) persons driving, attempting to drive, or in charge of animal-drawn vehicles;
(5) persons driving or attempting to drive a pedal cycle;
(6) persons found in public places who are affected adversely so as to be a danger to themselves or traffic.

At present, therefore, the law addresses the problem of intoxicated driving by setting out:

(1) how intoxication is established, i.e. the modes of proving guilt; and
(2) who is to be penalised and what penalties are to be applied to offenders.

4.9.5 Incapacity offences

4.9.5.1 *Offences in outline*: The following offences are governed by the incapacity test (para 4.9.4(i) above):

(a) driving or attempting to drive or being in charge of a mechanically propelled vehicle in a public place—ss 49 and 50 of the 1961 Act (as re-enacted by s 10 and s 4 of the 1978 Act);
(b) driving or attempting to drive or being in charge of an animal-drawn vehicle; or driving or attempting to drive a pedal cycle—s 51 of the 1961 Act (as amended by s 3(6) of the 1984 Act);
(c) persons found in a public place in such a condition due to intoxicating liquor or drugs as to be a danger to traffic or themselves—s 59 of the 1968 Act;

(d) persons found in charge of a mechanically propelled vehicle under influence of drugs to such an extent as to be incapable of having proper control of the vehicle—s 17 of the 1978 Act.

These sections (except s 17 of the 1978 Act) are set out in full above (para 4.9.3). In a charge of driving or attempting to drive, if a conviction should follow it should be based only on one offence, otherwise it will be void for duplicity (*State (Taylor) v CC Judge of Wicklow* [1951] IR 311). Charges of aiding and abetting can be brought, e.g. against the owner or passenger, but in *R v Kearnon & Anor* (1955) Crim LR 183 it was held that the owner, who was a passenger, was too drunk to have the necessary knowledge to aid and abet.

4.9.5.2 *Test of ability*. It is not legally wrong to drive while one has alcohol in one's body. Under the 1961 Act, however, a person shall not do any of the matters referred to at para 4.9.5.1 above 'while under the influence of intoxicating liquor to such an extent as to be incapable of having proper control' or to be a danger (s 49 of the 1961 Act and s 59 of the 1968 Act). The basic approach, therefore, is that of 'incapacity' resulting in lack of 'proper control' or 'danger'.

If the person does not have proper control, this deficiency must be shown to be due to the influence of an intoxicant, i.e. intoxicating liquor or drugs or a combination. It is readily appreciated that this is largely a matter of evidence. In applying this test the courts are concerned not so much with how much drink a person had but with its effect on him. It must be accepted that some people have a natural, and others an acquired, tolerance to alcohol. It was so referred to and accepted in *A-G v Regan* [1975] IR 367 (see para 4.2.5). A person's weight, health, eating habits, etc. affect the picture. Medical evidence is helpful to the court, but not essential, in making a judgment as to whether an accused person was incapacitated or a danger. The 'hip flask' drink, i.e. drink taken after detection or the accident but before the test, can cause confusion in this capacity test—it is now covered by the anti-evasion section dealing with specimens, i.e. s 18 of the 1978 Act which is discussed at para 4.9.6 below.

4.9.5.3 *Enforcement procedure*. Where a Garda is of the opinion that a person has committed an offence under s 49, 50, or 51 of the 1961 Act or s 59 of 1968 Act he can arrest the subject without warrant. He must, however, inform the suspect that he is being arrested and the reason for the arrest. The arrest should be made in clear and unambiguous language. In *Alderson v Boothe* [1969] 2 All ER 271 it was held that a request in the form of 'I shall have to ask you to come to the police station for further tests' was not sufficient.

In *DPP v O'Connor* (1984) ILRM 333 a Garda noticed a smell of alcohol on the defendant's breath and that his speech was slurred. The Garda told him he was arresting him under s 49(6) of the 1961 Act for offences under s 49(2) and (3). It was submitted successfully in the District Court that the Garda's observations did not go as far as to show that he had formed an opinion prior to arrest. The Supreme Court overruled that decision, holding there was a necessary implication when the Garda invoked the section that he had formed the required opinion.

The Garda usually notes the actions, speech, behaviour and demeanour of the suspect. As soon as a Garda makes up his mind that an offence has been committed, he administers the usual caution, i.e. that the suspect is not bound to say anything but anything he does say may be taken down in writing and may be given in evidence. The suspect is then arrested and taken to the Garda Station. At the Station, other Gardai will usually note the suspect's behaviour on the same lines. Normally, the Garda medical doctor is called, although the suspect should be informed of his right to call a doctor of his own choice at his own expense. If the doctor finds incapacity it strengthens the prosecution. The Garda doctor must warn suspect that he is not obliged to submit to an examination but that, if he does, the results may be used in evidence. Normally the Gardai give a similar warning. It is not an offence to refuse an examination, unlike the refusal of scientific tests as described at para 4.9.6.

If the suspect consents to a medical examination the doctor carries out a detailed test to ascertain the history, general behaviour, injuries, health, memory and mental altertness, physical condition, co-ordination, reflexes and gait of the suspect. (For a detail specimen examination, see British Medical Associations Booklet 1965 on '*The Drinking Driver*', p 18.) If no consent is given the doctor confines himself to observing the appearance and behaviour of the suspect, and these observations may be given in evidence. The doctor certifies his opinion to the Garda and verifies this in Court on oath later. When the suspect is considered fit to be allowed home he is normally released on recognisance, incorporating the charge, under the Criminal Justice Act 1951 and, now, the Criminal Justice Act 1984, s 26 (but see *State (Lynch) v Ballagh* (1987) ILRM 65 as the limitations in 'station bail'). See para 7.2.5.

All charges are tried summarily in the District Court. The prosecution relies on the medical and other evidence. Since the decision in *Kenny*'s case ((1960) 94 ILTR 185—see para 4.9.5.4) the courts rely more and more on opinion evidence, possibly too much so! Of course, in some cases no medical evidence is available, and then, if necessary, the Courts must rely on non-professional witness observations.

The accused has a right to cross examine and call his own witnesses. He can appeal to the Circuit Court where there is a complete re-hearing. The Circuit Court may affirm, vary or reverse the District Court decision. Where an indictable offence arises out of some incident (e.g. dangerous driving causing death), both offences can be charged in the one indictment to be tried by the jury in the Circuit Court or the Central Criminal Court.

Conviction figures under this capacity test, according to the Davitt Commission, showed 65% convicted under s 49 of the 1961 Act (main incapacity offence). Since the scientific tests were introduced these conviction rates have very substantially increased.

This approach now is normally only a 'back-up' charge by the Gardai, e.g. where the defendant refuses to give a specimen. The analysis test is now much more favoured as it largely replaces 'opinion' with 'science'.

4.9.5.4 *Case-law.*

(i) Tests must be shown to be voluntarily undergone. In *The State (Sullivan) v Robinson* [1954] IR 161 it was held that when a medical doctor, acting on behalf of the police, conducts an examination of, and carries out tests on, a person accused of driving while unfit, the court should not admit the results unless the prosecution affirmatively establish that the tests (and any statement in the nature of a confession) were voluntarily undergone. *R v Nowell* [1948] 1 All ER 794 establishes that a doctor's evidence following examination is expert evidence and is acceptable even if reasonable persuasion was used to get the defendant to agree to the examination.

A number of useful specific standards were laid down in the Scottish High Court case of *Reid v Nixon; Dunigan v Browne* (1948) SLT 295. The Court stated that:

(1) the police should caution the accused before examination and ought to ask his consent to examination by their doctor;
(2) the accused should be told of his right to have his own doctor and be given facilities so to have, but examination by a police doctor need not be delayed until the other doctor is present;
(3) the examination should normally proceed without the police present;
(4) interrogation by the doctor with regard to recent events should be for the purpose of testing the accused's memory and coherence and not for eliciting information bearing on his guilt;
(5) if such information regarding guilt is elicited it should not be communicated to the police;
(6) if consent to the examination is refused and the doctor gives evidence later at a hearing, he should confine himself to observations made without an examination or a test.

(ii) Caution. In *A-G v O'Keeffe* [1955] IR 24 it was stated that where a person charged with driving while drunk is told that a doctor called by the police is about 'to examine him as to his sobriety', he is not obliged to submit to the medical examination unless he wishes to do so, but if he does, the results may be given in evidence. He must also be informed that he is entitled to call another doctor, but the word 'tests' needs not be specifically mentioned. It was held that the warning is adequate. The tests are deemed voluntary and the results admissible evidence.

In *McCarrick v Leavy* (1964) IR 225; 98 ILTR 163 it was held that the absence of a caution, necessary under the Judges Rules after the Gardai have decided to charge a suspect with drunken driving before questioning, does not of itself render an admission inadmissible. The trial judge has a discretion. In *DPP v Farrell* [1978] IR 13 it was held that the trial Judge should consider the evidence of examination offered before exercising his discretion.

(iii) **Drugs.** *Flahive v Lawless* (1953-54 Ir Jur R p. 37) was an appeal against a charge of drunken driving. *Held*: appellant not guilty, his condition being due to drugs taken for medicinal purposes under doctor's orders. This decision has been overruled in relation to s 49 and s 50 offences under the new definitions of 'intoxicants' in the re-enactment sections by the 1978 Act. However, it remains a relevant decision in relation to offences under s 51 of the 1961 Act (animal and pedal cycle) and s59 of the 1968 Act (danger to traffic or self).

(iv) **Jurisdiction.** *A-G v Burke* [1955] IR 30 held that where a defendant enters into a bond to appear before a District Court on a drunken driving charge, a District Justice has jurisdiction to hear the case notwithstanding that the means adopted to procure his attendance are invalid—in this case recognizance entered into on a Sunday.

(v) **Non-professional evidence.** In *The State (Ruddy) v Kenny* (1960) ILTR 94 185 it was held that a garda or other ordinary person can give evidence of his opinion as to whether a person is unfit to drive. (Note that the position in Northern Ireland is the opposite—*Shearant v Jacob* (1965) NI 151 and noted NILQ 496.) So too may a doctor who has not medically examined the defendant (*A-G (Enright) v Reilly*, unreported, High Court, 30 January 1967) (1966 Act, s 5).

In *Murray v Muir* [1949] SLT 263, where consent to a medical examination was specifically refused, evidence of the doctor's observations was allowed.

(vi) **Constitutionality** *A-G v Conroy* [1965] IR 411 held that s 49 was constitutional, i.e. not repugnant to the constitution. It was argued that his was not a 'minor offence' and so should be tried on indictment. This argument was overruled. One cannot, with respect, read the Supreme Courts views without feeling a sense of unreality as to its conclusions. However, the 'scientific' test has brought more reality into this area of the law for the non-lawyer.

In *State (Collins) v Kelliher* (Supreme Court, 18 November 1983, unreported) it was held that a defendant may not be convicted under s 49(1)(a) and either s 49(2) or s 49(3).

4.9.5.5 *Davitt Report recommendation.* It is of interest to note that this Report (p 40) recommended that the wording of this test be changed to 'under the influence of intoxicating liquor to such an extent that his driving is likely to be a source of danger to the public or himself'. This is to avoid a defence of actual or apparent exercise of proper control of the vehicle even though the driver is really unfit to drive. This recommendation has not been enacted.

4.9.5.6 *Defences barred.* By s 20 of the 1978 Act the fact that the accused proves that the specimen analysis or breath test under the 1978 Act was not carried out is not a defence to a charge of driving while unfit under the 'capacity test' provisions of s 49(1) and 50(1).

4.9.5.7 *Provision of urine sample—drugs.* Section 17 of the 1978 Act extends the powers of a member of the Garda over a person in charge of a mechanically propelled vehicle, in relation to whom he has formed the opinion that he is under the influence of drugs to such an extent as to render him incapable of having proper control of the vehicle. The Garda may:

(i) require that person to accompany him to a Garda Station. If the person refuses, he is liable to up to six months' imprisonment and/ or up to £1,000 fine; plus discretionary endorsement and/or disqualification;
(ii) arrest that person without warrant;
(iii) require that person to give to a registered medical practitioner a urine sample. If the person refuses, the same penalties apply as in (i).

As to samples, see in particular para 4.9.6.6 and para 4.8.2 above. Note there is no requirement of a public place in this section. See para 4.9.8 *infra* re drugs.

4.9.5.8 *Refusal of blood/alcohol test.* By s 19(2) of the 1978 Act the refusal to supply a specimen of blood may be used in evidence in charges under ss 49 and 50.

4.9.5.9 *Charge.* A charge of driving under the influence of intoxicating liquor or drugs has been held good and not void for duplicity in the *State (McGroddy) v Carr* [1975] IR 275. The re-enacted ss 49 and 50, however, use the word 'intoxicant', i.e. which covers both drink and drugs or a combination. Nevertheless, the decision is of relevance in prosecutions under s 51 of the 1961 Act (animals or pedal cycle) and s 59 of the 1978 Act (danger to traffic or self). The conviction should only be for one element.

There is provision for a person charged under s 49 to be convicted under s 50 and s 50(4)(b), the opposite does now apply (see s 49(4)(b) at para 4.9.3).

4.9.5.10 *Persons found drunk.* The full text of s 59 of the 1968 Act (person found in a public place being a source of danger to traffic or himself) is set out in para 4.9.3 above. The incapacity test applies. As to 'person', 'public place' and 'traffic', see para 7.9

There are many old statutes which contain similar prohibitions, e.g. Licensing (IR) Act 1872, s 12; Licensing (IR) Act 1836; Towns Improvement (IR) Act 1854; Licensing Act 1874; Summary Jurisdiction Act 1908.

4.9.5.11 *Animals and pedal cycles.* The full text of s 51 of the 1961 Act (as amended by s 48 of the 1968 Act and s 3(6) of the 1984 Act) is set out above at para 4.9.3. It relates to animal-drawn vehicles and pedal cycles been driven by persons under the influence of drink or drugs.

Older provisions of a related nature still in force are:

(i) Licensing (Ireland) Act 1872, s 12;
(ii) Intoxicating Liquor (General) Act 1924, s 30, as to appeals of persons drunk in charge of any carriage, horse or cattle on the highway or in a public place—fine £4 and/or one month's imprisonment;
(iii) Summary Jurisdiction (Ireland) Act 1908, s 7, as to persons drunk in charge of any person, animal or vehicle—fine £2 or one month's imprisonment.
They are rarely, if ever, used now.

4.9.6 Intoxicant concentration offences

4.9.6.1 *Basic concept.* Part V of the 1968 Act, which dealt with the concentration tests approach, originally was brought in as a result of the Davitt Report. Its provisions extended the law to include:

(a) a new offence of driving (attempting to, or being in charge of) a mechanically propelled vehicle when the driver's (or person's in charge) level of alcohol exceeds a concentration of 125 mg of alcohol per 100 ml of blood or 135 mg/100 ml urine;
(b) requiring drivers in certain circumstances to submit to breath, blood or urine tests, designed to scientifically measure their blood or urine alcohol content.

The 1968 Act was amended substantially by the 1973 Act, which in turn was totally repealed by the 1978 Act. The 1978 Act overcame a number of court decisions on technical proof and replaced earlier provisions in the 1968 and 1973 Acts.

The 1978 Act goes further than the Davitt Report, as the Report recommended that this concentration of alcohol should only be *prima facie evidence* of guilt. The Report made this recommendation because of the known variation in effect of alcohol on people. The 1978 Act (following the 1968 and 1973 Acts), however, creates an *offence* on the part of a driver having such a concentration, with the same consequences as in the 1961 Act. However, the 1960 British Medical Association Report (*supra*), at p 32 states:

> 'The Committee wishes to emphasise that it is impressed by the evidence of the rapidity with which driving ability deteriorates, even in the most hardened drinkers and the most experienced drivers, at concentrations of alcohol in the blood of 100 mg/100 ml.'

Professor MD Hickey, the then Irish State Pathologist and a member of the Davitt Commission, carried out tests for the Report (Appendix V). He emphasises that these are general tests and conclusions. Assuming that an 11-stone person was drinking rapidly, he gives the following table to illustrate the minimum intake of (a) Irish whiskey or gin, or (b) average beer or stout capable of producing certain blood alcohol levels.

4.9.6.1 *Intoxicated driving*

Blood alcohol level (mg per 100 ml)	*Whiskey or gin in fluid oz.*	*Beer or stout in pints*
90	4	2
100	4½	2¼
110	5	2½
125	5½	2¾
135	6	3
150	7	3½

The Irish 'small whiskey' measure is equivalent to 1¼ fluid oz.

In summary Professor Hickey stated:

> 'As a general guide it may be stated that a man of 11-stone weight would be unlikely to exceed a blood alcohol level of 125 mg unless he drank more than 6 small whiskeys or gins in a period of approximately 2 hours, or more than 4 pints of stout or beer in the same period.'

To those readers with more than an academic interest in the subject, it should be stressed that this whole paragraph is the merest guide and no more, and that the level since the 1978 Act is 100 mg/100 ml blood (or 135/100 urine), so the position is stringent. It is now (1989) being suggested that the level be dropped to 80/100 in Ireland. The EEC proposal is for a drop to 50/100 throughout the European Communities.

4.9.6.2 *Outline of provisions.* The offences relate only to mechanically propelled vehicles and to alcohol/drugs in respect of this type of test. This is because the 1978 Act defines 'intoxicant' in both s 49(1) and s 50(1) as including or combining both alcohol and drugs; but s 49(2), (3) and s 50(2), (3) relate only to alcohol and s 17 of the 1978 Act relates only to drugs.

The Act's main provisions are set out above in para 4.9.3, and in outline they are as follows:

(i) There is—
  (a) a need for a Garda to form the opinion that liquor has been consumed, then
  (b) a requirement for drivers and others to give a specimen of breath in certain circumstances to Gardai, with
  (c) refusal or failure to take breath test being an offence, and
  (d) a power to arrest and being brought to a Garda Station.

(ii) Subsequently there is a requirement to give a specimen of blood/ or urine to the Gardai doctor. Refusal or failure is an offence. The procedure for dealing with a specimen is set out, including sending it for analysis.

(iii) A parameter is set up of 100 mgs alcohol/100 ml blood (or 135/ 100 urine) as the prescribed limit in a three-hour period of detection. If a driver's alcohol/blood (urine) limit exceeds the prescribed limit, he may be charged with the offence(s).

(iv) A Bureau is set up to carry out specimen analysis.
(v) There are severe penalties—£1,000 fine and/or six months' imprisonment; mandatory disqualification and endorsement.

All procedures must be followed and be properly conducted.

In a dissenting judgment in *DPP v Kenny* [1980] IR 160, the then Chief Justice O'Higgins said:

> 'Where a statute provides a particular form of proof or evidence in compliance with certain statutory provisions, in my view it is essential that the precise statutory provisions be complied with. The courts cannot accept something other than that which is laid down by the statute, or overlook the absence of what the statute requires. To do so would be to trespass into the legislative field. This applies to all statutory requirements; but it applies with greater general understanding to penal statutes which create particular offences and then provide a particular method of proof. The Act of 1978 is a penal statute.'

See also *Scott v Baker* [1968] 2 All ER 993.

If the prosecution therefore fails to prove the necessary items, or any of them (subject to certain presumptions where the onus rests on the defence), or the evidence is illegal, the court may reject the charge. Examples of this are found in *DPP v Joyce* (1985) ILRM 206 (see para 4.9.6) and *DPP v Greely* (1985) ILRM 320.

In *State (Collins) v Kelliher* (Supreme Court, 18 November 1983, unreported) it was held that a defendant may not be convicted of charges arising out of the same incident under both s 49(1)(a) and either s 49(2) or s 49(3). It should be remembered, however, that if a person is charged under s 49 he may be found guilty under s 50 of the 1961 Act (in charge).

4.9.6.3 *Formal proofs*. In charges under s 49(2) (driving/attempting to drive with excess intoxicant in blood), s 49(3) (excess in urine), s 50(2) (in charge—blood) and s 50(3) (in charge—urine) the following formal proofs apply:

(1) *Person*. See para 7.9.
(2) (i) *Drive*. See para 7.9.
(3) (ii) *Attempt to drive*. see para 7.9.
(iii) *In charge with intent to drive or attempting to drive*. See para 7.9 as to both 'in charge' and 'intention to drive or attempting to drive'.
(3) *Mechanically propelled vehicle*. See para 7.9.
(4) *Public place*. See para 7.9.
(5) *Quantity of alcohol*. See para 4.9.6.7.
(6) *Within three hours*. See para 4.9.3 as to the Act; para 4.9.6.5 below and *DPP v Clinton* (1984) ILRM 127.
(7) *Arrest*. See para 7.9.
(8) *Improper concentration*. See para 4.9.6.2, i.e. over 100/110 ml blood or 135/100 urine.
(9) *Due procedures* for taking samples by Gardai and doctor. See para 4.9.6.6. See (a) below.

(10) *Due analysis* by Bureau, certification and notification. See para 4.9.6.7. See (b) below.
(11) *Proper court hearing*.

Presumptions
There are a number of presumptions to ease the prosecution case:

(a) that equipment is correct (para 4.9.6.4);
(b) that procedures by the doctor and Garda in relation to many aspects of taking and dealing with specimens are prima facie valid and that the doctor was duly a registered medical practitioner—s 21(4) and s 23(4) of the 1978 Act, i.e. Item (a) (see para 4.9.6.5);
(c) in relation to Item (10) (samples) above, s 23(2) of the 1978 Act provides that the Bureau certificate is prima facie sufficient evidence of compliance (para 4.9.6.7).

See comments on proofs at para 4.9.6.2 above.

4.9.6.4 *Obligatory breath test.*

Breathalyser test (s 12 of the 1978 Act)
The current breath test (generally known as the 'breathalyser' test) is in the nature of a screening test. It is not an offence to have a positive breath test, nor is it essential for the Garda to do the test. However, it will, if the test is done and is positive, make it clear that the basis of arrest is valid. Such a positive result from a breath test leads only to further tests (see para 4.9.6.5). The following is provided by s 12 of the 1978 Act (as amended by s 5 of the 1984 Act) as to breath tests:

(1) Whenever a member of the Garda Siochana is of the opinion that a person in charge of a mechanically propelled vehicle in a public place has consumed intoxicating liquor he may require him to provide, by inhaling into an apparatus for indicating the presence of alcohol in the breath, a specimen of his breath and may indicate the manner in which he is to comply with the requirement.
(2) A person who refuses or fails to comply forthwith with a requisition under this section, or to comply forthwith with such a requirement in a manner indicated by a Garda Siochana, shall be guilty of an offence and liable on summary conviction to imprisonment for a term not exceeding six months or, at the discretion of the Court, to a fine not exceeding £1,000 or to both.
(3) A member of the Garda Siochana may arrest, without warrant, a person who, in the member's opinion, is committing or has committed an offence under this section.
(4) In a prosecution for an offence under this section, it shall be presumed until the contrary is shown that an apparatus provided by a member of the Garda Siochana for the purpose of enabling a person to provide a specimen of breath is an apparatus for indicating the presence of alcohol in the breath.

The wording of the section has some features on which the following comments are made:

(a) As to 'arrest', 'a person', 'in charge', 'mechanically propelled vehicle', and 'public place', see para 7.9.

(b) It is sufficient that the person is 'in charge'. This concept is wider than that of driving or attempting to drive. The basic concept is therefore wider than s 7 of the English Road Traffic Act 1972, but the decision in *Blacke v Pope* (1987) RTR 77 seems to have brought the English position close to the Irish one. Also, there is no limitation on the concept of 'in charge' under this section as there is in s 50, i.e. of intending or attempting to drive. See also para 7.9 as to 'In charge'.

The question of identity is often resolved by admission, e.g. *DPP v Leonard* (1980) (High Court), where the defendant identified himself as a driver of one of three vehicles involved in an accident. *Held*: the Justice was wrong in dismissing the charge on the basis that there had been no evidence of driving.

(c) There is an absence of the need for the Garda to be 'in uniform', which has been a fruitful source of litigation in England. However, s 111 of the 1961 Act requires a Garda not in uniform to produce his official identity card on request. See para 7.2.

(d) It is sufficient for the Garda to be 'of the opinion' that an offence has been or is being committed. There is no stated requirement of a reasonable cause for the opinion as in the English Act. The nature of the opinion is solely that the person in charge has consumed intoxicating liquor—no time limit as to when this was consumed applies, even though the major offences deal with consumption and having an intoxicant in the body during a three-hour period.

In *DPP v Donoghue* (1987) ILRM 129 the relevance of the breath test to the Garda's opinion was summarised as follows:

(1) A breath test is relevant only in so far as it provides evidence which assists a member of the Gardai in the formation of his opinion.
(2) In arriving at his opinion a member of the Gardai is entitled to rely on his observations alone.
(3) Where an opinion has been reasonably arrived at and is honestly held, it must be accepted.

In *DPP v Gilmore* (1981) ILRM 102 it was held in the Supreme Court that a positive breath test on its own is not sufficient to justify a Garda's opinion that a driver is incapable of having proper control of a vehicle, but it is sufficient to justify an opinion that his blood/alcohol or urine/alcohol levels are above the prescribed limits. An arrest will therefore be valid, but a defendant must be charged with an offence specific to blood or urine levels and not simply with an offence of incapacity to drive.

In *DPP v Gray* (1987) ILRM 4 the Garda observed the defendant's car been driven from side to side. When the driver got out he was unsteady and there was a smell of alcohol on his breath. He was unable to open the boot. The District Justice discounted this evidence on the basis that he was dissatisfied with the answers given by the Garda in cross examination as to the distance covered, and the speed and length of time, concluding there were mathematical inaccuracies. The High Court held the Justice erred in law in dismissing the case, when the matter came before the High Court on a case stated. The Justice's determination should have been whether the Garda had arrived at his opinion reasonably, and he erred in concluding that the possibility of innocent explanations for the matter which gave rise to the Garda's opinion was sufficient to invalidate that opinion. The Court directed the Justice to convict.

In *Hobbs v Hurley* (High Court, unreported) 10 June 1980, (and followed in *DPP v Donoghue* (1987) ILRM 129 *supra*) it was stated that 'The opinion arrived at must, of course, be a reasonable one, and must be one which results from an honest belief come to after facts had been ascertained and considered'.

It is normally necessary for a Garda to state in evidence that he reached an opinion and why. However, in *DPP v O'Connor* (1984) ILRM 333, where the Garda did not give specific evidence of the formation of any opinion, the Supreme Court allowed it to be inferred from his conduct because he told the defendant that he was 'arresting him under s 49(6) of the 1961 Act for offences under s 49(2) and s 49(3)'. The Garda also had given evidence that the defendant swung wide on turning off and swerved twice, that his breath smelled of alcohol and that his speech was slurred.

In England (s 7 of the 1972 English Act) in *Blake v Pope* (1987) RTR 77 it was held that the constable's suspicions need not arise whilst the driver was still driving, and that there need be no immediate connection between the driving and the arrival and suspicion of the constable. A constable was able to require a test from the person who had been driving or in charge. The suspicion can arise following a random stop in England (*CC of Gwent v Dash* (1985) Crim LR 674).

Two English cases on reasonable grounds for suspicion (which seems to a lower standard than 'opinion') are *R v Fardy* (1973) RTR 268 and *R v McCall* (1974) RTR 217, which show it is a question of fact how far bad driving, which is possible for all drivers, drunk or sober, can support a reasonable suspicion that the driver has consumed alcohol.

See **(h)** below also.

(e) In England a request to a person who had parked his car, locked it, and was about to enter a house, having completed his journey came too late (see *Cambell v Tormey* (1969) Crim LR 1950 and *R v Wall* [1969] 1 WLR 400). However, in Ireland he may well still be 'in charge' of the vehicle. See *DPP v Gaffney* as to private dwellinghouses at **(i)** (5) below.

(f) There is no specified place where the test it to be administered. The section seems to anticipate that the Garda will have the apparatus with him. If he does not have the equipment with him, and is of the opinion that the person is unfit to drive or will fail a 'concentration' test, he presumably will arrest him under his general power in s 49(6) of the 1961 Act. In *R v Clarke* (1969) Crim LR 441 a driver who drove off because the equipment was not at hand was held to have failed to take the test.

In *DPP v Joyce* (1985) ILRM 206 a breath test made in a private yard was inadequate, and rendered the subsequent arrest invalid, because the Garda formed his opinion on that basis (see **(i)** below as to *DPP v Gaffney*, etc.).

(g) A specimen of the driver's breath should be taken by his 'exhaling into an apparatus and (the Garda) may indicate the manner in which he is to comply with the requirement'. Under the earlier provisions there were regulations governing this procedure, but these regulations were repealed. The Garda should presumably provide an apparatus designed for the purpose of indicating the presence of alcohol in the breath, ensuring it is free from alcohol and following the instructions for the equipment. The person then exhales from his lungs into the apparatus so that the part of the apparatus designed to collect a specimen of breath is filled.

If the driver has, say, a lung condition that prevents him from complying with such directions, presumably it would provide a defence (see **(k)** below).

(h) 'Apparatus' is not defined in the Act, although the act of 1984 raises a presumption of the nature of the apparatus in s 12(4). It is presumed, until the contrary is shown, that it is an apparatus for indicating the presence of alcohol in the breath. However, that presumption is not all embracing.

There is no presumption that at the time of the specimen either the apparatus (a) was in order or (b) worked or was used properly. In *The State (Murray) v Clifford* (High Court, 4 February 1980 unreported) it was held by the High Court that generally there was no requirement to produce such apparatus in court. The Court did envisage production to be necessary, however, in cases where the accused, by reason of a patent defect or of appearance, considers that it was possibly not a proper apparatus or not of proper construction or design.

How will its suitability be disproved? How is the test result proved to be properly taken? These questions created considerable difficulty at first in England (*Scott v Baker* [1969] 1 QB 659). If the point is taken by the defence, the suitability of the device must be competently proved—*R v Gwillium* [1968] 1 WLR 1939 (label on box insufficient); *R v Holt* [1968] 1 WLR 1942 (evidence of an official with knowledge of approval of equipment sufficient). A useful review of the procedure on the administration of an alcotest device is found in *DPP v Carey* [1969] 3 All ER 1662. The provision of equipment generally is a matter for the Bureau (see para 4.9.6.12).

It can be commented that these provisions are rather vague now, as the more specific provisions of the 1968 Act and the regulations thereunder have been repealed.

In England it is held that if not following the instructions prejudiced the defendant, then the result may be inadmissible (see *Attorney-*

General's Reference No 1 1978 RTR 377; *DPP v Carey* [1970] AC 1072 (above)).

In *R v Holah* (1973) RTR 74 a person who did not fully inflate the bag, although the crystals turned green, was not held to have failed to supply a specimen (see **(k)** below also). In *Cotgrove v Cooney* (1987) Crim LR 272 a person who tried as hard as he could to blow but failed, was acquitted as having a reasonable excuse.

The Irish legislation has many presumptions raising the validity of actions and qualfications under the Acts (see para 4.9.6.3). No such far-reaching presumptions are found in the English legislation. It may well be challenged, under the 1937 Constitution, that these presumptions create an unfair onus on the defence. The defence have little control over the actions, equipment and procedures involved and face a virtually impossible task in challenging them.

The type of equipment used in Ireland in 1988 is the 'Alcolyser', which is supplied by the Medical Bureau of Road Safety, Department of Forensic Medicine, University College, Earlsfort Terrace, Dublin 2. Instructions are issued with each kit. These instructions read as follows:

'Wait 15 minutes after alcoholic drink before testing. Then—

(a) Cut and break off each end of the tube in the saw aperture provided. Remove mouth-piece cap.

(b) Push Red band end of the tube into the neck of the plastic bag, and insert the arrow end of the tube firmly into the exposed mouth-piece.

(c) Take a deep breath and blow steadily until the bag is fully inflated (blowing time 10–20 seconds), more than one breath may be used if necessary.'

And the instructions have diagrams as follows:

'Alcohol in breath turns yellow crystals green'.

Red	Green stain in the lower part of the tube but NOT EXCEEDING to the Red mark
Yellow	
Green	BELOW LIMIT

Red	Green stain extending UP to the Red mark
Green	ABOVE LIMIT

If the case of *Cracknell v Willis* (1987) NLJ 1061 is followed in Ireland, an accused will be allowed to produce indirect evidence (e.g. no alcohol consumption in fact) of the machine's non-function.

(i) Subsection (3) (para 4.9.6.4(3)) as to powers of arrest is curiously worded. The only offences under the section are in subs (2) (i.e. refusing or failing to comply with a requisition). The subsection seems to be aimed, therefore, at a power of arrest of a person who is *likely* to fail a breath test, i.e. a person who in the Garda's opinion 'has committed' an offence. Presumably, though, the subsection will be confined to allowing the arrest of persons failing to supply a proper breath test.

In *DPP v Corrigan* (1987) ILRM 575 the defendant was arrested in the driveway of his home after a chase. The Garda was of the opinion that he had consumed alcohol to such an extent that he was unfit to drive. The District Justice dismissed the charge under s 13 of the 1978 Act (failing to give a specimen in Garda Station). It was held in the High Court that an arrest without warrant under a statutory authority is not unlawful merely because it did not occur in a public place or because the Gardai were in law trespassers. A peaceful entry for the purpose of effecting an arrest is lawful, irrespective of whether any consent to enter is sought or given. This case might have had a different result if the Garda relied on other observations for the arrest. See also para 7.2.5 and 7.9 as to arrest.

It should be remembered that the request and arrest must be made in a public place (see para 7.9). Thus, a request in a private yard is invalid (*DPP v Joyce* (1985) ILRM 206). The following cases specifically relate to this area also:

(1) *Hobbs v Hurley* (High Court, 10 June 1980) held—

(i) It is not necessary for the Garda to have in mind any one of the specific offences under s 49 when effecting arrest once he has formed an opinion that an offence is committed under the section.

(ii) The Garda opinion must be a reasonable one, which results from an honest belief arrived at after the facts have been ascertained and considered.

(iii) The Garda's opinion is not dictated by positive scientific knowledge of the concentration of alcohol.

(2) In *DPP v Gray* (1987) ILRM 4, *Hobbs v Hurley* was specifically referred to and followed. See **(d)** above. In both cases, observations such as manner of driving, demeanour, smell of alcohol, bloodshot eyes and unsteadiness were sufficient to base an opinion on.

(3) In *DPP v Closkey* (High Court, 6 February 1984) (See Solicitors Gazette, May 1985, Green Pages) the defendant was arrested in his home, where he was apparently asleep. He had been involved in an accident a short time before. His sister resisted and obstructed arrest. The High Court considered the arrest in the specific circumstances lawful. See *DPP v Gaffney* ((5) below) which is

contrary. It distinguished on its facts the leading English case of *Morris v Beardmore* (1980) RTR 321, where the House of Lords held an arrest unlawful where the defendant himself had required the police to leave the house.

(4) In *DPP v Joyce* (1985) ILRM 206, where a Garda relied for his power to arrest on a test taken in a private yard, it was held to be an improper test and tainted with illegality and, therefore, the arrest was invalid.

(5) In *DPP v Gaffney* (1988) ILRM 39 the Gardai chased the defendant to his home. They were refused entry by his brother. Nevertheless they entered, looking for information under s 107 of the 1961 Act. It was held by the Supreme Court that there was a violation of Art 40.5 of the Constitution and unlawful.

As to arrests generally, see para 7.9.

(j) There is no set form of words in which the *demand* for a breath specimen must be made (*R v Clarke* [1969] 1 WLR 1109). In *R v O'Boyle* (1973) RTR 445 the words 'I intend to give you a breath test', were held to be sufficient.

If the police officer honestly believes, and is reasonable in his belief, that the person could hear and understand him, that is sufficient even if the person in fact did not (R *v Nicholls* (1972) RTR 308).

(k) The Act makes no provision as to the *quantity* of the breath test. The section says it must be by 'exhaling', presumably from the lungs, a 'specimen of his breath'. In *Brennan v Farrell* (1969) Crim LR 494 where the device was inflated by two breaths this was held sufficient. That was a Scottish case and is probably more akin to Irish thinking. A contrary decision was reached in England in *R v Chapman* [1969] 2 WLR 1004, where it was held that the approval of the Secretary of State of the test device included the approval of the instructions with it (one breath).

The Irish Act does not clarify the position. The English 1972 Act, s 12(3) does, by requiring a sufficient sample to enable the test to be carried out. However, in *Corp v Dalton* (1983) RTR 160, in construing 'fails to provide' in the English section the court held that where a driver fails to comply with the manufacturer's instructions in inflating the bag it is a question of fact and degree whether he fails to supply a specimen. The instructions referred to at **(h)** above specify 10–20 seconds, which is a relatively long time. See **(1)** below.

(l) There is on the face of the section no apparent defence of 'reasonable excuse' for failure to provide a breath test (e.g. lung complaint) as in the case of a blood test. If, however, the Courts apply the doctrine of *mens rea*, such a defence should arise.

In *R v Chapman* [1969] 2 WLR 1004 (*supra*) it was stated that being too drunk to inflate the bag is no excuse. In *R v Lennard* [1973] 1 WLR 483 it was stated that an excuse would not be reasonable unless the person was physically or mentally unable to provide the specimen or it provided a substantial risk to his health (see also *Teape v Godrey* (1986) RTR 213—asthmatic condition is insufficient unless the person does his best). In *McGrath v Ripas* (1983) Crim LR 628 it was held that a belief that a test was unnecessary because the suspect was not the driver was not a reasonable excuse. In *Cotgrove v Cooney* (1987) Crim LR 272 a person who tried as hard as he could to provide a breath specimen was acquitted even though he failed to supply it. He had a reasonable excuse of failure. In *Davis v DPP* Crim LR 249 it was held the test as to whether there is a medical Reason (asthma and a heavy cold started) for failure to provide a breath specimen is an objective one i.e. not the defendant's or the Police opinion. It is a question of fact to be decided by the Court.

In *DPP v Billington and others* (4 cases) 1988 Crim LR 772 held that one cannot refuse a specimen until the arrival of a solicitor unless police agree. These cases and commentary are useful as the Criminal Justice Act 1984 (P.A.C.E. English) are dealt with in principle.

There is doubt about the position where alcohol is consumed subsequent to driving—see *Glendinning v Bell* (1973) RTR 52 which was favourable to it being a defence; and *Williams v Critchley* (1979) RTR 46 which was against.

Contrast this position with s 15(2)(b) below ('Other obligatory breath tests') and s 19 (para 4.9.6.8).

(m) No special provision is made for taking tests on persons removed to *hospital*, unlike s 9 of the 1972 English Act. The Garda Station seems to be the only place for blood/urine tests, but apparently a breath specimen can be taken anywhere if it has resulted from a driver being in charge in a public place and the Garda is of the opinion that the driver has consumed intoxicating drink. No express power to enter private property is given (see *DPP v Gaffney* at **(i)** (5) above.

(n) It is difficult to know the *evidential value* of a positive breath test. A positive result is not in itself an offence. The Garda merely presses on to the more scientific tests of blood and urine. The Act is silent as to whether these breath tests are themselves admissible in evidence. Presumably, the Courts will consider them *relevant* evidence, but certainly not as *conclusive*. At present they are evidence only of the presence or absence of alcohol in the person's breath. A positive result is a base for the Garda opinion (see para 4.9.6.4**(d)** *supra*).

(o) There appears to be no bar to requiring a *second test* (*Owen v Morgan* (1986) RTR 151). See also *Nugent v Ridley* (1987) RTR 412 (para 4.9.6.6 below).

(p) The penalties for not giving a breath specimen are:

(i) up to six month's imprisonment—s 12(2) of the 1978 Act;
(ii) up to £1,000 fine—s 12(2) of the 1978 Act amended by s 5 of the 1984 Act;
(iii) optional endorsement (para 2.10);
(iv) optional disqualification (para 2.9).

Other obligatory breath tests (ss 15 and 16 of the 1978 Act)

The 1978 Act envisaged better equipment being available to the Gardai, whereby they could carry out an accurate test of alcohol content on the roadside or at the Garda Station. It was for this purpose that s 15 was enacted. Section 15 provides, with s 16, a base for a once-off test on the roadside or elsewhere using this more specific type of equipment.

The device known as the Lion Intoximeter 3600 is used under s 6 of the 1972 British Act for this sort of test in Britain. It is not yet in operation in the Republic of Ireland, but experiments on its use are being undertaken in Ireland in 1988 with three types of machines on a voluntary basis (Circular by the Department of the Environment of 27 April 1988). The type will be Intoximeter 30001 (Lion Labaratories); Camic XK 120 (Camic Limited); Datamaster II (Eastern Electronics). Each of these operate on the principle of infra red absorption at selected wavelengths. Each machine contains a calibration device called an *alcohol simulator*. This simulator is used to test the machine with a standard alcohol vapour before and after the person provides breath samples for analysis.

A standard sequence of testing for evidential purposes on such a machine would be (i) alcohol simulator test, (ii) test of first breath specimen from the person, (iii) second similar specimen from the person, and (iv) alcohol simulator test. If the results in either simulator test fall outside certain set limits, then the testing sequence as a whole is aborted and no print out is available. When acceptable simulator test results are obtained, a full print out of the results is provided by the machine.

The experimental voluntary testing is being carried out under the supervision of the Medical Bureau of Road Safety at six Garda Stations. The testing period will be concluded at the end of 1988 and the results will be evaluated by a group representing the Gardai, the Medical Bureau, the Department of the Environment, the Department of Justice and the Director of Public Prosecutions. It is to be anticipated that these machines will be introduced in 1989, as they are more accurate than the present machines and give more information.

The 1984 Act increases the penalties in the event of the system operating. In a leading English case of *Crackness v Willis* (1987) NLJ 1061, however, it was held that a driver who has provided specimens of breath for a Lion Intoximeter machine is entitled to adduce evidence which, although not direct evidence of the machine's malfunctioning, nevertheless provides material from which it may be reasonably inferred that the machine was unreliable In *Lodge v C.C.G. Manchester* [1988] Crim LR 533 a 23.1% discrepancy between 2 readings did not lead the court to disregarding the result. An odd decision.

Section 15 of the 1978 Act (as amended by s 5 of the 1984 Act) reads as follows:

> (1) Whenever a member of the Garda Siochana is of the opinion that a person in charge of a mechanically propelled vehicle in a public place has consumed intoxicating liquor, he may require him to provide, by exhaling into an apparatus for indicating the concentration of alcohol in breath or blood, a specimen of his breath and may indicate the manner

in which or the place (including a vehicle) where he is to comply with the requirement, or both the manner and the place.

(2)(a) Subject to paragraph (b) of this subsection, a person who refuses or fails to comply forthwith with a requirement under this section, or to comply forthwith with such a requirement in a manner or place indicated by a member of the Garda Siochana, shall be guilty of an offence and liable on summary conviction to imprisonment for a term not exceeding six months, or, at the discretion of the court, to a fine not exceeding £1,000, or to both.

(b) It shall be a good defence to a prosecution for an offence under this section to show that, as soon as practicable after the refusal or failure, the defendant offered to permit a designated registered medical practitioner to take from him a specimen of the defendant's blood.

(3) A member of the Garda Siochana may arrest without warrant a person who in the member's opinion is committing or has committed an offence under this section, and a person so arrested shall be deemed to be a person arrested under section 16(4).

(4) In a prosecution for an offence under this section it shall be presumed until the contrary is shown that an apparatus provided by a member of the Garda Siochana for the purpose of enabling a person to provide a specimen of breath is an apparatus for indicating the concentration of alcohol in breath or blood.

Many of the considerations referred to in para 4.9.6.4 above apply. However, the powers of the Garda are wider in that they allow him to indicate the manner and place (including a vehicle) of the test. There is also a specific defence in the case of refusal or failure to comply with the section that, as soon as practicable, the defendant offered to a designated medical practitioner a blood sample. The presumption of the type of apparatus does not extend to presuming that it is (a) working properly, or (b) worked properly.

Section 16 of the 1978 Act (as amended by s 5 of the 1984 Act) reads as follows:

(1) Where, consequent on a requirement under section 15 on him, a person provides a specimen of his breath and the apparatus indicates that he has committed an offence under section 49(2) of the Principal Act, he shall be supplied forthwith by a member of the Garda Siochana with a written statement indicating the concentration of alcohol in the person's blood.

(2) On receipt of the statement referred to in subsection (1) the person shall forthwith acknowledge such receipt in writing by his signature as requested by the member of the Garda Siochana.

(3) A person who refuses to comply with subsection (2) shall be guilty of an offence and liable on summary conviction to imprisonment for a term not exceeding three months or, at the discretion of the court, to a fine not exceeding £350, or to both.

(4) A member of the Garda Siochana may arrest without warrant a person who refuses or fails to comply with subsection (2).

(5) Where a person arrested under subsection (4) (or a person deemed under

section 15(3) to be a person so arrested) has been brought to a Garda Station, a member of the Garda Siochana may require the person to permit a designated registered medical practitioner to take from the person a specimen of his blood or, at the person's option, to provide for the designated registered medical practitioner a specimen of the person's urine.

(6) A person who, following a requirement under subsection (5)—

(a) refuses or fails to comply with such a requirement, or

(b) refuses or fails to comply with a requirement of a designated registered medical practitioner in relation to the taking under this section of a specimen of blood or the provision under this section of a specimen of urine,

shall be guilty of an offence and liable on summary conviction to imprisonment for a term not exceeding six months or, at the discretion of the court, to a fine not exceeding £1,000, or to both.

(7) Notwithstanding a refusal by a person to comply with subsection (2), the relevant statement referred to in subsection (1) may be tendered as evidence in a prosecution for an offence under section 49 or 50 of the Principal Act or an offence under this Part.

In relation to subs (5) there is a presumption that the person refused a sample to a registered medical practitioner (s 23(3) of the 1978 Act).

There is consequential mandatory disqualification for one year on a first offence and three years on a second and subsequent offence(s) under the 1961 Act, First Schedule, as amended by ss 24 and 25 of the 1978 Act. Oddly, endorsement is apparently discretionary.

It may well be that, notwithstanding the absence of equipment, the sections are not operated to date as they are curiously weak. They merely provide that the statement of the test result can be used in a prosecution under s 49 (intoxicated driving or attempt) or s 50 (in charge while intoxicated) as evidence. This is so even if the accused refuses to acknowledge receipt of the test result. However, the sections do not provide for an offence where that reading is over the limit, nor do they raise any presumption as to the evidential value of the statement of the result of the test. What weight is a court to attach to it?

Note also the provisions of s 13(4) and 14(5) of the 1978 Act, which envisage use of this type of equipment in Garda Stations after the present type of screening is carried out. These subsections raise a presumption of the validity of these pieces of equipment, i.e. that the apparatus is a valid measuring apparatus, until the contrary is shown. Again, refusal or failure to comply is an offence, but also no provision is made in those sections as to the exact evidential value, presumptively or otherwise, of the result.

4.9.6.5 *Specimens in a Garda Station.*

When a person is arrested under s 49(6) (intoxicated driving) or 50(8) ('in charge' while intoxicated) of the 1961 Act or under s 12(3) (fails breathalyser test) of the 1978 Act, he is taken to a Garda Station. In the unreported case of *DPP v Michael Sheehy* in the High Court, an arrested person was told he would be taken to a named Garda Station but it was found that there was no equipment there. He was taken to another Garda Station where the equipment was available. It was held that that was in order. The judgment was apparently extempore, and no reference to it is available at the time of writing.

At the Garda station the arrested person can be required to give both (or either):

(i) a further breath specimen into a machine an apparatus for indicating the concentration of alcohol in his breath. This is the type of machine envisaged under ss 15 and 16 of the 1978 Act and which is not in use in Ireland yet (1988), although undergoing tests (see para 4.9.6.4); and/or
(ii) a blood or urine specimen; under ss 13 and 14 of the 1978 Act.

These sections indicate that the arrested person should be brought to a Garda Station, and a Garda may at his discretion require the person to give either or both:

(a) a further screening breath test in the manner referred to in (i) above (or into an exhaling apparatus)
(b) require the person to permit a registered medical practitioner to take specimen of blood or, at the accused person's option, a urine specimen.

It is not necessary, nor indeed normally would it be proper to charge the person because he was arrested. Persons should only be charged if the available evidence (not suspicions) indicates that they have committed an offence. As the results of a test will not be known for some time, persons are not in fact normally charged.

In relation to a person taking or being refused specimens under s 13(1) or s 14(1), there is a presumption raised by s 23(3) of the 1978 Act that such a person is a registered medical practitioner.

Cases

In *DPP v Clinton* (1984) ILRM 127 it was held it is not necessary to prove the time of driving or of attempting to drive in a charge under s 13(3) of refusing or failing to comply with a requirement to provide a specimen, i.e. within three hours. That is a matter for the defence.

Refusal to give a sample can be direct or indirect. This was held in *Solesbury v Pugh* [1969] 1 WLR 114, where a person who insisted on the blood sample being taken from his big toe only, which the doctor was not agreeable to do, was held to have refused (see para 4.9.6.9).

A defendant who gave too small a specimen of urine for analysis was held to have failed to provide a specimen *(R v Coward* (1976) RTR 425).

A procedural point arose in *Moloney v Stanley* (High Court, 2 April 1984). The defendant opted for a urine test. He failed to give a sample after 20 minutes. He was asked to give a blood sample but refused. The charge sheet filled in at the Garda Station alleged that the accused had failed to permit the doctor to take a specimen of urine, or, at his option a blood sample. It was held this was not a fatal flaw and ought to be amended before conviction was entered by the Justice (see para 4.9.6.8 further in this case).

4.9.6.5 *Intoxicated driving*

In *Connolly v Sallinger* (1982) ILRM 482 it was held:

(1) The defendant's election to provide a blood or urine specimen is not irreversible.
(2) If the option to provide urine alone is made and the accused fails so to provide, he is failing to supply a specimen.
(3) Where the defendant had been informed that failure or refusal to provide a blood or urine specimen was an offence, the defendant failed to give a urine sample and then gave a blood sample; there was no need for a further caution that he was not obliged to give a blood sample which could be used to incriminate him. There is no need at any stage of the proceedings to give any caution, though the giving of a caution when the option was offered was 'very proper and very fair'.

In *State (Quinn) v Connellon* (High Court), 9 July 1984 it was held it was not necessary for the prosecution to prove that the doctor had used any particular equipment, or that the equipment was provided by the Bureau.

In instructions on the 1978 Act, issued by the Assistant Commissioner of the Garda, it is stated:

(1) Following the arrival of the Garda Doctor, the member of the Garda should formally identify the arrested person and the Doctor to each other.
(2) If the arrested person opts for a 'urine sample', the doctor will require that person to empty his bladder and then within 30 minutes approximately thereafter to provide him with a specimen of his urine in the urine jug provided.

If the accused fails to provide the urine specimen he can then, it appears, be required to give a blood specimen. The accused has the right to refuse or fail to supply the alternative blood test only for 'a special and substantial reason' (see para 4.9.8.7), otherwise he must be reasonable in his supplying of a sample. Thus, in *McPhail v Farbes* (1975) SLT 48 a driver who merely said 'please yourself' when asked for a blood or urine sample was held to have refused, as was a driver who offered his big toe to take blood from (*Solesbury v Pugh* (above)).

If the defendant refuses to provide a specimen and then changes his mind and offers a sample, the offence is committed (*Harris v Tudmore* (1985) SCCR 305). In *Ranston v Higgins* (1972) RTR 456 it was held that a person 'refuses' if he agrees to provide blood but in a different manner (e.g. capillary specimen from thumb) from that requested by the doctor (intravenous from arm requested).

Where a person consented to a blood test but the doctor could not extract enough, and then the person refused to give a urine specimen, there was no offence (*R v Taylor* (1974) RTR 554). Similarly, if police wrongly throw away a specimen of urine, the accused cannot be convicted for refusing when asked for a second one (*R v Hymas* [1972] 3 All ER 651).

In *Bayliss v Thames Valley Police* (1978) RTR 328 there was held to be no refusal by a defendant who allowed only his own doctor, who was present, to take a specimen. In *Wyllie v Crown Prosecution Service* (1988) Crim LR 753 the prosecution was allowed to amend an information by substituting a charge of failure to supply a blood sample for one of failing to supply a urine sample.

As to the size of a specimen, *Smith v Cole* [1971] 1 All ER 200 stated it must be 'of a quantity and quality capable of analysis by the use of ordinary equipment and ordinary skill by a reasonably competent analyst.'

In *Hobbs v Clarke* (1988) RTR 36 an appeal was allowed against a conviction where the defendant was not made aware of the alternative tests.

Oppressive behaviour by the police in obtaining samples gives a discretion to the court to exclude the evidence (*Matto v Wolverhampton CC* (1987) RTR 337).

In this regard the 1978 Act does not spell out how exactly the specimen is to be taken. In *Rowlands v Harper* (1972) RTR 469 the Sergeant assembled the syringe, needle and containers. The Justices dismissed the charge, having doubt that a true specimen was taken. The decision was upheld on appeal. (see doctors' duties below).

The principle of lawful arrest still applies in Ireland. *Scott v Baker* (para 4.9.6.2) has in reality been overruled in *Fox v Gwent CC* (1985) RTR 337 in England, as s 8(1) of the Road Traffic Act 1972, amended by the Transport Acts 1981 and 1982, allows a specimen to be taken in the course of an investigation. Modern English law diverges significantly from Irish law.

Penalties

If a person fails to give (by refusal or failure to supply) a breath sample, or blood or urine sample he is guilty of an offence with penalties of:

(a) up to six months' imprisonment; and/or
(b) £1,000 fine;
(c) endorsement—mandatory in s 13, but not under s 12 of the 1978 Act; and
(d) (i) disqualification, which is consequential under s 13(2) (failing to give breath sample in Garda Station); s 13(3) (failing to give blood or urine sample in Garda Station); Minimum of six months in s 17 (drugs) but one year in s 13 of the 1978 Act,
(ii) disqualification is also consequential under s 14 of the 1978 Act for a second and subsequent offence within a period of three years (and one adds previous offences under ss 49, 50 of the 1961 Act, s 30(3) of the 1968 Act and s 13 of the 1984 Act),
(iii) disqualification which is otherwise optional, e.g. under s 12 or for a first offence under s 14.

The Probation Act 1907 s 1(1) cannot be applied to either of these offences in s 49 charges (driving or attempting to drive) under s 13(8) of the 1978 Act. This presumably means it can be applied in the other offences.

Apparatus

A presumption of the correctness of an apparatus for taking breath specimens is provided for in both ss 13 and 14 in the same manner as discussed at para 4.9.6.4 **(h)**.

4.9.6.6 *Dealing with specimens at Garda Stations.* Where a person has been lawfully arrested and has been brought to a Garda Station, and has been required by a member of the Garda Siochana to give a specimen at that person's own option by either:

(i) permitting a designated registered medical practitioner to take a specimen of blood; or
(ii) providing for the designated medical practitioner a specimen of urine;

and that person has so provided a specimen; then there are statutory and regulatory provisions as to the procedure in dealing with the specimen—

(1) by the doctor;
(2) by the Garda;
(3) by the Bureau.

There have been a number of legislative attempts at defining the procedures for dealing with specimens. The present law as to doctors' and Gardai duties is basically in s 21 of the 1978 Act which, it should be said, is a brief section. The duties of the Bureau are set out at para 4.9.6.7 below.

Section 21 of the 1978 Act does not set out in any detail what procedure should be followed in any particular case. It merely provides general directives. In this, it is not like earlier Acts and Regulations.

The section deals with a specimen duly taken after a proper arrest and requirement has been made. Nowhere now is the actual procedure for taking a sample set out in the Acts. It imposes a series of duties on the designated registered medical practitioner (doctor) and on the Garda, with presumptions that they acted properly.

Doctors' duties (s 21(1) of the 1978 Act)
To take the specimen the Bureau provides two types of kit. The kit for blood samples is marked 'B' in red; and that for urine is marked 'U' in black.

The blood sample kit contains an unused disposable syringe and needle attached; an alcohol-free towelette; two specimen bottles in containers, each bottle containing sodium fluoride and potassium oxalate as preservative and anticoagulant; self-adhesive white labels for labelling the bottles and their containers; two red seals bearing the Bureau's crest for sealing the containers; and a certificate in duplicate for completion by the doctor. The doctor takes a specimen of venous blood using the syringe provided. The instructions say that it should, if possible, be 10 ml of blood, but a minimum of 4 ml is permitted. If 4 ml cannot be obtained, the doctor is instructed to record failure and no specimen is forwarded.

The urine sample kit contains two specimen bottles in containers, each bottle containing phenyl mecuric nitrate as a preservative; self-adhesive white labels for labelling the bottles and their containers; two red seals bearing the Bureau's Crest for sealing the containers; and a certificate in duplicate for completion by the doctor. The doctor requests the person to provide a specimen of urine in an unused disposable receptacle which the Garda will provide (although it might be asked how is it to be shown that this receptacle is uncontaminated?). The specimen should be of sufficient volume to fill both specimen bottles. If it is not, it is necessary for the person after an interval to give a further specimen to the required volume.

In *State (Quinn) v Connellan* (unreported, High Court, 9 July 1984) it was held there was no onus on the prosecution to show that the doctor used any particular equipment or that the Bureau provided it.

In *Nugent v Ridley* (1987) RTR 412 it was held that a third, or even later, sample, provided it was taken properly, may be sent for analysis.

If there is a mishap with a kit a second one should be opened. See also para 4.9.6.12 below as to Bureau equipment.

By s 21(1) (having duly taken or obtained the sample), the doctor divides the specimen into *two parts* which he places into two containers which are immediately sealed and one of which must be offered to the defendant by the Garda. The part given to the defendant must be capable of analysis (*Thompson v Charlwood* (1969) 113 Sol Jo. There is no duty at law to inform the accused to store sample (*Doctorine v Watts* (1970) RTR 305). In *A-G v Hollingsworth* 107 ILTR 77 it was held in the Supreme Court that merely stopping the container with a screw-on top did not constitute 'sealing'. However, Hench J said:

> 'There should be no difficulty in complying in future cases. All that is necessary is that the medical practitioner be provided with a sealing agent with which to seal the screw-on top, so as to ensure that the screw top may not be removed without breaking the seal'.

In the instructions issued to Gardai and doctors about these samples it is more specifically stated that the doctor should:

(i) divide the specimen into two parts by pouring half of the specimen into each of the specimen bottles provided. In urine samples both bottles should be full to their shoulder;

(ii) Place each part in a glass container, which he will close in the manner provided and identify by affixing a white adhesive strip containing the person's name and the date. In blood samples, before doing that it is necessary to close the bottles with the screw caps by repeated inversion—otherwise clotting may occur which would lead to the specimen being rejected by the analyst;

(iii) place each part into a separate, protective, cylindrical cardboard container which he will again identify as in (ii) and seal with the adhesive red coloured seal of the medical Bureau placed in a horizontal position on the cylindrical cardboard container so that the seal adheres to both parts of the container.

Having thus performed these procedures with regard to the specimen, the doctor must then complete the *form of certificate* (in duplicate) prescribed.

This form is set out in the Road Traffic (Amendment) Act 1978 (Part III) Regulations 1978 (SI 193/1978), First Schedule. It sets out the name and address of the person from whom the specimen is taken, the nature of the specimen taken, (Blood/urine), the Garda Station at which the specimen was taken, and the time. It also states that the doctor took the sample divided out into two parts, placed each part in a container, sealed and labelled those containers and gave both to the Garda.

There is no provision in the Act for the furnishing of a copy to the defendant of this form. In *The State (Higgins) v Reed* (1983) ILRM 310 the defendant's solicitor applied for and did not receive a copy of the form in advance of the District Court hearing. On a mandamus application for it to the High Court, it was held that the issue of its availability to the defence was a matter for the District Justice to consider. The decision does not clarify the issue, but the prosecution did in fact supply a copy of the certificate.

The manner of completing the form was considered in:

(1) *DPP v Collins* (1981) ILRM 447. The Doctor did not insert his name in the form in the place provided showing he was a designated registered medical practitioner, but he did sign it. He also omitted to delete in full a line referring to a specimen of urine, having taken a blood sample. The Supreme Court rejected the defence that the form was not duly completed. It stated the form must be looked at as a whole, the doctor's signature covering the first point and the second point was 'an obvious slip' of no misleading consequence.

(2) *DPP v O'Neill* (Supreme Court, 30 July 1984). The doctor filled in, in the space provided in the form, the time at 12.50, not specifying am or pm. The court held this was not fatal, as the defendant could not have been under a misapprehension as to the time or prejudiced by this omission. See also *DPP v McPartland* (1983 High Court) where it was held that an incorrect date of the medical certificate was not sufficient ground to merit dismissal.

Garda Duties (s 21(2)(3) of the 1978 Act

A member of the Garda shall (having received two samples from the Doctor—see above) offer to the person arrested one of the sealed containers, together with a statement in writing indicating that he may retain either of the containers; ('Pink slip') for blood ('Yellow slip') for urine.

The Gardai instructions by the Assistant Commissioner in 1978 state correctly that the arrested person's right to this option of accepting a sample should be emphasised. If the person opts to take one of the samples, it should be placed in an envelope stamped with the Station stamp. The instructions point out that there is no option about giving the slip of paper. Version of these slips in Irish are apparently available.

In *R v Kersberg* (1976) RTR 526 a conviction was quashed where there was a lingering doubt as to the correctness of the official analyst's (108 mg) result as against the defendant's sample analysis (70 mg).

Having performed the above duties, the Garda shall as soon as practicable cause to be forwarded to the Bureau the form referred to in s 21(1) (i.e. doctor's form completed) together with the relevant sealed container (or, where the person has declined to retain one of the sealed containers, both relevant containers).

In *DPP v Kenny* [1980] IR 160 the Garda sent a duplicate form of the

Doctor's certificate, being the lower one of a carbon set. The Supreme Court held it was sufficient.

The 1978 Instructions state that the specimen (or both parts if the arrested person declines to take a part) should be placed in a cardboard box from which the blood/urine containers were originally taken, together with the doctor's certificate, closed with the adhesive label already forming part of the box which bears the name and address of the Medical Bureau, and arrangements must be made for delivery to the Bureau by registered post as soon as practicable. They also state that the boxes containing blood equipment are to be clearly marked B (in red), and U (in black) in the case of urine. These instructions suggest that the Garda should give the doctor the Station stamp to be impressed on the part of the certificate on which he records the Station and that the Garda should check that the certificate is distinctly legible where the name and the address of the arrested person is set out.

As already mentioned there is a duty on the Garda to forward the specimen(s) and the doctor's form *as soon as practicable*. There is a similar duty on the Bureau to effect analysis and forward the result (see para 4.9.6.7 below). There has been considerable litigation about the time span this entails in regard to both duties. In *DPP v Byrne* (Supreme Court, 21 March 1984) the court held that it was for the defence to get over the presumption the statute raised that its requirements are met. In this case, evidence has not been adduced that it was practicable to forward the container and doctor's form sooner than they were in fact sent to the Bureau. In the event the Garda had delayed sending them for a number of days. See other cases at para 4.9.6.7 below.

Presumptions

(i) In any subsequent prosecution it shall be presumed, until the contrary is shown, that subs (1), (doctor's duties), (2) and (3) (Garda Duties) of s 21 have been complied with (s 21(4) of the 1978 Act);

(ii) There is, in addition to the presumption set out above, a presumption under s 23(1) of the 1978 Act that the doctor's form is sufficient evidence of the facts stated therein, without proof of any signature on it, or that the signatory was the proper person to sign it. That subsection also creates a presumption that the doctor complied with all the requirements he is obliged to comply with under the Acts. The drafting error in the subsection of referring to part III of the 1968 Act instead of part IV is not of importance. In view of a similar error under subs (2), it was held not to affect the validity of the Bureau's certificate (*The State (Murphy) v Johnson*—see para 4.9.6.7)

(iii) It is presumed that the person who took the sample is a registered medical practitioner (s 23(3) of the 1978 Act).

Points to watch in defence

(1) Was a proper arrest made and were other preliminary points properly

followed, e.g. opinion formed; proper words of arrest; proper place?

(2) Did the Garda make known to the defendant the sample options?

(3) *(a)* Did the doctor offer the sealed containers to the arrested person instead of the Garda? (Note that the Garda should make the offer).
(b) Did the doctor complete the form properly?

(4) Did the Garda give the statement in writing to the arrested person with the sealed container (pink or yellow slip)?

(5) *(a)* Was the option of blood/urine given by the Garda?
(b) Was the doctor designated (see para 4.9.6.11)?

(6) Whom does the Garda state sent the container to the Bureau? (must be a member of the Gardai not the doctor).

(7) Was the defendant offered his part of the sample? Was the part adequate (see *R v Wright* (1975) RTR 193)? Was it analysed, If so, did it differ from the official certificate and register below the Limit (*R v Kersberg supra*)?

(8) Was the defendant offered three refusals (if that is the legal position—see para 4.9.6.8) if he refused a sample?
(b) Did he have a special and substantial reason for refusal?

(9) Were specimens dealt with 'as soon as practicable' by (a) a Garda and (b) the Bureau?

(10) It is advisable to get a copy of the doctor's certificate, if legally obtainable (see *State v Reed* above at para 4.9.6.6). In England it has been held that each step in the procedure is only justified if every proceding step has been properly carried out, e.g. *Scott v Baker* [1969] 1 QB 659. The *Hollingsworth* decision (107 ILTR 77) above follows that view, as does *DPP v Joyce* (1985) ILRM 206 generally (see para 4.9.6.4(i) and *DPP v Kenny* [1980] IR 160 (see para 4.9.6.2).

(11) It should also be asked whether a proper cross examination was allowed? A solicitor has a right to follow a line of legal questioning regarding legal issues, e.g. whether an assault was committed. Improper comments by the District Justice will be subject to Judicial Review (*Gill v Connellan* (1988) ILT & Sol Jo 36).

4.9.6.7 *Procedure at Bureau.*There are two duties imposed on the Bureau under s 22 of the 1978 Act.

(i) As soon as practicable after receipt of specimen it is *to analyse* it and determine the concentration of alcohol or the presence of drugs in the specimen. If two specimens are forwarded to it, it is sufficient to analyse one of the two. See the text of the judgment of *Hobbs v Hurley* (High Court, 10 June 1980) as to how the analysis is performed i.e. two tests and a deduction of 6% from the mean figure.
In the case of *DPP v Collins* (1981) ILRM 447 the Supreme Court held there was no onus on the prosecution to disprove that the white substance in the containers created no error or might distort the result. The onus to produce such evidence is on the defence

and, if it does, the prosecution is entitled to call rebutting evidence. There is no minimis rule in law, but a small excess may effect the decision to prosecute (*McGarry v CC Bedfordshire* (1983) RTR 172).

'As soon as practicable' has been considered above at para 4.9.6.6 in the case of the duty of the Garda sending the container and form to the Bureau. The same considerations also apply to the duty set out in this paragraph and (ii) below. Thus, in *DPP v Corrigan* (High Court, 21 July 1980) the defendant was arrested on 24 October 1979. The Bureau certificate was issued on 13 November 1979. *Held*: this was 'as soon as practicable'

The cases have classified this duty as to proof as putting the onus on the defence *Hobbs v Hurley* (High Court 10 June 1980) laid down propositions in relation to Bureau's duty thus:

(1) The Bureau must comply with the duty, but the words do not mean as soon as possible, which is a more severe duty.
(2) The obligation, being in a penal statute, must be strictly construed.
(3) In considering any difficulties, the context and surrounding circumstances should be looked into, bearing in mind the nature and purpose of the obligation.
(4) The Bureau's certificate is obliged to be sent containing the result so as to enable the Garda Authorities to decide under which subsection of s 49, if any, to prosecute, and to enable the defendant to have an idependent analysis carried out and prepare his defence
(5) 21 days was, in the instant case, in conformity with the Bureau's duty of forwarding certificates, the court taking into account the practical difficulties of the Bureau. The Authorities and the defendant has ample time to deal with it.

(ii) As soon as practicable after that analysis the Bureau sends:

(a) to the Garda Station from which the specimen was forwarded, a complete *certificate* in the form prescribed by SI 193/1978 as amended. The signature of the analyst who carries out the test is required by the regulations. It is sufficient if one of the analysts signs (*Hobbs v Hurley supra*). The fact that signature is illegible is immaterial (*DPP v Collins (1981) ILRM 447)*;
(b) To the person named in the form accompanying the specimen as the person from whom the specimen was taken, a copy of the Bureau's completed statement.

There is no general duty or rule requiring the Bureau to ensure that the defendant receives his certificates; The duty is to send it. In *DPP v McGuoy* (High Court, 25 July 1983) the certificate was sent by registered post to the defendant but was returned. The Gardai knew this. A summons was issued, but the case was adjourned. The defendant's solicitor got a copy of the certificate from the Bureau. The District Justice dismissed the case on the basis the Bureau had not forwarded the certificate to the defendant. The High Court, on a case stated, held the District Justice had erred. Finlay P said 'I cannot construe the obligation to forward a copy of the certificate as being equivalent to an absolute obligation to ensure its receipt by the party concerned'. The Court also took the view that, as the defendant did not take her part of the specimen, there was no prejudice to her from the delay.

In *State v D J Plunkett* (1984) ILRM 347 it was held that where the prosecutor knew the defendant had not received the Bureau certificate, he was under duty to supply a copy (followed in *State (Walsh) v Murphy* [1981] IR 275), and in a realistic period, before the Court. As essential proof should not be withheld until the last minute.

In *DPP v Walsh* (1985) ILRM 243 the certificate was sent by registered post but returned marked 'not collected'. No further effort to get a copy to the defendant was made. The District Justice dismissed the charge on the basis that the Bureau had not fulfilled its obligation to forward as soon as practicable. The High Court held, on a case stated, that he was wrong in law in so doing.

Another point was dealt with in *DPP v McPartland* (1983) ILRM 411. In that case the Bureau's certificate gave the wrong address for the defendant. A summons was served on him with substantially the same address. The District Justice dismissed the case, the defendant appearing in Court. The High Court set this finding aside, regarding the error as not having been fatal in the circumstances. The typographical error of the date of affixing the Bureau's seal was also not a fatal error in the certificate according to Supreme Court in *DPP v Flahive* (1988) ILRM 133. The date of the seal according to the certificate was 6 May 1992—the correct date being 6 May 1982. This did not render the sealing invalid as it was a typographical error which could in no way be prejudicial to the respondent '(defendant) nor could it in any material way have misled her'.

As soon as practicable has been considered under (i) above.

The form of certificate is set out in the second Schedule of SI 193/1978 (as amended by SI 363/1983), being the Road Traffic (Amendment) Act 1978 (Part III) Regulations 1978 and 1983. In *Connolly v Sweeney* (1988) ILRM 35 it was held initially in the High Court that the certificate was flawed fatally as it was not a certificate expressed to have been issued under 23(3) of the 1978 Act. Despite the known fact that the decision was appealed, in *DPP v Fahy* (noted in 1987 ILT & Sol Jo 270) Brennan DJ following *State (Llewelly) v Donnchada* [1973] IR 151, held that he would dismiss a drunken driving charge on the basis that the existing High Court case represented the law as it stood. The Appeal in *Connolly v Sweeney* 1988 ILRM 490 was decided in the Supreme Court on 17 December 1987. The High Court decision was reversed, so the prescribed certificate was held to be in order.

Before the Supreme Court decision in *Connolly* the Minister for the Environment has in fact amended the statutory form of the certificate in SI 218/1987. This was unnecessary as events turned out, even though the Supreme Court made some criticism of the 1987 Regulations. These regulations now stand, but the validity of the certificates issued under the revoked statutory instrument—a case has been stated in 1988 to the Supreme Court—*DPP v Regan* which should be heard in 1989.

As to 'as soon as practicable', see para 4.9.6.6 also; 'The Bureau', see para 4.9.6.12; and 'registered medical practitioner' see para 4.9.6.11.

Presumptions
Section 23(2) creates a presumption, until the contrary is shown, that the Bureau's certificate is evidence of the facts certified in it without proof of the signature or that the signatory was a proper person to sign it. The certificate is sufficient evidence also, until the contrary is shown, that the Bureau complied with all its duties under the Acts.

The wording of the presumption contains a drafting error in referring to Part III of the 1968 Act. Part III of the 1968 Act deals with drivers licences. It was Part V of 1968 Act that should have been referred to. In *The State (Murphy) v Johnson* (Supreme Court, 27 March 1980), however it was held that the Bureau's certificate did not have to show compliance with Part V of the 1968 Act. It was sufficient if it complied with Part III of the 1978 Act despite the error of wording.

Under the 1968 Act the certificate was stated to be conclusive evidence of the alcohol concentration. This was held to be unconstitutional in *Maher v AG* [1973] IR 140.

In *DPP v Smyth* (1987) ILRM 570 a number of points on the certificate of the Bureau were clarified. It was held:

(1) There is no onus on the prosecution to prove that no change has taken place in the specimen between the time it was taken and the time it was analysed.
(2) The prosecution has discharged its burden of proof by establishing a prima facie case and, in so establishing, all the evidence must be looked at and not merely the certificate in isolation.

4.9.6.8 *Refusal of blood specimens—Defence.* A special defence is provided by s 19 of the 1978 Act to charges of refusing to provide a specimen of blood. It only arises when the accused has not exercised his option of giving a specimen of urine. Then it is a good defence to satisfy the court that there was 'a special and substantial reason' for the refusal or failure. In *AG v Jordan* 107 ILTR 112 it was held (Judge Deale in the Circuit Court) that failure to understand the prescribed caution—then necessary under the old regulations—was 'a special and substantial reason'. Such a caution does not appear to be necessary now.

It seems that, in reality, the defendant has to refuse three requests, i.e. Blood, Urine, Blood—*Procay v Johnstone* (1970) Crim, LR 110—but having so refused, he cannot change his mind, even before the charge. If one reads s 13 of the 1978 Act (or s 14), it seems the Garda gives a person the opportunity to make two refusals, i.e. by requiring him to provide either:

(a) a blood specimen, or
(b) a urine specimen

at his option. Then if one reads s 19 of the 1978 Act, i.e. where the person has not exercised his option to provide a urine sample, then, in a prosecution 'for refusing to permit a registered medical practitioner to take a specimen of blood' he is given the special defence of a special and substantial reason for his refusal or failure. Is it correct to read this last refusal as a third one in Irish Law? The case dealing with this point—*Connolly v Sallinger* (1982) ILRM 482—seems to be somewhat vague.

This question of options was looked at in *Hobbs v Clarke* (1988) RTR 36, where a conviction was quashed because the defendant was not made aware of the alternatives to blood and urine specimens of the breath test under the English legislation.

In *Molony v Stanley* (High Court 2 April 1984) the High Court directed the District Justice to amend a charge sheet and convict in the following circumstances, i.e. that it was not a valid reason for refusing that the defendant was charged inaccurately. The charge sheet alleged an offence of failing to permit the designated registered practitioner to take a sample of urine or, at the defendant's option, to take a specimen of blood, contrary to s 13(3) of the Road Traffic Act 1978. The defendant contended that the evidence was to the effect that he had been required to allow the doctor to take a specimen of blood, or, at his option, a specimen of urine. The High Court held that, while the charge was defective, the reference to the section was sufficient to cure the defect, and the Justice could amend and should convict. The Court acknowledge there was some confusion as to whether the Garda gave the option on the wording of the charge. The Garda gave the defendant the container for a sample of urine and allowed him 20 minutes to provide it. The Court does not appear to have dealt with what, it seems, are the two sets of options, i.e.:

(a) Requisition of blood or urine under s 13; then, on, a failure to supply urine, having taken that option,
(b) providing the option of giving a blood sample, as seems to be envisaged by s 19.

It can, of course, be argued that s 19 of the 1978 Act only applies where one opts for a urine sample, fails to give it, and then refuses a blood sample for a special and substantial reason.

In the case of *R v Garside* (1959) Crim LR 778 a sample urine was obtained without the warning, and the results of the analysis were accepted in evidence.

Other cases which considered the question of 'a special and substantial reason' include:

R v John (1974) RTR 332—Religious beliefs not a reasonable excuse.

Rowland v Thorpe (1970) RTR 406—Extreme mental conditions or physical injuries could constitute an excuse.

R v Knightly (1971) RTR 409—Confusion from concussion could provide a reasonable excuse.

Sykes v White (1983) RTR 419—dislike of the sight of blood not amounting to a phobia is not sufficient.

Spalding v Paine (1985) LR 673—Severe emotional distress rendering the driver incapable of providing a specimen was sufficient.

Law v Stephens (1971/115 Sol Jo 369—Desire to obtain a Solicitor's advice was not a reasonable excuse.

Fountain v DPP (1988) Crim LR 123—Fear of Aids not a reasonable excuse.

The English cases proceed on an objective standard being used as the basis of judging the capacity of the person to supply a sample, not on his beliefs as to whether he can refuse (See para 4.9.6.4. (1) above also).

4.9.6.9 *Prohibited defence*. Section 20 of the 1978 Act states it is not a good defence to a charge under s 49 (1) or s 50 (1) of the 1986 Act to show that, in relation to the facts alleged to constitute the offence, a specimen analysis or breath test was not carried out.

DPP v Donoghue (29 April 1986, 97 SS High Court) No breath test was administered. The Garda observed the defendant's conduct after an accident had been reported and formed the opinion under S 49 (6)—*Held*: the blood test alone was admissible in evidence.

4.9.6.10 *Anti-evasion*. Section 18 of the 1978 Act is an 'anti-evasion' Section to overcome what is known as the 'Hip Flask' defence. The Section eases the path of the prosecution by making it unnecessary to show that no alcohol was consumed after the time of alleged offence (under S 49 and 50) and before the specimen was provided. If the defence produces the evidence it must be disregarded, unless the court is satisfied by or on behalf of the defendant that, but for such consumption, his blood alcohol level would not have exceeded the 100 mg/100 ml level of blood or 135 mg/100 ml in urine.

Section 18(3) goes further. It provides a prohibition on a person taking or attempting to take any action (including the consumption of alcohol, but not the refusal or failure to provide a specimen) with the intention of frustrating a prosecution under s 49 or s 50 of the 1961 Act. If a person does take such action, or attempts it, he is guilty of an offence, which carries penalties of up to six months imprisonment and/or a £1,000 fine (s 5 of the 1984 Act) and the optional disqualification (See para 2.9) and endorsement (See para 2.10).

Section 18 (4) provides that any action intended to frustrate a prosecution under 49 or 50 of the 1961 Act is an offence and, if on the hearing of a charge under s 49 or s 50 the Court is satisfied that any action taken by the defendant (including the consumption of alcohol, but not the refusal or failure to allow a test) was taken with the intention of frustrating the prosecution under the section before the court, the Court could convict him of an offence under subs (3) above. In addition, the Court may convict him on other evidence of a s 49 or s 50 charge.

What amounts to an action intended to frustrate a prosecution? There will undoubtedly be divergent views. The Section itself specifically *includes* consumption of alcohol and specially *excludes* refusal to give a specimen. The exclusion is made because these matters are offences elsewhere in the Act.

In *Patterson v Charlton* (1986) RTR 18 it was held that once the sample showed excess alcohol the burden was on the defence to show the defendant had consumed alcohol after he ceased to drive (See 'Laced drink' case of a similar view in *Pugsley v Hunter* (1973) RTR 284. In *R v Walsh* (1973) RTR 478 a person who emptied the sample of urine down the sink was convicted of perverting the course of justice. Similarly in *R v Rothany* (1976) RTR 550 a person who gave a sample and then stole it was convicted of theft.

4.9.6.11 *Registered medical practitioner.* There was difficulty about proof of the doctor's rights and qualifications under the earlier 1968 and 1973 Acts. Registered medical practitioners are those persons who are entered in the register established under the Medical Practitioner Act 1978. Section 8(3) of that Act enables registration to be proved by production of a sealed certificate from the Medical Council.

The 1978 Road Traffic Acts deals with the position of doctors a series of presumptions which are set out in s 23(3) of the 1978 Act. This subsection states that in a prosecution under s 49 or s 50 of the 1961 Act, the person who took the samples, or the person who was refused the sample, under s 13(1), 16(5) or 17(4) is presumed to be a registered medical practitioner until the contrary is shown.

The Act does not say that the doctor is presumed to be designated, and that must be proved. Further, the presumption only arises when the prosecution is for an offence under s 49 or s 50 of the 1961 Act (as inserted by the 1978 Act). Thus, proof that the doctor is a duly registered medical practitioner is necessary in relation to offences under 13, 14,16 and 17 of the 1968 Act, i.e. failing or refusing to provide specimens to a doctor.

In *Martin v Quinn* [1980] IR 244 the Supreme Court held that the oral evidence of a doctor that he is a registered medical practitioner is prima facie evidence of the fact.

In *O'Connor v Bannon* (High Court, 15 December 1980) it was held that in s 49 and s 50 cases the presumption arises on a requirement under s 13(1) by a Garda that the Garda designated the doctor to take a specimen.

4.9.6.12 *The Bureau.* Mention has been made above of 'The Bureau'. The Medical Bureau of Road Safety was established by Ministerial Order (SI 241/1968) under 37-42 of the 1968 Act (as amended by the 1978 Act) to do the scientific and other work necessary to operate the Acts. It consists of between three and five members appointed by the Minister for The Environment. It can sue and he sued in its own name. Its Director manages the day-to-day business of the Bureau.

The Bureau has as its main functions, under s 38 of the 1968 Act, as amended by s 7 of the 1978 Act, the duties of:

(a) Analysis and Certification of Specimens and carrying out its functions as specified in the 1978 Act;

(b) Supplying equipment for taking such specimens and testing the same. In the unreported case of *The State (Quinn) v Connellan* (High Court, 9 July 1984) the Court held it was not necessary for the prosecution to show the doctor used any particular equipment in taking the specimen or that the Bureau had provided it.

The 1978 Instructions to Gardai by their Assistant Commissioner

(A 66/59/78) refer to the fact that complete units of blood/urine equipment assembled in cardboard boxes, marked B for blood and U for urine, and supplies of breathalyser equipment, are issued to Garda Stations by the Bureau. It would appear that not all Garda Stations are so supplied. However, the Act does not require the arrested person be brought to the nearest station. See also *DPP v Sheehy* at para 4.9.6.5 above;

(c) Approval of Apparatus for indicating the concentration of Alcohol in Breath or Blood, and arranging for the supply and testing of such apparatus. See para 4.9.6.4, i.e. ss 15 and 16 of the 1978 Act;

(d) With the consent of the Minister, arrranging research into the physical and mental fitness of vehicle drivers; medical aspects of Road Safety; the effect of Drink or Drugs on drivers and how to measure those effects; and the methods of determining the extent to which alcohol or drugs are present in the body (See para 4.9.6.4 above for the 1988 testing of new breath testing equipment);

(e) With the Minister's consent, rendering financial or other assistance to research in the Bureau's field of activity;

(f) holding meetings, appointing its own officers, etc.

The Bureau became operational under The Medical Bureau of Road Safety (Establishment) Order 1968 (SI 241/1968). This has been amended by SI 364/1983, which deals in some detail with the constitution of the Bureau, the terms of office, the Chairman, Director, and other members of the Bureau, its seal, minutes, accounts, majority, decisions, remuneration, etc.

The Director

The office of the Director of the Bureau is established by s 38 of the 1968 Act, as amended by s 8 of the 1978 Act. The Director is appointed by the Minister for the Environment. He may be a member of the Bureau. He is to manage the day-to-day functions of the Bureau, and has general supervision of specimens. He can appoint a Deputy and delegate powers to him. The Deputy must work *intra vires* his powers.

Under SI 241/1968, Act 16 (amended by SI 364/1983) the seal of the Bureau shall be authenticated by the signature of the Chairman, an authorised member, The Director or his Deputy.

Indemnity

An indemnity against Action or legal Proceedings is provided in favour of the Director, an employee or servant of the Bureau by s 42 of the 1968 Act, provided that they are carrying out an analysis or determination under the Act or Regulations.

Regulations

Ample powers to make various types of Regulations for implementing the 1978 Act provisions are contained in s 26 of the 1978 Act and, for the operation of the Bureau, in s 40 of the 1968 Act. The Regulations made to date have been referred to above.

Section 26 of the 1978 Act specifies, in particular, power to the Minister for the Environment to regulate the form which the doctor must complete under s 21 of the 1978 Act and the Certificate of the Bureau under s 22 of that Act. As mentioned at para 4.9.6.7, this form was successfully challenged in the High Court in 1987, but later that year in the High Court the decision was reversed (*Connolly v Sweeny* (1988) ILRM 483).

Section 40 1968 Act gives directions as to what is to be contained in the Bureau's establishment order. These directions are carried out in SI 241/1968, as amended by SI 364/1983, i.e. which sets out the terms and conditions of office of members of the Bureau; the Appointment of Officers and servants; meetings; regulating finances; Reports to the Minister; the Seal; and the provision of equipment.

In *DPP v Collins* (1981) ILRM 477 it was held that a judge is entitled to take judicial notice of these Regulations without their production in Court.

4.9.7 Penalties Generally

Imprisonment

The penalties imposed by the sections are set out above (para 4.9.3 et seq) They are, in relation to imprisonment, under:

(i) s 49 of the 1961 Act—six months maximum;
(ii) s 50 of the 1961 Act—three months maximum on a first offence, six months maximum on second or subsequent offences;
(iii) s 13 and 15 of the 1978 Act—six months maximum;
(iv) s 16 of the 1978 Act—three months maximum;
(v) s 12 of the 1978 Act—six months (no consequential disqualification or endorsement.

In the main section (s 49) the penalty is described by putting the term of imprisonment first.

In *A-G v Greene* (1952) 86 ILTR 31, under the similar section of the 1933 Act, it was held that the Court must give full consideration on any mitigating and extenuating circumstances, e.g. age, sex, health, the degree of incapacity, the deliberation with which the incapacity was produced, the general conduct, the time, the place, the opportunity, inducements and other attendant circumstances, and the length of time of driving. The frequency of the offence and the question of what harm may have been done must also be considered. In the case itself, imprisonment of a very incapacitated bus driver was upheld.

In *R v Wokes* (1978) RTR 101—a case involving 183 mg of alcohol, excessive speed, resisting arrest, bad behaviour on being analysed, and a bad motoring record,—six months' imprisonment was upheld. In *R v Newman* (1978) RTR 107, however, it was held that a high alcohol reading on its own may not be a sufficient basis for imprisonment; but if death or serious bodily harm results and the reading is high, imprisonment is likely (*R v Eadie* (1978) RTR 292).

In *State (Delaney) v Magee* (1983) ILRM 45, a conviction under s 49 of the 1961 Act the defendant was fined £250 with three months to pay, and was sentenced to six months' imprisonment in default of payment of the fine. This was in addition to three months' imprisonment for the offence itself, i.e. two penalties of imprisonment and a fine. In the High Court an effort to have the order quashed as being in excess of jurisdiction failed. The applicant contended he was open to nine months' imprisonment, while s 49 laid down a maximum of six months. The Court held that imprisonment for non-payment of a fine is different in character from imprisonment as a penalty punishment

Fines
The Acts stipulate that the following fines may be imposed:

(i) s 49 of the 1961 Act—not exceeding £1,000;
(ii) s 50 of the 1961 Act—£350 maximum a first offence; £1,000 on a second or subsequent offence;
s 12 of the 1978 Act—not exceeding £1,000;
(iii) s 13 of the 1978 Act—not exceeding £1,000;
(iv) s 14 of the 1978 Act—not exceeding £1,000;
(v) s 15 of the 1978 Act—not exceeding £1,000;
(vi) s 16 (3) of the 1978 Act—not exceeding £350; s 16 (6)—not exceeding £1,000;
(vii) s 17 of the 1978 Act—not exceeding £1,000;
(viii) s 18(3) of the 1978 Act—not exceeding £1,000.

See *State (Delaney) v Magee* (1983) ILRM 45 above as to imprisonment in default of payment.

Probation Act
Section 1 (1) of the Probation of Offenders Act 1907 cannot apply to the following offences under the Road Traffic Acts:

(a) s 49 of the 1961 Act—Prohibition in s 49(5) inserted by s 10 of the 1978 Act;
(b) s 13 of the 1978 Act—Prohibition in s 13(5) of the 1978 Act.

Disqualification
Consequential disqualification follows most convictions under the Intoxicant/Drink/Drugs provisions by virtue of s 26 and the Second Schedule of the 1961 Act (as amended by 1968 Act) specify four sets of offences.

(i) An offence under s 49—driving or attempting to drive a mechanically propelled vehicle. Minimum period is one year on a first offence and not less than three years on a second or subsequent offence. A four-year lapse allows any new offence to be deemed first offence;
(ii) An offence under s 50 ('in charge') being a second or subsequent offence within any period of three years, carries mandatory disqualification. Previous convictions under s 49 of the 1961 Act s 30(3) or 33(3) of the 1968 Act are counted as previous convictions. Period must be six months at least;
(iii) An offence under 13, 15, 16 and 17 of the 1978 Act—refusal to provide specimens. Periods as in (i) above for ss 13, 15 and 16(6); for ss 16(3) and 17, six months' minimum period;

(iv) An offence under s 14 of the 1978 Act—failure to provide a specimen under s 50 of the 1961 Act—being a second or subsequent offence. No consequential disqualification on a first offence.

Ancillary Disqualification can be imposed under s 27 in all other cases.

In England, Justices are encouraged by higher Courts to differentiate between drivers when considering disqualification. Thus, in *Sakluja v Allen* (1972) RTR 315 the Lord Chancellor said that 'They (the Justices) have a discretion to impose longer periods of disqualification when bad driving and bad behaviour follows drink'. See, however, para 2.9 as to excessive periods of Disqualification.

See para 2.9 as to Disqualifications generally, their removal, appeals, etc.

Endorsements

Endorsements are Mandatory in (i) to (iv) above; otherwise they are discretionary

Endorsements are also normally mandatory under s 36 of the 1961 Act (as set out above and see para 2.10)

Drivers licence refusal

It may be that a Licensing Authority may regard a number of convictions as evidence of Alcoholism (see chapter 2, especially paras 2.3.2 and 2.3.4) and it may subsequently refuse to issue a person with a drivers licence. If a doctor was aware of a number of such convictions it would place a substantial onus on him when issuing a Certificate of Fitness (See para 2.6).

Community service order

See para 7.1.2.

Multiple charges/penalties

It is often necesary to issue multiple charges, e.g. 49(1), (2) or (3) create separate offences, as do s 50(1), (2) or (3). There may be a necessity for two charges if there is danger of a technical defence to one. Often, dangerous driving under s 53 would also be involved.

The practice is to convict only of one of the 49 or 50 charges. The dangerous driving charge is regarded as a separate matter, but is regularly reduced to careless driving unless there is clear evidence of serious bad driving. This type of procedure is to some extent borne out by the instructions to the Gardai issued in 1978 by the Assistant Commissioner. These state: 'Though there is no legal objection to seeking a conviction for each offence it is felt by the Director (of Public Prosecution) that to do so, could be regarded as an oppressive act to the defendant.'

Further Reading

Marke De Blacam "Drunken Driving and the Law" The Round Hall Press (1986).

4.9.8 Drugs

4.9.8.1 *Drugs Generally*. A useful book on this subject is *'Controlled Drugs and the Criminal Law'* by Peter Charleton, which was published by An Clo Liuir in 1986. It basically deals with the Misuse of Drugs Acts 1977-84. It does not deal with the Road Traffic Acts. However, it provides a general view of the drug problems and its criminality.

4.9.8.2 *General Intoxicant Law Applied.* As seen above (para 4.9.3), the law on Road Traffic deals with drink and drugs under the same sections basically, as the definition of intoxicant covers both drink and drugs.

It was held in *Thomas v Knight* [1947] KB 336 that the words under the influence of drink or a drug do not create two offences—incapacity may be caused by either or both. See also *Watmore v Jenkins* [1962] 2 QB 572 as to whether the drug was the effective cause of the condition. '*Drink*' means alcoholic drink and '*Drug*' includes a medication or medicine, something given to cure, alleviate or assist an ailing body. In *Armstrong v Clarke* [1957] 2 QB 391, it was held that a diabetic who took a strong dose of insulin could be charged. However, a somewhat different view was taken in *Bradford v Wilson* (1984) RTR 116, where, while not defining a 'drug', it was stated that a substance taken into the body which was not a drink and was not food, but which affected the control of the human body, was capable of being a drug. If a proper dose was taken, and this was a mere predisposing cause and a change in body functioning produced the coma, the accused could be acquitted (*Watmore v Jenkins supra*). See also *Flahive v Lawless* (1953) IR Jur R 37 at para 4.9 54(iii) above.

4.9.8.3 *Incapacity concentration tests*. Section 17 of the 1978 Act specifically deals only with drugs (see para 4.9.5. *supra*). A Garda who is of the opinion that a person in charge of a mechanically propelled vehicle is under the influence of drugs so as to be incapable of properly controlling the vehicle, may require that person to accompany him to a Garda Station. Failure or refusal to comply is an offence, and the person so guilty is liable to severe penalties of up to six months' imprisonment and/or a £1,000 fine, mandatory disqualification and endorsement (s 17(2) of the 1978 Act). What is a requirement under the Section? It is not an arrest, but presumably the Garda would clearly have indicated what is required in unambiguous language. In the case of *Alderson v Boothe* [1969] 2 All ER 27 request 'I shall have to ask you to come to the police station for further tests' was held not to be sufficient to constitute an arrest. It probably would be a 'requirement', but use of the word 'require' and reference to the Act and a statement of the reason would be the best approach for the Garda. Section 17(3) does give an additional power to a Garda. In fact, to arrest a person who, in his opinion, is committing or has committed this offence, and the Garda must bring him forthwith to the Garda Station. There, the person can be required by the Garda to give a urine sample to a registered medical practitioner. Refusal or failure so to do is an offence with similar penalties as apply in 4.9.6.5 above, i.e. up to 6 months' imprisonment and/ or up to £1,000 fine.

This means that in this type of case the law applies both approaches, in that the Garda must form an 'incapacity' opinion and then require a 'concentration' test.

The question can arise of whether it was an illness or the drug that was the effective cause of unfitness to drive. This would be a mixed question of fact and law. Example of acquittal is found in *Watmore v Jenkins* [1962] 2 QB 572 (*supra*). *Flahive v Lawless* (1953) IR Jur R 37 (*supra*).

In *R v MacKenzie* [1971] 1 All ER 729 it was held that once a driver has provided a sample he may leave the station, unless he is detained under the section (English 1972 Act s 11).

In *Duffy v Tadhope* (1984) Sol Jo 107 it was held that a driver whose capacity to drive was impaired by inhaling solvents cannot claim that such solvents are not drugs if in fact they had the drugging effect.

It should be noted that s 17 of the 1978 Act has no requirement that the events take place in a 'public place'.

4.10 Taking a vehicle without authority

Section 112 of the 1961 Act, as amended by s 65 of the 1968 Act and s 3 of the 1984 Act, deals with this crime. It is improperly often denoted as 'Joy Riding' in the Press. The section, as amended, also deals with illegally allowing oneself to be carried in or on a vehicle taken without authority.

4.10.1 Using and Taking without Authority

Mechanically propelled vehicles—s 112(1) of the 1961 Act
A new subs (1) of s 112 was inserted by s 65 of the 1968 Act. It creates two offences, i.e.:

(i) A person must not use or take possession of a mechanically propelled vehicle without the consent of the owner thereof, or other lawful authority (s 112(1)(a), i.e. 'Joy Riding' offence); and
(ii) Where a vehicle has thus been taken a person who knows of the taking shall not allow himself to be carried in or on it without the consent of the owner or other lawful authority, (i.e. 'Carried on' offence).

As to 'mechanically propelled vehicle', 'Owner' and 'Use', see para 7.9. As to penalties see para 4.10.7 below.

Pedal Cycle—s 112(3) of the 1961 Act
A person must not use or take possession of a pedal cycle without the consent of the owner thereof or other lawful authority. If convicted, the general penalty applies (See para 7.1).

A motor cycle is classified as a mechanically propelled vehicle and not as a pedal cycle (*Floyd v Bush* [1953] WLR 242).

4.10.2 What is taking unlawful possession

The offence is usually charged where the prosecution cannot prove that there was an intent permanently to deprive the owner of the vehicle, i.e. the vehicle was taken for a 'joy ride' and then abandoned. In these circumstances it appears to be improper to charge a person with Larceny of petrol also (see 1968 Crim LR 282 and *R v Burnham* J.J. (1959) 3 AER 505), but there is a different concept in the English Theft Act 1968 to the Larceny Act 1916 which is still in force in Ireland (See para 4.10.6).

'Use' means use as a conveyance (*R v Stokes* (1982) Crim LR 695—pushing a vehicle around corner as a prank not 'use', but intention to use is enough (*R v Marchant & Anor* (1985) 80 CAR 361). See para 7.9 as to 'Use'.

In *R v Roberts* [1964] 2 All ER 541, releasing the brake on a lorry and leaving it to run down the hill driverless was held not to constitute taking and driving away.

The consent to use, if obtained, must be freely given (*R v Hogdon* (1962) Crim LR 563). If a person has consent (e.g. an employee), and then goes outside the terms of the consent on a 'frolic of his own', he may not be guilty of an offence under the section (*Moore v Perraton* [1952] 1 All ER 423); but this non-liability does not apply if use of vehicle is made after taking it back to garage and after working hours (*R v Wibberley* [1966] 2 QB 214). More modern decisions take a strict view, i.e. if the character of control and consent is changed by his personal use, the defendant then 'takes' the vehicle (*McKnight v Davies* (1974) RTR 4; *R v Peart* [1970] 2 QB 672) if the consent of the owner is obtained by intimidation it is void (*R v Hogdon* (1962) Crim LR 563). A subsequent declaration by the owner that he would have given his consent if he had been asked is not a defence (*R v Ambler* (1979) RTR 27, but see para 4.10.4 below.

As to *mens rea* generally, see (1980) Crim LR 609—An article by White, *'Taking the Joy out of Joy riding; The mental element of taking a conveyance without Authority'*.

There is presumed consent to and liability for user in certain circumstances (see s 118 of the 1961 Act at para 6.4.7).

4.10.3 Allowing to be carried

Where possession of a vehicle had been taken in contravention of s 112 (1), a person who knows of the taking shall not allow himself to be carried in or on it without the consent of the owner thereof or other lawful authority (s 112(1)(b), as inserted by s 65 of the 1968 Act).

In order to convict a passenger there must be some evidence to show that each of the accused was a party to the taking, or that each knew of the unlawful taking; mere entry into the car after the unlawful taking, without further evidence of partaking in the taking or knowledge of it, is not sufficient to convict (*R v Stally* [1959] 3 All ER 814). In *R v Hume* (1979) Crim LR 328 it was stated that a juvenile under 14 should not be convicted unless he was shown to have known he was doing something wrong. In *Ross v Rivenall* [1959] 2 All ER 376, there was some judicial variance as to what amounted to sufficient evidence to make a case against a passenger. It was held, in that particular case, that, where the car with driver and passenger was found without petrol at 2 am and no satisfactory reason was given, the driver and passenger had a case to meet. In *R v Richardson* (1958) Crim LR 480 it was held to be immaterial whether the driver or passenger took vehicle, so long as they were acting in concert.

This offence apparently is not committed unless the vehicle is moved, i.e. it is not an offence under this Section merely to get into a car (*R v Diggin* (1981) RTR 83) (but see s 113 of the 1961 Act at para 4.11 as to interference with the mechanism).

4.10.4 Defence

It is a good defence to any of the three offences outlined above if the defendant shows that, at the time of the alleged offence, he believed, and had reasonable grounds for believing, that he had lawful authority for doing the act (s 112(5) of the 1961 Act).

In *Shimnell v Fisher* [1951] 2 All ER 672 it was held that moving an obstructing vehicle for one's own convenience was a defence. In that case two men pushed a parked lorry, while a third person steered it. See a similar Defence under s 113(4) of the 1961 Act, referred to at para 4.11.2.

In *R v Diggin* (1981) RTR 83 (above) the defendant found that because of drink and the similarity of the vehicle (same year and type), the vehicle was not the one he thought he was being carried on. It was held he did not have the necessary knowledge. In *Boldizer v Knight* (1980) Crim LR 653 the defendant learned of the taking during the journey. It was held that he should not be convicted as it was not a joint enterprise (Insurance case).

Taking by a mistake is probably a defence—J Crim L 1963 at p 1951 i.e. absence of *mens rea*; and in the same Journal at 1968 a case is noted in which a defendant was acquitted, where the owner said he would normally have consented to the defendant, a friend, taking the car (but see *R v Ambler* (1979) RTR 27, para 4.10.2 above).

In the case of a car on hire-purchase, the consent of the hirer is sufficient (*R v Tolhurst* (1962) Crim LR 489).

The onus on the defence is the proof on the balance of probabilities (*R v Corribriant)* [1943] 2 All ER 156)

4.10.5 Arrest

A Garda can arrest without warrant any person he has reasonable grounds for believing has committed or is committing an offence under the section (s 112(6) of the 1961 Act, as amended by s 65 of the 1968 Act).

As to arrests generally, see para 7.9.

4.10.6 Larceny charge

By virtue of the provisions of s 112(7) of the 1961 Act, if a person is charged with the larceny of the vehicle, and the Court (or jury) is of the opinion that he is not guilty of larceny under the Larceny Act 1916 but is guilty of an offence under s 112 of the 1961 Act, then he can be convicted under s 112. This applies whether it is a summary trial or an indictment.

In *Tolley v Giddings* [1964] 1 All ER 201 it was held that a person who drives or travels in a stolen car, knowing it to be such, is guilty of the offence.

In *Kilna v HM Advocate* (1960) SC (J) 23 it was held that, on an indictment for stealing, it is essentially within the judge's discretion to decide whether he should, in the circumstances, direct the Jury that they have a right to convict under this section.

4.10.7 Penalties

(1) The position when a firearm is involved is set out at para 4.10.8 below
(2) A person who uses, takes possession of, or allows himself to be carried in or on a mechanically propelled vehicle without the owner's consent is liable under s 112(2) of the 1961 Act, as inserted by s 3(7) of the 1984 Act:
   (i) On summary conviction, to up to a £1,000 fine and/or 12 months' imprisonment;
   (ii) On conviction on indictment, to a fine of up to £2,000 and/ or five years' imprisonment.
(3) The General penalty under s 102 (See chapter 7) applies to using or taking possession of a pedal cycle without the owners consent.
(4) Disqualification from driving and/or Endorsement is optional in all cases (See paras 2.9 and 2.10).

In fact, this crime, which has often led to death and destruction in recent years, is severely dealt with in Irish Courts. It is appropriate to disqualify a pasenger in a joint venture case (*R v Reed v Saunders* (1975) RTR 313 and 315).

4.10.8 Firearms Act 1964

A person who has with him any firearm or imitation firearm at the time of committing an offence under s 112(1) above is liable on conviction on indictment to a fine of up to £500 and/or five years' penal servitude. This is specified in s 26 of the Firearms Act 1964, which also allows as a defence to such a charge the fact that the accused shows he had the firearm with him for a lawful purpose at the time.

4.10.9 Summons

In *State (McCarthy) v Governor of Mountjoy Prison* Supreme Court, 20

October 1967, unreported) it was held that a summons charging the offence could specify either subs (1) or (2) as its basis (presumably now subs (1)(a) or (1)(b).

In *State (Comerford) v Kirby* (High court 1986, 23 July 1986; Noted at ILT & SJ 1986, p 247) the defendant was charged with being carried on a vehicle contrary to s 112 as amended. He was tried in the District Court. His Solicitor submitted that there was no evidence of the DPP consenting to that mode of trial. On an application of *certiorari* to quash his conviction, it was held there was no statutory requirement for trial on indictment if requested by the accused (applied *State (McEvitt) v Delap* [1981] IR 125).

4.10.10 Attempts

Where a person was sitting in the driver's seat, fiddling with the dash board (which was lit), and he admitted he would have gone off with the car, it was held that he could be convicted of an attempt (*R v Cook* (1964) Crim LR 423). See also *Prendergast v Porter* (1961) IR Jur R 14 which is noted under heading of 'attempt' in para 7.9.

In *Police v Bishop* (1956) Crim LR 569 it was held that an attempt to commit the offence is a Common Law offence also; But in *R v Pence* [1953] 1 QB 30 it was held to be incorrect to give a longer sentence for the attempt that could be given for the substantative offence under the section.

4.10.11 Unlawful seizure

By s 10 of the Criminal Law Jurisdiction Act 1976 a person who unlawfully by force or by any other form of intimidation, seizes or exercises control of any vehicle is guilty of an offence. Up to 15 years imprisonment can be imposed.

4.11 Unauthorised interference

Three types of interference with vehicles are covered by the 1961 Act;

(1) Mechanical interference;
(2) Getting in or on a vehicle
(3) Holding on to a vehicle

4.11.1 Interference with the Mechanism and Getting on a vehicle

It is an offence under s 113(1) and (2) of the 1961 Act, as amended by s 3 of the 1984 Act, for a person without lawful authority or reasonable cause to;

(i) Interfere or attempt to interfere with the mechanism of a mechanically propelled vehicle while it it stationary; or

(ii) Get on or into or attempt to get on or into the vehicle while it is so stationary.

There appears to be little case-law on this section or its British counterpart (s 30 of the 1972 Act and s 9 of the Criminal Attempts Act 1981, (formerly s 219 of the 1960 Act), but in *Reynolds and Anor v Metropolitan Police* (1982) Crim LR 831 it was held that merely looking into vehicles is not interfering with them.

The cases mentioned in connection with the unauthorised 'Taking' of vehicles at para 4.10 above are of some relevance. If damage is done to the vehicle, the defendant may be guilty of malicious damage.

As to 'mechanically propelled vehicle' See para 7.9.

The earlier requirement of the interference being done in a public place was removed by the 1984 Act, so that now interference in private property is illegal as well.

4.11.2 Non-application and Defence

(1) It is stated in s 113(4) that the section does not apply to a person taking, in relation to a mechanically propelled vehicle which is obstructing his lawful ingress or egress to or from any place, such reasonable steps as are necessary to move the vehicle by human propulsion for a distance sufficient to terminate the obstruction. This follows the case of *Shimnell v Fisher* [1951] 2 All ER 672, mentioned in connection with taking a vehicle without authority in para 4.10.4

(2) Section 113(5) of the 1961 Act states that it is a good defence to show that, at the time of doing the acts alleged to constitute the offence, the defendant believed, and had reasonable grounds for believing, that he had lawful authority for doing that act, e.g. if he believed reasonably that it was his own property (*R v Smith* [1974] 2 All ER 632).

4.11.3 Arrest

Any Garda can arrest without warrant any person he has reasonable grounds for believing is committing or has committed an offence under this section (s 113(4) of the 1861 Act). As to arrests generally, see para 7.9.

4.11.4 Penalty

The General Penalty applied until 1984, but, at amending subs (2), by s 3(8) of the 1984 Act the defendant is now liable to a fine not exceeding £350 and/or three months' imprisonment.

Disqualification and/or endorsement is optional (See paras 2.9 and 2.10).

4.11.5 Holding on to a vehicle

Two sections of the 1961 Act deal with holding on to vehicles illegally:

4.11.5 *Unauthorised interference*

(1) s 99 of the 1961 Act makes it an offence for any person to hold on to, or get on or in to, a moving vehicle in a public place.

It is a Defence to have either (a) Lawful Authority, or (b) reasonable cause for the act complained of. As to 'public place' and 'vehicle' see para 7.9.

(2) S 100 of the 1961 Act makes it an offence for a person on a bicycle or a tricycle in a public place to hold on to any other vehicle which is in motion or to hold on to any person or thing on, in or attached to any such vehicle. There is an exception for holding on to another pedal bicycle which no person is driving.

The general penalty (para 7.1) applies in both cases.

4.12 Excessive driving periods

4.12.1 Control

The social control exerted against prolonged driving under the Road Traffic Acts is contained in a long section s 114 of the 1961 Act, as amended by Sch 1968 Act. It came into operation on 1 October 1961, replacing s 169 of the 1933 Act, but now the main provisions are contained in regulations which are largely influenced by EEC limits and requirements. The problem is dealt with by prohibiting excessive periods of driving of certain types of vehicles, and by requiring the keeping of records (manual and mechanical) of driving periods.

Section 114 of the 1961 Act does not apply to carriage by road in circumstances in which the EEC Council regulations apply under Act 13 of the European Communities (Road Transport) Regulations 1986, (SI 392/1986). However, these regulations are discussed below, as are the European Communities (Road Transport) (Recording Equipment) Regulations 1986 (SI 392/1986), in view of their importance in the control of this area of users of vehicles.

Section 114 of the 1961 Act really now applies only to domestic journeys or work outside the scope of the EEC Regulations. Ireland has to introduce these EEC measures under Arts 74 and 75 of the Treaty of Rome, which were directed to a common Transport Policy. Action had been taken by the EEC to force the United Kingdom to implement the regulations (*Commission of European Communities v UK* (1979) RTR 32).

The control in this area is now as follows:

(1) As to drivers' and their crews' hours and the recording of these the law basically is found in EEC. Rules applied by Regulation in Ireland. They apply to most commerical vehicles over 3.5 tonnes. They apply to domestic and international journeys. See para 4.12.7 below.

(2) Where (1) does not apply s 114/1961 Act as amended and the regulations thereunder may apply.

The various exceptions and exemptions would have to be looked at carefully in each case.

4.12.2 Prohibition

Section 114 of the 1961 Act, as amended, reads:

> A person shall not drive, or cause or permit any person employed by him or subject to his orders to drive, for an excessive period a mechanically propelled vehicle which is either (I) a large public service vehicle; or (II) is intended or adapted solely for the drawing of another vehicle or is fitted with a body intended or adapted solely for the carriage of goods or two or more such vehicles successively.

It should be remembered that SI 392/1986 now limited severely the application of the section. This regulation (See para 4.12.7 below), subject to exceptions therein specified, applies to the carriage of goods and passengers by road within the European Community. Further, the section does not apply to State vehicles or those used for military or police purposes, or to persons in the public service driving or using them. (s 114(8) of the 1961 Act).

As to 'drive', 'mechanically propelled vehicle' and 'large public service vehicle', see para 7.9

In *Beer v Fairclough* (1937) 101 JP 157 it was held that if proper rest periods were allowed, the employers did not have to check to see that the time was actually spent resting. However, in *Grays Haulage Co Ltd v Arnold* [1966] 1 All ER 896 it was stated that it was no defence that the driver drove for excessive periods against his master's orders without any supervision.

In *Witchell v Abbot* [1966] 2 All ER 657, where the driver drove the full permitted period and then used his employers' car to get home, rather than taking up a genuine option provided by the employers of staying overnight at the terminal, it was held that no offence had been committed. This case was, however, distinguished in *Porter v Gorbould* [1969] 3 All ER 828, where the employer provided alternative non-driving work during an insufficient rest period. *Held:* the employer was guilty of an offence.

In *Carter v Walton* (1985) RTR 378 it was held that the question of whether breaks and recreation periods, whether paid or unpaid, should be considered off duty, is a question of fact.

As to 'permitting' see *Forsyth v Phillips* (1964) 108 Sol Jo 36, i.e. knowledge was imputed to the defendant by virtue of his wife's knowledge and his not seeing the obvious. The employer must take proper steps to ensure that his employee knows the law, and he could be guilty of 'permitting' if he does not do so (*Dixon Bool Transport v Forsyth* (1966) III Sol Jo 52). See also *Knowles v Russell* (1975) RTR 87 at para 4.12.7. See also para 7.9 under 'cause or permit'.

4.12.3 What are excessive periods

General Rules

A period, or series of periods is stated to be excessive for the purpose of 114 of the 1961 Act if it is either:

(a) Continuous for over 5½ hours in any one period;
(b) Continuous for over 11 hours in any period of 24 hours beginning two hours after midnight; or
(c) Any period or series of periods which is arranged so that the driver has not at least ten consecutive hours' rest in every period of 24 hours from the start of the driving period.

Modifications

Those are the general rules, but they are modified and explained, as follows, by s 114(2):

(i) If a driver has had at least nine hours' rest consecutively in a 24-hour period commencing with the driving period, it is reckoned as ten hours, provided the driver gets 12 hours' continuous rest in the 24 hours in the day after the said 24 hours' driving period.
(ii) Periods of driving are deemed consecutive unless separated by a minimum half-hour period in which the driver can obtain rest and refreshment.
(iii) Periods of work (other than driving) in relation to the vehicle or load thereon are to be reckoned as driving time. In the case of any public service vehicles, work, such as being a conductor, etc, in a capacity other than a driver or passenger is reckoned as driving time.
(iv) If the work is done in connection with Agriculture or Forestry with a vehicle used for or in the course of any operation, time spent driving on any other than the public road is not to be reckoned as a driving period.
(v) Those variations set out at para 4.12.4 below under Regulations. In *McCallum v Adair* (1937) SC (J) 114, time spent in canvassing and delivering during a journey was held to be driving time.

4.12.4 Regulations

Two sets of powers are given by 114(4), as amended by Sch, 1968 Act, and s 114(7) to make regulations to enable the Section to have effect. The subsections give powers to the Minister for Labour as follows:

(a) A general power to make regulations to give effect to the section is conferrred by s 114(4) of the 1961 Act, as amended by Sch, 1968 Act, with particular powers to deal with the keeping, in respect of a person engaged in driving vehicles under the section, and the form of, records and the production of records to a Garda or officers of the Minister; exhibiting of a specified notice on vehicles; and the exclusion of specified classes of vehicles from the Regulations.

It should be noted that, by the section, the Minister for Industry and Commerce has this power to make regulations. However, by SI 164/1966 (Labour (Transfer of Departmental Administration and Ministerial Function) Order 1966) the functions under both subs (4) and subs (7) were transferred to the Minister for Labour.

(b) A power to vary or suspend in any manner any excessive period, with different regulations for different classes and different circumstances, is given by s 114(7) provided representatives of Employers and Employees are satisfied with the change.

Current Regulations
The Regulations now in force are those made under the 1933 Act, i.e. The Road Traffic (Variations of Excessive Periods of Driving) (No 1) Order 1934 (SI 128/1934) and The Road Traffic (Variations of Excessive Periods of Driving) Order 1936 (SI 27/1936).

These orders arose out of submission made by Trade Unions. Their effect is to vary to 6½ hours the continuous period of driving on certain days and on certain conditions for bus drivers in the County Borough of Dublin, the Borough of Dun Laoghaire and certain other specified routes around Dublin. The days on which the variation operates are Sundays, Christmas Days, St. Patricks Day, Easter Monday, Whit Monday, August Monday and St. Stephens Day. The conditions of the variation are:

(a) The driver must be allowed 30 minutes at the terminus during the period of 6½ hours; and;
(b) the driver does not drive a public service vehicle further on that day.

4.12.5 Defence

A defendant who can show, on a charge of excessive driving or of causing or permitting such driving, that the act on which the charge is based was due to unavoidable delay caused by unforeseen circumstances in completing the journey, has a good defence under s 114(6) of the 1961 Act.

4.12.6 Penalties

The General Penalty under s 102 of the 1961 Act (para 7.1) applies to offences under s 114 and the Regulations thereunder.

Disqualification and/or endorsement is optional

4.12.7 Irish Regulations under EEC Regulations

The European Communities requirements dealing with these matters are introduced to Irish Law by making provisions under Irish Regulations. These are SI 392/1986 (periods of driving) and SI 393/1986 (tachographs)

(1) *Irish regulations on EEC periods of driving*
The purpose of the Irish regulations, i.e. the European Communities (Road Transport) Regulations 1986 (SI 392/1986), is to provide

for the implementation and enforcement of EEC Council Regulations (EEC) No 3820/85 (see (2) below) in Ireland. The EEC Regulations apply directly, and the Irish regulations merely implement certain facets of it.

These Irish regulations:

(a) Provide for the powers of authorised officers for the enforcement of the Council Regulation. Authorised officers are Gardai, Custom Officers or Transport Officers appointed by the Minister for Communications. The powers include entering premises, inspecting vehicles and records, etc. Obstruction of authorised officers is an offence;
(b) State that documents and records can be demanded by Notice by Registered post at a designated place;
(c) Provided that offences may be prosecuted by a Garda or by the Minister. Article 15 goes very far by Irish standards in admitting evidence in written form, i.e. all entries and records by an authorised officer are admissible, as are all recordings by a tachograph, etc. without the normal proofs (see below);
(d) Prescribed penalties for infringements of the Regulations which are a fine of up to £1,000 and/or six months' imprisonment;
(e) Allow certain presumptions in prosecutions to be raised to ease the onus of proof that, for example the weight of the vehicle is over the Limit; that the driver's age is less than the minimum age, or non-possession of the relevant age, i.e. that the defendant driver is not within the exceptions, etc. and the onus passes to the Defence to prove they are;
(f) Specify those vehicles which shall be exempt from the Council Regulations when engaged in national transport operations, i.e.

(i) Passengers vehicles capable of carrying less than 17 persons,
(ii) Public Service vehicles not in competition with professional road hauliers after 1 January 1990,
(iii) Agricultural, Horticultural, Forestry or Fishery Undertakings vehicles operating within 50 km of base,
(iv) Vehicle carrying animal waste or carcasses not for human consumption (see *Paterson v W Wedell* (1984) 2 CMLR 540),
(v) Vehicles used for carrying farm animals to and from the local market or slaughterhouse (See *DPP V Sidney Hackett Ltd* below),
(vi) Farm and forestry tractors after 1 January 1990,
(vii) Specially fitted vehicles, used as shops at markets for door-to-door selling, or as bars, or for worship, or for lending books, records and cassettes, or for cultural events (See *R v Scott* under 'Specialised vehicles' below) In *Creek v Fossett* (1986) Crim LR 256 a circus tent used for a musical event was held to be used for a cultural event,
(viii) Vehicles used by a driver to carry his material or equipment within 50 km of base, the unladen weight not to exceed 3,040 kg and

the driving of the vehicle not to be his main occupation. As to unladen weight see para 1.7,

(ix) Vehicles on islands of up to 2,300 sq. km,

(x) Gas or Electrical vehicles up to 1,524 kg unladen,

(xi) Vehicles used in bona fide driving instruction.

EEC Regulations as to Excessive driving periods
The Council Regulations (EEC) No 3820/1985: O J No 1370, 31 December 1985 which are applied by (1) above state as follows:

(a) They apply to the carriage of goods and passengers by road within the European Community. Basically, they apply to commercial vehicles on international journeys or works. There are both EEC and national exemptions and exceptions possible and specified in these Regulations.

(b) They apply the provisions of the 'European Agreement concerning the Work of Crews of Vehicles engaged in International Road Transport' (AETR) to certain international road transport operations (Art 2). The parties to the AETR agreement include the EEC members, Austria, Czechoslovakia, the German Democratic Republic, Norway, the Soviet Union, Sweden and Yugoslavia.

'International journeys' includes the part of the journey which takes place in Ireland (*Paterson v Richardson* (1982) RTR 49). As to the meaning of an 'international operation', the EEC Commission issued an opinion to the Irish Government on 16 May 1974, stating, *inter alia*, 'The community has always understood international transport to be all transport between the beginning of the journey and the destination'.

(c) They provide for the ages of drivers of vehicles affected to be at least 21 years normally, but 19 in the case of lighter goods vehicle (Art 5). This article also requires experience in driving before using certain passenger vehicles.

(d) The prescribed maximum periods of daily and fortnightly driving, together with minimum breaks and daily and weekly rest periods for drivers (Art 6-9). Basically, these articles provide for driving periods not exceeding 4½ hours continuous and 9 hours a day; Not more than 90 hours a fortnight; a 45-minute rest period after 4½ hours driving; and 11 consecutive hours rest in 24 hours. Records must be kept by the driver and driver's mate in a prescribed record book. In *Kelly v Shulman* (1988) Crim LR 755 it was held that 'Day' meant successive periods of 24 hours beginning with the resumption of driving after the last weekly rest period. It also illustrated what is meant by weekly Rest period.

(e) They Exempt—

(i) goods vehicles of less than 3.5 tonnes,

(ii) passengers vehicles carrying less than nine persons, including the driver,

(iii) passenger vehicles for regular service of less than 50 km,
(iv) vehicle with less than the authorised maximum speed of 30 kph,
(v) Army, Civil Defence, Fire and Police, certain Public Corporations vehicles, emergency services, medical vehicles, and specialised breakdown vehicles, being tested. As to a 'specialised breakdown vehicle' see *Universal Salvage Ltd v Boothly* (1984) RTR 285 (must be built, adapted and kept for that purpose),
(vi) island vehicles,
(vii) vehicles used for non-commercial personal use, and
(viii) milk collection vehicles. These vehicles on domestic journeys may be subject to s 114 of the 1961 Act and regulations. It will be noticed that, generally, the EEC regulations are more stringent, e.g. $4\frac{1}{2}$ hours (Irish limit $5\frac{1}{2}$ hours).

(f) They prohibit certain types of payments to wage-earning drivers (Art 10), i.e. bonuses and supplements related to distance travelled, unless they do not endanger safety.
(g) They prescribe the use of duty rosters and service timetables on certain regular passenger services (Art 14).
(h) They oblige transport undertakings to ensure compliance with the requirements of the regulations and of Council Regulations. (EEC) No 3821/85 (Recording Equipment), (Act 15) (see below).
(i) They allow exceptions for lower times, for ensuring the safety of persons, vehicles or loads—see *Geldard v Browne* (1986) RTR 106—by National Governments on a specified scale (see above at (1)).
(j) The regulations do not apply to vehicles when engaged in certain specified operations (Art 4). They also provide that Member States may exempt vehicles when engaged in certain national operations (Art 13 of Council Regulations and 5 of these Regulations). This ended some of the exemptions referred to at (1) above.

(a) *'Specialised vehicles'*. The leading case on specially fitted vehicles is *R v Scott* (1984) RTR 337, a decision to the European Court which held that 'specialised' referred to the vehicle and was intended to cover exclusively vehicles whose construction, fitments and other permanent characteristics guaranteed that they were used primarily for the operation in question. In that case the vehicle had been specifically adapted for the transport of bread and cakes by putting in interlocking trays. It did not have a special engine or viewing facilities, or the produce arrangements usual in door-to-door selling vehicles. It was held not to be 'specialised vehicle' . This case was followed in the Irish case of *Devine v Fitzgerald,* 3 December 1985, Solicitors Gazette July 1986, Green pages V, where the defendant was a salesman for a frozen food firm calling at shops on a speculative basis. The new regulations (EEC No 3820/85 and Irish SI 392/1986), however, now use the wording 'specially fitted', and this is covered in the exception.
(b) *'Local Market'*. The EEC Court of Justice held in *DPP v Sidney Hackett Limited* (1985) RTR 40 that a 'local market' means a market which, having regard to geographical circumstances, was the nearest

to a particular farm and at which it was possible to buy and sell according to the needs of a normal organised farm in the area

(c) *'Causing or Permitting'* As to an employer 'causing of permitting', knowledge is essential—*Knowles v Russell* (1975) RTR 87—but where the defendant is a corporation, such guilty knowledge must be imparted to a 'responsible officer' i.e. one whose duty includes some measure of control of the company business see also para 4.12.2 above.

In the case of exceeding the daily period (9 hours now under EEC rules) a strict view is taken, e.g. *Whitly v Stead* (1975) RTR 169, where delay in helping out at an accident scene was not a good defence.

See para 7.9 under 'Cause or permit'.

4.12.8 Tachographs

(1) Irish regulations under EEC law

This equipment is now governed by the European Communities (Road Transport) (Recording Equipment) Regulations 1986 (SI 393/1986).

The purpose of these regulations is to provide for the implementation and enforcement of aspects of Council Regulations (EEC) No 3821/85 on recording equipment (tachographs) (see (2) below) in vehicles in road transport. The EEC regulations, of course, apply directly.

Broadly, the Irish regulations:

(a) provide for the installation, proper functioning and periodic checking and inspection by the owner, and use by the driver, of the equipment, and allow for and requires the keeping of record sheets. The purpose is to prevent excessive periods of driving and reduce accident risk. The vehicles that require tachograph installation are those specified in Art 3 of the EEC regulations (below) that are not exempt (below, (e)),

(b) Established and specify the powers of the competent authority (Currently Institute of Industrial Research and Standards: IIRS—now renamed Eolas, the Irish Science & Technology Agency, Glasnevin, Dublin 9) for the approval and control of fitters and workshops for the installation, repair and inspection of recording equipment (tachographs). In a prosecution it is presumed that a person or workshop is not approved;

(c) Provide for the powers of authorised officers for the enforcement of the regulations by entering premises, inspecting vehicles, records, and books, requiring production of records, examining them, etc.;

(d) Create a number of offences—

(i) non-installation and non-use of tachographs,

(ii) non-display of an installation plaque,

(iii) obstruction, etc. of officers,

(iv) false entries,

(v) interference with equipment, etc., and prescribe penalties for infringements of the regulations i.e. a fine of up to £1,000 and/ or six months' imprisonment.
There are a number of presumptions raised in case of a prosecution as in para 4.11.7. It is a defence to show that a tachograph had been working properly, and that when it broke down reasonable steps were taken to fix it;

(e) specify those operations which shall be exempt from the regulations when engaged in national transport operations. There are a number of these specified, and they are identical to those specified as being exempt under para 4.12.7 (1)(f) above, e.g. not more than 17 passengers, public service vehicles, agricultural vehicles, travelling shops, etc.

(2) EEC regulations

The Council Regulations (EEC) No 3821/85 (OJ No 1730, 31 December 1985)) apply directly to Ireland, and the Irish regulations above only implement, enforce and apply aspects of the EEC regulations.

The main provisions of Regulations No. 3821/85 EEC are:

(a) They provide for the installation and use of recording equipment in certain types of vehicles registered in a Member State, which are used for the carriage of passengers or goods by road (Art 3). Recording equipment is normally called a 'tachograph', and is defined in Annex I as 'equipment intended for installation in road vehicles to show and record automatically or semi-automatically details of the movement of those vehicles and of certain working periods of their drivers or driving mates. The equipment must be capable of recording the distance travelled, the speed, driving time, other periods of work or availability, breaks from work and daily rest periods. and allow for the opening of the case containing the record sheet.'

(b) Basically the same rules as to tachographs apply to both passenger vehicles and goods vehicles, and in both cases there are a considerable number of exemptions.

An employer is generally liable for using, or causing or permitting to be used, a vehicle in which a tachograph is not properly installed or not used as specified (see *Knowles v Russell* at para (4.12.7) re knowledge). An employer and employee can be guilty of a conspiracy to contravene the regulations (*R v Blamires* [1963] 3 All ER 170), but in *Cassady v Reg Norris (Transport) Limited* (1975) Crim LR 398 it was held that an employer shall not be convicted unless he knowingly encouraged the breach in some way. Records may be admissible evidence against employers—*Beer v Cleach* [1936] 1 All ER 449—and this view is strengthened by the considerable number of presumptions in the Irish regulations referred to in (1) above.

'Recording Equipment' is specified in Regulations 382/85 EEC (OJ

No 370, 31 December 1985), as set out above at para 4.12.7 (h), as being necessary, and the regulations (EEC and Irish) require compliance with the provisions for their installation and use

(c) Procedures are prescribed for the approval of types of recording equipment and model record sheets, and for the approval and control of fitters and workshops for the installation and repair of the recording equipment (Arts 4–12. See IIRS (Eolas) at (1)(b) above as to their controlling function.

(d) The regulations lay down the responsibilities of undertakings, employers and drivers regarding use of the equipment (Arts 13–16). In *Auditer du Travail v Duford* (1978) RTR 186 an employment agency had supplied a driver. It was held it was the responsibility of the undertaking which got the driver to see that the regulations were complied with.
The employer is responsible for the proper functioning of equipment, its repair, and the giving of record sheets daily; the driver for keeping them properly, and clean; and every crew member must keep his information properly recorded, i.e. odometer reading dates, places, etc.

(e) In Annex I of the regulations the requirements regarding the construction, testing, installation and inspection of recording equipment are specified, as set out briefly above.

(f) The regulations do not apply to vehicles when engaged in certain specified operations (Art 3). The regulations also provide the Member States may exempt vehicles when engaged in certain national operations (Art 3 and R 4 of these regulations). These exemptions are set out in the Irish regulations at (1)(e) above. The same type of exemptions generally apply in both Irish regulations and EEC regulations, as both have similar provisions.

(g) Council Regulation (EEC) No 3821/85 replaces council Regulation (EEC) No 1463/70. The European Communities (Road Transport) (Recording Equipment) Regulations 1979 (SI 214/1979) are revoked by the 1986 European Communities (Road Transport) (Recording Equipment) Regulations.

4.13 Duties on an accident

4.13.1 Duties

The importance of a clear statement of the duties of drivers and users of vehicles, and the rights of other persons on the occurrence of an accident is obvious. These are contained in s 106 of the 1961 Act, as amended by the Sch, 1968 Act, with increased penalties for breaches under s 3 of the 1984 Act.

The duties are broadly:

(i) to stop:
(ii) to remain stationary at the scene;
(iii) to give information; and
(iv) (a) in certain circumstances, to report to the Gardai, and/or
(b) certain persons also are given rights to what is called the 'appropriate information'.

The Gardai are also empowered to obtain information on where vehicles are kept, and to get search warrants—See para 4.13.9 *infra*.

The duty to produce the drivers licence is dealt with in Chapter 1. The duty to give information to and about the insurers under s 72 and s 73 of the 1961 Act is covered in para 6.10.

There are provisions which make it an offence to be in breach on any one or more of these duties under s 106. See also generally as to Garda powers at para 7.2. As to investigation of accidents generally, see para 5.13, i.e. a Ministerially ordered investigation. As to the removal of a vehicle, see para 5.3 under General Bye-laws and Regulations.

4.13.2 Stopping stationary and giving information

Under s 106(1) of the 1961 Act, as amended by Sch, 1968 Act, where injury is caused to a person or property in a public place, and a vehicle is involved in the occurrence of the injury (whether the use of the vehicle was or was not the cause of the injury), then:

(a) The driver must stop the vehicle, if not already stationary; and
(b) the driver, or any other person in charge, must keep the vehicle at or near the place of the occurrence for a period which is reasonable in all the circumstances of the case and having regard to the provisions of the section; and
(c) The driver or, if he is dead or incapacitated, the person in charge, of the vehicle must give on demand the appropriate information (as set out at para 4.13.7 below) to a Garda, if present, or, if no Garda is present, to a person entitled under the section (as set out at para 4.13.8 below).

Note again that it is not necessary that the vehicle was in fact the cause of the injury for these duties to come into operation.

As to 'vehicle', 'public place', 'use' and 'in charge', see para 7.9. As to 'driver', under a similar English section (s 25 of the 1972 Act) (2) the word 'driver' was widely construed as meaning the person who takes out the vehicle until he finished the journey (*Jones v Prothere* [1952] 1 All ER 434, i.e. in this case the door was opened on the off side when vehicle was stationary and knocked down a cyclist). See also para 7.9.

An offence is committed if the driver fails to stop or fails to give the appropriate information (*North v Gerrish* (1959) 123 JP 313) or if he both fails to stop and fails to give information (*Roger v Sullivan* (1978) RTR 181). A bicycle is a vehicle under the section (*Ennis v Nott-Bower* 60 JP 760).

4.13.3 What is stopping

In *Lee v Knapp* [1966] 3 All ER 961 'stop' was construed as including remaining at the scene (See para 4.13.4 below), and the duty to remain cannot normally be delegated. See also *Ward v Rawson* (1978) RTR 498 below.

It is no defence to a charge of failing to stop to prove that the defendant reported the accident subsequently to the Gardai (*Dawson v Winter* (1932) 149, LT 18). If the driver drives around but remains at the scene, that is not an offence (*R v SIC Board)* (1981) RTR 122).

In *Hampson v Powell* [1970] 1 All ER 929 a driver of a lorry was held not guilty of failing to stop and failing to report, when he was unaware of the accident, even though he was convicted of careless driving. No damage was visible on the lorry, and immediately on being questioned by the police the defendant had admitted being in the area but denied all knowledge of the accident. It is for the defendant to prove absence of knowledge (*R v Carrbriant* [1943] 2 All ER 156) on the balance of probabilities.

In *Harding v Price* [1948] 1 All ER 283 it was also held that a driver who was unaware that his vehicle has collided with anything was not guilty, i.e. absence of *mens rea* was a defence. See also *Butler v Whittaker* (1955) Crim LR 317 (cow struck while driving through herd).

In *R v Breingan* (1966) 3 SA 410 it was held if the driver is aware of the accident, ignorance of the consequences is not a defence unless it is established that be believed honestly on reasonable grounds that the accident was not one within the section, i.e. no injury to person or property.

In *Ward v Rawson* (1978) RTR 498 it was held that 'stop' means remaining at the scene near the vehicle for a sufficient period to allow a person, having reasonable grounds for doing so, to ask for the appropriate information. The driver does not, however, have to wait indefinitely (*Norling v Woodacott* (1964) SASR 377). See para 4.13.6 also. In another Australian case, *Jarmon v Walsh* (1936) SASR 25, it was held that a driver who had gone on for 300 yards and then returned to the scene has failed to 'stop'. A learner driver was convicted of failing to stop, and his instructor of aiding and abetting, in *Bentley v Mullen* (1986) RTR 7.

4.13.4 Stationary

In *Lee v Knapp* [1966] 3 All ER 961 it was held under a British statute that requiring a driver to 'stop' meant that he must remain at the scene stationary for such a length of time as in the prevailing circumstances was sufficient to enable those persons entitled to get the appropriate information. The circumstances to be looked at in particular are the character of the road or place where the accident occurred. This decision implies that if the vehicle is stationary when the accident occurs, then it must remain where it is.

If no-one comes on the scene it is not necessary to go around knocking at doors at 2.30 am to find out if anyone is entitled to the appropriate information (*Mutton v Bates* (1984) RTR 256). A person is not entitled to use force to prevent a person leaving the scene (*R v Jackson* (1985) RTR 25).

4.13.5 Reporting to Garda

Under s 106(1)(d) of the 1961 Act (inserted by Sch, 1986 Act), where injury is caused to person or property in a public place, and a vehicle is involved in the occurrence of the injury (whether it is the cause or not), then if;

(1) the driver has injured someone else's property and he (or if he is incapacitated or dead, the person then in charge) has not given the appropriate information to a person entitled (see para 4.13.8) below; or
(2) the driver has injured a person other than himself; he; the driver, must, or if he is dead or incapacitated, the person in charge of the vehicle shall, either—
(a) give the appropriate information (see para 4.13.6) to a Garda; or
(b) as soon as possible, go to report the occurrence to a Garda and, if necessary, go to the nearest convenient Garda Station and give, on demand, the appropriate information to a Garda there.

Tremelling v Martin (1971) RTR 196 held that this means remaining on hand long enough to allow the information to be noted, etc (in this case it was information about certificates). The reporting must be made officially (*Mutton v Bates* (1984) RTR 256) and not to a Garda friend informally.

Where the driver stops and gives the information to an entitled person on the scene, then (unless there is an injured person) there is no duty to report to a Garda. Where a person was stopped by the police 24 hours afterwards and gave information, that was held to be insufficient *Dawson v Winter* (1932) 149 LT 18. Where there is delay in reporting and no explanation is given, the defendant should be convicted (*Balman v Larkin* (1981) RTR) 1.

The duty to report arises where there is a connection between the presence of the vehicle and the accident (*Quelch v Phipps* [1955] 2 QB 107—passenger falling off a bus platform). Once relevant injury or damage is proved, the onus shifts to the defendant to show that he did not know of the accident (see *Selby v CC Avon*, *The Times,* 18 February, where absence of *mens rea* and *actus reus* was claimed).

In the Australian case of *Clements v Gill* (1953) SASR 25 it was held that actual physical injury was not necessary—it was sufficient that a pedestrian was knocked to the ground, shaken and dazed, though not physically injured.

A telephone call to the Gardai is not sufficient reporting as such—*Wisdom v McDonald* (1983) RTR 186—but it might be a consideration on the issue of whether reporting occurred soon as possible and on a decision as to whether to prosecute. In *Britton v Loveday* (1981) Crim LR 49 dealing with a duty under a similar English statute requiring reporting as soon as practicable, it was held that a dismissal was correct where a motorist had failed to take a bend and collided with a fence at 11 pm. He left the car at the scene with his name and address on it. He was interviewed by police at 8.30 am the following day.

Reporting the incident to the Garda properly does not prevent an offence being committed of failing to give the appropriate information at the scene (*Dawson v Winter* (1932) 149 LT 18 (para 4.13.3 above)).

Failing to stop and failing to report are two separate offences (*Johnson v Finlow* [1983] 1 WLR 879).

4.13.6 Giving appropriate information

The duty to give the appropriate information to a Garda or other entitled person rests on the driver, or on the person in charge if the driver is dead or incapacitated.

The scope of this duty was considered by the Supreme Court in a case stated in *A-G (Supt Lynch) v Horton* (unreported, 25 October 1968). The accused was driving a motor car when he collided with a pedestrian, injuring her by breaking her leg. The injured girl was 16 years old and was accompanied by three other children (her cousin, a brother and a sister) aged respectively 14, 6 and 8 years old. The accident occurred 196 feet from a crossroads where a number of men were standing. The defendant drove on 100 yards after the accident, when he stopped on being told by a back seat passenger of the collision. He walked back to the point of impact, stayed for 15 minutes, and then drove away without indentifying himself to anyone on the scene. During the 15 minutes the father of the injured girl arrived and a number of people gathered. Nobody requested any information from the defendant and no Garda was present. *Held.* not guilty of a charge s 106(1)(d). There had been no finding that the father was suffering from disability because of mental distress. The father was entitled under s 106(1)(c) to the information. It appeared his difficulty in identitying the driver had been due to the fact that the car was 100 yards away. A prosecution proposition that, as the father was not present at the time of the accident, he was not the person entitled to the information was not acceptable to the Court. The phrase 'for the time being having charge' is not the same as 'the time' when the injury was inflicted. It was also held that the men at the crossroads would be the persons who are 'present when the injury was inflicted', if no relation was present. The decision appears to run counter to the English decision of *Peek v Towlie* [1945] KB 458.

There is no time limit imposed on the giving of information but in *Lowe v Lester* (1986) Crim LR 339 it was held it meant giving it as soon as reasonably practical. If the person from whom the information is requested denies his vehicle was at the scene, then the police must prove its presence (*Neal v Fior* [1968] 3 All ER 865).

4.13.7 Appropriate information

The driver or person in charge is bound, on certain occasions as set out above, to give the 'appropriate information'. The nature of this information is defined by s 106(4) of the 1961 Act as being:

(i) The name and address of the person required by the section to give such information, i.e. the driver or person in charge; and

(ii) The name and address of the owner of the vehicle; and

(iii) The registration number of the vehicle, i.e. the identification mark of the vehicle under the Roads Act 1920 (see para 1.11) or other such enactment (i.e. the Local Government Act 1955, which deals with vehicles not registered in the State but circulating here under their own numbers. The 1955 Act allows the Minister to make orders allowing these to circulate, i.e. International Circulation Orders (SI 269/1964), as amended by SI 12/1962; 193/1963; 59/1964; 99/1966; 71/1976; 346/1980; 215/1983) and

(iv) Particulars of the insurance of the vehicle. The section refers to guarantee 'particulars' but this has been rendered obsolete by the 1968 Act. See Chapter 6 as to insurance.

Curiously, the section does not apparently require particulars of a vehicle operating under exemption under s 60 of the 1961 Act, as inserted by s 54 of the 1968 Act, e.g. vehicles of State-sponsored bodies (see para 6.6).

4.13.8 Persons entitled

The categories of persons who are entitled to demand the appropriate information vary, depending on the circumstances of the accident. They are set out in s 106(5) of the 1961 Act:

(i) in the case of injury of a person, the injured person; or

(ii) if a person is killed or incapacitated, then if, by virtue of a family relationship or master and servant relationship or otherwise, there was or is someone in charge of the dead or incapacitated person, the person so in charge is entitled to the appropriate information (see *A-G v Horton* at para 4.13.6 above).

(iii) where the injury is to property, then—

(a) the owner, or

(b) if the owner is absent, killed or injured, the person in charge of the property is entitled to the information;

(iv) If none of foregoing persons is available, then any one person who was present when injury was inflicted is entitled to the information, provided he is not the employer, or employee or in the company of the person required to give the information. See *Horton*'s decision referred to at para 4.13.6 above, i.e. by-standers at a bridge nearby;
(v) the Garda (see para 4.13.5).

4.13.9 Location of vehicle

(1) Questioning whereabouts

To help investigation of accidents the Gardai are given power under s 106(2) of the 1961 Act to request the owner to state where the vehicle is kept. The owner must comply with the request or he will be guilty of an offence (as to penalties see para 4.13.11 below). A request made to a Company Secretary is sufficient (*Blake v Sullivans Cars Ltd, The Times*, 26 June 1986).

Before exercising this power a Garda must not be aware of where the vehicle is being kept, and must have reasonable grounds for believing that a person or property was injured in a public place and that the vehicle was involved. It is not necessary that the Garda believes that the vehicle was the cause of the injury. As to 'public places', see para 7.9.

Privilege against self-incrimination cannot be claimed (*Bingham v Blake* [1962] 1 All ER 136) nor can professional privilege (*Hunter v Mann* (1974) RTR 338—medical ethics claim by doctor who treated the person involved.

The Garda does not appear to be bound to state the nature of the alleged offence when applying for the information (*Pulton v Leader* [1949] 2 All ER 747). It may be obstructing the police to give false information (*R v Field* [1964] 3 All ER 269).

This power is in addition to the following rights of:

(a) obtaining the appropriate information, as set out in para 4.13.7 above;
(b) demanding information as to insurance (para 6.3 and 6.10) and the drivers licence (para 2.7);
(c) obtaining information about user under s 107 of the 1961 Act (para 7.2.2);
(d) obtaining information as a result of a search warrant as at (2) below:
(e) his general powers as a Garda (see para 7.2, e.g. stopping vehicles, etc.); and
(f) demanding the drivers licence (para 2.7)

(2) Search Warrant

Where a Garda has obtained information as to the location of a vehicle he believes, on reasonable grounds, was involved in an accident causing injury, he may apply by information on oath for a search warrant to a District Justice or Peace Commissioner. It can be applied for an information obtained under (1) above or from another source. The right of a Peace Commissioner to grant the warrant may be somewhat suspect, however, in view of *State (Clarke) v Roche* (1987) ILRM 309 which deemed powers they had in relation to the issue of summonses as being judicial in nature and unconstitutional.

The warrant may authorise:

(a) any specified member or members of the Gardai to enter within one week the premises it relates to and, if necesary, to so enter by use of force;

(b) any person(s) so entering to search the premises, and examine and take possession of any vehicle found during the search.

4.13.10 Penalties: Fines and Imprisonment

Section 106 of the 1961 Act has special penalties in subs (3) for failures to stop, to give information, to report to the Gardai or to state where the vehicle is, etc. The special penalties are:

(i) In the case of personal injury, a fine of up to £1,000 and/or up to six months' imprisonment;

(ii) In any other case up to £350 and/or three months' imprisonment.

The fines were increased to those levels by s 3 of the 1984 act (from £100 and £50 respectively).

4.13.11 Disqualification Penalties:

(a) On a first offence or in the case of injury to person or property, disqualification is discretionary.
(b) Disqualification is consequential, i.e. mandatory, on a second or subsequent conviction involving injury to a person by the driver of a mechanically propelled vehicle (s 26 of the 1961 Act and para 10 of the Second Schedule).
(c) Otherwise disqualification is optional, e.g. a second or subsequent offence involving injury to property only.

The mandatory minimum period is six months.

In *Joyce v Circuit Court Judge for the Western Circuit* (1987) ILRM 316 it was held that there was no necessity for the Judge to reconsider the evidence after conviction and before making judicial determination to disqualify. This was on the basis that the Judge has heard such evidence in dealing with the charge, and the defendant was allowed an opportunity to present evidence as to whether the disqualification should be made. (See also para 2.9.1 above).

4.13.12 Endorsement

Endorsement is mandatory in all offences involving personal injury by the driver of a mechanical propelled vehicle, as in para 4.13.11(b). Endorsement is optional in all other cases. See para 2.10 generally as to Endorsements.

Chapter 5

Control of traffic

The Rule of the Road is a paradox quite
In riding and driving along;
If you keep to the left you are
sure to be right;
If you keep to the right you'll be wrong
But in walking a different custom applies
And just the reverse is the rule
If you keep to the right, you'll be right
Safe and wise
If you keep to the left, you're a fool.

Erskine (1812)

5.1 Introduction

5.1.1 Control

This chapter deals with the control and regulation of traffic. The law in the main is contained in part VIII of the 1961 and 1968 Acts. The Road Traffic General Bye-laws 1964, as amended, made under these parts of the Acts are of such importance that they are discussed at some length. Many other Regulations and bye-laws are made under the Acts.

The main features of the Acts, Regulations and Bye-laws are:

(a) Flexible control through statutory instruments; and
(b) Control being vested in different levels of authority—the Minister, Garda Commissioner,Local Authority and Gardai. Therefore, where

possible, change and consultation are allowed for, particularly in resolving local control needs.

5.1.2 Methods of Control

The methods of control are numerous and interlocking. At times different sections can, in certain circumstances, overlap and be used together. Sometimes one set of powers specifically overrules others

The main types of controls are:

(1) General Regulations or Bye-laws controlling Traffic, which are covered in detail at para 5.3 below;
(2) Specified Area Bye-laws, i.e. controlling special areas such as the Urban roads (para 5.4 below);
(3) Parking regulations with provision for meter, disc or attendant parking (para 5.5);
(4) Large assemblies directions, e.g. Race meetings, Fleadh Cheoil (para 5.6);
(5) Fairs and Markets Bye-laws (para 5.7);
(6) Traffic Signs (Para 5.8);
(7) Wardens at school crossings, i.e. School Patrols (para 5.9);
(8) Closing roads (para 5.10);
(9) Control of car parks and their provision (para 5.14);
(10) Erections of ramps and bollards (para 5.14);
(11) Control of construction sites (para 5.14);
(12) Control of road works (para 5.14);
(13) Motorways (para 5.15);
(14) Preventing holding on to vehicles or illegal getting on to vehicles (see para 4.11 *supra*);
(15) Fixed penalty procedure, i.e. 'on the spot' fines (para 5.11);
(16) Removal of vehicles abandoned or unlawfully parked (para 5.12) and 5.14.2);
(17) Investigation of accidents (para 5.13);
(18) Promotion of road safety (para 5.16);
(19) Dealing with persons on the road who are a danger to traffic because of intoxication (see para 4.9 above);
(20) Other statutory controls (para 5.17). Harbours, Animals etc.

5.2 Administration

5.2.1 Garda Commissioner

In this chapter much of the power of regulating traffic and making bye-laws and rules for that purpose is conferred on the Garda Commissioner—these powers are in sections 84, 85, 86, 89, 90, 93, 94, 95 and 96 of the 1961 Act, as amended. This is because the Gardai are the main regulators of traffic and enforcers of traffic laws. These powers are referred to in the text.

The Minister and local authorities also exercise powers of control. The 1987 Act increased these, i.e. The Dublin Transport Authority (Dissolution) Act 1987 (see para 5.14).

The growth of traffic wardens' and school wardens' systems has taken some of the routine work of enforcement from the Gardai's hands (see paras 5.9 and 5.11 and para 5.2.2 below).

5.2.2 Transfer of functions

Sections 62 of the 1968 Act, recognising this need to relieve the Gardai of some traffic duties and the greater need for local participation in traffic planning, enables the Minister for the Environment to transfer specified functions from the Commissioner to Road Authorities and to transfer certain functions from one Road Authority to another. The Minister may by order transfer to a specified Road Authority (i.e. County Council and Corporation, County Borough or Urban District Council) for specified area, whether within its functional area or not, a specified function of The Commissioner which he holds under s 84 (bye-laws for street service vehicles), s 85 (stopping places and stands for buses), s 86 (bye-laws for bus stops and stands), s 89 (bye-laws for specified areas), s 90 (parking vehicles on public roads), s 93 (protection of bridges), s 94 (closing roads), s 95 (traffic signs) or s 96 (school patrols) of the 1961 Act.

Under s 62 of the 1968 Act the Minister can also transfer certain functions in relation to urban roads in an Urban District Council's area. The functions that can be so transferrred are those under s 90 (3) (meter parking places), s 93 (protection of bridges), s 94 (closing roads) and s 95 (traffic signs) of the 1961 Act.

The order of transfer of functions can modify the 1961 Act by reasonably necessary consequential and ancillary provisions. The order can be amended or revoked by the Minister. No such order has to date been made by the Minister (1988).

5.3 General bye-laws regulations

5.3.1 Power to Make

Section 88 of the 1961 Act originally covered such general bye-laws and regulations, the bye-laws being made by the Commissioner of the Garda, with the Minister's for the Environment consent. That section has been repealed by s 5 of the 1968 Act and replaced by s 60 of that Act.

Section 60 (1) of the 1968 Acts reads: 'The Minister may make regulations for the general and control of traffic and pedestrians in public places.' Note that there is a distinction drawn between traffic and pedestrians, and this is emphasised by s 60(6), which states that traffic in the section does not include pedestrians. As to 'public place', see para 7.9. Different regulations can be made for different classes of traffic, different circumstances, different areas and different classes of roads. In addition to these general powers, s 60(2) sets out particular powers in these regulations to deal with use of roads; parking rules; the side and part of road to be used; priority of passage (including dual and multiple carriageways); prohibiting the use of parts of the road, including footpaths; stopping, reversing; turning, overtaking or passing animal-drawn vehicles; control of junctions; animals on the road, assigning parts of roads to pedestrians; signals, Garda powers to conduct traffic controls; signs; horn use; restricting races; trials and rallies; and the regulation of speed.

The 1968 section states specifically that regulations made under the former s 88 of the 1961 Act are deemed to be made under the new section and to continue in force. These are the 1964 Regulations set out at para 5.3.3. which had some minor amendments made to them by s 1 281/1975 and a further part added by SI 275/1983 to deal with motorways.

Under s 6(1) of the 1961 Act, every Bye-law under s 88 was required to be laid before each House of Oireachtas and could be amended by resolution of either House within 21 sitting days of its laying, but without prejudice to the validity of everything done thereunder. This also seems to apply too under s 60 of the Act bye-laws. See para 7.6 re Bye-laws.

5.3.2. Offence

Contravention of any regulations is an offence. The general penalty applies under s 102 of the Act (para 7.1). Disqualification is optional but, of course, if the Court decides to disqualify there is endorsement automatically (see paras 2.9 and 2.10).

Proof of the bye-laws is helped by the provision of s 7 of the 1961 Act (see para 7.6), i.e. by use of the Documentary Evidence Act 1925.

5.3.3 Existing Bye-laws

The Road Traffic General Bye-laws 1964 (S1 294/1964) are the main existing regulations. They have been amended by S.1 281/1975 and S1 275/1983. They are so important that they are set out in some detail below, but not fully. Specific queries can only be answered by going to the actual text of the relevant bye-law.

Part I General Provisions

BL 1: Gives the citation of the bye-laws as the Road Traffic General Bye-laws 1964. It repeals former similar bye-laws.

BL 2 Definitions: Many terms are defined. Many of these are mentioned under main appropriate rules below. References to signs are to those in the Road Traffic (Signs) Regulations 1962, as amended (see para 5.8 below). 'Traffic' is stated for the purpose of the bye-laws as not including pedestrians.

Drivers of animals, or persons riding or leading them are considered 'drivers', and a drover accompanying an animal on a road is deemed to be 'in charge'.

BL 3: Signals and directions by the Garda Siochana override the bye-laws if given to preserve order, or for regulating or controlling traffic.

BL 4 Conflicts: The following overrule these bye-laws where there is a conflict—

(a) Special Traffic Regulations made in relation to Street Service Vehicles (paras 1.12 and 1.16) under s 84 of the 1961 Act (see Chapter 1 part 2);
(b) Area traffic bye-laws and rules under s 89 of the 1961 Act (see para 5.4 below);
(c) Public Road parking bye-laws and rules under s 90 of the 1961 Act (para 5.5 below); and
(d) Fairs, and Markets rules under s 92/1961 Act (para 5.7 below).

BL 5: Exemption from bye-laws is granted where compliance is not possible by reason solely of road work, building operations or obstruction of road traffic, or an unexpected emergency confronting a driver, pedal cyclist or pedestrian which he could not reasonably anticipate. See BL 3 and 4 above also as to other ways or overruling the Bye-laws.

Part II Traffic signs and roadway marking

This part legally defines the effect of some of the signs referred to in para 5.8 of this chapter.

BL 6 Junctions: Stop signs and yield right of way signs show that the next road ahead is a major road. The effect of a stop line is to require the driver to stop at it. The vehicle should be brought to a standstill at the stop line if there is one, or if not, before the major road, i.e. at its edge with a view and not at the sign itself (*Tolhurst v Webster* (1936) All ER 1020 and *Brooks v Jefferies* (1936) 3 All ER 232). If any part of the vehicle enters the major road without stopping at the stop sign the offence is commited (*Ryan v Smith* (1967) 1. All ER 611).

As to yield signs, see *Lord V Wolley* (1956) Crim LR 493.

BL 7: Deals with signs indicating the *directions* to be taken at junctions—

(a) A signal prohibiting through traffic is indicated by an authorised sign showing a black arrow and diagonal red line;
(b) a similar sign without a red line means you must follow the arrow.

Both signs must be obeyed. See BL 3,4, and 5 above as to exceptions and exemptions.

BL 8 Dual carriageway signs: A sign bearing a curved black arrow means you must drive on the left hand carriageway of the dual carriageway. In *Brazier V Alabaster* (1962) Crim LR 173, at the end of a dual carriageway the defendant made a 'U' turn, 62 feet from a traffic roundabout, so as to be able to drive back in the opposite direction. *Held:* no offence.

BL 9 Continuous White Line cannot be crossed except for the purpose of leaving or entering land or premises at the other side, and one must always drive to the left of such a white line. See BL 11 as to double lines. See also BL 3, 4, and 5 as to Exemptions and Exceptions.

In *Bensley v Smith* (1972) Crim, LR 239 it was held that crossing a white line can be dangerous driving in the circumstances (see para 4.2)

BL 10: Similar provisions apply as to driving to the left of a Broken white line, except when it can be crossed without danger to other traffic or pedestrians. See BL 9 as to continuous white lines. See BL 3, 4 and 5 as to exemptions; BL 11 as to continuous and broken lines together, and BL 12. as to traffic lines.

BL 11: Driver must keep to the left of double white lines, except for crossing to enter or leave premises on the opposite side. If there are continuous and broken lines combined, then the driver on whose side the continuous line is cannot cross (except for entering or leaving land or premises on the other side); whereas the driver who has the broken line on his side can cross the line to enter or leave land on the other side, but only if by so doing he creates no danger to other traffic or pedestrians. See BL1, 3, 4, and 5 as to exemptions.

In *Davies v Heatley* (1971) RTR 145 where the lines are not as specified regulations, a person contravening them commits no offence even though the lines are recognisable.

BL 12: A broken white line also indicated the boundary of a traffic lane and arrows on such lanes indicate the permissible directions to be followed, i.e. straight ahead, left or right turns, or a combination of such directions. See BL3, 4 and 5 as to Exemptions.

BL 13 Traffic Lights: The rules are

(1) If red, the driver must stop at the stop line, or at the sign if no line;

(2) If *non-flashing amber,* then the driver must stop at the line, or at the sign if no line unless the vehicle is so close to the line that he cannot stop safely at the line;

(3) If it *is* a flashing amber light the driver can proceed beyond the stop light or line but must yield to crossing pedestrians (amended by SI 281/1975);

(4) If green, the driver may proceed past the light. If an arrow only is green, then the driver must proceed as the arrow directs.
This bye-law was amended by SI 281/1975. It would be difficult to make the Exemptions in BL 5 apply. See BL 3 and as to a Garda signal overruling lights (see also *R v Watts* (1955) Crim LR 787).

In *Doyle v HF Murray* (1967) IR 390 the Supreme Court held that if the light is green on approach, the onus on a driver is not as heavy as if the junction was uncontrolled. However, he must use a reasonable standard of care, commensurate with the circumstances existing at the relevant time, particularly in regard to keeping a proper look out.

In an interesting District Court decision, the not too unusual difficulty that faces a motorist when the lights are 'stuck' was dealt with. The Dublin District Court decided that, after waiting a sufficient time, the driver could ignore the lights and proceed through the junction with caution (decision referred to in (1959) Jo Crim L 224).

Wheeling a bike against a red light is an offence (*Police v Wetherill* (1955) Crim LRV 322). It is also an offence to cross the line with any part of the vehicle when the red light is showing (*Ryan v Smith*) (1967) 1 All ER

611). The absence of a line affords no defence to a defendant who has actually passed the lights (*Costelloe v Farry*) 74 ILTR 251).

There is a duty placed by BL 34 (*infra*) on pedestrians to comply with this regulation.

In *Piel v Dublin United Tram Company Ltd* (1939) Ir Jur R 88 it was held that a driver who enters a controlled junction on the green light, but the light turns to amber and red before he completes the crossing, is entitled to complete his crossing maintaining, however, a proper look out for other traffic. Similarly in *Sudds v Honscombe* (1971) RTR 212, a civil case, the defendant, who failed to notice the lights change to red, was fully liable to the plaintiff who entered the crossing on a green light.

BL 14: Requires a driver approaching a level crossing in a railway to stop if so signalled by a set of two red lights.

Part III Control of Vehicular traffic

BL 15: A driver shall not drive wholly or partly on the *footpath,* except to cross it to get to another place. Prams and invalid carriages are exempt. The fact that the driving on the footpath is only for a few seconds is no defence.

(M'Arthur v Jack (1950) SC (J7 29). The defence of emergency, etc. Under BL, 3, 4, and 5 may be open. See para 7.9, as to what is a footpath.

BL 16: Has a similar prohibition against driving a vehicle other than a pedal cycle over a *cycle track,* except to cross to or from adjacent land. See also BL 28 below as to who can use Cycle Tracks. See BL 3,4 and 5 as to Exemptions generally.

BL 17:

(1) The *Left side* of the road is the one to use, and one must keep as near as is practicable to the left to allow, without danger or inconvencience, passage to traffic and pedestrians approaching or overtaking to the right; and a driver must keep to left side of traffic refuge also except in a one-way roadway. This left-hand rule was introduced in Ireland on 1 January 1810 (49 G. III, C. 84, s 30).

(2) Crossing from *traffic lanes* is prohibited except for a good cause, and a driver must yield to traffic in that other lane, See BL 3, 4, and 5 Exemptions.

BT 18: This sets out an important general obligation that a person shall not drive at a *speed exceeding* that which will enable him to halt within the distance he can see to be clear. Breach of this Bye-law is regularly referred to in Civil Cases. *Scott v Warren* (1974) RTR states that a driver following another vehicle should take up a position and drive so as to be able to meet all reasonably anticipated traffic emergencies. (See para 3.5).

BL 19 Overtaking rules:

(1) No overtaking (or attempt to overtake) is to be done by a driver unless he sees clearly a portion, sufficiently long and wide, of the road, free from approaching traffic, pedestrians and obstruction,

so as to enable him to complete the passing without danger of inconvenience to other traffic or pedestrians.

(2) A driver must overtake on right and move back into the left when safe to do so.
Overtaking on left is permissible, however

(a) If the driver in front has signalled he is going to turn right, and the overtaking driver intends to go straight ahead or left after overtaking:
(b) where the driver of the overtaking vehicle intends, after having overtaken, to turn left at a road junction and has signalled this intention; and
(c) in slow moving traffic, when vehicles in the traffic lane to the driver's right are moving more slowly than the overtaking vehicle.

These rules do not affect the position of persons *vis-à-vis* dangerous and careless driving, but would be a guide as to proper procedure. *Taylor v Rogers* (1960) Crim LR 270 shows that failure to exercise due care may be a deliberate act, e.g. overtaking on a curve in the belief that the driver in front has signalled that it is safe to pass. A driver must ensure that the person giving signals can see the road properly (*Lidon v Stringer* 117 NLJ 464). In *Squire v Metropolitan Police* (1957) Crim LR 817 it was held there was a prima facie case of dangerous driving where a person on a four-lane road pulled out to overtake and so made a third lane on the wrong side of the road. See BL 3, 4, and 5 exemptions. See paras 5.2 and 5.3 regarding dangerous and careless driving decisions where overtaking was involved.
BL 20 Turning at Junctions: Here the Rules are (unless a traffic sign requires differently)

(i) Keep to left side of the road if you intend to turn left;
(ii) if you wish to go right, keep to the centre of the road or, if it is a one-way street, to the right of the street.

BL 21: It is, of course, also necessary to give and obey signals and signs. A driver shall enter a *roundabout* by turning to the left.
BL 22: Covers the yield right of way rules, which are

(i) A vehicle *starting* from the stationary position must yield to all traffic and pedestrians;
(ii) At junctions, approaching traffic must yield to actually turning or crossing traffic in accordance with bye-laws, or to pedestrians who have commenced crossing;
(iii) When entering a public road, from a place which is not a public road, a vehicle must yield to all traffic on the road from both directions;
(iv) Where there is a stop sign at an entrance to a major road, the vehicle must stop at or near the sign, and yield to all traffic on

the major road; its front wheels must not cross stop line, if there is one.

(v) Where there is a yield right of way sign, the vehicle must yield to all traffic on the major road;

(vi) If there is no sign but the vehicle is entering a major road from a lesser road, then it must yield to traffic on the major road. In this respect the definition 'of major roads' in BL 2 (i) is relevant, i.e. a road so indicated by a sign to be such or the road carrying the greatest volume of traffic normally.

(vii) If no major road is involved and rules (iv), (v) and (vi) do not apply, then the vehicle must yield to traffic from the right. See *Byrne v Sheedy* (1965) IR 1 concerning the civil effect of this bye-law. The decision is now somewhat out of date, however, in view of the provisions of the Civil Liability Act 1961. See also, regarding yielding to traffic from the right as a general rule, *McIntyre v Coles* (1966) 1 All ER 723;

(viii) If one intends turning right at a junction one must yield to traffic approaching from the opposite direction and proceeding through the junction;

(ix) A vehicle must yield to pedestrians on zebra crossings, i.e. a crossing which is marked and beaconed. The fact that the driver thinks the pedestrian will let him pass is irrelevant (*Neal v Bedford* (1966) 1 QB 505. The presence of parked vehicles obscuring the view is no defence (*Gibbons v Kahl* (1956) 1QB 59). As to pedestrian's duties at these crossings see BL 38 below. The Authorised signs for these crossings are governed by Act 9 of SI 171/1962 (see para 5.8) In *Burns v Bidder* (1967) 2 QB 277 it was decided it was not an absolute offence if failure to accord precedence was due to something outside the driver's control, i.e. latent defect, pushed from behind, etc., can be a defence.

See also BL 3, 4, and 5 as to Exemptions, and BLS-38 below
BL 23 Signal by drivers: Wherever a driver intends to slow down, stop or alter course he must give a direction indicator or stop lamp signal, or a hand signal. See BL 3, 4, and 5 as to Exemptions.

The signals that may be given by hand are as follows:

(a) Slowing down or stop—extend right arm and move the palm up and down slowly. The palm of one's hand must be turned downwards;

(b) If turning left—extend right arm and rotate the hand anti-clockwise. If using cycle or animal-drawn vehicle, extend a left arm horizontally;

(c) If turning right—extend right arm, palm to front, in rigid horizontal position straight out from the right side;

(d) If a driver is signalling to a pointsman his intention to go:

(i) straight ahead—extend forearm and hand upwards with palm to front,

(ii) left—point right forearm with extended fingers to left. If a cycle, extended left arm,
(iii) right—extended right arm, palm to front, in rigid horizontal position.

See BL 24 below as to signals by pointsmen. See also BL 3 as to pointsmen overruling bye-laws.
These signals should be given in sufficient time before altering course and be clearly visible. It is forbidden to give simultaneous contradictory signals. Many of these hand signals are unnecessary through use of direction indicators. If a driver does not see that his signals are understood he can be guilty of careless driving (*Sorrie v Robertson* (1944) SC (J) 95). A driver who signals he will turn right but instead turns left, without taking precautions to see whether anything is coming up behind, is guilty of careless driving (*Pratt v Bloom* (1958) Crim LR 817) In *Another v Probert* (1968) Crim LR 564 the defendant indicated he intended to turn but did not do so. *Held:* careless driving: As to careless driving generally, see para 4.3 above.
BL 24 Signals by pointsmen: The duty of drivers and pedestrians approaching a pointsman (who is, under BL 2 (i), a Garda in uniform on traffic control duty) is to act in accordance with his signals. If the pointsman—

(i) Extends his right arm and hand at full length above his shoulder, the duty is to halt if approaching from in front of him;
(ii) Extends his left arm and hand horizontally, the duty is to halt if approaching from behind him;
(iii) Extends his right arm and hand and holds his out horizontally, the duty is to halt if approaching from the front or back;
(iv) Beckons with his hand and forearm, the duty of the driver is, if approaching from the front, left or right, or if stopped by him, to proceed as beckoned;
(v) Points to a traffic lane, the driver must move into that lane.

A pointsman can use a baton for giving signals, and a whistle to warn of any change of signal. If a driver is signalled to stop, his front wheels should not cross a stop line if there is one. These signals override other bye-laws (BL 3). See BL 4 and 5 as to exemptions, but these are unlikely to apply if the pointsman is alert.
BL 25 Reversing rules: The rules for a driver are—

(i) To ensure (by sufficient vision, etc.) that he/she can reverse without endangering other traffic or pedestrians.
(ii) A driver cannot reverse on to a main road from another road, or when his vision is such (i.e. the lack of it) that he/she would be likely to endanger other traffic or pedestrians. If relying on signals from another, the driver must be satisfied that other person has that proper vision (*Liddon v Stringer* (1967) Crim LR 371).

BL 26 Parking rules:
Drivers must ensure when parking that the vehicle will not—

(a) Cause (or be likely to cause) inconvenience, obstruct or endanger other traffic or obstruct the view of a driver at or near a road junction, corner, bend, brow of a hill, or block view of traffic signs;
(b) Obstruct or interfere with the entrance to a fire brigade or ambulance station;
(c) Interfere with normal flow of traffic;
(d) Be on, or within 30 feet of the approach side of a zebra crossing, or pedestrian lights, on the side of the road on which traffic is approaching;
(e) be in marked areas near traffic lights;
(f) Obstruct the entrance of premises for vehicles, save with the occupier's consent;
(g) Be on an appointed stand for street vehicles, unless it is a street service vehicle (see para 1.16) (Fixed penalty procedure applies under s 103—see para 5.11.2);
(h) Project over or interfere with a footpath or cycle track such as to prevent free movement;
(i) Be where there is a single or double white line in the centre of the road. There are exceptions for pedal cycles and motor bikes without side cars.

The regulation does not apply to ambulance vehicles, police vehicles, vehicles on road work or telephone duty, or vehicles removing an obstruction to traffic.

A vehicle may stop within 30 feet, of pedestrian lights to take up or let down a passenger, load or unload, or while being attended at a service station.

As to dangerous parking, see para 4.7. Many of the above rules can amount to dangerous parking if the circumstances so warrant, e.g. where a double white line. See BL 3, 4, and 5 as to Exemptions.
BL 27 Removal on Breakdown/Accident: A driver or person in charge must as soon as possible remove a vehicle which is parked in contravention of bye-laws, or which is an obstruction because of breakdown, accident of mishap. If the vehicle has a warning device, then this must be placed properly on the road until the vehicle is removed. The device is to be removed when the vehicle is removed.

Exemption from compliance can operate in the events specified in BL 3, 4, and 5 above.

Part IV Cycle Traffic.
Mention of special types of signals by cyclists, etc. has been made above. 'Traffic' includes cyclists in the bye-laws generally, therefore almost all the regulations apply to cyclists. This part deals only with two special aspects, i.e. cycle tracks and cycling abreast. Other rules about cyclists' behaviour are mentioned where specially needed, e.g. holding on to vehicles at para 4.11 above, etc. Generally, cyclists are subject to much the same laws as mechanically propelled vehicle drivers.
BL 28 Cycle tracks: No other vehicle (except a non-mechanical invalid carriage) may use the cycle tracks. See also BL 16 above, which prevents

drivers from using cycle tracks where it is provided that they must be used by cyclists. A cycle track is defined by BL 2 as part of a road designed for use by pedal cycles only.
See BL 3, 4 and 5 for Exemptions.
BL 29 Driving abreast: Pedal cyclists cannot drive more than two abreast, except when overtaking another cyclist, and when so doing must not endanger other traffic or pedestrians. In fact, the bye-laws say that cyclists shall cycle in single file when overtaking other traffic.

An autocycle, if its engine is disconnected, can be a cycle (*Lawrence v Howley* (1952) 2 AllER 74). See BL 3, 4 and 5 for Exemptions.

Part V Animals

An animal, for the purpose of the bye-laws, does not include dogs or cats (BL 2). Also under BL 2(2) and (3), a person leading or riding an animal (with or without a vehicle attached) is deemed to be a driver, and every driver is deemed to be in charge of the animal he is accompanying. See also para 1.31 as to animals and vehicles.
BL 30: A driver of a vehicle meeting or passing an animal on a road shall either reduce speed or halt the vehicle on being requested or signalled to do so by a person in charge.
BL 31: Drover-duties are to drive animals, taking all reasonable steps to ensure that

(a) the Animals do not obstruct other traffic or pedestrians;
(b) an Animal does not go on the footpath or cycle path, except to cross them to or from land;
(c) traffic can safely get past, i.e. has room to pass.

'Driving' means conducted without rein or lead. See BL 3, 4 and 5 for Exemptions. See BL 33 for driving at night.
BL 32 Leading horses: Horses must be led on the right side of the road. See BL 3, 4 and 5 for Exemptions. The Summary Jurisdiction Act 1851, s 13(2) provides that any person riding any horse, and leading any other horse, who does not keep such led horse on the side farthest away from any carriage or person passing him on any public road, will be liable to a fine of 50p.
BL 33 Driving in the dark: Driver must carry effective warning lamp, showing white to the front and red to the rear, when driving animals during lighting up hours. Bye-law 2(1) states that these hours are between one-half hour after sunset and one-half hour before sunrise. See also BL 31 above. See BL 3, 4 and 5 for Exemptions. See para 1.31 also on animals on the road.

Part VI Pedestrians.

Parts II, III and IV dealt with aspects of traffic control under BL 2. Traffic does not include pedestrians. Part VI, therefore, is a special part dealing with pedestrians.
BL 34 General duty of care: Pedestrians must exercise care and take all reasonable precautions to avoid causing danger or inconvenience to traffic or other pedestrians. They must also obey BL 13 regarding traffic lights signals. What is danger or inconvenience is a matter of fact.

BL 35: The general rules for Pedestrians (including a person pushing a pram) are—

(i) They must use the footpath, except when crossing the road, if there is one. If there is no footpath, they must keep as near as possible to the right-hand edge of the road. For exceptions see (ii) below.
(ii) If a group of 20 or more is walking, then it must keep as near as possible to the left-hand edge of the road. At night, at least one of the group must have a lamp showing white to the front and red to the rear from a reasonable distance.

As to footpath, see para 7.9.

Exemptions may apply under BL 5 where there are road works, an emergency, etc. They are also possible under BL 3 and 4 (Pointsmen, Garda directions and special regulations). See BL 36-38 regarding crossing roads.

BL 36, 37 and 38 Crossing roadways: The rules applicable to pedestrians crossing roads are as follows:

(i) To remain on the roadway only for as long as is necessary. Each lane of a dual carriageway, or where a refuge (traffic island) is deemed a separate roadway;
(ii) To obey pointsmen and traffic lights, crossing with traffic proceeding in same direction but yielding to traffic turning in front of pedestrians;
(iii) Where there is a pointsman in control of traffic, to cross only when he permits;
(iv) Where pedestrian lights are provided to cross only when the facing light is green and non-flashing (Amended by SI 281/1975). These lights are erected under R 14 of the 1962 Signs Regulations (See para 5.8 below).
(v) If there is a zebra crossing, then pedestrians cannot cross within 50 feet of it—they must use the crossing. They cannot step on to the crossing if it is likely to cause an approaching driver to brake suddenly or to swerve.
Zebra crossings are provided for in R 9 of the 1962 Signs Regulations (See para 5.8). See also BL 22 above.

Zebra crossings give priority to pedestrians. A driver must stop and allow pedestrians to cross, and has very limited defence if he does not. In *Burns v Bidder* (1966) 3 All ER 29 it was said that being pushed by another vehicle on to a crossing, or the vehicle having a latent defect, may provide a defence. The crossing markings and signs must be strictly in accordance with the law *Power v Davidson* (1964) LGYR 320) or there is no offence. See also *Moulder v Neville* (1974) RTR 53 for a similar result. In *Kayser v LPTB* (1950) 1 All ER 231 it was held that where a driver is satisfied that the persons crossing are out of danger, he may proceed at a reasonable speed. See the contra decision in *Burns v Bidder* above, where it was stated that the duty on a driver to give pedestrians precedence is absolute except for where there is a latent defect or outside force is applied. In *Gibbons v*

Kahl (1955) 3 AER 345 it was held the duty of the driver is to stop before he gets to the crossing, unless he sees there is no-one on it. *Dakley Moore v Robinson* (1982) RTR 74 is another example of the almost absolute approach—a person who stopped within the approach limits, thinking he was out of petrol, was convicted as he was not out of fuel in fact.

Exemptions to all these rules (except (iv)) are provided under BL 5 where there are road works, an emergency etc. The general overriding validity of pointsmen and Garda directions and the special Regulations in BL 3 and 4 should also be borne in mind.

Part VII Motorways
This part was added by The Road Traffic General Bye-laws (Amendment) Regulations 1983 (SI 275/1983). As to motorways generally. See para 5.15 below.
BL 39 Definitions: definitions for the part are given—Direction of Flow of Traffic, Left hand, Right hand side, medium strip, Motorway and Carriageway. These call for no special explanation here.
BL 40 Prohibitions: A driver on a motorway shall not—

(1) Drive against the direction of traffic flow;
(2) Drive on or across any part of the motorway which is not a carriageway;
(3) stop or park on the motorway;
(4) Drive a vehicle with a 40 mph speed limit or less (See Chapter 3) on the right lane of the motorway, except when necessary due to obstruction or closure of other lanes, or where stopped by an obstruction.
Exceptions to Rules (2) and (3) are—

(a) Vehicles removing obstructions or engaged in maintenance;
(b) State or Local Authority vehicles repairing or altering the motorway and equipment for the same;
(c) Fire Brigades, Garda Vehicles and Ambulances in the course of their duty;
(d) A vehicle which has broken down, or been damaged in an accident or in an emergency;
(e) A vehicle parked as set out below (BL 42) off the road.
(f) A vehicle required to stop by a Garda.

BL 41 Accident/Breakdown:
Where, due to an accident, breakdown or emergency, a vehicle cannot proceed, the driver or person in charge must-

(i) Drive or move the vehicle off the carriageway and on to the left margin;
(ii) Notify the Gardai by the nearest telephone;
(iii) Accept assistance (and pay for it) for the removal of the vehicle off the carriageway by the Gardai or Road Authority.

BL 42 Obstruction: If any object likely to cause a danger or obstruction to traffic is thrown, falls, or is deposited from a vehicle, the driver must notify the Gardai by the nearest telephone and park his vehicle in the left margin.

As to obstruction generally, see para 4.8.

5.4 Control of Traffic In Specified Areas

5.4.1 Specified Area Bye-laws

The power to make local Bye-laws to control traffic is in s 89 of the Act 1961 Act (as amended by sch, 1968 Act). These bye-laws are usually made with parking bye-laws under s 90 Act (See para 5.5. below and, in particular, the list of bye-laws at para 5.5.9)

Section 89 gives the Commissioner of the Gardai power to make, in respect of any specified area, bye-laws for the regulation and control, and to facilitate the movement, of traffic and pedestrians. 'Traffic' does not include pedestrians. These bye-laws overrule the General bye-laws under para 5.3 in a conflict (See General Bye-laws 1964 BL 4). See however, bye-laws 26 and 16 of the 1964 bye-laws as to general rules of parking. See also Dangerous Parking at para 4.7 and obstruction at para 4.8.

Before making the bye-laws s 89 the Commissioner must:

(a) Get the Minister for the Environment to consent; and
(b) Consult with the local authority concerned, under the Road Traffic (Bye-laws and Temporary Rules) Regulations 1961 (SI 219/1961).

To comply with these requirements the Commissioner must send two copies of the bye-law to the Minister for his consideration. The Commissioner must also send with those copies evidence that the local authority has been consulted and that the provisions of s 6 (5) of the 1961 Act have been complied with (See para 7.7). These regulations further require the Commissioner to publish after Ministerial approval is obtained, in three newspapers circulating in the affected areas (of which one at least must be a daily newspaper), a notice of the making of the bye-laws. This notice must state the Section under which the bye-laws are made, the area they operate in, and the place where and price at which Bye-laws can be bought. Amending SI 60/1962 does not affect bye-laws under this section.

Special powers in s 89 (2) in respect of these bye-laws allow them to deal with specifying the course of traffic; its turning and crossing public roads; prohibiting or restricting entrance to or passing along specified public roads; direction control, size, length and breadth of vehicles; conduct of pedestrians; load restrictions on certain roads; the restriction of animals on certain roads; the depositing of goods on footpaths or roads; washing of footpaths; controlling queuing; prohibiting stopping, reversing, turning or overtaking, as specified; and (by amendments made by the 1968 Act Schedule) control by Traffic signs. Different bye-laws can be made for different classes of traffic and different circumstances. The existing bye-laws are set out in paragraph 5.5.10 below.

5.4.1 *Control of Traffic In Specified Areas*

Most bye-laws contain many of the above types of clauses, and are usually combined with parking bye-laws under s 90 of the 1961 Act (See para 5.5.3). The procedure to be followed by the Commissioner is set out above and at para 7.6. That paragraph also deals with the making of these bye-laws and the question of their proof.

Under 89 of the 1961 Act controls of one-way streets, no entry, no right turn, etc, are also operated.

It is an offence to which the General penalty applies (para 7.1.) and to contravene a bye-law. It is a defence under s 89 (8) to show that the act was done bona fide and reasonably to save some person or property from death, destruction or injury.

In relation to the power of the Garda Commissioner, the Minister may, under s 62 of the 1968 Act, transfer this power to a specified Road Authority by Order (See para 5.2.2 above). In fact, there has always been considerable discussion between the Gardai, Local Authorities and interest groups about such bye-laws.

In *DPP v McDonald and Ord* (1983) ILRM 223 it was held that Bye-laws under this section and s 90 (see para 5.57) are not, and are not intended to be, effective to regulate traffic and parking at a lawful Fair or Market. This can only be done under s 92 (1) where evidence raises an inference that the conduct complained of may consist of trading in a lawful market, the prosecutor must rebut that inference if he is to secure a conviction for breach of bye-laws under s 89 and 90.

5.4.2 Power to make Local Temporary Rules to control traffic

Under s 89(3) and (4) the 1961 Act, the Commissioner of the Gardai has similar powers to those described at para 5.4.1 to make temporary rules on more or less the same matters. These would be for test periods normally. Different rules can be made for different classes of traffic and in different circumstances. The rules are intended to last a maximum of one year, unless revoked before that. They overrule bye-laws while operational. The Commissioner must give prescribed notice before operating any of the rules, and they cannot come into operation until a week after their being made. It is during that week the Commissioner must give notice of the rules (see below). The general procedure to be followed by the Commissioner for making of temorary rules is set out at para 7.6. The existing temporary rules, which are often combined with temporary parking rules, can be ascertained by local enquiry. They are normally of short duration for experimental purposes.

The procedure in relation to giving notice is governed by SI 219/1961. It requires notice to be published in at least three newspapers circulating in the area of operation of the Rules, and one such newspaper must be a daily one. The notice must specify the section under which it is made, date and area of operation, and where Rules can be bought at what price. Persons who contravene a rule are guilty of an offence to which the general penalty applies (para 7.1). It is a good defence to show that the act done bona fide and reasonably was to save some person from death or injury, or to prevent property destruction or injury.

The same right given to the Minister to transfer functions by Order as described above exists in relation to these temporary Rules, i.e. from the Commissioner to the Road Authority under s 62 of the 1968 Act. (See para 5.2.2 above).

5.4.3 Fixed Penalty

By virtue of 103 of the 1961 Act, the system of fixed penalties or on-the-spot fines applies to breach of bye-laws or rules under s 89 (See para 5.11.2).

5.5 Power To Make Local Parking Bye-laws

5.5.1 Parking Bye-laws

By virtue of s 90 of the 1961 Act (as amended by Sch 1968 Act), the Commissioner of the Gardai may make bye-laws for the control and regulation of the parking of vehicles on public roads in any specified area. See para 5.4.1 as to the limits of that power in relation to fairs and markets (*DPP v McDonald and Ord* (1983) ILRM 223). See para 5.5.3 as to rules of parking, i.e. use of car parks, and para 5.14.1 as to the provision of car parks.

The Bye-laws under s 90 of the Act normally specify and regulate one or more of three types of parking in public places

(a) meter parking;
(b) disc parking (the 'Disc' being a printed document);
(c) supervised or attendant parking.

These bye-laws overrule the General Bye-laws 1964, as amended, in the event of conflict (1964, BL 4—See para 5.3.). Bye-laws under ss 89 and 90 are usually made together (See list at para 5.5.10).

The Commissioner must first consult with the Local Authority concerned and also get consent to the making of the bye-law from the Minister for the Environment. The procedure to be followed is set out in SI 219/1961. It requires the Commissioner to send two copies to the Minister, with proof that the local authority has been properly consulted (See para 7.6) under s 6 of the 1961 Act. When Ministerial approval has been obtained the Commissioner must publish a notice in three newspapers circulating in the area affected (one at least being a daily newspaper) of the making of the bye-law. This notice must state the Section under which the bye-law is made, the area it operates in, and the place where a copy can be bought and its price.

The bye-laws under 90 (2) may deal in particular with the places on public roads for parking; duration of parking, e.g. indefinitely or for specified periods; fees for parking by means of meters, discs, or to parking attendants;

conditions on and/or periods for which parking will be allowed; prohibiting parking in certain areas (including parking places); prohibiting unofficial parking attendants; and regulating and controlling the erection of signs about parking. This latter power was inserted by Sch, 1968 Act.

5.5.2 Meter Parking

A parking meter means, under s 90 (15), an apparatus for collecting fees at a parking place and for indicating payment of such fees and the periods that have elapsed since they were paid. If parking meters are used, then the local authority (County Council, Corporation, County or other Borough Urban Council or Town Commissioner, as defined in s 5(15)(b) and (c)) must provide the meters to collect and specify the fees; specify the periods covered by these fees; prohibiting parking without paying these fees; make rules for administering the meter parking system to deal with the class or type of vehicle of parking; specify what happens when meters are out of order; that vehicles can use spaces; exempting vehicles and specifying how these vehicles may be identified to allow suspension of operation of meters; and allowing the indications given on meters to be treated as proof of facts, e.g. red arrow on a time meter. The Minister's consent is necessary for these rules.

Meter parking is operating in one city (Dublin) in the Rebublic. Disc parking is now a more popular system in smaller cities and towns. The rules made for Dublin are the Dublin Meter Parking Places Rules 1985-87 (SI 27/1985 and SI 366/1985 and SI 232/1987). Parking meter rules are specifically stated in s 90(16) to come within the Statutory Instruments Act 1947 (See para 7.5.6). Different bye-laws can be made for different classes of vehicles and circumstances.

In a prosecution a meter is presumed, until the contrary is shown by the Defendant, to be duly placed, accurate and in good working order (s 90 (12). In *Strong v Dawtry* (1961) I All ER 926 it was held that a coin must be put in the meter immediately on parking. In that case the driver had gone for change. He was convicted. A similar view was taken in *Riley v Hunt* (1981) RTR 79, where it was held that the latest time for paying the initial charge was before the driver left the car. In *Wilson v Arnott* (1977) 2 All ER 5 the placing of a red bag over the meter suspended the bay from normal use.

The fixed penalty or 'on-the-spot' fine procedure of s 103 of the 1961 Act applies to meter parking breached (See para 5.11.2)

5.5.3 Disc Parking

If the Commissioner, in making bye-laws as under para 5.5.1, considers its necessary to operate disc-parking places, he can specify, by his additional powers under s 90 (4) of the 1961 Act, the fees to be paid for discs, how they are to be paid, who issues the discs, the duties of persons parking and how the discs are displayed. Different bye-laws can be made for different classes of vehicles and circumstances.

Normally these discs (which are made of paper) have printed on the back detailed instructions as to their use. They are sold in local shops, garages, etc. and are issued by the Local Authority. They usually allow a vehicle to move around a city or town to different parking areas during the time specified or allowed by the disc, e.g. within one hour.

5.5.4 Attendant Parking

Should the Commissioner allow licensed parking attendants to operate in an area, he may in the bye-laws made under s 90(1) (5) and (6) specify the fees chargeable by the attendant and the manner of payment to such attendants. He may set up a licensing system for attendants and determine the fee for their licences; provide for the issue of badges (and the fee for same) to be worn; specify the duties of attendants; and prohibit persons interfering with, obstructing or molesting them. Different bye-laws can be made for different classes of vehicles and circumstances.

Under s 90(14) a licensed car park attendant is not considered for the purpose of the Act to be in charge of the vehicles in the parking place at which he is the attendant.

5.5.5 Temporary Rules

The Garda Commissioner, under s 90(7) of the 1961 Act, with the consent of the Minister for the Environment can make temporary rules in respect of any specified area for all or any of the purposes set out in s 90 of that Act, i.e. the control and regulation of parking of vehicles in public roads. These are in the nature of experimental rules. Different rules can be made for different classes of vehicles and circumstances.

The general procedure for making these rules is referred to at para 7.6. The section specifically states that the temporary rules must be made at least a week before they become operational, and during that week the Commissioner must give the prescribed notice. Under SI 219/1961. Act (5) this means publishing a notice in at least three newspapers (of which one at least shall be a daily newspaper) circulating in the area where the rules are to have effect. The notice must specify under what section they are made, the date of operation, the area of operation, and where copies are on sale and the price thereof.

The rules operate for a year at maximum, unless revoked sooner. They overrule corresponding bye-laws in their area.

Existing temporary rules (Under ss 89 and 90)
All temporary rules prior to 1986 were repealed and replaced by the 27 sets of Bye-laws referred to at 5.5.10 below. Enquiries from the Local Authority or Gardai will establish the actual position, of whether any temporary rules have been made since then for the particular area or part of it.

5.5.6 Breach

Contravention of a bye-law or temporary rule is an offence, with the general penalty (para 7.1) applying. The fixed penalty procedure under s 103 of the 1961 act, as amended, applies to breaches of parking a mechanically propelled vehicle (See para 5.11.2).

The registered owner, hirer under a hire-purchase agreement, or the person parking is liable for breach of a bye-law or rule, or each of them under an amendment made by the new subsection (9) introduced by Sch 1968 Act. The new subsection (9) reads:

> Whenever there is a contravention of a Bye-law or Rule under this section and a mechanically propelled vehicle is involved, each of the following persons shall be guilty of an offence:
>
> (a) the registered owner of the vehicle
> (b) If the vehicle is the subject of a hire-drive agreement on the occasion in question, the hirer under the Agreement and
> (c) If the person parking it is not the registered owner or the hirer under a hire-drive agreement, the person parking the vehicle.

This subsection seems to have been re-enacted in this wide format to overcome the decision of *O'Toole v Life Association of Scotland* (1979) IR 53. There the High Court held dealing with the old and more narrowly worded subs (9) and (10), that the words 'used and use' referred to use which was related directly to the particular act or omission which constituted the contravention of the bye-law. The Court held, in the circumstances of an employee of the Defendant parking the defendant's vehicle unlawfully in contravention of his contract, that a District Justice was correct is dismissing the complaint against the Defendant company/vehicle owner.

In *DPP v Clancy* (1986) ILRM 268 the High Court supported a restrictive interpretation of bye-laws under ss 89 and 90 of the 1961 Act dealing with traffic, parking and signs. The then Limerick Traffic and Parking Bye-laws 1975 provided, in R 18: 'A driver shall comply with a prohibition, restriction or requirement indicated by means of a sign'. Both courts held this was not a 'catch all' Article but a rule requiring the driver to obey other valid Bye-laws, and the mere placing of a sign did constitute making a bye-law. The sign must, however, be validly designated and prescribed by a bye-law.

If no vehicle is involved, then the person contravening the bye-law is liable (s 90(12).

In a prosecution for any offence in relation to a parking meter it is prima facie presumed to be correctly placed, accurate and in good order.

The only statutory defences under s 90(10) are unauthorised use or the fact that the car is on hire-purchase defence for the hire-purchase firm.

5.5.7 Protection from Liability

The Commissioner and Local Authority are protected by s 90(13) from any claims arising from loss or damage to a vehicle or its contents in any parking place. As noted at para 5.5.4 a licensed parking attendant has somewhat similar protection.

5.5.8 Disposal of Fees

The disposal of fees collected is to be regulated by the Minister for the Environment. The present regulations are the Road Traffic (Parking Fees) Regulations 1969 (SI 169/1969), which state the fees are firstly to be applied for the cost of administering and maintaining car parks, meters and disc-parking places, and then towards capital expenditure on the provision of car parks, road improvements and traffic improvements.

5.5.9 Immobilisation

Section 101(B of the 1961 Act (inserted by the Dublin Transport Authority (Dissolution) Act 1987 provides for the immobilisation by devices of mechanically propelled vehicles on a public road, which are parked in contravention of any prohibition or restriction imposed under s 90 of the 1961 Act.

In cases of such unlawful parking:

(a) An authorised person can fix a device to the vehicle.
This is a device or appliance designed or adapted for fixing to a vehicle for the purpose of preventing it from being driven or otherwise put in motion. The authorised person can move the vehicle to another place for that purpose.
(b) Exceptions are ambulances, fire brigades, Garda vehicles used in the course of duty, or a vehicle with a validly displayed disabled drivers permit.
(c) When a device is attached a notice is also attached—this informs the owner what steps he is to take to secure removal of the device. Removal of the device is by authorised persons only. Removal of the Notice by a person not so entitled is an offence (General Penalty, para 7.1).
(d) Removal of the device is normally only made at the request of a person who shows he is the owner, and on payment of the prescribed fees. If the owner shows the parking was authorised, the fee will be waived. The device can also be removed for the purpose of removal of an abandoned vehicle (See para 5.12).
(e) Obstructing the placing of such a device or its unauthorised removal is an offence (General penalty, para 7.1).
(f) Authorised persons are those persons or classes of persons prescribed in regulations.
(g) Regulations are to be made by the Minister for the Environment, after consultation with the Minister for Justice, specifying who are authorised persons, the types of devices, notices and fees. No general regulations have been made as yet. Regulations under the repealed

5.5.9 *Power To Make Local Parking Bye-Laws*

Dublin Transport Authority Act 1986 s 34 remain in force but affect the Dublin area only

See also para 5.12 on immobilisation and removal.

5.5.10 Existing Bye-laws

These bye-laws provide for a wide range of traffic management measures, including bus-lanes, pedestrianisation, parking prohibitions and restrictions, clearways, meter and disc parking, parking permits for disabled drivers, parking discs for residents, etc,:

County of Carlow Traffic and Parking Bye-laws 1986 (SI No 177 of 1986).
County of Cavan Traffic and Parking Bye-laws 1986 (SI No 178 of 1986).
County of Clare Traffic and Parking Bye-laws 1986 (SI No 179 of 1986).
Cork (County Borough and County) Traffic and Parking Bye-laws 1986 (SI No 180 of 1986).
County of Donegal Traffic and Parking Bye-laws 1986 (SI No 181 of 1986).
Dublin Area Traffic and Parking Bye-laws 1986 (SI No 182 of 1986) and amending Bye-laws of 1987 (SI No 292 of 1987).
County of Galway Traffic and Parking Bye-laws 1986 (SI No 183 of 1986).
County of Kerry Traffic and Parking Bye-laws 1986 (SI No 184 of 1986).
County of Kildare Traffic and Parking Bye-laws 1986 (SI No 185 of 1986).
County of Kilkenny Traffic and Parking Bye-laws 1986 (SI no 186 of 1986).
County of Laoghis Traffic and Parking Bye-laws 1986 (SI No 187 of 1986).
County of Leitrim Traffic and Parking Bye-laws 1986 (SI No 188 of 1986).
Limerick (County Borough and County) Traffic and Parking Bye-laws 1986 (SI No 189 of 1986).
County of Longford Traffic and Parking Bye-laws 1986 (SI No 191 of 1986).
County of Louth Traffic and Parking Bye-laws 1986 (SI No 190 of 1986).
County of Mayo Traffic and Parking Bye-laws 1986 (SI No 192 of 1986).
County of Meath Traffic and Parking Bye-laws 1986 (SI No 193 of 1986).
County of Monaghan Traffic and Parking Bye-laws 1986 (SI No 193 of 1986).
County of Offaly Traffic and Parking Bye-laws 1986 (SI No 195 of 1986).
County of Roscommon Traffic and Parking Bye-laws 1986 (SI No 196 of 1986).
County of Sligo Traffic and Parking Bye-laws 1986 (SI No 197 of 1986).
County of Tipperary (NR & SR) Traffic and Parking Bye-laws 1986 (SI No 198 of 1986).
Waterford (County Borough and County) Traffic and Parking Bye-laws 1986 (SI No 199 of 1986). Amended by SI No 16 of 1988.
County of Westmeath Traffic and Parking Bye-laws 1986 (SI No 200 of 1986).
County of Wexford Traffic and Parking Bye-laws 1986 (SI No 201 of 1986).
County of Wicklow Traffic and Parking Bye-laws 1986 (SI No 202 of 1986).

5.5.11 Defence Forces

It appears that by virtue of the Interpretation Act 1937, 113 of the Defence Forces Act 1954 operates to exempt from certain local controls a member of the Defence Forces while on duty during a period of emergency so decided by Government order.

5.6 Large Assemblies Control

5.6.1 Power to Regulate Traffic

To meet unusually large volumes of traffic on occasions (e.g. race meetings, Fleadh Cheoil, etc) attracting assemblies of persons, special powers are given by s 91 of the 1961 Act (as amended by Sch, 1968 Act) to Gardai in uniform to preserve order in traffic and persons. Their powers are to divert, regulate and control traffic, and regulate and control parking. This can be done by oral or manual direction, or by the use of portable signs (of any size, colour and significance as may be prescribed). A Garda is given power to prohibit the passage of traffic, indicate the direction in which traffic is to proceed, prohibit, regulate, or limit parking or places as stands for public service vehicles, and generally to make such prohibitions or indications which he (Garda) considers necessary to prevent obstruction or disorder in traffic (subs (2)(e).

These powers are also applicable in the event of traffic congestion following a fire, flood or other similar occurrence. In addition, an officer of the Gardai may authorise any person to temporarily act, for the purpose of the section, as a parking attendant.

It should be noted that it is stated in 126 of the 1961 Act that nothing in the Act prejudices or derogates from the general power and duty of the Commissioner and Garda Siochana to preserve order in public places and to regulate and control traffic therein.

The permissible signs used on these occasions are specified in the Road Traffic (Signs) Regulations 1962 (SI 171/1962), Part V, R 19 (inserted by SI 127/1979, R 6) as amended, being regulatory signs prohibiting through traffic or turning, and indicating particular directions and stating whether parking is permissible or not (See para 5.8 as to signs).

5.6.2 Offence

Section 91 (3) of the 1961 Act (as amended by the 1968 Act, Sch) states:

> A person who contravenes a direction given by a member of the Garda Siochana under this section or a person who contravenes a prohibition, restriction or requirement indicated by a sign referred to in subsection (2) of this section shall be guilty of an offence.

The general penalty (para 7.1) applies.

5.6.2 *Large Assemblies Control*

On a strict reading, this subsection provides no penalty for disobeying a temporary parking attendant.

5.7 Fairs and Markets

5.7.1 Bye-laws

Bye-laws for these occasions can be made under 92 of the 1961 Act (as amended by the 1968 Act, Sch). Local Authorities have power to make the necessary bye-laws to secure the free passage of vehicular traffic through public roads on the occasions of fairs or markets in their functional areas.

As seen above (para 5.4.1), *DPP v McDonald or Ors* (1983) ILRM 223 held that the power to regulate is limited. See also *Skibbereen UDC v Quille & Ors* (1986) ILRM 170 as to the nature and duration of old established Fairs and Markets, despite road traffic and casual trading legislation.

5.7.2 Procedure

The provisions of 219, 221 and 223 of the Public Health (Ireland) Act 1878 apply to s 92 bye-laws. These provisions of the Health Act relate to making the consent of the Minister for the Environment necessary. As to the procedure under the Public Health Act for making, publishing, etc. bye-laws, see para 7.6.

The section recognises the existence of street fairs in towns by custom or charter. Few bye-laws have been made, as the fairs are gradually being replaced by marts (See para 5.7.4).

5.7.3 Local Authorities

The Local Authorities who are expected to act under the section are Corporations of a County or other Borough, County Councils, Urban Councils or Town Commissioners. Where a County includes a Borough, urban areas or town (with Commissioners therein presumably), then the County Council in the area is deemed not to include these boroughs, urban areas or towns.

5.7.4 Contravention of Bye-laws

It is an offence, with the general penalty (para 7.1) applying, to contravene a bye-law under the section. Proof, etc. of by-laws is covered at para 7.6.

5.7.5 Existing Bye-laws

Only two sets of bye-laws have been made:

(1) Ballyshannon Town Commissioners Bye-laws 1964—applying to the town of Ballyshannon:

(2) Longford Urban Distric Council Bye-laws 1969—applying to the town of Longford.

5.8 Traffic Signs

Section 95 of the 1961 Act (as amended by Sch, 1968 Act) provides for signs on roads and is largely a re-enactment of s 69 of the Local Government Act 1946, as amended by s 36 of the Local Government Act 1955, both of which sections are replaced by the 1961 Act. However, signs erected under those Acts are deemed to be provided under the 1961 Act.

5.8.1 Provisions of Signs

Road Authorities are required to provide traffic signs where indicated on any public roads in their charge at the written request of the Garda Commissioner and may, with the consent of the Commissioner, provide on roads such traffic signs as they consider desirable. The signs shall be transferred, altered and removed as the Commissioner requests. These may be permanent or temporary signs or for particular occasions, at the discretion of the Commissioner. The Local Authority must maintain and operate any signs as well as erect them.

The mere erection of an authorised sign and its contravention is not sufficient to create an offence. Thus in *DPP v Clancy* (1986) ILRM 268, dealing with the then Limerick Traffic and Parking Bye-laws 1975, Act 18 (which reads 'A driver shall comply with a prohibition, restriction or requirement indicated by a traffic sign.'), the court held it was not a 'catch all' article that the sign had to be designated and prescribed by a bye-law and it was the contravention of that which would create an offence.

5.8.2 Definitions

'Traffic sign' is defined, enlarging somewhat on its normal meaning, so as to include signs, devices, notices, road markings or signalling instruments operated by mechanical means which do one or more of the following:

(i) Gives information as to where Public Roads lead to and from, give distances or otherwise, i.e. signposts (called Informative Signs);

(ii) Warn of dangers and/or suggest precautions (called Warning Signs);

(iii) Indicate the existence of a Road Regulation in relation to a Public Road, or implement such a regulation, or both, or indicates the existence of a provision in an enactment relating to Road traffic (called Regulatory Signs). A 'Road Regulation' is an order, Regulation, Bye-law or rule under an enactment relating to traffic on a road, other than those made under s 86A (Bus stops and stands), s 91 (Large Assembly) s 93 (Bridges Protection) s 94 (Road Closing) or s 96 (School Crossings) Under the 1961 Act. See para 5.6.1 in relation to some of these other enactments.

5.8.3 Erection of Signs

5.8.3.1 *Entry on to land.* Special powers of entry on to private property adjacent to a road, but not being a part of a public road, are given to the Road Authority by s 95 (6) for the purpose of erecting a road sign where such provision is reasonably necessary. Before entry a 21-day notice must be served by registered post on the occupier and other persons with an interest in the land. Any person with an interest may apply under s 95 (6) on notice on the Road Authority, to the Minister for the Environment to direct removal of the sign, which the Minister may do if satisfied that it causes an unnecessary or unreasonable hardship. The Minister may direct its removal to another position by the Road Authority, or may refuse the application to remove the sign. The Road Authority is bound to remove the sign if the Minister so orders.

If a person wilfully obstructs or interferes with the erection of such a sign, or without lawful authority removes, defaces or otherwise injures such a sign, he is guilty of an offence. The general penalty (para 7.1) applies.

5.8.3.2 *Expenses.*The expenses of a Road Authority in providing traffic signs for a public road shall be part of the expense of maintaining the road.

5.8.4 Prohibition of Private Signs

It is normally an offence for any person other than a Road Authority to provide a sign. The general penalty applies (para 7.1) It is presumed, until the Defendant shows to the contrary, that the sign is erected by a person other than a Road Authority and without consent. The exception is where there is consent given by the Commissioner. A person shall not provide a sign, device, notice or light which is not a traffic sign, if it is visible from the public road and is either (a) capable of being confused with a traffic sign, or (b) it makes a lawful traffic sign less visible, or (c) it obstructs the view of road users dangerously. To do so is an offence and the General Penalty applies (para 7.1).

If such a sign is erected, the occupier or owner (if unoccupied) is guilty of the offence unless he shows, under s 95(20), that the sign, device, notice or light was not provided by him or with his consent, and that he had it removed as soon as practicable after it came to his notice.

5.8.5 Validity of Signs

To obviate the need in prosecutions to prove (a) that the Road Authority actually provided the sign, and (b) that the Commissioner consented thereto to the request of the Road Authority, s 95(18) of the 1961 Act states that a traffic sign on or near a public road shall be taken as having been lawfully placed until the contrary is shown by the Defendant. Should doubt arise, the prosecution are normally entitled to an adjournment to prove validity (*Royal v Prescott Clarke* (1966) 2 All ER 366). It is no defence that a person did not see the sign (*Hill v Baxter* (1958) 1 All ER 193).

Signs and their meaning are strictly construed (*Brazier v Alabaster* (1962) Crim LR 173). Thus, a non-conforming sign or a sign not erected under the proper authority cannot give rise to an offence if they are disobeyed (*DPP v Clancy* (1986) ILRM 268). *MacLeod v Hamilton* (1965) SLT 305 is authority for the proposition that if a sign is not in conformity with the regulations then no offence arises; and this was taken further in *Davis v Heatley* (1971) RTR 145, in that, even if the sign is clearly recognisable to a reasonable man as a sign of that kind, no offence arises unless the sign complies with the size, colour and type prescribed. This would not be so where there was only a trivial departure from the regulations (*Cotterill v Chapman* (1984) RTR 73). Also, even if the sign itself is all right, the offence can be recorded if the back of the sign is wrong (*Sharples v Blackmore* (1973) RTR 249).

As disobedience of signs is an offence if they are properly and lawfully erected, there can often be a double summons, e.g. additional dangerous driving. If, however, a Court on such a charge took disobedience of signs into account, this conviction would be a bar on further proceedings (*Welton v Taneborne* (1908) 72 JP 419).

5.8.6 Regulations as to Signs

Under s 96(2) of the 1961 Act, the Minister for the Environment has wide powers to make regulations as to signs. Many of these signs now display international standards and symbols.

Where a sign is a type specified by Regulations, the Road Authority must use that type of sign. Signs can be with or without words. If a Road Authority is providing a traffic sign, and it is not a sign specified by the Minister's regulation, e.g. a Tourist sign, then it must, under subs (16), be in conformity with any general or particular directions that the Minister has given. The Minister issued a Memorandum on this matter in October 1962.

In *Levine v Morris* (1970) 1WLR 7 it was held that the English Minister for Transport owes a duty to motorists when siting large signs to choose the site with care and, if there is an option, not to choose a more hazardous site.

Temporary or local signs displaying hours or days of parking must be clear and precise (*James v Carey* (1967) 2QB 676). A portable sign of an authorised nature must be obeyed even though person using it is not a policeman in uniform (*Langley Cartage Co v Jenks* (1937) 2 All ER 523). In *Murray v Sturrock* (1951) SLYT 34 a sign reading 'no waiting this side today' was held not to be deficient through ambiguity.

It should be noted that under s 5 of the Tourist Traffic Act 1952 Bord Failte Eireann may supply Local Authorities with local signs outside the scope of s 95, i.e. direction signs to monuments or to places of local interest or amenity (e.g. a Golf Club; Youth Hostels); and Route notices (See 1962 Memorandum referred to above).

There are also controls under the Local Government (Planning and Development Act) 1963, as amended, in relation to certain advertisements, landscape maps and indicators on or near public roads (See, *inter alia*, ss 53 and 89 of that Act).

The present regulations are in a somewhat confused state because of successive amending regulations to the 1962 Principal Regulations. It it to be hoped that a new, comprehensive regulation will be introduced in due course. Existing regulations are:

(1) Road traffic (Signs) Regulations 1962 (SI 171/1962);.
(2) Regulations Amending (1) are—

SI 56/1964	SI233/1966
SI 217/1969	SI 164/1970
SI 127/1971	SI 188/1971
SI 256/1971	SI 247/1974
SI 280/1975	SI 66/1977
SI 51/1979	SI 329/1979
SI 413/1979	SI 358/1980 (Bus Lanes)
SI 333/1981 (Bus Lanes)	SI 276/1983
SI 182/1985	SI 292/1988

Road Traffic (Signs) Regulations 1962 (SI 171/1962)
These regulations are 33 pages long and have been amended regularly. They describe the signs with specification as to colour and symbols, etc. It is not feasible to set them out in detail here. Reference should be made to the Regulations themselves, as amended. The following is an outline of their contents:

Definitions of many terms are set out in R2. These include Bus Stop sign, Informative sign, Regulatory sign, Traffic sign and warning sign.

Section 95 signs are divided into different types as stated above. Each type is described in the Regulations, i.e.—

(a) Informative signs (R 3) are upright signs giving information about the road, including distance and where the road leads. The specifications require a white background and black lettering, etc in Irish and English, but in Gaeltacht areas it can be Irish only (SI 164/1970, R 2 amending).
(b) Warning signs (R 4) are to be a yellow diamond in shape and display black symbols as laid down by the Schedules of the regulations. The Dimensions of such signs are also regulated and set out. A warning sign means an upright sign which warns persons of danger in relation to a road, or which advises the precautions to be taken against such danger, or both, e.g. to indicate that a dangerous corner is ahead.
(c) Regulatory signs (R5-8) are to be used to indicate a major road, stop, and the end of a speed limit, as specified in the Schedules, and include other signs, e.g. to yield right of way. The definition in R 2 of such a sign is one which is an upright sign which indicates the existence of a road regulation (as in s 95 (1) of the 1961 Act) in relation to a road, or implements such regulation, or both, or

which indicates that a built up area speed limit applies or ceases to apply to a road or roads.

Specific Signs are covered by R.9.

Pedestrian Crossing—Roadway markings, beacons, refuge, etc, are set out (amended by R 3, SI 233/1966). Where the markings are to be on the road, the colour of the beacons and details of the pedestrians crossing equipment, the signs and their format are also specified. See also SI 329/1979 as to pedestrian crossing complex signs (*infra*).

Road markings are covered by RR10 to 12. Specifications are given for stop lines, continuous white lines, double continuous white lines (R3, SI 56/1964), broken white lines, white arrows, two bended arrows, curved arrows, place names and arrows, parking prohibitions, meter parking, lots, cycle parks, broken yellow lines, continuous yellow lines, and double yellow lines (amended by 1964/66/69 Regulations). See para 5.3.3 as to the meaning and observance of these under the General Bye-law.

Traffic lights and signals lamps, their type, size, colour, etc, are specified in RR 13 and 14, e.g. lamps coloured red, amber and green with their height from the ground. Arrows in lamps, etc. are also provided for. In *Doyle v HF Murray* (1967) IR 390 the Supreme Court laid down the principle of care at such lights (see para 5.3.3, BL 13).

Section 86 signs are covered by RR 15 and 16 i.e. Bus Stop signs regulated. R 15 has been amended and replaced by R 7 of SI 233/1966 (see chapter 1, part 2). See para 5.3.3. as to observance.

Section 96 signs (see para 5.9), i.e. Traffic Warden signs and the Wardens uniforms are specified in RR17 and 18. See also para 7.2.

Section 91 signs (see para 5.6 *supra*) are covered by R19, This deals with Temporary Garda signs and was added by SI 127/1969.

Schedules—Set out scale specimen signs, with the specifications, the type of text to be used, etc. These Schedules have been extensively amended by the 1964, 1967 and 1969 Regulations (below) and also by other regulations.

Amending Regulations

These extensively amend the 1962 Regulations and add some additional signs and markings. Some direct amendments are noted above briefly.

1964 Amending Regulations (SI 56/1964)

These provide for the use of certain signs to ports; warning signs for unprotected waterways, canals and rivers; roadmarkings; information plates and roadway markings in meter parking areas. SI 217/1969, R 7 amends these regulations by adding a regulation (R8) to deal with meter parking bays.

1966 Amending Regulations (SI 233/1966)

These provide for new roadway markings to indicate a prohibition to entry to a street for the alteration of Road markings; and for the use of other native language bus stop signs.

1966 Amending Regulations (SI 217/1969)

As noted above, these deal with signs for meter parking and signs under s 91 of the 1961 Act, which are used by Gardai for the temporary control of traffic, i.e. portable signs.

1970 Amending Regulations (SI 164/1971)
These regulations allow the Irish versions of signs in Gaeltacht areas.
1971 Amending Regulations (SI 127/1971)
Provide for the use of 'box junction' road markings and enable loading bays to be provided outside meter parking places.
1971 Amending Regulations (No 2) (SI 188/1971)
These allow plates showing information, e.g. prohibited times or days, to be erected and signs dealing with the prohibition of Traffic, e.g. one-way streets. The signs involved are Nos. 204, 205 and 206.
1971 Amending Regulations (No 3) (SI 256/1971)
Create a new type of sign (No 216) indicating that traffic, or a specified traffic is prohibited in both directions. They also alter the significance of signs 204 and 209, and allow information plates with signs 207, 208, 209 and 216.
1974 Amending Regulations (SI 247/1974)
Allow for markings and signs for disc parking and meter parking.
1975 Amending Regulations (SI 280/1975)
These deal with a pedestrian crossing controlled by traffic lights, and enable a Road Authority to introduce flashing Amber and Green lights there.
1977 Amending Regulations (SI 66/1977)
Allow for the reduction in size of sign 213 when fixed to a parking meter.
1979 Amending Regulations (SI 51/1979)
Provide for sign 217, indicating the prohibition of vehicles exceeding a specified weight.
1979 Amending Regulations (SI 329/1979)
Provide for 'Pedestrian crossing complex' signs and dual carriage junction signs.
1980 Amending Regulations (SI 358/1980)
Provide for a bus lane marking and contra-flow bus lanes to show that part of a roadway is a bus lane on which specified vehicles only are permitted.
1981 Amending Regulations (SI 333/1981)
Provide for the use of Irish on information plates, road markings, bus lanes, and bus only streets.
1983 Amending Regulations (SI 276/1983)
Provide for a series of road markings to be used on motorways. See para 5.15.4. as to these.
1985 Amending Regulations (SI 182/1985)
Allow 'box junction' controls to have effect, whether or not the junction is controlled by Traffic Lights.
1988 Amending Regulations (SI 292/1988)
Provide that name signs in Irish be in Italic letters, and that in English be in Roman letters.

5.9 School Crossings

Section 37 of the Local Government Act 1955 is repealed and replaced by s 96 of the 1961 Act. Section 96 (amended by Sch. 1968 Act) provides that local authorities may appoint school wardens, with the consent of the Garda Commissioner, whose duties are to patrol and control places where school children cross public roads. As to 'public road', see para 7.9.

The school warden, if in prescribed uniform (which term includes any garment, armlet or cap), can by authorised sign stop traffic (not including pedestrians) to enable school children to cross the road in safety. Failure by a person to stop his vehicle or animal is an offence involving the general penalty (para 7.1). In legal proceedings a person acting as school warden is prima facie presumed to be acting properly, in accordance with regulations. The sign and uniform are prescribed by the Road Traffic (Signs) Regulations 1962 (SI 171/1962), Part IV (See para 5.8.4). The sign is a white disc with a red border mounted on a pole, with the word 'stop' and the symbol of children crossing. The uniform is a white or off-white overcoat. A person is not bound to stop unless the warden exhibits the sign so as to be visible to traffic (*Hay v Smith* (1964) 1WLR 1377). The earlier case of *RV Greenwood* (1962) Crim LR 639 stated that a vehicle was not bound to stop *even if* the sign was exhibited, unless children were actually crossing or seeking to cross the the road. It is unlikely that this would now be regarded as correct law, and the wording of s 96 (2) only requires the school warden to exhibit his sign requiring traffic to stop and remain stopped to enable school children to cross the road in safety. Therefore, it is an offence in Ireland for traffic not to stop as required, and not to remain stopped accordingly, so long as the sign is exhibited.

In *Franklin v Langdown* (1971) 3 All AER 662 and *Wall v Walwyn* (1974) RTR 24 it was held not to be necessary to show that the children were impeded, i.e. overruling *Greenwood* above in reality.

For the purpose of the section local authorities mean County Councils, Corporations of a County or other Borough, Urban Districts Councils or Town Commissioners. The Commissioners have the functions of the section vested in them, even though their areas are also in the physical area of the County Council (Subs (5)). This provision is necessary because County Councils usually have control of national roads going through towns and cities.

Under s 62 of the 1968 Act, the Minister for the Environment may make an Order making this function of school wardens the exclusive domain of the Local Authority, i.e. doing away with the necessity of the Ministers consent.

5.10 Closing Roads

5.10.1 Closing Order

It is obviously important that the public road system be open to the public. Under the 1961 Act, s 94, a road can normally only be permanently closed after a public inquiry. If, as a result of a public inquiry s 94, the Minister for the Environment is satisfied that it has been proved that the driving of vehicles, or any class of vehicle, would endanger traffic on a specified public road, or that the road is unsuitable for such vehicles or class, he may Order, prohibit (subject to such exceptions or conditions as may be specified in the Order) the driving of all vehicles or any class of vehicles on it. Where such an Order is made, then it is forbidden to drive on the road in contravention of the Order, the driver/owner both being liable to the general penalty (para 7.1). It is a good defence by the owner to show that the vehicle was used on the occasion by another person and that such use was unauthorised.

5.10.2 Notices and Signs

The Road Authority responsible for the maintenance of such roads must erect and maintain notices at places specified in the Order, in an approved form, stating the effect of the closing Order. The Road Authority may also erect signs informing drivers of the prohibition—this becomes mandatory if the Garda Commissioner requires such signs to be erected. The signs are to be of such sizes, shapes, colours and character as may be prescribed. No general Regulations have yet been made on these, but they can be specified in the closing Order.

5.10.3 Revoking and Amending the Order

The Minister may revoke or amend his closing Order, on giving notice to the Road Authority and considering its representations. If the Minister revokes or amends the Order the Road Authority must revoke or alter the notices it erected. The making of representations is a 'reserved functions' under the County of City Management Acts, i.e. the representations are a result of a decision by the elected councillors, not the Manager or officials.

Under s 62 of the 1968 Act, the involvement of the Garda Commissioner may be dispensed with by Ministerial Order.

There is no specified procedure as to how a public inquiry is conducted under s 94. Only one such inquiry has been held, in fact, under the Act, and the procedure used was that used in compulsory purchase inquiries.

5.10.4 Temporary Closing

It should be remembered that at events that attract large assemblies of people, or in certain emergencies, the Gardai can prohibit the passage of Traffic (see para 5.6) through a Road.

Under s 4 and s 35 of the Local Government Act 1955 and the Temporary Closing of Roads Regulations 1956 (SI 30/1956), the local authority charged with the maintenance of a road may, after giving the prescribed notice, close a road or part of it for such period and in such conditions as it sees fit. Use of such road then without due authority can attract a £5 fine.

This section enables local authorities to close the road specifically for road races. The Minister for the Environment can vary or annul the local authorities' decisions. The regulations (SI 30/1956) specify that the Minister must be notified, a newspaper notice must be inserted, and, if a road race is being held, the Gardai must be notified also. In cases of urgency the Minister only need be notified.

5.10.5 Extinguishment/Abandoment

At common law it is difficult to either extinguish or abandon a public right of way. Almost any user, however irregular, keeps the right alive. However, when a public right of way over a public road is extinguished, the right to pass and repass is terminated, and the Road Authority is relieved of responsibility for the road.

A road (other than a main road) may be abandoned, and this also relieves the local authority of responsibility for the road, but it does not affect the right of way of the public

A public right of way may be extinguished under a number of legislative provisions. The most commonly used are s 76 of the Local Government (Planning and Development) Act 1963 (as amended by s 43 of the Local Government (Planning and Development) Regulations 1977 (SI 65 of 1977), s 10 of the Local Government (No 2) Act 1960 (as substituted by 86 of the Housing Act 1966) and 84 of the Local Government Act 1946.

5.11 Fixed Penalty Procedure

5.11.1 Regulations

The cost and effort of court proceedings for rather obvious and not too serious offences can be avoided under s 103 of the Act, 1961 as amended by s 64 and Sch, 1968 Act. This section allows the Minister for the Environment to specify by regulations offences under the Road Traffic Acts and road-related offences (e.g. no tax) to which the system of what is commonly, but somewhat incorrectly, described as 'fines on the spot' can be applied. The existing regulations are Road Traffic Act 1961 (Section 103) (Offences) Regulations 1976 (SI 188/1976) ('The Principal Regulations') and amending regulations, SI 90/1983, 443/1986.

The section is supplemented by the provisions of the Local Authorities (Traffic Wardens) Act, which specifies offences for which local authority traffic wardens can impose 'fines on the spot'. The Wardens' range of offences is not as wide as a Garda's (see paras 5.11.4 and 7.2.7).

5.11.2 Existing offences

The existing offences, declared to be offences to which the section applies, are:

(1) breaches of bye-laws and rules under s 84 of the 1961 Act, which prohibit street service vehicles from standing for hire except at appointed stands—£10 fine as from January 1987 (See para 1.16);

(2) breaches of bye-laws under s 86 of the act, which prohibited the stopping or parking of cars or machines within certain marked areas for bus stops or stands, or other mechanically propelled vehicles within certain marked areas—£10 fine (see para 1.17);

(3)(a) breaches of bye-laws or rules under 89 and 90 of the Act, which prohibits the parking of mechanically propelled vehicles in a specified place, time, manner or without paying a fee (e.g. parking meter)—£10 fine (see para 5.4 for s 89; para 5.5 for s 90),

(b) Offences of stopping or parking on a clearway during a prohibited time under a bye-law made under s 90 of the Act 1961 and s 6 of the 1968 Act—£15 fine,

(c) parking on a bus lane in contravention of a bye-law or rule under s 90 of the Act and s 6 of the 1968 Act—£15 fine;

(4) Non-display of a proper insurance disc under s 11 of the 1968 Act—£50 fine (see para 6.4.11).

(5) Certain Offences under s 12 of the 1961 Act, i.e. overloading under the maximum weight section—£50 fine (see para 1.7);

(6) Tax offence of non-displaying of a tax disc under s 73 of the Finance Act 1976—£50 fine (see para 1.11).

There is power in the section to enable different amounts of fines to be specified for different offences, classes of vehicles or areas. This is under s 103 (6A) of the 1961 Act, inserted by Sch, 1968 Act. There has, in fact, been a substantial increase in the number of 'on the spot' offences and of the amount of the fines. The first set of regulations introduced in 1962 (S I 91/1962, which have long since been repealed) has three sets of offences with a fine of 50p. A touch of 'The good old days' even in reasonably recent times!

5.11.3 Procedure

If a Garda or authorised person (see below) reasonably believes a person has committed an offence, or finds a vehicle, the use of which vehicle amounts to an offence, in the circumstances to which s 103 applies, he must deliver to the person or affix to the vehicle a notice in the form prescribed in the Schedule to SI 188/1976, stating that the offence has been committed. The form specifies that the person has an option to pay the fixed fine to a Garda at a specified Garda Station within 21 days on sending in the notice, and, if he does, then he will not be prosecuted for the alleged offence. A receipt is issued on payment. It appears, under a rather curious phrase in subs (4)(b), that if you pay the fine you cannot get it back under any circumstances.

If the person elects to pay, the matter ends there, but, should prosecution be brought, the onus of proof of payment is on the defendant, i.e. if an ordinary summons issues. There is unfair provision in the District Court rules (1948 as amended) that one cannot normally get costs or expenses against the Garda (See *Dillane v AG & Ir*—Supreme Court (1980) ILRM 167 which upheld this rule), although these rules do not appear to extend to authorised persons.

It is an offence (General penalty applies, para 7.1) for any person, other than the person to whom the notice applies, to remove or interfere with a notice affixed to a vehicle.

5.11.4 Authorised Person

These were introduced by the 1968 Act to relieve the burden on the Gardai in relation to work on the beat dealing with parking and minor offences. An authorised person means a person appointed by the Garda Commissioner to be such—normally known as a 'Traffic Warden'. Their number, pay and conditions are determined by the Minister for Justice with the approval of the Minister for Finance. They do not, however, have Civil Service status and the Acts and Regulations of the Civil Service do not apply to them.

Authorised persons have power to demand the name and address of a person who they reasonably believe has committed an offence to which the section applies. To refuse, fail, or to give a false or misleading name and address to an authorised person is an offence (General Penalty applies, para 7.1). As to their appointment and powers, see also para 7.2.7.

5.11.5 'Previous conviction'—Bar

As on payment of the fixed penalty no prosecution follows, no question of conviction arises. therefore, these offences are not mentionable as 'previous convictions' in subsequent prosecutions. If, however, the fixed penalty is not paid and the matter is then brought to Court successfully, a conviction does arise and becomes one which could be mentioned in later criminal charges.

Where a fixed penalty is payable under the section it is so payable only if the vehicle is parked unlawfully. Should a summons for such parking be dismissed (on its merits or because no evidence is offered), that dismissal is a bar to recovery of the fixed charge (*Metropolitan Police Commissioner v Mellar* (1963) 107 S.J. 831; (1963) Crim LR 856).

5.12 Removal of Vehicles

A procedure to deal quickly with an abandoned or unlawfully parked vehicle is found in s 97 of the 1961 Act (as replaced by s 63 of the 1968 Act). The procedure is to remove the offending vehicle, store it for a time, and then to dispose of it in the manner set out in the relevant regulations.

5.12.1 Offending Vehicles

The power can be exercised in respect of two sets of vehicles:

(a) vehicles which have been, or appear to have been, abandoned on a public road or in a Local Authority car park (See para 5.14) provided under s 101 of the 1961 Act; or
(b) vehicles which have been parked in contravention of the Act or any regulation, bye-law or rule made under the Road Traffic Acts.

'Vehicle', for the purpose of the section, is stated to include a part of a vehicle or an article designed as but being a non-functioning vehicle, and a load on or in a vehicle. There is no definition of 'abandon' or 'appear to have been abandoned' in the Act, so each case will depend on its own facts, although these phrases are equated to each other in fact in regulations (See next paragraph).

5.12.2 Regulations

The Minister for the Environment has a general power to make regulations authorising and providing for the removal, storage and disposal of such offending vehicles—this power includes regulating who does the removal, etc; how the vehicle is stored; charges for removal and storage to be demanded from the owners; the disposal or sale of offending vehicles; and how money so collected is disposed of. The regulations may apply generally or in specified circumstances, and different regulations may be made for different circumstances. However, the Minister's power to regulate the disposal of removed vehicles is limited by subs (4) of the section, which makes it mandatory to retain the vehicle for six weeks at least from the time of removal, or for two weeks after notice had been given in the prescribed manner, whichever is the longer.

The present regulations are The Road Traffic (Removal, Storage and Disposal of Vehicles) Regulations 1983 (SI 91/1983).

The main provisions are as follows: An offending vehicle which has been abandoned on a public road or in a car park can be removed by the Gardai and, in certain circumstances, by or on behalf of a Road Authority (i.e. County Council, Corporation or Urban Council). If a Road Authority is requested by a Garda officer or Inspector to remove an abandoned vehicle, it must do so. Power is given to the Road Authority to take steps and to make arrangements with others (e.g. garage) for the removal and storage of abandoned vehicles. It should be noted, as stated in the last paragraph, that there is no definition of 'abandoned' or 'appears to be abandoned' but there is a curious provision in R 3(2) which says that reference to an abandoned vehicle is to be intended to include a vehicle which appears to be abandoned.

Unlawfully parked vehicle (R6). These may be removed by or on the authority of a Garda or other person appointed by a Road Authority (presumably persons who are traffic wardens or the like) after consultation with the Garda Commissioner. The Garda or such person can take such steps or make such arrangements with other persons (e.g. with a garage) as are necessary for the removal or storage of the offending vehicle. Removal can be to a non-storage place and thence to a storage place, e.g. an obstructing vehicle can be moved to a convenient spot off the road at first and thence to a proper place of storage.

If an immobilisation device under 101B of the 1961 Act is attached, it can be removed by an authorised person (see para 5.5.9).

Charges (R7). The removal charge is £20 and storage costs £2 for each day or part of a day (measured in periods of 24 hours). These charges are payable on vehicle being reclaimed by the owner, who can take his vehicle away on his producing satisfactory evidence of ownership. The charges may be remitted if the owner shows that the vehicle was unlawfully parked by another person whose use of it was unauthorised. Any charges unpaid can be recovered as a simple contract debt in any court of competent jurisdiction, e.g. up to £2,500 in the District Court. The charges are payable to the Garda Commissioner or the Road Authority, as the case may be.

Disposals (R8 and 9). This can be arranged by the Road Authority or the Garda Commissioner where a vehicle is unclaimed or charges are unpaid, having first either (a) notified the owner of the intended disposal, having held the vehicle for not less than six weeks, or on two weeks' notice presumably, or (b) where it is found not to be reasonably possible to trace the owner, after a notice of intention to dispose has been published in at least one daily newspaper. See the meaning of 'owner' in para 7.9.

Under R 10 (see below), if within a year of disposal the owner satisfies the Road Authority or the Garda Commissioner that he is the owner of the vehicle, he can be repaid the proceeds of sale less charges and expenses of disposal.

Money from disposal (R10). The money collected as above is to be used by Road Authorities to defray their operational costs of the scheme and then for works of the relevant county or municipal fund.

If the money is collected by the Gardai, it is paid into the Exchequer for use as the Minister for Finance directs.

5.12.3 Offence

A person who obstructs or impedes (or assists in such conduct) the removal of a vehicle under s 97 is guilty of an offence. The general penalty (para 7.1) applies.

5.12.4 Damages

The section, i.e. s 97(6) of the 1961 Act specifically provides a bar against an action for damages in respect of anything done in good faith and without negligence in the course of the removal, storage or disposal of a vehicle under the section.

5.12.5 Planning Acts

The deposit of car bodies and other parts of vehicles on land is subject to control under the Local Government (Planning and Development Act)

1963. Section 3(2)(b)(iii) of that Act includes such operations specifically within the meaning of 'Development' under that Act. This means that a Local Authority has powers over such anti-social behaviour under that Act too.

5.12.6 Litter Act

The Litter Act 1982 also grants wide powers to local authorities to prosecute for abandoned vehicles and to dispose of them (see para 1.29.4 (b)).

5.13 Investigation of Accidents

Section 66 of the 1968 Act introduced a power for the Minister for the Environment, through authorised persons, to investigate accidents and the vehicles involved in them. The section is operational under SI 169/1969 but is not used in fact, and specific regulations allowable under the Section have not been made. The principle is that investigation of particular accidents may produce valuable research material or explanations, or may satisfy a disturbed public in the case of a particularly striking accident.

5.13.1 Investigation

Where a vehicle has been involved in an accident in a public place the Minister can appoint a person in writing to investigate its circumstances (S 66). If the Minister considers it necessary, the inquiry will be in public. The authorised person reports on the cause and circumstances of the accident to the Minister and may make recommendations. This report cannot be used as evidence in legal proceedings—as to its privilege generally, see *Speigelman v Hocker* (1933) 150 LT 256. However, it can obviously, if it is detailed, provide valuable material for a civil case.

There was a useful manual on the subject of accident investigation and its technical aspects in 1980—*Manual of Road Accident Investigation* (2 Vols) *Byratt & Watts,* Pitman Publishers Limited.

5.13.2 Powers

The following powers are given to the authorised person for the conduct of an inquiry:

- (i) To enter at any reasonable time any premises where there is a vehicle which was involved in the accident. If requested by the owner or person in charge of the premises, he must produce his authority;
- (ii) to inspect, examine and test vehicles as reasonably necessary for the investigation;
- (iii) to summons witnesses, administer oaths, and require the production of books, papers or documents relating to the subject matter of the inquiry and retain them. If a witness does not comply with these powers, e.g. does not attend or refuses information, the

authorised person may certify the witness for contempt to the High Court. The High Court is empowered to hold such inquiry as it sees proper and punish in the same way as if guilty of contempt in the High Court. Somewhat similar powers under Dail Eireann Public Accounts Committee (Privilege and Procedure Act) 1970 were considered in the case of *A-G v Padraic Haughey* (1971) IR 217 in which the powers were held to be unconstitutional. Therefore, presumably, these provisions will have to be redrafted;

(iv) to do such things and make such requirements as appear to him to be reasonably necessary for the purpose of the investigation.

5.13.3 Offences

A person who contravenes a lawful requirement of an authorised person under the above powers, or obstructs him in the performance of his duties, is guilty of an offence (General Penalty (para 7.1) applies).

5.13.4 Regulations

The Minister for the Environment has power to make regulations generally for the operation of the section by subs (8). In particular, he can make regulations under subs (4) to enable:

(a) The payment of witness expenses and other expenses incurred by a person in connection with the section;

(b) Recovery by the Minister from any person of the costs incurred by him (Minister) in connection with an inquiry. It is difficult to see how this power can be exercised or is constitutional, unless the provision in the regulation is carefully drafted.

No regulations have yet been made under the Section.

5.14 Other Local Authority Controls

5.14.1 Car Parks

5.14.1.1 *Powers to Provide Car Parks.*A Local Authority has power under s 101 of the 1961 Act, which is an unnecessarily complicated section (as amended badly by Sch, 1968 Act), to provide one or more car parks to relieve or prevent traffic congestion, and to provide access to them. This power specifically includes (with the Minister's for the Environment consent) the power to erect car park buildings, such as waiting rooms, cloak rooms, a petrol station and shop facilities in any of their car parks.

The Local Authority can adapt land for use as a car park, e.g. a building site. It is further entitled to terminate the use of land as a car park if it thinks it should be used for one of its other lawful purposes. The Local Authority can sell or lease its car park, with the Minister's consent, to any person, subject to such conditions as it thinks proper, e.g. give it over to commercial interests.

The operation of a car park leased by a local Authority is not a business within the Landlord and Tenant Acts 1931-1967 (now the Landlord and Tenant Act 1980).

The Minister, with the consent of the Minister for Finance, can make grants and loans to local authorities for the provision of car parks under the Road Fund. Under Part V of the Housing Act 1966, a local authority may acquire land by agreement or compulsion for car parks. It also appears that a Planning Authority (usually the local authority) has general powers to provide car parks under the Local Government (Planning and Development Act 1963, Part VII.

Local authority car parks may not form part of the public road and may not have a public right of way over them. Where casual trading operates in any of the car parks, it is usual to allow such activity to continue by means of a 'saver' clause in the bye-laws.

A Local Authority is stated in s 101(1) to be defined for the purpose of the section as being an authority which is a sanitary authority under the Local Government (Sanitary Service Acts) 1878 to 1952. This unusual equation arises from the historical position about acquisition of land by local authorities under the Public Health Act 1978. The original s 101 (5) of the 1961 Act, referring to these old powers, has been deleted by Sch, 1968 Act, which, incidentally, also deletes s 101 (4) which required the Minister's consent in a number of situations on purchasing and leasing.

Local authorities now have a general power of acquiring land for any of their lawful purposes. As the 1968 Act did not repeal the definition of local authorities being equivalent to sanitary authorities, the position is that the above bodies can operate under the section.

The connections with the old Public Health Acts were therefore not deleted in full, and, indeed, are incorporated in part in the 1961 Act, also with reference to Bye-laws (see para 5.14.3).

5.14.1.2 *Power to assist provision of car Parks.* A Local Authority can assist any person in providing a car park, provided the Minister for The Environment consents. This assistance may be by money contributions, by doing work, or by granting or leasing land.

5.14.1.3 *Bye-laws on Car Parks.* A local authority can make bye-laws as to the use of any of its car parks. In particular, it can restrict admission to certain classes of vehicles; specify charges for and periods of parking; and the conditions of use of the car park by vehicles. A person who contravenes a bye-law is guilty of an offence and the general penalty applies (para 7.1).

The provisions of 219, 221 and 223 of the Public Health (Ireland) Act 1978 apply to any such bye-laws, and so the Minister's for the Environment consent is necessary to the bye-laws

Current Bye-laws

Bye-laws made under this section so far are:

Arklow Urban District Council Car Park Bye-laws 1987.
Birr Urban District Council Car Park Bye-laws 1980.
Clonmel Corporation Car Park Bye-laws 1986.
Cork Corporation Car Park Bye-laws 1979.
Drogheda Corporation Car Park Bye-laws 1971.
Dungarvan Car Park Bye-laws 1976.
Galway Corporation Car Park Bye-laws 1982.
Amendment of Galway Corporation Bye-laws 1982.
Killarney Car Park Bye-laws 1977.
Kilkenny Corporation Car Park Bye-laws 1985.
Laoighis County Council Car Park Bye-laws 1980.
Longford County Council Car Park Bye-laws 1970.
Macroom Urban District Council Car Park Bye-laws 1975.
Navan Car Park Bye-laws 1975.
New Ross Urban District Council Car Park Bye-laws 1984.
Roscommon Car Park Bye-laws 1986.
Skibbereen Urban District Council Car Park Bye-laws 1980.
Sligo Car Park Bye-laws 1976.
Tipperary (North Riding) County Council Car Park Bye-laws 1987.
Trim Car Park Bye-laws 1987.
Waterford County Council Car Park Bye-laws 1976.
Waterford Corporation Car Park Bye-laws 1987.
Westmeath County Council Car Park Bye-laws 1970.
Wexford Corporation Car Park Bye-laws 1987.

5.14.2 Immobilisation/removal

The Immobilisation of unlawfully parked vehicles under s 101B of the 1961 Act by devices is discussed in para 5.5.9 above. The removal of such vehicles under s 97 of the 1961 Act is covered at para 5.12.

5.14.3 Control of bollards and ramps

A Road Authority may, in the interests of the safety of road users, provide or remove bollards and/or ramps under and by virtue of 101A of the 1961 Act, inserted by 9 of the Dublin Transport Authority (Dissolution) Act 1987. A bollard is a pole, post or similar device inserted into or affixed vertically, or nearly vertically, to the surface of a roadway or footway. A ramp means an artificial hump in or on the surface of a roadway. When erected they are deemed to be structures forming part of the public road.

The road authority must follow a lengthy procedure under the section before providing such bollards or ramps. The decision must be made by the elected local authority representatives, as it is a reserved function not a management function. The Road Authority must:

(1) Give prescribed notices of intention to provide or remove bollards or ramps. By SI 32/1988 this must be by notice in a daily newspaper circulating in the functional area of the Road Authority;

(2) Consider written objections and appoint a person to hear objections;
(3) Consult the Garda Commissioner, who has two months to submit observations;
(4) On making its decision, give public notice of its decision and notify objectors;
(5) Comply with Ministerial Regulations and only provide bollards or ramps in accordance with the Act and Regulations.

It is an offence carrying the general penalty (para 7.1) to attempt or to remove or damage a ramp or bollard, and the Road Authority itself can prosecute in addition to the Director of Public Prosecutions.

The Minister for the Environment is given wide powers to make regulations under 101A(b) to prescribe procedures. Notices, types of bollards and ramps, lighting, signs and the types of roads on which bollards and ramps are or may not be erected. Regulations under s 32 of the Dublin Transport Authority Act 1986 remain in force. These are the Road Traffic (Bollards and Ramps) Regulations 1988 (SI 32/1988). They provide for the publication of required notices in a circulating daily newspaper in the functional area of the Road Authority; give the requirements as to the provision of bollards, their size, shape and location; and give similar specifications as to ramps. They have been amended by SI 291/1988 to the effect that a Ramp shall not be provided unless it is within 5 metres of a street light.

5.14.4 Control of construction sites

As damage can be done to roads, nuisances created by dirt and material, and disruption of traffic caused by large construction sites, specific powers of control in relation to these are given to the Road Authorities (See para 7.9 as to Road Authorities and para 1.7.8 as to extraordinary traffic).

Section 101C of the 1961 Act (inserted by s 9 of the Dublin Transport Authority (Dissolution) Act 1987 gives this control over access and egress from construction sites by vehicles by means of bye-laws. The bye-laws can be general ones, or relate to a specified site or a specified class of vehicle, e.g dumpers. The Garda Commissioner must be consulted by the Road Authority. The section does not apply to widening public roads or construction work on, to, above , or under public roads.

The bye-laws can relate to general matters of access/egress but can, in particular:

(a) Limit times of access/egress;
(b) Limit numbers of vehicles;
(c) Require vehicles to be cleaned.

A person who contravenes a bye-law is guilty of an offence and the general penalty applies (para 7.1). As to bye-laws generally, see para 7.6.

Sections 219, 221 and 223 of the Public Health (Ireland Act 1878 apply to these bye-laws. This means the Minister for the Environment must consent to them. Bye-laws under the Dublin Transport Authority Act 1986 were continued until revoked by the repealing Act of 1987. These are the Dublin Area Traffic and Parking Bye-laws 1987 (SI 292/1987).

5.14.5 Control of road works

Local authorities are given power to issue directions in writing to any person carrying out road works in their functional areas. These powers are contained in the lengthy 101D of the 1961 Act, inserted s 9 of the Dublin Transport Authority (Dissolution) Act 1987. The local authorities are those prescribed County Councils, Corporations and Urban District Councils set out in Regulations by the Minister for the Environment. By SI 220/1988, the Road Traffic (Co-ordination of Road Works) Regulations 1988 Dublin Corporation, Dublin County Council and Dunlaoghaire Corporation are designated Local Authorities for the purposes of s 101 D. See also para 1.7.8 as to extraordinary traffic.

Road works are divided into two kinds:

(a) emergency road works; and
(b) other road works.

A direction can apply to all or some of the road works and can be amended or revoked. It can specify the periods during which the road works can be carried out, and the manner, standards, security for, and control of traffic and road works.

The power must have regard to:

(a) the need to minimise disruption of traffic;
(b) the urgency of Road works;
(c) the cost resulting from the direction;
(d) The need to co-ordinate the periods of these and other road works, including works it is itself doing; and
(e) regulations by the Minister (which it must comply with).

Emergency road works are basically exempt from control. These are road works the carrying out of which is immediately required in order to prevent or reduce risk of loss, injury or damage to persons or property.

The law on directions does not apply to the carrying out of road works by a local authority.

The Minister for the Environment is given a general power to make regulations to give effect to the section, and specific powers to regulate which local authorities may operate the section, the requirement of advance notice of road works, notice of emergency works, information to be given about road works, time limits, reinstatement of roads, and control of traffic. Different regulations can be made for different local authorities, different areas within functional areas, different types of road works, and different circumstances. SI 220/1988 above are the only Regulations so far under the section.

A person who contravenes a direction or regulation is guilty of an offence, as is the Director, Manager, Secretary or other officer of a body Corporate who consents or connives to its commission. The penalties on summary conviction are fines of up to £1,000 and/or one year's imprisonment; on indictment, £50,000 and/or five years' imprisonment. The penalties in s 13 of the Criminal Procedure Act 1967 are amended. That section deals with a plea of guilty to an indictable offence in the District Court.

Local authorities or the Minister are not to be liable for any loss, injury or damage, or any expenditure incurred by another person by reason of the performance or non-performance of their functions under the section. The constitutionality of this type of global exemption must be suspect. See also *Kelly v Dublin Co. Co.* (High Court 21 February 1986) where the County Council was held liable in nuisance for using vehicles which created dust, noise and smells.

5.15 Control of Motorways

5.15.1 Statutory Provision

Under the Local Government (Roads and Motorways) Act 1974, the Minister for the Environment can declare a public road or proposed public road to be a motorway. These motorways are normally constructed under the Act by Local Authorities. As motorways involve speeding up traffic, there are various controls in the Act and regulations thereunder.

Section 11 of the Dublin Transport Authority (Dissolution) Act 1987 extends the scope of the 1974 Act to enable busways to be created and to regulate such busways. Motorways and Busways involve two different types of roads use, with different restrictions and prohibiting as to the type of vehicles which can and cannot use them, e.g. ordinary passenger cars are excluded from a busway but not from a motorway.

The 1974 Act is extensively amended by SI 221/1988, the European Communities (Environmental Impact Assessment) (Motorways) Regulations 1988. The effect of the amendments and the Statutory Instrument is to provide for an environmental assessment to be done as part of the preparation of a Motorway Scheme. The various forms of Notices for these types of studies and other forms are set out and prescribed by the Local Government (Roads and Motorways) Act 1974 (Prescribed Forms) Regulations 1977 SI 395/1977 and amended by SI 222/1988.

5.15.2 Controls

(1) *The 1974 Act*
Under the Local Government (Roads and Motorways) Act 1974:

(a) s 8 prevents direct access to motorways from adjoining land. Construction of such access, or interfering with any boundary of the motorway is an offence—fine £200;
(b) s 9 gives power to make regulations as to the types of mechanically propelled vehicles that can use the motorway; with subs (2) preventing pedestrians, pedal cyclists, certain classes of mechanically propelled vehicles and animals being brought on to motorways—fine up to £50. (See (2) below);

(c) s 10 prevents State Authorities or Statutory Undertakers from laying pipes, etc. in, under or over motorways, except with the Minister's consent;
(d) s 11 allows the Minister to give binding directions to Local Authorities on the management of motorways, e.g. as to the provision of signs. 'Traffic Signs' has the same meaning as under the Road Traffic Acts (see para 5.8)

(2) *Regulations under s 9*
The Local Government (Roads and Motorways) Acts 1974 (Prescribed Traffic) General Regulations 1977 (SI 396/1977) allow the following vehicles, or combination of vehicles (other than an invalid carriage), to use a motorway:

(a) A vehicle which is driven by the holder of a full licence under s 22 (1) of the 1961 Traffic Act (see para 2.3.1); and
(b) is constructed so that its entire weight is transmitted to the road surface by circular pneumatic tyres as defined in the regulations (see chapter 1); and
(c) is propelled by at least a 50 cc internal combustion engine and is capable of doing at least 50 kilometres per hour under its own power.

Other mechanically propelled vehicles which can use motorways in certain circumstances under the said Regulations are all or any vehicles:

(i) In an emergency or directions from a Garda;
(ii) By special permit under Art 17 of the Road Traffic (Construction, Equipment and Use) Regulations 1963 (see para 1.5) and use as in accordance with such permit);
(iii) engaged in maintenance, repair, clearance or construction work on the motorway

5.15.3 Prohibitions

It follows, therefore, from the Act and Regulations that the following are prohibited from using a motorway:

(1) pedestrians,
(2) pedal cyclists,
(3) invalid carriages,
(4) animals,
(5) certain mechanically propelled vehicles, including motor cycles of limited cylinder capacity and speed,
(6) vehicles driven by learner drivers,
(7) general bye-law prohibitions referred to at para 5.3.3. and the next paragraph, e.g. stopping, parking, obstructions.

5.15.4 General Bye-laws

The General bye-laws 1964 set out at para 5.3.3. apply, and, by the Road

5.15.4 *Control of Motorways*

Traffic General Bye-laws (Amendment) Regulations 1983, were amended with specific bye-laws for motorways. (See in particular, RR 39-42 at para 5.3.3, specifically dealing with motorways).

5.15.5 Signs

The Road Traffic (Signs) (Amendment) Regulations 1983 (SI 276/1983) provide for a series of road markings to be used on motorways. See para 5.8 above.

5.16 Promotion of road safety and research

5.16.1 Local Authorities

Power is given by s 120 of the 1961 Act to County Councils, Corporations, Urban Councils and Town Commissioners to incur expenditure for the purpose of promoting road safety. Local authorities are therefore acting *intra vires* in promoting shows and displays in connection with safety on the roads. As will be seen below they can be reimbursed for any expenditure for this purpose in whole or in part by the Minister.

5.16.2 Minister

The Minister for the Environment is entitled under the same section to make grants from the Road Fund for road safety promotion by:

(i) Awarding the expenses of a Local Authority, as mentioned above, incurred in the promotion of road safety

(ii) Giving awards also towards the expenses of an association or body, where the advancement of road safety is among its primary objectives.

The Minister's own expenditure on road safety is, under s 8 of the 1961 Act, recouped from the Road Fund.

Grants are in fact made to local authorities towards expenditure on their activities in relation to national campaigns and to the Safety First Association of Ireland to operate a scheme of 'Road Safety Officers' throughout the Country.

5.16.3 Medical Bureau of Road Safety

This body is discussed at para 4.9 in relation to the law covering intoxicated driving. Research into medical aspects of road safety is one of the specified functions of the Bureau under s 38 (3)(b) of the 1986 Act. The Bureau is established by the Minister for the Environment.

5.16.4 National Safety Council

Under the Road Traffic Acts and the Local Government Services (Corporate

Bodies) Act 1971 and SI 103/1974, a National Road Safety Association was established as a body corporate under the aegis of the Department of the Environment. It produced periodic reports and recommendations on road traffic problems, the construction of roads, safety, etc. From January 1988 its functions were transferred to a new National Safety Council under SI 327/1987. This body continues the same work. Its stated objective is the promotion of measures, including the advancement of education, relating to the prevention of accidents caused on the roads. It can organise conferences, provide advice, develop safety codes, conduct examinations and courses, and co-operate with local authorities, etc.

The former National Road Safety Association was abolished as such by SI 328/1987. It has produced a large number of leaflets, teachers' notes, posters and badges in an imaginative way. Many of these are still available, though some are out of date, especially the Rules of the Road (1979). (Write to 4 Northbrook Road, Ranelagh, Dublin 4). Its more recent publications reflected the growing impact of EEC law on Irish Law. It also engaged in radio, press and television advertising. Its report for 1985 showed that 410 people were killed on Irish roads and 7,327 injured during that year, at a cost estimated at £220,000,000 per annum to the nation, and generally assessed the values and method of the State's objective of road safety. Approximately 30% of health care expense is used in caring for road victims.

There are 92,000 km of public roads in the Republic, with annual additions of about 600 km (i.e. new public roads built, and estate roads taken over). An interesting publication on this subject is *'Road Development Plan for the 1980s'*, PRL7967, obtainable from the Government Publications Office. In 1988, with EEC funds available many improvements and new motorways are promised for the road system.

5.16.5 Environmental Research Unit

An Foras Forbartha, was an important advisory body, charged with carrying out research into accident prevention and road safety. It has an internal bureau, the road safety records bureau, which was set up in 1968.

An Foras Forbartha was disbanded and some of its functions, including the road safety records bureau, transferred to the Environment Research Unit. This unit was established under SI 20/1988 (Environment Research Unit (Establishment) Order 1988.

5.17 Provisions of other Acts on traffic control

Some statutes provide for controls of traffic within places (including public places) for which particular public authorities are responsible; others may apply, in a limited respect, to public roads. Examples are given in paras 5.17.1 to 5.17.5 below.

5.17.1 Harbours

A Harbour Authority may make bye-laws for the good rule and government of its harbour. This includes the prevention of obstruction of or interference with traffic within the limits of the harbour (Harbours Act 1946 s 60).

5.17.2 Aerodromes

The Minister for Transport and Power may make, in relation to any state aerodrome, bye-laws for the regulation on traffic within the aerodrome, (Air Navigation and Transport Act 1950, s 16).

5.17.3 Transport Authorities

CIE (now Bus Eireann or the Irish Bus Company) and Dublin Bus may make bye-laws for maintaining order in, and regulating the use of the stations, depots or other premises occupied by them and the approaches thereto (Transport Act 1950, s 22, Amended by 1963 Act s 18(2)). This power now seems to be vested in both 'The Dublin Bus Company' and 'The Irish Bus Company' under the Transport (Reorganisation of Coras Iompair Eireann) Act 1986.

5.17.4 Defence Forces Land

(i) The Minister for Defence may make bye-laws regulating the use of state land vested in him (except the Curragh of Kildare) and, further, may, with the consent of the Road Authority concerned, make bye-laws for the restriction of the use of a road which crosses or runs near such land 276 and 279 of the Defence Act 1954.

(ii) The Officer in command of the Curragh Camp may restrict or control the use of the public road through the Camp in specified circumstances (Curragh of Kildare Act 1961, s3)

(iii) In an area specified in a Manoeuvres (Authorisation) Order made by the Minister for Defence, or in the vicinity of any place used for artillery, etc. practice, the officer in command may temporarily stop all traffic so far as is necessary for safety and the conduct of the manoeuvres or practices (s274 of the Defence Act 1954).

(iv) During a period of emergency, certain provisions of the 1961-1968 Acts (speed limits, traffic bye-laws, road closing orders) do not apply to a member of the defence forces while on duty (113 of the Defence Act 1954, as applied by 20 of the Interpretation Act 1937)

(v) Also, as has been noted throughout this book, there are various exemptions for members of the defence forces and their vehicles in the course of their duties.

5.17.5 Animals

(i) Wandering animals may be impounded (See Summary Jurisdiction (Ireland Act 1851) The Pounds (Provision and Maintenance) Act 1935 deals with the provision of pounds. The Animals Act 1985 ss 4 and 5 increase the impounding powers of the Gardai and local authorities.

(ii) It is an offence to exercise or lead a greyhound in a public place unless he is under control, or for one person to exercise on a lead more than 4 greyhounds at a time (Protection of Animals (Amendment) Act 1965.

(iii) The Minister for Agriculture and Fisheries may make orders regarding the keeping of dogs under control, their indentification etc (Diseases of Animals Act 1966).

(iv) The Minister for Agriculture and Fisheries may make orders for the purpose of the prevention, or checking or eradication of diseases of animals, by prohibiting, restricting and regulating their movement and transport and that of other items; the local authorities are to enforce the Act and the Minister may by order authorise them to make regulations accordingly (Diseases of Animals Act 1966) See also para 1.31 as to animals and para 5.3.3. with regard to animals in relation to general bye-laws.

Chapter 6

Control of user: Insurance

'An insurance policy is like old underwear. The gaps in its cover are only shown by accident.'

David Yates (1984)

6.1 Introduction

The benefits of the mechanically propelled vehicle are obvious; so are the ravages it inflicts on members of the community (see para 5.16.4). With the emergence of these vehicles, courts applied the principles of the Common Law tort of negligence to the 'accidents' resulting from this new phenomenon. The damages awarded from an early date were substantial because the injuries were often serious. For the first quarter of this century 'the motoring car' was primarily the acquisition of the rich, who could usually meet the damages. Still, from early on vehicle owners insured on a voluntary basis. The 1933 Road Traffic Act first introduced compulsory insurance in Ireland, as a result of the recommendations in the report of the Interdepartmental Committee on the Control and Regulation of Road Traffic 1928. The 1933 Act's requirements have been substantially re-enacted in the 1961 Act and somewhat simplified by the 1968 Act. The 1961 Act and its regulations have sharply improved passenger cover. EEC regulations have enhanced the insurance requirements in relation to property damage.

The justification for insurance is that a driver must arrange that the victims of his potentially hazardous activity will be adequately compensated. We are more conscious now that society as a whole benefits from good road infrastructure and vehicle use—it is therefore sometimes suggested that the nation, in the form of State Insurance, should compensate the victims. Up to 1988 major cases were heard by Civil Juries in the High Court. Civil Juries in this regard were abolished from 31 July 1988.

In the Dail Debates of 24 February 1988 there were some proposals in relation to insurance mentioned, i.e. that in 1989 or later a Bill may be introduced to enable Gardai to seize and impound uninsured vehicles. It was stated that approximately 76,000 such vehicles were on Irish roads at that time, costing £28,000,000 in lost insurance premiums. The total premiums in 1986 were £335,000,000 among the 24 insurers operating in Ireland. It was also suggested that uninsured drivers should be automatically disqualified as in the manner of intoxicated drivers.

The insurance provisions of the Road Traffic Acts are, of course, more important in the realm of civil law than in the criminal law elements of road traffic legislation. The traditional concept of negligence in civil law is paramount. Establishing a breach of the Road Traffic Acts alone may not suffice to ground civil liability if it does not establish a breach by the motorist of his duty of reasonable care towards fellow road users. On the other hand, a driver may well find his insurance policy coming under fire if he has been wanting in reasonable care on the balance of probabilities, even though he has not been in breach of the Road Traffic Acts. It should be noted, however, that the Civil Liability Act 1961 provides in s 57 that it shall not be a defence in an action for tort merely to show that the plaintiff is in breach of the civil or criminal law.

The inclusion of these insurance provisions in the Road Traffic Acts shows that the legal rights of the individual and social protection interact in this sphere of the law. They also represent a striking example of State limitation on the old doctrine of freedom of contract. The nature of civil liability covered by the compulsory insurance is now defined. There is social control of the terms of the contract of insurance.

The entire law can only be found by a study of the Common Law, the Civil Liability Acts 1961-64, the Road Traffic Acts and other sources, but it is not proposed to deal with other than the Road Traffic Acts here. We will examine the Road Traffic Acts and regulations, and some of the case-law which has evolved around these provisions.

6.2 Outline of provisions

6.2.1 Acts

Under Parts VI of the Road Traffic Acts 1961 and 1968, a mechanically propelled vehicle, subject to certain exceptions, cannot be used in a public place unless covered for liability for negligence by proper insurance issued by an approved vehicle insurer. The insurance must be issued by the vehicle insurer in the form of an approved policy, which must comply with certain provisions, requirements and legal limits. A certificate of insurance must be issued to the insured, to be produced when lawfully required. Where certain bodies carry their own insurance they may have, in lieu of certificates of insurance, documents called certificates of exemption. The vast majority of vehicles meet the requirements of the Acts by being covered by such insurance under an 'approved policy' issued by a 'vehicle insurer'.

In many cases where no effective insurance cover exists, personal injuries (and limited property amounts) negligently inflicted may be paid for by the Motor Insurance Bureau. Certain rights of an extra statutory nature exist in the event of refusal of cover by vehicle insurers.

In reading the Acts one must bear in mind there are substantial amendments of the 1961 Act particularly, sometimes by the doubtful expedient of Statutory Instruments, e.g. of s 56 of the 1961 Act.

6.2.2 Regulations

The Minister for the Environment is given wide powers to regulate matters relating to insurance (s 75 of the 1961 Act). These are referred to throughout the text. The current regulations are:

(a) Road Traffic (Compulsory Insurance) Regulations 1962 (SI 14/1962) as amended by SIs 58/1964, 359/1977, 321/1987;
(b) Road Traffic (Insurance Disc) Regulations 1984 (SI 355/1984) as amended by SI 277/1986;
(c) European Communities (Road Traffic) (Compulsory Insurance) Regulations 1975 (SI 178/1975 as amended by SI 322/1987.

6.2.3 Guarantee

The provisions of the 1961 Act as to approved guarantees were repealed by s 53 of the 1968 Act.

6.3 Obligation to insure

6.3.1 Duty to have cover

By virtue of s 56 of the 1961 Act (as amended by the 1968 and 1984 Acts), a person may not use (or owner allow use of) a mechanically propelled vehicle in a public place unless:

(a) a 'vehicle insurer' or 'exempted person' is liable for negligent use of the vehicle by him, with two exceptions as below; or
(b) an approved policy of insurance covers any negligence of the user, or other person liable, or their personal representatives for injury so caused for all sums without limit of the vehicle (save as below):

Excepted persons
The liability to pay is owed to all persons except 'excepted persons' (see para 6.7). (A 'person' includes a company—*Briggs v Gibbons Bakery* (1948) N Ir 165.) As to the phrases 'use', 'public place' and 'mechanically propelled vehicle', see para 7.9. The sums covered include damages and costs; but there are also exceptions as to the vehicle.

Excepted vehicles

(a) A pedestrian controlled vehicle (see para 7.9 which is excepted (s 79—see para 6.3.6); or
(b) State owned/driven vehicle (see para 6.3.7).

6.3.2 Limits

The insurance cover under (a) or (b) above must be without limit of amount, except that:

(i) There was a £1,000 limit in respect of injury to *property* from one act of negligence or a series of acts of negligence collectively constituting one event. However, by the European Communities (Road Traffic) (Compulsory Insurance) (Amendment) Regulations 1987 (SI 322/1987) the limit is increased to £40,000 for accidents in the period 31 December 1987 to 31 December 1990, and thereafter to £80,000. This will affect visitors and their vehicles mostly, as the Irish insurance practice has been to grant full damage cover, except for commercial vehicles where the usual limit has been £10,000 per accident.
(ii) *Special liability* in addition to common law or statutory liability undertaken by an insured or principal debtor is also excepted. In respect of this limitation, where the regulation does not require passenger cover, e.g. for motor cycles, special cover for this liability would be an additional extra but in reality is unobtainable.

The above provisions are contained in s 56(2) of the 1961 Act, as re-enacted by SI 322/1987 above. That instrument also amended its parent instrument—European Communities (Road Traffic) (Compulsory Insurance) Regulations 1975 (SI 178/1976). There has been added to 56 of the 1961 Act an additional subsection (2A) and also subs (7) and (8) (re-enacted by SI 322/1987) and (9), extending the terms of an approved policy to use in any *EEC Country* and to Austria, Finland, Norway, Sweden, Switzerland, Hungary, Czechoslovakia and the German Democratic Republic (called 'designated territories'). This is to cover the damage and costs required to be covered by compulsory insurance in the country where they are incurred in any of the designated territories. As to defining the territory in which a vehicle is normally based, the reference is to be—

(a) until 31 December 1988, to the state where vehicle was registered or, if none, the state where it got its insurance plate or similar plate or, if none, the state where the person with custody of the vehicle is permanently resident,
(b) from January 1989, it is to be the territory of the state of which the vehicle bears a registration plate or, if not so plated, then, if it has an insurance plate or analogous mark or sign, the state that so issues it, or, if none such, then the territory of the state in which the person who has custody of the vehicle is permanently resident.

6.3.2 *Obligation to insure*

These provisions facilitate the Irish Visiting Motorists Bureau (IVMB) (see para 6.9 below) in dealing with compensation for innocent victims of road accidents which involve vehicles fitted with false number plates, etc. The IVMB will be able to recoup the compensation and costs from the Bureau of the state whose national plate was falsely displayed. (See also para 6.9 below).

The insurance must cover *trailers* also. This applies in Ireland and these other above-mentioned territories, i.e. the countries known as 'designated territories' for the purpose of this Part of the Act dealing with insurance. SI 178/1975 gave effect to EEC Directive 72/166; SI 322/1987 gave effect to the Second Council Directive on Motor Insurance (84/5/EEC).

Contract aspects

Insurance is a contract and must be accepted by both sides. Hence, if a cover note is issued by a company after the insured has communicated an intention not to renew a policy, then there is no policy in force (*Taylor v Allen* [1966] 1 QB 304). A voidable policy of insurance is good until avoided (*Goodbarne v Buck* [1940] 1 KB 771). In *Sands v O'Connell* (1980) RTR 42 a person under 21 was allowed to drive, although under the hire company's stipulated age, by the hirer, who was over 21. *Held*: the driver was uninsured as he was driving without the hire company's permission.

An insured must have an insurable interest (*O'Leary v Irish National* (1958) Ir Jur R 17; *Coen v Employer's Liability Assurance Co* [1962] IR 314). The burden of proof for establishing the existence of proper insurance is placed on the accused. This is based on the principle that it is a fact particularly within his own knowledge (*John v Humphreys* [1985] 1 All ER 793). A Notice to Produce is not necessary at a court hearing if the accused does not produce a certificate of insurance on demand to the Garda (see para 6.4.6) *Williams v Russell* (1933) 97 JP 128).

An offence is committed if the car is used before the certificate of insurance is issued to the assured or his agent (*Starkey v Hall* [1936] 2 All ER 18). An offence is also committed where there is in fact no insurance, though the insurance company, as an act of grace (because of a letter), covers the risk (*Egan v Bowler* (1939) 63 Lloyds Rep 266). As to contribution between Insurers, where there is double insurance see *Zurich Insurance v Shield Insurance* (Supreme Court 18.12.1987: ILL 1988 p 88).

6.3.3 Penalties

The penalties for breach of this obligation to be insured are a maximum £1,000 fine and/or six months' imprisonment (s 56 of the 1961 Act and by s 3(8) of the 1984 Act); and the disqualification provisions which apply are:

(1) discretionary on a first offence; and
(2) automatic for a second offence or subsequent offence within three years (see para 2.9).

Each conviction must be endorsed on the drivers licence (see para 2.10). To omit in the court order the endorsement of a licence or disqualification from driving is not fatal to the order as these do not form part of the conviction (*State (Carthew) v D J Dunleavy and others* (unreported), Supreme Court, 26 April 1967). It *is* mandatory to endorse the licence, however, (A-G v Keane 106 ILTR 5). In addition, it was enacted under s 57 of the 1961 Act that a Court could award to any negligently injured party, with his consent, through means of a fine on the convicted uninsured person, an amount which, in the opinion of the Court, would be the damages which the injured party would get in a civil action on the basis of that injury being one which should be insured against. This provision was held to be unconstitutional in *Cullen v A-G* [1979] IR 394. In that case s 57(1) and (2) were declared contrary to Art 38.2 of the Constitution and void. It is a pity that these provisions have not been redrafted, if only to the extent that a District Court could specifically adjourn the imposition penalty pending the payment of the civil claims where the civil case has not been determined and paid.

There is, however, still remaining in s 57(3) an additional penal sanction to deal with the convicted uninsured offender, against whom a civil award to the extent the damages should be insured is made. The Court making the award may order that he be imprisoned for not more than six months (or until the damages are paid, if shorter) if the damages and costs are not paid within a stated period fixed for their payment, which must be within 14 days, or such longer period fixed by the Court, or a sum lodged in Court fixed by the Court. This provision was not in contention in the *Cullen* case.

6.3.4 Defences

An owner or driver has the following defences for non-compliance with his obligation to insure under s 56 (in subs (5) and (6) respectively):

(1) *Owner*. If the owner shows that the vehicle was used without his consent and he had taken all reasonable precautions to prevent its use, *or* if he shows that it was being used by his servant in contravention with his orders, he has a full defence. In *Lyons* v Cooney [1978] IR 41 the Supreme Court put a heavy onus on the owner. He must clearly show he comes with the statutory defences and that he has taken all reasonable precautions to prevent the vehicle's use without his consent.

(2) *Servant*. A servant of the owner has a good defence if he shows that he was using the vehicle on the express orders of the owner. In *A-G (Hayes) v Downes* (1959) 93 ILTR 121 a servant acting on orders drove a car covered by a policy although he never had held a drivers licence. The servant was able to avail himself of the special defence. The defendant/master was guilty of an offence, as there was the usual condition in the policy (see para 6.4.2 below) of the need for a drivers licence. In the English case of *Davey v Toule* (1974) RTR 329 a driver was convicted even though he was not the owner and had been unable to get a certificate of insurance or a policy

from the owner. The Court held he was under liability to show that cover existed. The burden of proof is on the defendant on the balance of probabilities *R v Carr Briant* [1943] 2 All ER 156.

It may be relevant here to note briefly the provisions of s 112 and 118 of the 1961 Act. Section 112 penalises a person taking a vehicle without authority (see para 4.10) and, therefore, driving without insurance. It provides that it is a good defence to such a charge if the person doing the act alleged to constitute the offence believed on reasonable grounds that he had lawful authority to do that act. Section 118 states that user of a mechanically propelled vehicle with the consent of the owner shall be deemed user by a servant, if the user is within the terms of the consent for the purposes of determining the liability, if any, of the owner or any other person for injury to the vehicle, persons or property by negligent use. In *Buckley v Musgrave Brook Bond Ltd* [1969] IR 440 the defendants lent a van to a lorry driver, the employee of another company, to enable him to return home for the weekend to Cork. He was required to return the van to the defendants on Sunday night or early Monday morning. On Sunday he used the van for his private purposes, was involved in an accident and was killed. The plaintiff, his passenger, was injured. The defendants claimed there was no consent to user under s 118, a claim which was upheld by the High Court Judge who withdrew the case from the jury. The Supreme Court held this withdrawal was incorrect. Where there was evidence of consent to general or some user, the defendants were obliged to discharge the onus of establishing that their consent did not apply to the particular use which gave rise to the claim made against them. See also articles (and cases in them) by Nial Osborough in *Solicitors Gazette*, May 1971, Vol 65, p 7 and *Irish Jurist* (NS), Winter 1971. In *Kelly v Lombard Ltd* [1974] IR 142 the driver used an improper drivers licence when hiring a car from the defendants. *Held*: their consent to use was vitiated by fraud of driver.

A modern English case on consent is *Singh v Rathour* [1988] All ER 16. See an article on it in *New Law Journal* (1988) p 519.

(3) *In all cases* it is a defence that the owner or driver was not given ten days to produce a certificate of insurance (*State (McDonagh) v Sheerin* (1981) ILRM 149 (see para 6.3.5 below).

(4) *In all cases* it is a defence that the owner or driver had insurance or exemption.

(5) It is a defence that the owner or driver was an *excepted person* or the vehicle was an *excepted vehicle*.

6.3.5 Presumptions

In a prosecution for driving with no insurance under s 56 a presumption of non-insurance against the defendant exists, *provided* that:

(a) a demand is made under s 69 of the 1961 Act. That section briefly states that a Garda can demand production of certificate of insurance or exemption within a month of user of the vehicle. The person has ten days to comply with the demand or, alternatively, he must prove he did not use the vehicle on the occasion, or that he was a servant acting under express orders; and
(b) the person on whom the demand is made refused or failed to produce the appropriate certificate or, if he did produce it, failed to allow its examination.

In *A-G v Shivman* (1968) IR 369 it was held that a motorist complies with s 69(1)(a) if he produces either type of certificate, and that the demand for such production must be so expressed as to require the production of either of the said documents, i.e. certificate of insurance or certificate of exemption. In *State (McDonagh) v Sheerin* (1981) ILRM 149 it was held that a conviction was invalid when, at the date of the trial, the driver could not be said to have failed to produce a certificate of insurance before the specified ten days provided for, i.e. conviction before that period (ten days) had expired was bad. See further discussion of s 69 at para 6.4.6 below.

It was held in the Northern Ireland case of *Reid v Hull* (1975) NI 171 that permitting another person to use an uninsured motor cycle was an absolute offence and involved no element of *mens rea*.

Applying the principle as to production stated in *A-G v Carville* (1961) ILTR 41, the State has to prove absence of insurances in the event of a proper demand not being made. The presumption of no insurance only arises where a demand is made properly under s 69.

In *Lyons v Cooney* [1978] IR 41 it was held that once a demand is made on the user under s 69 of the 1961 Act, the owner is liable in the event of non-production, unless he comes within the defences envisaged by s 56 as set out at para 6.3.4.

It is not necessary for the prosecution to serve a notice to produce when the defendant has failed to procure the relevant document to the Garda—*Williams v Russell* (1933) 97 JP 128.

6.3.6 Excepted pedestrian controlled vehicles

Section 79 of the 1961 Act excepts from the provisions dealing with insurance, pedestrian controlled vehicles as specified in Ministerial regulations.

Under Art 4 of the Road Traffic (Compulsory Insurance Regulations 1962 (SI 14/1962), the types of vehicles so excepted are those which are neither constructed nor adapted for use for carrying the driver or a passenger and which do not exceed 8 cwt unladen. The first specification as to construction is already contained in the definition of this type of vehicle in s 3 of the 1961 Act (see para 7.9). By virtue of an amendment effected by Sch, 1968 Act, these vehicles are now called 'Pedestrian controlled vehicles'.

6.3.7 Other excepted vehicles

Tucked away in s 4(2) of the 1961 Act are three exceptions to the general application of the insurance provisions of Part VI of the Act. They are:

(a) State-owned vehicles used by a person in the course of his employment;
(b) vehicles seized by a State employee in the course of his duty or a person using such vehicle in the course of his employment;
(c) vehicles used by members of the Gardai or Ministerial officials for the purpose of a test, their removal or disposition under the Acts or regulations thereunder. It should be remembered that under the Civil Liability Act 1961, s 59 the State is liable in tort, for example, for the negligence of the driver of a state vehicle. The State carries its own insurance, so to speak, on the assumption that the Minister's for Finances resources are as adequate as any insurance company's;
(d) other exceptions—
    (i) certain pedestrian controlled vehicles as noted in the last paragraph (para 6.3.6),
    (ii) insurance is also not necessary if any exempt person is answerable for claims (para 6.6),
    (iii) similarly, if a vehicle is owned by an insurer for which the insurer is liable, i.e. insurance company-owned cars.

As to injury to person and property in certain circumstances where the MIBI covers see para 6.8 infra.

6.3.8 Transitional provisions

Section 81 of the 1961 Act has transitional provisions to carry over deposits made and certificates issued under the repealed 1933 Road Traffic Act.

6.4 Extent and effect of cover: approved policies

6.4.1 Minimum requirements

To qualify as an approved policy of insurance, under s 62 of the 1961 Act (as amended by SI 178/1975 and SI 322/1987) the policy:

(i) must be issued to a named person (referred to in the Act as 'the insured') by a vehicle insurer. Vehicle insurers are discussed more fully at para 6.5; and
(ii) the insurer must cover the insured and his personal representative for an unlimited sum of damages and costs on a personal injuries claim and, until 31 December 1987, for £1,000 on a damage and costs to property claim to all persons caused by negligent use of the stated vehicle (unless they are 'excepted persons'—see para 6.7), for the period of cover specified in the policy. The liability must extend to the designated territories (see para 6.3.2) for negligent use there.

The £1,000 limit is not in fact used by Irish insurance companies to limit property damage cover for Irish approved policies. There was no limit for third party property damage in the case of private car policies. There was usually a limit of cover of £10,000 in the case of third party damage by commercial vehicles. The limit has been raised to £40,000 from 1 December 1987 to 31 December 1990, and thereafter to £80,000 by SI 322/1987

(iii) it must contain no limitations other than those in (ii) above, allowed by s 56(2) (as inserted by SI 322/1987); and restrictions prescribed by Ministerial regulations shall not be inserted in approved policies, i.e. no prohibited conditions, restrictions or limitations (see para 6.4.2).

By virtue of SI 178/1975, a policy of insurance issued in accordance with the national laws on compulsory insurance in any of the designated territories where vehicles are based is also an approved policy.

It should be remembered, however, that insurance is an indemnity, i.e. that is its maximum 'return', and the insured is not entitled to make a windfall profit from a claim (*St Albans Investment Co v Sun Alliance* [1983] IR 362). The doctrine of subrogation applies to all indemnity contracts, i.e. insurers are entitled to all the rights of the insured on payment of the loss (*Lister v Romford Ice* [1957] 1 All ER 125, approved by the Supreme Court in *Sinnott v Quinnsworth* (1984) ILRM 523). See also *Zurich Insurance v Shield Insurance* (Supreme Court 18.12.1987: ILL 1988 p 88) on what happens when there are two policies.

6.4.2 Prohibited conditions

The prohibited restrictions on policies are set out in the First Schedule of The Road Traffic (Compulsory Insurance) Regulations 1962 (SI 14/1962), as amended by the 1964 Regulations (SI 58/1964) and the 1987 Regulations (SI 321/1987).

These 1962 Regulations were challenged in *Greaney v Scully* (1981) ILRM 340. It was claimed that they were *ultra vires* the Minister's powers. In that case the defendant was convicted of driving without insurance under s 56 of the 1961 Act. A policy of insurance was in force in respect of the vehicle, but it was restricted to driving by the defendant's father only. It was held in the Supreme Court that in drafting the regulations the Minister did not exceed his delegated powers under the Road Traffic Act and that he had acted *intra vires*.

The prohibited conditions are of the following kinds, i.e. conditions which cannot be inserted as they would reduce the third party rights required to be covered by compulsory insurance:

(a) One which depends on something being done or omitted after the 'accident' covered by the insurance—see *McCarthy v Murphy* [1938] IR 737 as to such a condition, prohibited under similar provisions of the Road Traffic Act 1933.

(b) A condition which limits the drivers covered, except—

(i) by naming the drivers covered or not covered, or persons whose employees are covered, or requiring a person so covered to be accompanied by a named person or an employee of a named person (see *Greaney v Scully* above);

(ii) by requiring persons so covered to have the consent of a named person to such driving (and see (v) below); or

(iii) by requiring drivers to be accompanied by specified persons, by requiring drivers to have the consent of a named person; or

(iv) by requiring that a driver shall hold a driving licence or a provisional licence, or (having held one) that he is not disqualified by the Courts. In *National Farmers v Dawson* [1941] 2 KB 424, a case of a drunken chauffeur, it was held that a condition that the assured should use only steady and sober drivers was not a condition by reference to the age or physical condition of persons driving the vehicle;

(v) by SI 321/1987 Road Traffic (Compulsory Insurance) Amendment Regulations 1987, these conditions, i.e. (ii), (iii) and (iv), shall provide that the limitations or restrictions shall not apply with respect to a claim by a person to receive moneys from the insurer under s 76 of the 1961 Act. Section 76 deals with the right of a judgment creditor/claimant to collect directly from the insurers, and is covered at para 6.4.7 below;

(vi) by requiring a driver to hold a public hire vehicle licence or, having held such a licence, that it has not ceased.

(c) A condition specifying that maximum or minimum ages of the persons to be so covered is allowable now (inserted in the 1962 Regulations by SI 359/1977—Road Traffic (Compulsory Insurance) (Amendment) Regulations 1977). It was not allowable prior to 1977.

In *A-G v Daniel Reilly* (unreported, Supreme Court, 17 November 66) it was held that a clause in a policy restricting cover to a person holding 'a licence to drive such a vehicle or who, having held such a licence, is not disqualified . . .' was not more restrictive than was permitted by these regulations. It allowed for a driver holding a provisional licence to drive. The Supreme Court reversed the High Court decision.

In *A-G (Wren) v O'Brien* (unreported, High Court, 16 July 65) a policy covered the insured and any person driving with his consent who held a licence to drive 'such a vehicle' or having previously held such a licence, was not disqualified. The High Court held a provisional licence holder, who had previously driven while accompanied and now drove while unaccompanied, to be covered. See also *Rendlesham v Dunne* (1964) 1 Lloyds Rep 192, where this was so even though the learner was driving in breach of his provisional licence.

In *Brady v Brady* [1938] IR 103, a case taken under the Road Traffic Act 1933, it was held that a driving licence obtained by the insured for a person, through the making of a false statement, was inoperative. Therefore, a policy which excluded vehicles 'driven with the general consent of the insured by any person who to the insured's knowledge does not hold a licence to drive such a vehicle unless such person has held and is not disqualified from obtaining such a licence' was also inoperative. See also *Adams v Dunne* (1978) RTR 281—disqualification concealed but policy valid until avoided.

In *A-G (Hayes) v Downes* 93 ILTR 121 a servant who drove on the orders of the defendant never held a drivers licence. *Held*: the defendant (owner) was convicted and the servant was entitled to the special defence of acting under orders (see para 6.3.4).

(d) A condition specifying that the vehicle must not have been stolen or obtained by violence, or taken without the consent of the owner or other lawful authority (or hold a driving licence). This exception was inserted in the 1962 Regulations by amending SI 321/1987 and operates only from 31 December 1988. The effect will be in these cases to transfer liability for relevant compensation of 'joy riders' victims' and other innocent victims to the Motor Insurance Bureau of Ireland (MIBI) under the newly drafted 1988 Agreement between the Bureau and the Minister (see para 6.8.13).

(e) A condition under which liability depends on—

(i) the weight, construction, equipment, maintenance or state of repair of the vehicle;
(ii) the speed at which the vehicle is to be driven;
(iii) keeping or carrying anything on it;
(iv) the times or areas when it operates or is used;
(v) the number of persons carried (except where it is a cycle); or
(vi) the weight or physical characteristics of the goods to be carried in such vehicle.

On a similar provision in regulations under the Road Traffic Act 1933, it was held in *Higgins v Feeney* [1953] IR 45; 88 ILTR 152 that it did not prohibit a condition that the policy would not cover use of a motor cycle while carrying a passenger unless a sidecar were attached; the sidecar would not be 'equipment' for the purpose of the regulations.

In *Haughton v Trafalgar I Co* [1953] 2 All ER 1409 a policy which prohibited carrying a load in excess of that for which the vehicle was constructed was held to refer to the weight load specified for lorries and vans and was infringed by carrying excess passengers.

As to maintenance, see *McInnes v National Motor* (1963) 2 Lloyds Rep 415, where it was stated that such a condition means that the vehicle should be capable of doing what is normally and reasonably required of it. Thus, in *Conn v Westminster* (1966) 1 Lloyds Rep 407 a car with threadbare tyres was not so maintained.

(f) Any condition requiring the existence or amount of the liability of the insurer to be determined by arbitration. Apparently, such a clause, while a prohibited condition as regards third parties, may be valid as between insured and insurer (*O'Donnell v Yorkshire Insurance Co* [1949] IR 187, a case on a similar provision under the Road Traffic Act 1933).

(g) A condition which makes the liability of the insurer depend on any policy except an approved policy.

(h) A condition which would in effect extend in favour of the insurer the provisions of s 76(1)(e) of the 1961 Act, i.e. section dealing with executing judgment directly against the insurance company (see para 6.4.7(b)). That subsection bars an insurer from raising against third parties fraud, misrepresentations or false statements by the insured when called on to pay judgment, unless there has been a criminal conviction. This provision does not rule out a condition operative against the insured himself, nor a condition requiring the insured to reimburse to the insurer part of a claim ('excess payment'), nor a clause confining cover to specified uses such as 'social, domestic and pleasure'. In relation to this latter purpose, giving a lift out of courtesy to a person on business rounds is use for social purposes (*Passmore v Vulcon* (1935) 52 TLR 193). Carrying turf for a neighbour under an agricultural policy was covered (*A-G v East* (1964) ILTR 33).

6.4.3 Obtaining

As 'vehicle insurers' are associations or companies of a non-State owned nature, the obtaining of insurance is basically a matter of private contract negotiation, albeit enforced by statute law. As with all insurances, road traffic insurances are contracts *unberrimae fidei.* Full and honest disclosure must be made. This is reinforced by the provisions of s 64 of the 1961 Act (as amended by Sch, 1968 Act and s 3 of the 1984 Act) which makes it an offence if a person, for the purpose of, or in the course of obtaining insurance for himself or any other person, commits any fraud, or makes a written or verbal representation or statement, or makes a representation by conduct which to his knowledge is false or misleading in any material respect.

It was held, in relation to the similar provision in s 65 of the 1933 Act, in *A-G v Sheane* (1955-56 Ir) Jur R 55 that this creates two offences, the word 'or' not being conjunctive. That case held that, in a prosecution under this section, evidence must be forthcoming (a) that the accused sought to obtain the issue of an approved policy, and (b) that the statement or representation is false or misleading in some material respect. The question as to whether a representation is material must be proved by expert evidence. As a side issue on a practice note, this case, it was held that a District Court Summons charging, as one offence, what a statute states to be the doing of a number of different acts in the alternative may be good having regard to rule 44 of the District Court Rules 1948. However, the court order must be for one offence only or it will be bad.

In general insurance/contract Law, a policy obtained by misrepresentation of a material fact insures no-one and it would not be a policy within the section (*Guardian Assurance Co v Sutherland* [1939] 2 All ER 246, but, however, see para 6.4.7 as to rights of third parties under the Act). A policy normally lapses on the sale by the insured of his vehicle (*Peters v General Accident* [1943] KB 139).

In a prosecution under s 64, a proposal form, application form or similar document purporting to be signed by the defendant is presumed to be such and signed by the defendant until the contrary is shown by the defendant.

A prosecution under s 64 of the 1961 Act as amended by the 1968 Act may be instituted within one year, notwithstanding the normal six months' limit of the 1851 Petty Sessions (Ireland) Act. Conviction carries a maximum fine of £1,000 and/or six months' imprisonment. The normal position as to ancillary disqualification and endorsement (optional) applies. See also para 7.4 as to false declarations, misleading information, etc.

In respect of proposal forms the following decisions should be noted:

(a) In *Re Sweeney and Kennedy's Arbitration* [1950] IR 85; (1951) 85 ILTR 31 a proposal form contained the following Question 9 and answer—

Q. 'Are any of your drivers less than 21 or with less than 12 months' driving experience?
A. 'No';

and a statement 'I agree that this declaration shall be held to be promissory and so form the basis of the Contract'. A driver of the lorry aged under 21 was involved in a fatal accident. The insurance company repudiated cover. *Held*—

(i) that the declaration was not 'promissory' and was referable only to facts then existing;

(ii) the answer to question 9 was not a warranty as to the age of drivers to be subsequently employed;

(iii) where an insurer uses ambiguous language, such language will be strictly construed against him.

(d) On the question of full disclosure it is relevant to mention *O'Leary v Irish National Insurance Co Ltd* (1958) Ir Jur R 1. It held that where a person purports to effect a policy of insurance in respect of a vehicle of which he is not the owner, it being represented to or understood by the insurers that he is the owner, no valid contract of insurance exists. See also *Coen v Employer's Liability Co* [1962] IR 314, where it was held the motorist had an insurable interest.

(e) *Chariot Inns Ltd v Assicurazioni* [1981] IR 199 deals with the test of materiality of disclosure. It is an objective test and only information which would be of importance to the prudent insurer will be relevent.

The provisions of s 115 of the 1961 Act (see para 7.4) should be borne in mind as to declarations, and also as to forging, altering, fraudulently lending or using certificates.

6.4.4 Certificate

The vehicle insurers must, under s 66 of the 1961 Act, on the issue and renewal of a policy under the Act give to the insured in the prescribed form a certificate of insurance. A disc must also be provided (see para 6.4.1) normally.

This certificate is prescribed in the Road Traffic (Compulsory Insurance) Regulations 1962-64, R 7, which requires a certificate to be issued for each vehicle, or to each person if use is to be made of an unlimited number of vehicles by one or more persons, or the number of certificates needed by the policy holder if other liabilities are covered. All certificates must be duly authenticated. Under s 70 of the 1961 Act the insured must deliver up the certificate within seven days if the insurance is terminated or suspended by any means before its expiration by effluxion of time. If he does not he is guilty of a criminal offence with the general penalties under s 102 of the 1961 Act applying (see para 7.1). The policy may not be terminated by the insurer before expiration, however, except by seven days' notice in writing.

If the certificate is altered in its particulars after issue, except on alteration of the address of the person to whom it is issued by the insurer, it is invalid. If it is lost or destroyed, the insured can apply to the company for a new one, application being on a prescribed form; but, if the new one is issued and the old one found, the old one must be returned to the insurers for cancellation. If the certificate becomes obliterated or defaced, similarly, it must be returned for cancellation and a new one issued. See R 7 of the 1962 Regulations (SI 14/1962). The provisions of s 115 of the 1961 Act as to forging, altering, fraudulently using, or lending a certificate apply (para 7.4).

These Regulations (R 9 of SI 14/1962) also requires vehicle insurers to keep records of particulars of a policy, of the issue of a certificate, its loss, destruction, obliteration or defacement for 12 months from the expiry of cover in the State in premises where it can be inspected. Such premises and the name of the person in control of the records have to be notified to the Minister for the Environment. A Minister's authorised officer or a Garda is entitled to information from the insurer about any policy or certificate. In *Murphy v PMPA* (HC, No 539 SS 1977, unreported) Doyle J cast doubt on the provisions of Reg 9 as to the production of information, regarding the contract as a confidential one being one *uberrimae fidei*. He said, dealing with setting aside a conviction of failing to furnish all information, that the regulation was in conflict with the natural right of the insurers (to maintain confidentiality) and the regulation was not clear enough to do this.

Most of the regulations are penal and carry the general penalty (para 7.1). In Court a letter from the insurance company will not suffice to prove the terms of the policy (*Egan v Bowler* (1939) 63 Lloyds LR 266).

In *Samuelson v National Insurance* [1986] 3 All ER 417 it was held that there is nothing inherently objectionable in maintaining a contract of insurance in such a way as to put the insurers on or off risk at short or recurring intervals. This deals with the problem of 'cover notes'. See also *Smith v Alexander* (1965) 1 Lloyds Rep 283.

Where cover is extended by a certificate, beyond the period when it should have run out, the cover is effective if relied on by the defendant, e.g. days of grace (*Taylor v Allen* [1965] 1 All ER 557).

6.4.5 Effect of certificate

The result of the issue of a certificate of insurance (s 67 of the 1961 Act) is to prove to third parties that a policy on the terms of the certificate exists. The policy document overrules the terms of the certificate when issued. Until a policy is issued, the certificate shows the extent of cover (s 67(i)(a)).

There is a decision under 1933 Act of *O'Donnell v Yorkshire Insurance Co Ltd* [1949] IR 187; ILTR 43 to the effect that a certificate, where no policy had been issued at the time of the accident, represents the contract. It also held that the costs of the insured are not payable in the absence of the insurer's consent.

6.4.6 Production of certificate

The certificate of insurance (or exemption) must be produced:

(a) On 'taxing' the vehicle, i.e. paying annual duty under the Excise Acts (see para 1.11);

(b) on demand to a member of the Garda who has reasonable grounds for believing that a vehicle was used by a person, within one month of the alleged user, from the driver (or the owner). If that person fails to produce it on demand, then he has ten days to produce it to a named Garda Station. There is a presumption against him until he proves he did produce it at that station.

This law (b) above, is contained in s 69 of the 1961 Act (see para 6.3.5 above and cases on same). The provision for disc display (para 6.4.11) should also be borne in mind, and the provisions in para 6.10 below as to information on insurance by a claimant.

If the driver or owner is not given the ten days to produce the certificate he cannot be convicted (*State (McDonagh) v Sheerin* (1981) ILRM 149). In *Lyons v Cooney* [1978] IR 41 a District Justice had dismissed a charge under s 56 of the 1961 Act (i.e. no insurance) against an owner as no demand under s 69 had been made on the owner. The demand had been made to the other person who was using the vehicle on that occasion. The Supreme Court held the Justice was wrong and that, subject to the defences in s 56, the owner was liable and that there was no justification for ignoring the ordinary meaning of the phrase 'a demand is being made under section 69' contained in s 56. Interestingly, the High Court had upheld the District Justice but the decision was reversed by the Supreme Court.

In *A-G v Shivman* (1968) IR 369 the Supreme Court held that a demand for production should be so expressed as to require the production of any one of the documents mentioned in the section. At that time that meant either insurance, exemption or guarantee. The guarantee provisions were subsequently deleted by the 1968 Act. This decision now means that the Garda asks for production of a certificate of insurance or a certificate of exemption (see para 6.6).

Section 69 provides certain limited defences to each party, i.e. the person alleged to use the vehicle and the owner. These are:

(i) Defence of user—that he did not use it, or he used it as the servant of the owner on express orders;

(ii) defence of owner—that the vehicle was not used, or it was used without his consent by another and either used in contravention of his orders by his servant or he had taken all reasonable precautions to prevent its use (see para 6.3.4).

If the certificate has all the requirements of the Act a court can act on it (*Borders v Swift* (1957) Crim LR 194), but it is for the defendant to prove proper cover (*Leathley v Dromond* (1972) RTR 293). The policy overrides the certificate if there is an inconsistency between the two. This is different from the English position (*Biddle v Johnston* (1965) 104 Sol Jo 395). Section 67 of the Act (1961) confirms the effect of a certificate of insurance and that (i) issue of the certificate is sufficient to prove cover to third parties even if no policy is issued, and (ii) the particulars in the certificate, if more favourable, overrule those in the policy in favour of third parties.

Visiting vehicles–production of insurance

By SI 178/1975 (European Communities (Road Traffic) (Compulsory Insurance) Regulations 1975) s 69A is added to the Act. This allows a Garda or an officer of the Customs and Excise to demand production of insurance covering use of the vehicle in the State and the designated territories. If not produced, the vehicle must not be used in the State, and it can be removed or be directed to be removed or retained by the officer until evidence of such insurance in produced. A person using the vehicle, or who uses it without such insurance, or who disobeys a lawful direction is liable to a fine of (only) £50.

Arrest

If the certificate is produced to the Garda and he is not allowed to read it, an offence is committed (general penalty applies, para 7.1) and the Garda can arrest the person without warrant and/or demand the person's name and address (s 69(3) of the 1961 Act). If that information is not given, or is falsely or misleadingly given, the Garda can arrest the person without warrant and that person commits an offence (s 69(4).

6.4.7 Liability of insurers

If a person claims damages against the owner or user of a mechanically propelled vehicle, or has a Court award arising from such a claim and the insurers had notice of the case, he (the injured party) can serve on the insurers of the vehicle a notice of that claim (by registered post) and then, under s 76 of the 1961 Act, the following rights arise:

(a) *Unexecuted judgment*. The insurer shall not pay to the owner or user more than that person (owner or user) has to pay the claimant. If judgment has been obtained the insurers may, in the event of non-payment by the insured, pay the claimant, and this payment is valid discharge of the contractual liability of the insurer to its insured (s 76(i)(c)). The claimant can apply in the event of non-payment to the Court in which he obtained judgment for leave to execute the judgment, i.e. damages and costs, against the insurer.

In *Whelan v Dixon* (1963) 97 ILTR 95 the Supreme Court held under similar section of 1933 Act that the burden of proof is on the claimant to show that the judgment is for a sum against the liability for which the driver or owner is insured. In this case the policy was limited to social, domestic and pleasure use, and the plaintiff had to show that the vehicle was used within these limits. See (f) below as to defences.

Precedent—s 76(i)(c) see 2.5.8.

The District Court

District Court Area District No

Between

AB Claimant

and

CD 1st Named Respondent

and

XY 2nd Named Respondent

Notice of motion

Take Notice that AB of in the County of intends to apply to the District Court sitting at on the day of 19 at 11 am or the next opportunity thereafter for leave to execute against the 2nd Named Respondent under s 76(i)(c) of the Road Traffic Act 1961 a Judgment obtained by him on the day of at District Court against CD of for £ and £ costs the 1st named Respondent being the owner/user of a mechanically propelled vehicle who was insured by the 2nd Named Respondent under an Approved Policy of Insurance.

Dated the day of 19

Signed: ....
Solicitor for Applicant

TO The District Court Clerk

	At
and	
TO	CD 1st Named Respondent
	at
and	
	XY Insurance Co./2nd Named Respondent

Notes

(1) Ten days' service is required by registered post. Declaration of service and the Original Notice must be lodged with the Court Clerk at least four days before the hearing.

(2) The Court Area is the Court where judgment is obtained.

(b) *No judgment and defendant missing*. If a Court is satisfied that the owner or user is not in the State, cannot be found or served with the process of the Court, and no judgment can be obtained against him, or for any other 'just and equitable' reason, it can give liberty by the claimant under s 76(i)(d) of the 1961 Act to proceed against the insurer as if it was the owner or user, to the extent that liabilty must be covered compulsorily under the Acts. An example of 'just and equitable' is seen in the case of *Hayes v Legal Insurance Co Ltd* (1941) Ir Jur R 49. Consequent to a two-car collision, the driver of one vehicle died. No representation was raised to his estate within six months. The Court allowed the other driver to proceed against the insurers directly.

A precedent District Court application in these circumstances would be as in (a) above, except that relief would be for 'Leave to institute and prosecute proceedings in the above mentioned court area and district against the 2nd named respondent in lieu of the 1st named respondent (owner/user)'.

(c) *Misrepresentation*. Insurers by the same section are prohibited from raising against the claimant any invalidity of the policy arising from fraud, misrepresentation or false information once the claimant is not a party to it, and in respect of which no conviction has resulted under the Act. This is a limitation of the normal law of contract. In *Guardian Assurance Co Ltd v Harris* 75 ILTR 43 it was held that where the policy provided that the insured should refund the insurer, this refund extended to all costs, even though the insured did not approve of the line of defence. In the English case of *Merchants and Manufacture's Insurance Company v Davies and Anor* [1938] 1 KB 196 discovery was refused as to documents about non-disclosure of a previous conviction.

The policy must be otherwise valid, e.g. there must be an insurable interest (*O'Leary v Irish National Insurance Co* (1958) Ir Jur R 1, where the policy was held to be inoperative because the person who represented himself as the owner had no insurable interest).

The section does not apply where the risk is a valid risk, e.g. an employee (*Gray v Blackmore* [1934] 1 KB 95). The judgment must be on the insured person by the third party (*Crown v Herbert* (1950) 100 LT 597). The insurers may apply to set aside the judgment in certain circumstances (*Windsor v C Rolcraft* [1939] 1 KB 279) (see (f) below).

Notice can be given to the agent of the insurers but it must be reasonably informative and certain (*Herbert v Railway Passengers Insurance Co* [1938] 1 All ER 650). Where a third party is found, and he makes a claim against the insured, notice of this must be given (*Cross v British Oak* [1938] 2 KB 167).

(d) There is a *limit*, in addition to the restriction that the insurer's liability is to pay, to that liability which is compulsory insurable under the Act. Insurers are also safeguarded by s 76(2) of the 1961 Act in relation to more than one claim arising from one event or act of negligence. In these latter circumstances the insurer is liable only to the statutory limit and claims are abated proportionately to that amount, and these claims are so abated *inter se*. This in reality applies only to property damage. It should be remembered that cover of £1,000 was only necessary (s 56(3)) in relation to injury to property. This £1,000 figure became inadequate, but was unused in relation to Irish insurers, in fact, except as to a £10,000 limit in commercial vehicle policies. By SI 322/1987, to give effect to EEC requirements, this figure was raised to £40,000 for the period 31 December 1987 to 31 December 1990 and thereafter to £80,000 (see para 6.4.1).

(e) On the question of the *notice of the Court proceedings* which the insurers must have, the Act merely stipulates *prior* notice. A similar provision (omitting the word 'prior') was contained in the 1933 Act, and was interpreted in the Supreme Court as referred to proceedings of the existence of which the insurers had reasonable notice. It was not necessary that such notice should be given to the insurers before the institution of the proceedings (*Herlihy v Curley* [1950] IR 15; 83 ILTR 155, decided a few years earlier on this point). Now, however, under the 1961 Act, the section specifies prior notice. The MIBI should also get prior notice in case of any doubt (see para 6.8).

For the purpose of s 76 of the 1961 Act, a reference to an owner or user is construed as also being a reference to and including his personal representative.

(f) *Defence (s 76 application)*. Any defence available to the defendant can be relied on by the respondent (*Stanbridge v Healy* (1985) ILRM 29, where £9,000 judgment execution was refused against the insurance company as the accident occurred in a 'non-public place').

In a further civil case application against insurers under s 76—*Boyle v McBride* (1987) ILRM 95—it was held:

(1) a third party cannot claim against insurers, save where specially allowed by statute, e.g. s 76 of the 1961 Act;
(2) s 76 did not apply to the circumstances of that case where a claim was brought against the deceased driver of a vehicle in collision with the plaintiff's vehicle, the owner of the vehicle not being the personal representative of the driver.

The High Court ordered the insurers to nominate a defendant or, if they did not, that they be joined as co-defendants. The Supreme Court allowed an appeal against that order on the basis that there was no estoppel (as there had been in *Doran v Thompson* [1978] IR 223) and the order would be fruitless as the liability of the insurers lies in contract and not in negligence. See also *Whelan v Dixon* referred to at (a) above.

(g) *Stolen vehicle uninsured.* By a discussion document issued by the Department of the Environment in July 1987 on the implementation of the Second EEC Directive on Motor Insurance (84/5/EEC), it is proposed to amend s 76, if necessary, to give the victim of an accident involving an uninsured or stolen vehicle the right to seek compensation directly from the Motor Insurers' Bureau of Ireland. The victim already had the right, under the existing 1964 Agreement, to seek execution against the MIBI of a judgment made against the driver of an uninsured or stolen vehicle after a period of 28 days has expired following judgment. See para 6.8 below.

(h) *Determining consent.* A presumption of consent to use as a servant is raised by s 118 of the 1961 Act, which can extend the liability of insurers. This section reads:

> 'Where a person (in this section referred to as a user) uses a mechanically propelled vehicle with the consent of the owner of the vehicle, the user shall, for the purpose of determining the liability or non-liability of the owner for injury caused by the negligent use of the vehicle by the user, and for the purposes of determining the liability or non-liability of any other person for injury to the vehicle or persons or property therein caused by negligence occurring while the vehicle is being used by the user, be deemed to use the vehicle as the servant of the owner, but only in so far as the user acts in accordance with the terms of such consent'.

As to the limitations on the section, see *Kelly v Lombard Ltd* [1974] IR 142. There, a driver obtained a car on hire from the defendants on production of a false licence. The plaintiff, a passenger, was injured by his negligence. *Held*: the defendants were not liable as their consent was vitiated by the fraud of the driver. See also *Buckley v Musgrave Brook Bond Ltd* [1969] IR 440, referred to at para 6.3.4 above—general consent to use by servant put the onus on the owner to show it did not apply to the plaintiff.

6.4.8 Insured's insolvency, death, etc—set off

In certain circumstances the funds available under policies are given to the victims of accidents in priority. Section 62 of the Civil Liability Act 1961 provides that money payable to a person who becomes bankrupt, dies, or, if a corporate body or group, is wound up or dissolved, under the proceeds of an insurance policy covering liability for a wrong is to be applied to the discharge of valid claims against the insured. This section repealed s 76(4) of the 1961 Road Traffic Act and reversed the decision in *Re Harrington Motor Co, ex parte Chaplin* (1928) Ch 793, which had treated such moneys as part of the assets of the bankrupt.

The provisions of ss 36(4) and (5) of the Civil Liability Act 1961 (inserted by 1964 Civil Liability Amendment Act) should be borne in mind also. These allow the insured to collect from the insurers any deduction or non-payment made by way of set off by the insurers when paying the claim, by reason of the person making claim to payment owing such sums to the insured.

Nevertheless, it should always be borne in mind that insurance is primarily a contract between the insurers and the insured. Thus, in *Boyce v McBride* (1987) ILRM 95 it was stated that a third party cannot claim against an insurer under the policy, save where that is specially allowed by statute, as under s 76 of the Road Traffic Act 1961. The insurers will not be estopped by mere discussions (*Doran v Thompson* [1978] IR 223).

6.4.9 Regulations

Under s 75(1) of the 1961 Act, the Minister for the Environment may regulate the issue of certificates of insurance and exemption, of copies and new certificates when lost or destroyed, the keeping records of the same, the cancellation of certificates and their surrender, and the furnishing of records and of information to Gardai and Ministerial officers. It is an offence punishable under s 102 of the 1961 Act (general penalty, see para 7.1) not to obey the regulations under s 75(3).

The Road Traffic (Compulsory Insurance) Regulations 1962-64 (SI 14/1962 and SI 58/1964) provide for the form of certificates (R 7) and the issue of duplicates (R 8) (and see certificates of exemption order R 9). Regulation 7 also requires records to be kept. The powers of the Gardai to inspect these, etc. are discussed at para 6.4.5. Other provisions as to prohibited conditions, etc. have been noted at para 6.4.2.

6.4.10 Construction of policy

The lawful terms of the policy must be observed. The document will normally be construed against the insurers if there is ambiguity or doubt (see in *Re Sweeney and Kennedy Arbitration* [1950] IR 85; 85 ILTR 31). Policy disputes are referred to arbitration under the clauses of the policy normally.

In *McCarthy v British Oak Insurance Co* [1938] 2 All ER 1 the question of what amounts to 'hire' was considered. The assured lent a car to the driver, who paid for petrol only at the assured's garage. The assured made no profit. The policy excluded use while on hire. *Held*: the insurance company was liable to passengers (who had in fact reimbursed the driver and gave him two quarts of beer) injured due to the driver's negligence, as 'hire' meant a genuine contract for reward.

As this practice of 'expense sharing' is common, it is relevant to point out that separate payments to the driver can, even if small, be deemed to constitute carrying for hire and reward (*East Midland Traffic Area Commissioners v Tyler* [1938] 3 All ER 39). See also, on the distinction of hire and reward, *Baraam v Zurich Insurance Co* [1944] 2 All ER 573 and *Lyons v Denscombe* [1949] 1, All ER.

6.4.10 *Extent and effect of cover: approved policies*

Examples of the construction policy of insurance contracts are to be found in:

(1) *Kelleher v Christopherson* 91 ILTR 191—carrying swill in a container in lieu of on the back seat was not use for 'business or trade';
(2) *A-G v East* 100 ILTR 4—an insurance policy allowing haulage of agricultural goods was sufficient to allow a farmer to bring home a neighbouring farmer's turf for domestic consumption;
(3) the decision of *Whelan v Dixon* 97 ILTR 195 largely reverses the case of *Pattison v Martin* 81 ILTR 155 by holding (Supreme Court) that it was for the claimant to establish that the vehicle was being driven within the limits of cover;
(4) *McComiskey v McDermott*, 26 July 1973, SC, 149/1970—a passenger may have waived the right to claim in certain circumstances, e.g. by accepting a notice displayed in a vehicle which states that passengers travel at their own risk.

6.4.11 Disc display

There was for many years a system of displaying a taxation disc in Ireland. The system was extended to displaying an insurance disc by the Road Traffic (Insurance Disc) Regulations 1984 (SI 355/1984). These regulations were amended by SI 227/1986 (Road Traffic (Insurance Disc) (Amendment) Regulations 1986).

These discs are issued by insurance companies on granting or renewing policies and are normally displayed on windscreens.

The Minister claimed in Nov 1988 that these discs had reduced by two-thirds the number of uninsured drivers.

6.4.11.1 *Duty to display*. Under Art 5 of the 1984 Regulations (inserted in redrafted form by Art 4 of SI 227/1986), a person shall not use a vehicle in a public place, after ten days from the authentication of the certificate of insurance, unless he displays in the proper position an insurance disc. The owner, if not the user, is also liable, but the owner has a good defence to such a charge if he shows the use of the vehicle on the occasion in question was unauthorised. As to 'public place', 'use' and 'vehicle', see para 7.9.

6.4.11.2 *Position of display*. The disc must be carried on the windscreen of the vehicle in a conspicuous position. The display must be such that it is visible and readily accessible for inspection; also, its location must be such that it does not obscure the vision of the driver.

If the vehicle does not have a windscreen, the disc must be displayed in a conspicuous position on the near side of the vehicle.

6.4.11.3 *Issue of a disc*. A vehicle insurer must issue a disc for each vehicle (other than those exempted—see below) when issuing an insurance certificate, and issue a replacement disc on being satisfied that the original disc has been lost or destroyed, or, on the return of the original, if available, that it has been mutilated, discoloured, defaced or is illegible.

6.4.11.4 *Form of the disc.* The size of the disc must be 85 mm to 95 mm by 70/80 mm. Its colour must be white with a green band.

The disc must be in the form as set out in Schedule, 1984 Regulations. It must display the name of the fleet owner (five or more vehicles being a fleet) if the vehicle is a fleet vehicle, and must give the vehicle's registration number, or chassis number if the vehicle is not registered.

6.4.11.5 *Exempted vehicles.* The regulations apply to all mechanically propelled vehicles except:

(a) a mechanically propelled motor cycle with or without a side car;
(b) an agricultural tractor (see Finance (Excise Duties) (Vehicles) Act 1952 as to these);
(c) a vehicle exhibiting a trade licence (see Road Act 1920, s 9, as amended by s 15 of the Finance Act 1922);
(d) a vehicle owned or used by an exempted person (see para 6.6);
(e) a vehicle registered outside the State.

6.4.11.6 *Fixed penalty.* By virtue of s 103 of the 1961 Act, the fixed penalty procedure ('on the spot fines') apply to non-display of a tax disc (see para 5.11.2 above).

6.5 Vehicle insurers

6.5.1 Who are vehicle insurers?

An approved policy can be issued only by a vehicle insurer and, therefore, under ss 58 and 78 of the 1961 Act (as amended by Sch, 1968 Act), such an insurer must comply with two conditions, viz:

(a) be an Assurance Company or Syndicate under the Insurance Acts 1936-85 (see below), carrying on the business of a mechanically propelled vehicle insurer operating under licence from the Minister of Industry and Commerce under those Acts; and
(b) be a member of the Motor Insurers' Bureau of Ireland, or have given an undertaking, approved by the Minister for the Environment, to deal with third party claims on vehicles insured by it on similar terms to those standing agreed between the Minister and the Motor Insurers' Bureau.

Under the Assurance Companies Act 1909 (as amended by s 74 of the 1961 Act) and the Insurance Acts (1936-85):

(i) an insurer must maintain a substantial deposit in the High Court which can be available to meet judgments otherwise unpaid;

(ii) the insurer must contribute to an Insurance Compensation Fund, which is maintained to meet certain liabilities of insolvent insurers (see para 6.5.3 below). Note, however, that this is a different fund from that providing for uninsured personal injury claims dealt with by the Motor Insurers' Bureau of Ireland (para 6.8);

(iii) the insurer must annually present a statement of its business to the Minister for Industry and Commerce, and these statements are published annually by the Stationary Office.

As noted at para 6.4.9, under s 75 of the 1961 Act the Minister for the Environment has power to regulate such matters as the form of certificates and their issue, the keeping of records, and other controls on insurers. The present regulations are the Road Traffic (Compulsory Insurance) Regulations 1962-87 noted above.

Following recent EEC decisions, it is expected that the Irish market will be opened up substantially, i.e. that non-Irish companies will have greater access to becoming vehicle insurers. The position up to now has been regulated by the Insurance Acts 1909-81, but mainly by the Insurance Act 1936, which basically regulated 'assurance licences'. These were extended to EEC members by the European Communities (Non-life Insurance) Regulations 1976 (SI 115/1976) made under s 3 of the European Communities Act 1972. These regulations give effect in turn to the EEC Council Directive of 24 July 1973 (73/239/EEC.

The regulations cover all authorised non-life insurance bodies doing business in Ireland. They specify the conditions of admission to the market, opening it to EEC Member States where authorisation is granted by the Minister for Industry and Commerce. All undertakings, once authorised, must comply with the rules laid down for financial security, etc. Undertakings from countries outside the EEC are subject to special provisions in Part III of the regulations.

The 1976 Regulations have been extended and amended by SI 401/1977, SI 322/1987 and SI 144/1988, and were further extended to cover administrators appointed under the Insurance (No 2) Act 1983 (see para 6.5.3.3).

Section 74 of the 1981 Act made a number of consequential amendments to the Assurance Companies Act 1909 and The Insurance Act 1936 to widen the scope of those Acts in relation to mechanically propelled vehicles and to allow for annual statements to be presented to the Minister of its mechancally propelled vehicle Insurance business. See para 6.5.3 below.

6.5.2 Rights of vehicle insurers

Vehicle insurers are specifically given three sets of rights under ss 71, 72 and 72A of the 1961 Act (as amended by 1968 Act and SI 178/1975). They are:

(a) *Notice by insured*—s 71 of the 1961 Act. The insured or principal debtor must, as soon as practicable after the occurrence of an event which might place liability on the insurer to pay money to any person, give to the insurer notice in writing of such event, with such particulars as are in his knowledge or procurement and are reasonably required by the Insurer. If the event did not occur in his presence, the insured must give this notice within 48 hours of the event coming to his knowledge. The policy may relieve the insured of this liability under the Act, but in practice it never does.

(b) *Notice by user*—s 72 of the 1961 Act. Where a similar event occurs and the insured is not the person using the vehicle at the time and is not present, then the user must give notice and full particulars to the insured and also give all reasonable particulars that are in his knowledge or procurement to the insurer on demand.

(c) *Notice to IVMB Limited*—s 72A of the 1961 Act. Under SI 178/1975 a new s 72A was inserted in the 1961 Act. It requires, in the event of an accident, that the user of a vehicle from a designated territory (see para 6.3.2.) notifies the Irish Visiting Motorist Bureau Ltd. The user must give full particulars as to the vehicle, his own name and address and insurance, as well as particulars of the accident. The current address of the Irish Visiting Motorists Bureau is 5/9 South Frederick Street, Dublin 2.

The provisions of this additional section and SI 178/1975 were necessary to implement Directive No 72/166 EEC. It seems unusual to have amended the Act by regulation. The result of the regulation is, of course, to give preferential treatment to EEC based vehicles and vehicles from certain other designated countries.

Directive 72/166 EEC, Art 3 requires Member States to take all appropriate measures to ensure that civil liability in respect of the use of vehicles normally based in their territories is covered by insurance, including covering loss occurring in other Member States. Notices and particulars can be sent by post in all cases.

Failure to comply with the sections is an offence with the general penalty applying under s 102 (para 7.1). Disqualification and endorsement are optional.

The aim of these sections is obvious, i.e. to enable insurers to proceed with investigation of the event at an early date. Similar provisions as to notice are usually contained in the actual policy documents. The question of giving notice 'as soon as practicable' was considered in *John Butler, Applicant* [1970] IR 45, where it was held that the insured had failed in his duty, even though he believed it was futile to give notice as the insurance company was insolvent. Notice given 13 months after the accident was not binding on the liquidator.

Following a dictum in *O'Donovan v A-G* [1961] IR 114, at p 132, 'practical' is 'what is capable of being carried out in action', having regard to all the circumstances. See also the cases at para 4.9, dealing with 'as soon as practicable' in relation to a Garda and the Bureau.

The general law of contract applies with special regard to the nature of an insurance contract as being one *uberrimae fidei*, and so provides special rights to insurers. Standard books on this subject should be referred to. See para 6.4 above also. Similarly, the law and the terms of the policy, in so far as they do not conflict with the Road Traffic Acts, may confer special rights on the insurers. Thus, in *Hibernian Insurance v Eagle Star Insurance* 17 February 1987, High Court, 1985/6700P) a right of subrogation was involved. This case is under appeal at present.

6.5.3 Insurer's insolvency

6.5.3.1 *Insolvency/Liquidation.* To prevent frustration of claims for damages, a tight control is maintained by Government authorities over insurance companies. This is done under the Insurance Acts 1909-81. A fund is available under the Insurance Act 1964 to meet unpaid claims by insurers who become insolvent. Insurers maintain deposits in the High Court and present accounts, etc. to ensure the avoidance of insolvency and the monitoring of solvency under the 1936 Insurance Act.

In the *Equitable Insurance Company Ltd (in liquidation)* 1964 Monthly Notes, 98 ILT & Sol Jo 465 it was held by the Supreme Court that the deposit under the 1936 Insurance Act formed part of the general assets of the company and so was for the benefit of policy holders equally. The Dublin Corporation's claim for a priority payment was refused.

6.5.3.2 *Compensation Fund.* The *Equitable Insurance* case was pre-1964 Act. The 1964 Insurance Act, amended by the Insurance (No. 2) Act 1983 and the Insurance (Miscellaneous Provisions) Act 1985, set up the Insurance Compensation Fund, i.e. a fund to meet certain liabilities of insolvent insurers, contributed to by insurers. The Acts give liberty to the Minister for Finance to make grants and advances to the fund. As a result, claimants in *Sandys and Irish Agricultural Machinery Ltd* [1965] IR 489 were fortunate. A company which was compromised by an action by an employee was reinbursed by the Insurance Compensation Fund. The company had been insured by the Equitable Insurance Company.

The Insurance Compensation Fund is administered by the President of the High Court (s 2). It is maintained by licensed insurers paying a percentage fixed by regulation by the Minister for Industry and Commerce and by grants and advances by the Minister for Finance from State Funds (s 4). Section 3 of the Insurance Act 1964 empowers payment from the Fund to the liquidator of an insolvent insurer of 'such amounts as may be necessary to pay any sum (other than a sum payable in respect of the refund of a premium) which is due to a person under a policy issued by the insurer in the State' with reasonable costs and expenses, subject to a limit of one million pounds in resepct of any one insurer. If the Motor Insurers' Bureau has paid any claim, the Fund is not liable; if the Bureau has paid it in part, the Fund is liable only for the balance.

6.5.3.3 *Administrations.* In the 1980s there was again a crisis in parts of the insurance industry. In the main, two companies, the PMPA and the ICI insurance companies, got into difficulties. The device used to shore them up and keep them going was to put them into administration.

To deal with the difficulties of the PMPA insurance company, the

Insurance (No 2) Act 1983 was passed. It allows the Minister for Industry and Commerce to petition the High Court to appoint an administrator to administer a company's affairs. The administrator takes over the management of the business of the insurers, with a view to putting it on a sound financial and commercial footing. While an administrator is appointed, no proceedings to wind up the insurers can be brought without the Court's permission. The Minister can make regulations under the Act for the purpose of ensuring the proper regulation of non-life insurance business, with heavy fines of up to £20,000 for breach. The European Communities (Non-life Insurance) Regulations 1976 (SI 115/1976) to 1988 (SI 144/1988) apply to an administrator under the 1983 Act (see para 6.5.1).

The difficulties the Insurance Corporation of Ireland plc found itself in in 1985 led to virtual emergency legislation, i.e. Insurance (Miscellaneous Provisions) Act 1985, to enable the Minister for Industry, Trade, Commerce and Tourism to rescue it by capital and cash injections and guarantees, as well as putting it under administration.

6.6 Exempted persons and vehicles

6.6.1 Who and what are exempted?

By s 4(2) of the 1961 Act, Part VI (Insurance) does not apply to:

(a) a vehicle owned by the State, or a person using such a vehicle in the course of his employment;

(b) a vehicle seized by a State servant in the course of his duty or used in the course of his employment;

(c) a Garda or officer of any Minister using a vehicle for the purposes of tests, removal, or disposition under the Road Traffic Act or regulations thereunder.

In *Jones v CC of Bedfordshire* (1978) Crim LR 502 an appeal was allowed against a conviction of driving without insurance, as the defendant policeman was driving his private car while on police duty.

A Government employee who uses a State vehicle for purposes other than the public service without insurance is guilty of an offence under s 56 (*Salt v McKnight* (1947) SC (J) 99). The State carries its own insurance and, under s 59 of the Civil Liability Act 1961, is liable for the negligent use of its vehicles. That section actually repealed and replaced s 116 of the Road Traffic Act 1961;

(d) in addition to the State's general exemption, in certain circumstances persons of bodies can be declared 'exempted persons' for insurance purposes, i.e. exempt from having their vehicles covered by an approved policy. They in fact fund compensation cases from their own revenue as self-insurers. These bodies are regarded as similar to the State *vis-à-vis* insurance, and are recognised by the European Convention on Compulsory Insurance 1959.

6.6.1 *Exempted persons and vehicles*

The original provisions on exemption of persons as 'exempted persons' in the 1961 Act (repeating the 1933 provisions) underwent a radical change in the 1968 Act, when ss 60 and 61 of the 1961 Act, which contain the basic conditions of those exempted persons, were redrafted in s 54 and s 55 of the 1968 Act. The new concept is that only State sponsored bodies will be permitted in future to be 'exempted persons'. This change reflects the growth in numbers and financial strength of these organisations. The only exempt 'person' under the old system was, in fact, a state sponsored body—Coras Iompair Eireann (CIE). However, to date since 1968 Act, the following are 'exempt' persons—Bord Telecom Eireann, Coillte Teo, Bus Eireann, Bus Atha Cliath, and Iarnrod Eireann.

Note that ss 54 and 55 of the 1968 Act inserted new ss 60 and 61 in the 1961 Act, and these sections (54 and 55) of the 1968 Act were brought into operation on 26 October 1970 by SI 244/1970 Commencement Order.

See also 6.8 below as to application of MIBI Agreement in certain circumstances.

6.6.2 Who can qualify?

By the new redrafted ss 60 and 61, and under s 78 of the 1961 Act, to become 'exempt person' under (d) above a body must comply with the following requirements:

(a) The body must be either—
  (i) a statutory company, i.e. one especially established under the Act of the Oireachtas; or
  (ii) a State sponsored company; or
  (iii) a company controlled by either of the former types, in respect of which the Minister for the Environment issued a certificate that it is an exempt person for the purposes of the Road Traffic Acts.

  The Minister must be satisfied that such a body would be able to meet claims in relation to liability from the use of its vehicles which require compulsory insurance in regard to other ownership if such vehicles are negligently driven, and, in so judging, the Minister must take into account any deposit paid under (b) below.

(b) The body must pay a deposit to the account of the High Court of Justice where the Minister requires it. The Minister specifies the sum and issues a warrant to enable the Accountant of the High Court to receive it. The Accountant invests it in authorised securities, as directed by the depositor, and the income goes to the depositor. The Minister is given powers which seem to conflict with those normally vested in the Accountant by s 61(4) in controlling the investment, income, etc. of these deposits. This subsection enables the Minister to control the withdrawal and transfer of such deposits. The more detailed provisions as to deposits are contained in The Road Traffic Act (Deposits by Vehicle Guarantors and Exempt Persons) Order 1933 (SI 178/1933) which is still in force. It was made under s 61 of the 1933 Road Traffic Act, which required a deposit of £15,000 in the High Court. Regulation 4 of the Order enables the warrant to be issued to enable the deposit be lodged. The deposit may be in cash or authorised securities. This Order obviously needs replacing. No deposit existed in the case of CIE. The figure of £15,000 is hopelessly out of date.

(c) The body must give to the Motor Insurers' Bureau of Ireland under s 78 of the 1961 Act an approved (by the Minister for the Environment) undertaking to deal with third party claims in respect of its vehicles on terms similar to those agreed between the Minister and the Bureau in respect of the Bureau (see para 6.8).

6.6.3 Certificates of exemption and their production

An exempted person may issue certificates of exemption in the prescribed form, certifying that he owns the vehicle and giving particulars of his liability for the negligent use of the vehicle (s 68 of the 1961 Act). This certificate is required as a policy equivalent to an insurance policy under the Insurance Act 1936.

The form of the certificate; the need to keep it in the vehicle; keeping cancelled certificates; keeping records; and similar provisions as apply to insurance certificates are contained in the Road Traffic (Compulsory Insurance) Regulations 1962 (SI 14/1962), especially R 2. The regulations are penal and the general penalty (para 7.1) applies.

Similar provisions to those outlined above (para 6.2.5) in relation to certificates of insurance apply to the production of certificates issued by exempt persons.

6.6.4 Application of deposit

(a) If a person recovers judgment in any Court against an exempt person who has furnished a deposit under s 61 of the 1968 Act above, the High Court, under s 77 of the 1961 Act, can order its payment (i.e. judgment sum and costs of order) from the deposit (para 6.6.2 (b)) if satisfied that the depositor has no goods which can be taken in execution to satisfy the judgment. The Accountant of the High Court pays out the money accordingly. Until the depleted deposit is made good to the full required amount the depositor is not an exempt person. The liability in respect of which the deposit will be so paid out is only that which would require compulsory insurance as outlined in this chapter.

(b) If the depositor is wound up or becomes bankrupt, insolvent or dies (if an individual, as was previously possible, although there does not appear to have been any such person), the deposit is applied:

(i) in payment of liabilities in respect of which compulsory insurance is required under Part VI of the 1961 Act;
(ii) as general assets of such person or body.

Similar application occurs if the exempt person, being a corporate body, partnership or an incorporated association, is dissolved.

6.6.4 *Exempted persons and vehicles*

These provisions are contained in s 77 of the 1961 Act, as amended by s 6 and sch, 1968 Act (brought into operation by SI 6/1971).

6.7 Excepted persons

6.7.1 No need to insure

Reference has been made above (para 6.3.1) to the fact that it is unnecessary to insure certain persons who are referred to as 'excepted persons'. Section 65 of the 1961 Act, as amended by Sch, 1968 Act, is the basic provision as to who these people are. The position is also governed by some of the provisions of the Road Traffic (Compulsory Insurance) Regulations 1962 (SI 14/1962).

Basically, it is unnecessary to cover 'excepted persons' who are as follows:

(a) Certain persons making personal injury claims (as set out at para 6.7.2); and
(b) certain property damage claims (see para 6.7.3).

6.7.2 Personal injury claims

The Acts themselves allow as an 'excepted person' in relation to a personal injury claim:

(a) Any person claiming for personal injury to himself while in or on (or entering, or getting on, being put on or into, alighting from or being taken off or being thrown out of or off) a mechanically propelled vehicle or vehicle drawn by it to which the relevant document relates (i.e. an insurance policy using the expression 'exempted persons'), *other than* such a vehicle, drawn vehicle, or combination of vehicles of a class specified in Ministerial regulations;
(b) a person claiming for injury to another person who was, if dead, an excepted person under (a) unless the injury caused his death, or if the person who was himself claiming (i.e. other injured person) was an excepted person.

The series of negatives used creates difficulty, but basically everyone has to be insured for personal injury, as set out in Ministerial regulations, unless they are excepted persons, i.e. those persons travelling in vehicles not specified by the Minister's regulations to require compulsory cover.

The personal injury claim at present under the Acts and regulations which can therefore be legally excluded from cover are those by:

(i) Certain passengers who are not covered. Passenger insurance cover need not be effected in reality, except in relation to those types of vehicles for which it is specified in Ministerial regulations as being obligatory. The current regulation is R 6 of SI 14/1962, i.e. The Road Traffic (Compulsory Insurance) Regulations. Under this regulation compulsory passenger cover must be effected for three classes of vehicle:

(a) Public service vehicles (see para 1.12),

(b) vehicles constructed primarily for the carriage of one or more passengers, e.g. the ordinary motor car basically (therefore, pedestrian controlled vehicle operators are not covered—see para 6.3.6 on this principle),

(c) station wagons, estate cars and other similarly constructed or adaptable vehicles with actual or potential passenger seating accommodation. There is a special definition of 'passenger' in the regulations with a view to excluding the driver or a person being conveyed by a cycle, whether in a side car or otherwise.

Therefore, injury to persons, other than those in or on the vehicle or a trailer drawn by it set out above, can be excluded, e.g. lorry passengers, motor cycle passengers. There has been much discussion about making compulsory insurance on motor cycle passengers, and it will probably be made so;

(ii) the driver, in view of the fact that the definition of 'passenger' excludes the driver under the 1962 Regulations;

(iii) persons claiming through injury to persons who are exempted persons, e.g. the personal representatives of excepted persons as above.

6.7.3 Property damage claims

The following need not by law be covered by compulsory insurance under s 65 of the 1961 Act (as amended by Sch, 1968 Act);

(i) injury to property in or on the vehicle, or a trailer drawn by it, to which the insurance policy relates, in that it shows it to be 'excepted'. 'In or on' includes entering, getting into, being put into or on, alighting from or being taken out of or off, and being thrown out of or off the vehicle;

(ii) injury to property owned by or in the possession, control or custody of the insured or principal debtor in the relevant document, i.e. a policy which states they are excepted.

It should be remembered that, in any event, at present the limit of compulsory insurance is £1,000 under s 56 of the 1961 Act for property damage in respect of any one act of negligence or a series of acts constituting one event. However, in practice that limit is not availed of in policies issued in Ireland, except in relation to commercial vehicles on which a £10,000 limit is placed. If insurance is intended to protect victims, this was obviously an inadequate bottom line for cover in law. In 1987, to meet EEC requirements, by SI 322/1987 the figure was raised to £40,000 for the period from 31 December 1987 to 31 December 1990, and thereafter to £80,000 property damage.

6.8 Motor Insurers' Bureau of Ireland

6.8.1 Membership

As can be seen above under s 78 of the 1961 Act (as amended by s 53 of the 1968 Act) a Vehicle Insurer (para 6.5) must be a Member of the Motor Insurers' Bureau of Ireland (MIBI) or have given an approved form of undertaking to deal with claims from vehicles insured by him on certain terms. A similar provision is contained in the Act for 'exempted persons' (para 6.6) and in relation to administrators of insurance companies continuing under Administration (para 6.5.3) under their statutory provisions.

The MIBI is a body set up to deal with the terms of an Agreement made between that body (MIBI) acting on behalf of the insurance companies operating in the State, and the Minister for The Environment. The Agreement sets out a scheme of compensation in respect of injuries to persons by uninsured or ineffectively insured motorists. It is of considerable importance.

The Address of the MIBI is 3/4 South Frederick Street, Dublin, 2.

6.8.2 History

The first such Agreement was made in 1955 and was amended in 1962. The Bureau was set up as an incorporated company limited by guarantee and not having a share capital, under the Companies Acts 1908–24 on the 26 October 1955 (Company no. 156/61). Interestingly, the Memorandum contains the names of 43 Insurance Companies and 185 syndicates at Lloyd's, and admitted them as members and records a duty on each member to subscribe £2. annually. There are now 26 licenced insurers. These Agreements (1955/62) were replaced by an Agreement, which was dated the 30 December, 1964 and operated from the 1 January 1965. This has been replaced by a new Agreement in 1988 operating from 1 January 1989. The 1964 Agreement is ended from that date save in relation to accidents occurring before 31 December 1988. The 1988 Agreement gives effect to some of the provisions of EEC Directive 84-5-EEC. The scheme set out in the 1988 Agreement is designed to secure compensation in respect of personal injuries (and property damage) to third party victims of road accidents where, notwithstanding the requirement for compulsory insurance under the 1961–87 Road Traffic Acts, the victim of the accident is deprived of compensation by the absence of third party motor insurance or the absence of effective insurance. For the purpose of compensating such victims, the MIBI can be sued and undertakes to pay, in certain circumstances, the amount of the unsatisfied judgment against the motorist who was not insured or was not effectively insured, in so far as it relates to injuries to the person and property, with certain exceptions, coming within the compulsory insurance sections of the Road Traffic Acts. The text of the Agreement can be got from the Government Publications Sales Office, Sun Alliance House, Molesworth Street, Dublin, 2.

The Agreement in 1988, changes the basis of claims somewhat in relation to personal injuries giving entitlement in three types of cases where only *ex gratia* payments were made previously and allows claims for property damage in certain cases. These changes are noted in the following paragraphs, but the full text of the 1988 Agreement should be looked at for any problem in future.

6.8.3 Validity of Agreement

The Agreement can be terminated by the Minister at any time or by the MIBI on 2 years' notice. If such notice is given it will not prejudice the continued operation of the Agreement up to the date of termination.

The Agreement is an unusual legal document. It is a contract between the Minister for the Environment and the MIBI. It creates solely third party benefits, and this is outside the doctrine of privity of contract. In Great Britain a similar Agreement exists.

The courts have specifically admitted these agreements to confer rights (*Gurtner v Circuit* [1968] 1 All ER 328) in that they have turned a blind eye to the situation, and held indirectly they were entitled to assume there was valid consideration unless the Bureau raised the issue as such (see also *Albert v MIBI* [1971] 2 All ER 1345). In *Gardner v Moore & Ors* [1984] 1 All ER 1102 Lord Hailsham LC says, referring to the British Agreement, 'Their foundation in jurisdiction are better not questioned any more than were the demise of John Doe and the behaviour of Richard Roe in old ejectment proceedings'.

An example of an Irish Court getting around the difficulty of privity is found in *McEneaney v Minister for Education and Smythe* [1941] IR 430.

The Bureau has not pursued the point in Ireland prior to 1989, even though it has been raised. In *Hardy v M.I.B.* [1964] 2 QB 745 the redoubtable Lord Denning said he hoped the point would never be taken i.e. at no consideration.

In 1987 as part of the renegotiation of the Agreement the MIBI gave an undertaking to the Minister for the Environment that it would not in future raise the privity point.

6.8.4 Compensation

Compensation must be made to victims of road accidents in three cases under the 1988 Agreement i.e. in relation to:

(a) uninsured vehicles, (including stolen vehicles),
(b) ineffectively insured vehicles,
(c) unidentified or untraced motorists who cause personal injury or death or damage, but not property damage in cases under (c) however.

6.8.5 The main provisions of the 1968 Agreement (clause 4) states

'(1) Subject to the provisions of subclause (2) of this clause "if judgment in respect of any liability for injury to person or damage to property which is required to be covered by an approved policy of insurance under Section

56 of the Act is obtained against any person or persons in any court established under the Courts (Establishment and Constitution) Act, 1961 (No. 38 of 1961) whether or not such person or persons be in fact covered by an approved policy of insurance and any such judgment is not satisfied in full within 28 days from the date upon which the person or persons in whose favour such judgment is given become entitled to enforce it then MIBI will so far as such judgment relates to injury to person or damage to property and subject to the provisions of these presents pay or cause to be paid to the person or persons in whose favour such judgment was given any sum payable or remaining payable thereunder in respect of the aforesaid liability including taxed costs (or such proportion thereof as is attributable to the relevant liability) or satisfy or cause to be satisfied such judgment whatever may be the cause of the failure of the judgment debtor to satisfy the same.

(2) Where a person has received benefit or compensation from any source in respect of damage to property, MIBI may deduct from the sum payable or remaining payable under Sub-clause (1) of this Clause an amount equal to the amount of that benefit or compensation in addition to the deduction of any amounts by virtue of Sub-clauses (4) or (5) of Clause 7.

(3) Where a person applies to the MIBI for compensation and no judgment has been obtained or is obtainable, MIBI shall, as soon as is reasonably practicable, give a decision on the application and shall give reasons for the decision.

(4) Where MIBI and the claimant agree an amount in respect of compensation, MIBI shall pay such amount to the claimant within 28 days of such agreement being reached."'

Notes

(i) 'Injury to person,' however, does not include any injury by way of loss of services of the person injured (Clause 14). Death is included in injury to person.

(ii) Clause 7 referred to at Clause 4 (2) relates to property damage (see para 6.8.9 *infra*).

The 1964 agreement excluded payment for property damage. The 1988 Agreement allows for property damage claims by third parties up to substantial amounts but only in relation to the accidents on or after 31 December 1992.

It should be remembered that the Bureau only comes in when the Judgment is unsatisfied or when the judgment is not against itself or it is not settling the case. The plaintiff's normal rights against the tortfeasors were and to some extent in law still are the primary rights. The plaintiff is entitled to collect from the tortfeasor and to negotiate with him. In practice, there are usually negotiations with the Bureau. This had been done by the Bureau getting a mandate signed by the tortfeasor or owner and, sometimes, where possible, getting a contribution to payments. The 1988 Agreement gives the MIBI an automatic right to represent drivers of stolen or uninsured vehicles without mandates. This arrangement is to overcome the difficulties of securing mandates.

However, as is seen below, the MIBI can be both initially contacted and negotiated with and also sued directly on its own or jointly with the owner and/or user.

'Judgment' means the net amount recoverable after deduction of any sum allowed on a counterclaim or set off or benefit.

A person in breach of his duty to insure does not escape his personal liability because the MIBI does step in to pay (*Corfield v Groves* [1951] All ER 485). Felonious offences are covered by the Agreement (*Hardy v MIBI* [1964] 2 QB 745). However, the Bureau is only liable to meet claims requiring compulsory insurance under the Act, so in *Lees v MIBI* [1952] 2 All ER 511 an employee's claim excluded under compulsory insurance was not payable by the Bureau.

In the case of State vehicles or 'exempted persons' vehicles such claims are dealt with by State (see para 6.8.11) and the 'exempted person' (see para 6.6) respectively in a manner similar to the MIBI Agreement pursuant to arrangements and undertakings given by the Minister for Finance on behalf of the State and the exempt persons (see para 6.6) to the Minister for the Environment. It should be noted that the MIBI also accept liability under clause 11 in respect of a vehicle, owned by or in the possession of the State the use of which is required to be covered by an approved policy of insurance purporting to cover the said vehicle, and that, for the purpose of determining liability, a vehicle which has been unlawfully removed from the possession of the State or an exempt person shall be taken to continue in that possession while so removed. (Clause 11 of 1988 Agreement).

6.8.6 Conditions precedent

The conditions precedent necessary under Clause 3 of the 1988 Agreement before the MIBI will accept liability to deal with the matter are as follows:

(i) Notice of the proceedings must be given in writing by registered post to MIBI (and the insurers where a policy was in existence purporting to cover the vehicle and its existence is known to the plaintiff), before the commencement of the proceedings. This is normally done by a detailed solicitor's letter initially and then by sending a copy of Summons, Civil Bill or Process.

If there is a Policy of Insurance (ineffective) in existence, the claim is normally handled by the company issuing the policy on behalf of the MIBI as 'Insurers Concerned'. If no policy exists, the Bureau handles the claim, but it usually gets one of the MIBI member insurance companies to process the claim 'Handling Office'.

There is a duty placed on the claimant to try to establish if there is insurance that covers the incident (Clause 3(4)). This is done under s 73/1961 Act—see para 6.10 *infra* by demanding the information.

The Irish Visiting Motorists' Bureau Limited deals with claims against visiting vehicles' claim (see below).

(ii) The claimant must give the MIBI all reasonably required information about the claim i.e. of the time and place, vehicles, persons, the injuries, damage, personal expenses, professional fees, copies of correspondence, statements, pleadings, notification of claim etc.

(iii) If required by the MIBI the person bringing the proceedings shall take all reasonable steps against the defendant(s) i.e. tortfeasors. Any plaintiffs so doing will receive a full indemnity from the MIBI i.e. The Bureau must indemnify the person as to costs in this situation. If a dispute arises as to whether or not reasonable steps were taken, the Minister for the Environment decides on the reasonableness of the steps taken. This decision is final. This apparently has only arisen once in practice in Ireland, the MIBI settled the claim and a formal determination by the Minister was not necessary. The MIBI can request the assignment of such judgment or judgments to itself or its nominee. If it does, the request must be complied with.

(iv) The person bringing the action must give credit to the MIBI for all amounts paid to him by the defendant. This appears to cover payments made also in respect of property damage (Clause 3(9) of the Agreement).

(v) The 1988 Agreement has revised time limits for notification of claims to the MIBI, of three years in personal injury claims and one year in property damage claims.

6.8.7 Refusal to pay

There are three specific exclusions:

(1) The MIBI was entitled to refuse to pay or to accept liability under the terms of the 1988 Agreement, Clause 5 where, at the time of the accident, a vehicle was being used without the consent of the owner (See para 4.10) or other lawful authority or stolen, or obtained by violence, or threats of violence, and judgment is obtained against the owner or user of the vehicle in respect of injury or death or property damage resulting to a person who so obtained the vehicle or stole, was in or on such vehicle in collusion with such person or knew it was stolen or so obtained.

(2) Where the injured person suffering the loss, or the deceased victim at the time of the accident knew or ought reasonably have known that there was no insurance the MIBI need not pay a claim while such person was by his consent in or on such vehicle or consenting to its use e.g. number of persons taking a car on a 'joy ride' but only one driving.

Payments must, however, be made under the terms of the Agreement by the MIBI, in respect of any judgment in any case where the person injured or killed was not aware, or could not have reasonably known, that the vehicle was used without the consent of the owner of the vehicle (see para 6.8.13). The 1988 Agreement requires payment in the events above as of right in future, i.e. not on an *ex gratia* basis only as previously. Also see SI 321/1987, referred to at para 6.8.13 below.

(3) The Agreement clarifies the fact that there is an exclusion of liability on the MIBI where both vehicles are uninsured i.e. neither user can claim

for injury, death or damage even though all the fault may be on one user (Clause 5(3)). One must wonder about the fairness (constitutionality?) of this e.g. a motorist who in all innocence is driving an uninsured vehicle is seriously injured by another uninsured vehicle. Under the 1988 Agreement Clause 5(3) he gets nothing. Presumably this subclause will be challenged at some stage.

6.8.8 Procedure

You notify the MIBI of the claim. They can settle it. You give the required information. If no settlement is made then you can sue the MIBI on its own or jointly with the owner and/or user where it refuses compensation or makes an inadequate offer. Where an application is made and no judgment obtained the MIBI must give a decision as soon as practicable and must give the reasons for the decision. Where agreement is reached the amount must be paid within 28 days.

A system akin to lodgment in court exists to enable the Bureau to make an offer in satisfaction after notices duly given by the Bureau to the claimant up to and within 14 days of the closing of his pleadings in a case. If the offer is refused and the subsequent award is less than the offer, the Bureau has only to pay the award and costs to date of the offer, and the Bureau can set off against the award its cost from the date of the offer (Clause 10). This offer in satisfaction is usually made by open letter by the Solicitor acting for the Defendant and the Bureau.

The money of the offer does not have to actually be tendered or lodged in court. Clause 10 which deals with this says at the end 'MIBI reserves the right to vary the amount offered in satisfaction'.

The Government Publication referred to at para 6.8.2 above contains useful notes on procedure and practice.

6.8.9 Property claims

The 1964 Agreement did not allow for property claims.

The 1988 Agreement does but only from 31/12/1992 onwards and with the following deductions:

(a) In the case of an accident between 31/12/1992 and 31/12/1995 a sum of £1,150 will be deducted by the Bureau on payment of any property damage claim to the legal limit.

(b) After that date there will be payment of the sum to the legal limit with two exclusions or 'excesses':

(i) of the first £175 where the vehicle was negligently used having been stolen or obtained by violence or threats of violence or without consent of the owner or other lawful authority.

(ii) of the first £350 where damage due to negligent use.

In relation to (a) and (b) the legal limit under s 56(2)(a) applies (see para 6.7.3) i.e. £80,000 in reality under SI 322 of the 1987 Act. The limits and excesses apply to any one owner/claimant.

However, there is no liability on the MIBI to pay for property damage caused by a vehicle the owner or user of which remains unidentified or untraced.

6.8.10 Visitors

In respect of visiting motorists doing damage the Irish Visiting Motorists Bureau 3/4 South Frederick Street, Dublin 2, deals with claims in these types of case i.e. no insurance or ineffective insurance cases. These are handled on the principles and in the same circumstances as at para 6.8.6 above.

In relation to injury, death, property damage to visitors by Irish vehicles the MIBI would deal with the claim as above. It is being suggested at present that these two Bodies (MIBI and IVMB) be amalgamated.

6.8.11 State vehicles/Exempted person

The State will normally make payments where a vehicle owned by or in the possession of the State is used without insurance, such liability usually being outside the 1988 Agreement (as such vehicles are not covered by s 56 of the 1961 Act normally – see para 6.6.1).

These circumstances in which this will apply are:

(i) there is not an approved policy in force (where there is see para 6.8.5);
(ii) the claim is for personal injury or property damage in circumstances similar to those in which the MIBI makes a payment;
(iii) if the claim is made by a State employee, any other payments made to him by the State as a result of injury are set off;
(iv) the conditions as to notice, assignment of judgment and offers of satisfaction apply as in the case of the Bureau.

The payment is under and by virtue of an arrangement made between the Minister for Finance on behalf of the State and the Minister for the Environment and, as stated above, is generally on the same criteria as the MIBI payment, i.e. that Plaintiff did not know, or could not reasonably have known, of the absence of consent to use the vehicle, untraced or unidentified driver.

6.8.12 Recoveries

Vehicle insurers can provide, by condition in their policies or by collateral agreements, that all sums paid by them on behalf of the MIBI or by the MIBI in or towards the discharge of the liability of their policy-holder shall be recoverable by them for the MIBI from the policy-holder or from any other person. The 1988 Agreement Clause 9 specifically states that it does not prevent or effect those agreements.

6.8.13 Stolen vehicles—passengers

Where, prohibited conditions would otherwise apply so that the innocent victim of a road accident arising out of the negligent use in a public place of a vehicle stolen, obtained by violence, or without consent or lawful authority (as 'Joy Riding') would have failed in a claim, such person will now be compensated by the MIBI, under SI 321/1987 and 1988 Agreement as of right. That statutory instrument limits prohibited conditions in policies so as to prevent insurers from refusing or reducing a claim by a third party victim where the driver of an insured vehicle (e.g. family member or employee) did not have the consent of a named person, or the driver did not hold a valid driving licence or a public service vehicle licence—these cases will be the liability of the MIBI no longer, but will be the liability of the Insurers (para 6.4.2 above).

Thus a passenger in a stolen vehicle which he genuinely was unaware of its being stolen now has a right to compensation for injury etc., from the MIBI or insurer as the case may be.

6.8.14 New 1988 agreement

This new 1988 Agreement will probably impose an extra burden on the MIBI. This body paid out £14 million in 1987, and had outstanding estimated liabilities of £51 million. The growth of uninsured payments can be seen by contrasting those 1987 figures with £1.8 million paid five years previously in 1981.

It was estimated that about 76,000 vehicles or between 6/8 per cent of all vehicles were uninsured at the beginning of 1987 (see Dail debates, 24 February 1988). Later in 1988 the Minister for the Environment claimed that this number was substantially reduced due to the successful operation of the display of Discs system (see para 6.4.11) from about 15 per cent of drivers to 8 per cent in December, 1988. Certainly from 1992 the property damage claims will impact on insurance premium levels.

6.8.15 1964 Agreement

This Agreement continues in force in relation to accidents prior to the 31 December 1988 only. It is on similar, but more restricted lines, than the 1988 Agreement. It did not give a right to apply to or sue the MIBI directly. It did not give a right to compensation to victims of (a) unidentified or untraced motorists (b) certain passengers in stolen or unauthorised vehicles. The 1988 Agreement does. The 1964 Agreement should be studied (with notes attached) in relation to cases prior to 1989.

6.9 Non-residents

6.9.1 Minister's control

The insurance problems of visitors are dealt with by regulation mostly. This is to enable quick changes in international rules to be brought into effect here. This is an obvious benefit to a tourist country such as Ireland.

Section 80 of the 1961 Act provides that the Minister for the Environment may make regulations to facilitate the application of the insurance provisions of the Act to non-residents. It also enables the Minister to modify Part VI of the Act in relation to non-residents, but this modification must not be such as to substantially exempt any persons from this obligation under Part VI. This 'Henry VIIIth' clause is a curious provision and, some day, presumably, with the growing volume of tourist traffic, will provide an interesting law case. However, the Minister's position is strengthened, in relation to EEC members at least, by Directive 72/166/EEC, as amended by 72/430 EEC and 84/51 EEC, which requires the approximation of the laws of Member States relating to insurance against civil liability in respect of the use of motor vehicles and to the enforcement of the laws.

6.9.2 EEC position

The approximation of laws required by the EEC Treaty of Rome as to road transport has, *inter alia*, resulted in the approximation of road traffic insurance laws. This was done by amending s 56 of the 1961 Act through the media of regulations in 1975 and 1987, and by extending those provisions to designated territories (see para 6.3.2 above). There is considerable progress in having a uniform code of motor insurance in the EEC and designated territories.

6.9.3 The international regulations

The regulations made by the Minister under the Local Government Act 1955 to date are parts of the Mechanically Propelled Vehicles (International Circulation) Orders 1961 (SI 269/1961); 1962 (SI 12/1962); 1963 (SI 193/1963); 1964 (SI 59/1964); 1966 (SI 99/1966); 1976 (SI 71/1976); 1980 (SI 346/1980); and 1983 (SI 215/1983). These orders deal with other aspects of international circulation, such as motor taxation, driving licences, construction, use and equipment, and insurance, etc.

Under Art 13 of the 1961 Order, as amended by Art 5 of the 1962 Order, what is known internationally as the 'Green Card System' is operated in Ireland. It is provided that an International Motor Insurance Card (Green Card) is deemed to be a certificate of insurance with Part VI of the 1961 Act issued to the insured named thereon in respect of the vehicle referred to in the card. The Irish Visiting Motorists Bureau (IVMB) of Dublin is deemed to be the vehicle insurer. The contents of the Green Card are specified in the second Schedule of the 1962 Order. On the Green Card EIR or IRL can be used to indicate the name of the State.

The system is operated by the IVMB and corresponding bodies in the EEC and elsewhere. The Green Card is issued by the insurance Company and covers driving on visits to other countries in the scheme.

An injury caused by a motorist without a Green Card is now automatically covered against third party claims while driving in EEC countries and designated territories as mentioned above and also in para 6.3.2.

6.10 Information as to insurance

Where a notice is served by registered post by or on behalf of a claimant against a person whose liability should be compulsory insured under the 1961-87 Acts, this latter person is bound by s 73 of the 1961 Act to state, as appropriate:

(a) whether the liability is so covered, and to furnish the name and address of the insurers and particulars of the policy (see R 7 of the Road Traffic Act (Compulsory Insurance) Regulations 1962 as to particulars at para 6.4.4); or

(b) the name and address of insurers concerned who have avoided, cancelled or terminated the policy which would have covered the liability; or

(c) that he is a vehicle insurer or exempt person himself and, if so, the particulars required by s 68 of the 1968 Act ('exempted person' is discussed at para 6.6 above); or

(d) if none of the foregoing apply, state that fact.

The particulars can be sent by prepaid post, and failure to furnish them is an offence for which the general penalty is prescribed under s 102 (para 7.1). The section regrettably places no time limit on the giving of these particulars.

Normally in accident cases, if the Gardai are called they will have demanded production of the insurance or exemption certificate (see para 6.4.6) and checked and recorded the particulars. These particulars can be obtained from the Gardai on request by an injured party or his solicitor. They will also appear on the Garda abstract of the accident, to be obtained from the Garda Superintendent's office of the area where the accident occurred. This abstract (and copy statements) will not normally be released until after any prosecutions arising from the accident have been disposed of, or it has been decided not to prosecute. However, particulars of insurance will usually be given earlier on request.

Again, if there is an accident the insurance disc on the vehicle will give the name of the insurance company and the policy number (see para 6.4.1).

6.11 Refusal to cover

6.11.1 The Declined Cases Committee

Since the law requires that a mechanically propelled vehicle must be covered by insurance, an arrangement exists whereby cases of refusal (or cases equivalent to refusal) of the minimum cover required by the Road Traffic Acts will be investigated. In such cases the Minister for the Environment refers a complaint of refusal to a committee of representatives of motor insurers, working under an agreement with the Minister. This committee examines the case and arranges cover if possible. It is known as 'The Declined Cases Committee'.

Except where it is clear that it would be entirely unreasonable to afford cover through a particular company, as an outrage to the public interest, e.g. repeated drunken driving convictions, cover will be arranged. This is a non-statutory arrangement, but it is understood that the Committee in fact has never refused to investigate a case. Complaints of refusal, unreasonable terms, etc. should be referred to the Minister for the Environment, Road Traffic Section, O'Connell Bridge House, Dublin 1.

6.11.2 Report: future

There is a fairly comprehensive report, called the '*Motor Insurance Report of Enquiry into the methods of providing motor insurance* 1982'—available from the Stationery Office (Government Publications Office) Molesworth St, Dublin 2—, which gives a good idea of the changing needs of the insurance market. The publication number is PL 1323. It comments on the Declined Cases Committee, uninsured driving, the MIBI, and other factors that have effected the cost. It was prepared by the Prices Advisory Committee.

Further enquiries have been held and will continue to be held. The impact of EEC legislation will also affect Irish legal requirements as to insurance in the future.

Chapter 7

Control of user: Enforcement

'The Police are like jam in a sandwich.'

Peter Wright

7.1 Penalties

7.1.1 General penalty

Many sections throughout the Acts and regulations create offences and do not specifically say what penalty the Courts may impose as a result of a finding the offence has been committed. This position is, in fact, covered by the imposition and creation of a general penalty by s 102 of the 1961 Act (as amended and substantially increased under s 2 of the 1984 Act).

Section 102, as amended, provides that where a person is convicted of an offence under the Acts and no particular penalty is provided for in the section, then, on summary conviction, the following are the maximum penalties:

(a) on a first offence under the section or subsection, £150;
(b) on a second offence under the section or subsection, £350;
(c) on the third or subsequent offence under the section or subsection—
 (i) within any period of 12 months, £350 and/or three months' imprisonment,
 (ii) otherwise (i.e. not within 12 months), £350.

This section does not, of course, include reference to the disqualification and endorsement provisions of the Act—such matters are additional to the above penalty, i.e. usually discretionary but sometimes mandatory. See para 2.9 on disqualification and para 2.10 on endorsements. See para 7.1.2 below also as to penalties generally.

As to 'second' or 'subsequent' offences, in *A-G (McConville) v Brannigan* [1962] IR 370 it was held that this means second or subsequent *similar* offence or offences.

7.1.2 Penalties generally

(1) *Fines*

(a) The special maximum fines have been stated, where possible, throughout the text. Many fines are considerable, and the 1984 Act brought in £1,000 as the maximum fine in a number of offences. The fine can be imposed in addition to imprisonment in most cases, even for a first offence. This is not so in the case of the general penalty (above). In the appropriate place in the text, reference has been made to the fines imposed in actual cases as a very rough guide. Each case is different, especially those dealing with serious offences, as is the treatment by the Court of each defendant. The Court always hears evidence and/or submission on these matters. There are no suggested fines in Ireland like those of the Magistrates Association in England.

(b) Fixed penalties are discussed at para 5.11 above. The range of offences that they cover, and the amount of the penalty, has substantially increased over the years.

(c) Disposal of fines is considered at para 7.7.2 below.

(2) *Imprisonment*

This is the most severe penalty, and is stated in the Acts as the first penalty only in one case, i.e. intoxicated driving. In reality, it is rarely used in Irish Courts, except where the offence includes a high degree of bad behaviour, e.g. joy riding (see para 4.10), or the serious consequences of death or serious injury from bad driving (see paras 4.2.7 and 4.2.9 where some cases are cited), or where the accused has a bad driving history of a serious nature, e.g. continuous driving while disqualified.

The sentence can be suspended (e.g. *R V Barnes* (1986) Crim LR 573) and often is in addition to the imposition of a fine (*R v Leigh* (1969) 113 Sol Jo 897).

Penal servitude is not mentioned in the Road Traffic Acts, except in relation to dangerous driving causing death or serious bodily harm under s 53 2(b) of the 1961 Act. Under the Criminal Justice Act 1960, a male juvenile defendant aged between 16 and 19 years may be sent to St Patrick's Institution if he is fit to be so sent in lieu of imprisonment or penal servitude.

(3) *Disqualification*

The Courts have held that this is not a penalty as such. This matter is dealt with fully at para 2.9.

(4) *Endorsement*

This is discussed fully at para 2.10.

(5) *Probation Act 1907*

This statute can be applied in most cases. However, it is excluded in relation to the main intoxicant offences (see para 4.9).

(6) *Compensation*

The Acts now unfortunately have no provision for payment directly of compensation. The provision made for this in 'no insurance' cases (s 57 of the 1961 Act) was declared unconstitutional (see para 6.3). Compensation must be sought by separate civil remedy.

The Act does, in its insurance provisions (see Chapter 6, enable compensation to be collected on a judgment directly from the vehicle insurer and, under an agreement, in certain cases from the Motor Insurers' Bureau of Ireland (para 6.8).

(7) *Community Service Orders*

The Criminal Justice (Community Service) Act 1983 enables a Court to make a community service order in respect of any offender over 16 years of age who has been convicted of an offence which would merit penal servitude or detention in St Patrick's Institution, Dublin. The order will require between 40 and 240 hours unpaid community work to be done by the offender.

Before making the order, the court:

(a) must get the consent of the offender;
(b) must consider the offender's circumstances and have a report on him to say he is fit for the work;
(c) ensure that a probation officer is available to supervise the work; and
(d) must explain to the offender that if he fails to perform the work he will be guilty of a further offence (s 7 of the 1983 Act).

In *R v Bushell* (1988) Crim LR 259 a youth (17) was sentenced to 180 hours of Community Service. He had pleaded guilty to taking a conveyance and crashing it. This sentence was upheld on appeal and it was stated that it would only be in exceptional cases that the Appeal Court would interfere with the length of a Community Service Order.

(8) *Forfeiture*

There is no provision for the forfeiture of vehicles used for criminal purposes as under s 43 of the English Act. Some Irish Acts do contain this type of provision, e.g. Fishery Acts, but questions of constitutionality may arise if there is a double penalty. Also, it may render a charge not a minor charge fit to be tried summarily. See para 5.12 as to the removal and, in certain circumstances, sale of vehicles.

(9) *Costs*

The power to grant costs is limited and infrequently used in criminal cases. The Supreme Court and the Circuit Courts have inherent jurisdiction to grant costs to an acquitted person (see *The People v Bell* [1969] IR 24). However, Legal Aid, which is granted in serious cases to certain people, may have covered the problem, i.e. under the Legal Aid Act 1962. See also the decision in *Dillane v Ir. & A-G* (1980) ILRM 167, holding valid under the constitution a District Court rule not allowing costs against a Garda. The decision is far from the layman's notion of equality before the law.

(10) *Penalty points*

There is no system of penalty points and totting up in Ireland as there is in England. However, in many sections, and in the general penalty above, higher penalties apply to second and subsequent offences.

(11) *Remission*

There is a general power to remit penalties vested by his constitutional office (Article 13.6.9 of the 1937 Constitution) in the President acting on the advice of the Government. By s 23 of the Criminal Justice Act 1951 this power is exercised by the Minister for Justice. The procedure is by written petition to the Minister. By s 124 of 1961 Road Traffic Act, however, disqualification orders cannot be remitted under the 1951 Act.

7.1.3 Increased penalties

Each amending Act normally brings increased penalties, especially to the more serious offences. The 1984 Act increased penalties substantially. These increases took effect only for offences committed after the Act commenced, i.e. 18 July 1984 for the 1984 Act.

While the Constitution of 1937, Art 15.5 prevents retroactive criminal legislation, it may not preclude retrospective increases in criminal sanctions. Other Articles on personal rights might come into play, however, and the European Convention on Human Rights, to which Ireland is party does prohibit such action (see Art 7 of the Convention and *R v Deery* (1977) NICCA 164).

7.2 Powers and rights of Garda

7.2.1 General powers

Throughout this book the various powers of a Garda as to arrest, requiring information, directing traffic, etc. are set out. However, there are some general powers given to the Gardai in Part IX of the 1961 Act which require specific mention. These are:

(a) right to demand information (ss 107 and 108 of the 1961 Act);
(b) right to stop a vehicle (s 109 of the 1961 Act, as amended);
(c) right to dispose of vehicles temporarily (s 110 of the 1961 Act); and
(d) also it is appropriate to deal briefly with the powers of arrest without warrant, identification of Garda and related matters.

7.2.2 Right to demand information

Section 107 of the 1961 Act deals with the power to require certain information in connection with the use of a mechanically propelled vehicle, and s 108 with pedal cyclists.

As to 'use', 'vehicle', 'mechanically propelled vehicle' and 'public place', see para 7.9.

7.2.2.1 *Information on use of a mechanically propelled vehicle.* Section 107 of the 1961 Act gives the following powers to any member of the Garda Siochana:

(**a**) Information as to name of users. A Garda has the right to demand the name and address of a person using a vehicle where the Garda alleges to that person that he suspects that such person has committed a specified offence under the Acts. If the person refuses or fails to give his name and address, or gives a false or misleading one, he is guilty of an offence under the section. It is not necessary for owner to be satisfied that the suspected offence was committed (*Poulton v Leader* [1949] 2 All ER 747).

(**b**) Information as to identity of user. Where the Garda has reasonable grounds for believing that there has been an offence under the Road Traffic Acts involving the use of a mechanically propelled vehicle, he can require information from:

(i) the owner, and
(ii) other persons.

As to (i) above, the owner must state, on request from the Garda, whether or not he was actually using the vehicle at the material time. If the owner does not give the information he is guilty of an offence under the section.

If the owner states he was not so using the vehicle at the material time, he must give all required information to the Garda as to the identity of the person who was actually using it at that time. Again, if that information is not forthcoming, he will be guilty of an offence, unless he shows he did not know, or could not with reasonable diligence have ascertained, who was using the car at the material time.

The section (s 107 of the 1961 Act) was discussed, at length in *People (A-G) v Gilbert* [1973] IR 383; 107 ILTR 89, where the accused had been convicted in the Circuit Court on indictment for receiving a motor car under the Larceny Act 1916, s 33(1). He had been asked by a Garda under s 107 of the 1961 Act to state who was using the car at the particular time, the Garda having first told him the penalty under the section. The answer was that it had been the accused himself. The accused appealed his conviction and the Court of Criminal Appeal set it aside, holding:

(1) that the statement made under s 107 was not a voluntary statement and that evidence of the statement should not have been admitted in evidence at the Trial;
(2) the other evidence was not sufficient to support the conviction.

As to what is 'reasonable diligence', see *Record Tower Crane Ltd v Gisley* [1969] 1 WLR 148, where it was held that enquiry by the owner from less that 50% of the owner's drivers was not sufficient.

Neil v Fior [1968] 1 WLR 1875 dealt with the onus of proof and held:

(1) The Court must first decide if the defendant's vehicle was involved in an offence;
(2) then it was for the defendant to show that he did not know, or could not have ascertained with reasonable diligence, who the driver was.

The obligation on the owner is a personal obligation and usually cannot be discharged by another person (e.g. his solicitor) on his behalf (*Hodgson v Burn* (1966) LR 1361; 110 Sol Jo 151). In *R v Hanbey* (1905) JP 219 it was held that it was not necessary that the driver had refused his name and address before the owner was required to give information.

As to (ii) above other persons, *any person*, other than the owner, must give to the requesting Garda any information which it is in his power to give leading to the identification of the user of the vehicle at the material time. If he does not he is guilty of an offence.

In *Bingham v Bruce* [1962] 1 All ER 136 it was held that any other person includes the driver. In *Hunter v Mann* [1974] 1 WLR 742 a doctor was held guilty and was not entitled to claim professional confidence. In *Hawkes v Hinckley* (1956) 120 JP Jo 642 it was held that the obligation to give information continues after the person himself is charged with dangerous driving. The information must be supplied within a reasonable time, which normally will mean immediately (*Lowe v Lester* (1986) Crim LR 339).

The Supreme Court limited the power to enter dwellings for information and arrest under the Constitution in *DPP v Gaffney* (1988) ILRM 39 see (c) below and para 7.2.5 below.

(**c**) Arrest under s 107(2). A Garda can arrest without warrant the person he reasonably believes has used a vehicle without a registration mark under the Roads Act 1920 in the commission of an offence under the Act, or which the Garda has reasonable grounds for believing was committed.

A Garda can also arrest without warrant a person who refuses or fails to give his name and address, or who gives a name and address which the Garda has reasonable grounds for believing is false or misleading, when required under (a) above. In *DPP v Gaffney* (1988) ILRM 30, however, it was held to be unlawful to arrest a person in his own house where the defendant has sought refuge and the defendant's brother had refused the Gardai entry. The Gardai claimed the right to enter under s 107 of the

1961 Act for information and arrested the defendant. See para 7.2.4 as to disposition of a vehicle in those circumstances. See para 7.2.5 as to arrest without warrants generally under the Acts.

As to the consequences of arrest, see general criminal law books and the Criminal Justice Act 1984. There is a commentary on that Act in 'Irish Current Law Statutes Annotated', a most useful series.

(d) Offence and penalty. A person guilty of an offence under (a) or (b) above is liable to a fine of up to £350 and/or up to three months' imprisonment. This is under s 107 of the 1961 Act, as amended by s 3 of the 1984 Act.

Disqualification and endorsement are optional (see paras 2.9 and 2.10).

7.2.2.2 *Information from pedal cyclists.* When a Garda suspects a person in charge of a pedal cycle has:

(a) committed any crime or offence; or
(b) was concerned or involved in a collision or other event in a public place causing injury to person or property;

The Garda can under s 108 of the 1961 Act demand the person's name and address. If the person refuses, or gives one the Garda reasonably believes to be false or misleading, the Garda can take the cycle (by force if necessary) and retain it until he is satisfied as to the identity of the person.

The section has a curious *non sequitur* air about it—the Garda does not arrest the person but seeks to establish his identity through a largely unidentifiable cycle.

The section also rather curiously provides for no offence or no penalty in itself. Presumably, in certain circumstances a general type of offence, such as obstructing a Garda in the due execution of his duty, may be invoked. The similar English section (s 164 of the Road Traffic Act 1972) has a power of arrest and penalties.

As to 'in charge', 'pedal cycle' and 'public place', see para 7.9.

7.2.3 Stopping vehicles

7.2.3.1 *Power.* There is inherent in many sections of the Acts the need for Gardai to have power to stop vehicles and persons to carry out their duties and rights under the Acts. Section 109(1) of the 1961 Act, as amended by Sch, 1968 Act, gives a general power to stop vehicles and requires the driver to keep the vehicle stationary for a reasonable period as follows:

> 'A person driving a vehicle in a public place shall stop the vehicle on being so required by a member of the Garda Siochana and shall keep it stationary for such period as is reasonably necessary to enable the member to discharge his duties.'

As to 'person', 'driving', 'public place' and 'vehicles', see para 7.9.

There is no specific signal prescribed in the section as to the requirement to stop, but obviously guidance can be obtained from the General Bye-laws 1964 (see BL 24 as to signals, e.g. from a pointsman; see para 5.3.3). Such signals, at night particularly, often lead to a good deal of contention in Court. The Gardai normally use torches, and may be wearing special scotchlight belts or other equipment.

In the unusual case of *R v Waterfield* ([1964] 1 QB 164 the defendant drove his car at a policeman, when the policeman was trying to prevent its removal but without authority so to prevent. The Court held that the similar English section created a power as opposed to a duty. In the case in question the officer was seeking to do something he had no power to do. The charge of assaulting the officer in the due execution of his duty was dismissed. In *Beard v Wood* (1980) Crim LR 384 it was held that, while a policeman must not act capriciously, there is no need for him to be acting under any of his Common Law powers when acting under a similar English section. Nevertheless, both these cases were questioned in *Steel v Goacher* (1983) RTR 98, where it was held that, having stopped a driver, there was nothing in the English s 159 to require him to detain his vehicle. This view was upheld in *Lodwick v Saunders* [1985] 1 All ER 577, but in *Sanders v DPP* 1988 Crim LR 605 held a police officer was acting within the execution of his duty in stopping a vehicle under s 159/1972 (Eng) Act (s 106/1961 Act SR.) on reasonable suspicion that it might then have been stolen. The driver who struggled with him was convicted. The commentary on the case is useful. The Irish section says there is a duty to keep the vehicle stationary for sufficiently long for the Garda to discharge his duties.

The position as to the visibility of signals arose in the Scottish case of *Keane v McSkimming* (1883) SCCR 220. It was held that if the prosecution show the signal ought to have been obvious, they do not have to prove the defendant driver saw it. It is clear, however, that, as the wording of the section creates a positive duty, a Court would have to be satisfied beyond reasonable doubt that the driver saw the signal. See *R v Ellis* [1947] 1 WWR 717 a Canadian case to that effect, *R v Barber* (1963) 3 SALR 700 (a South African case) and *Harding v Price* [1948] 1 All ER 283, an English case on 'stopping and knowledge'.

See also para 4.13 above as to stopping after an accident.

7.2.3.2 *Remaining stationary*. The 1968 Act in its Schedule amended the original s 109 of the 1961 Act to require the driver who has stopped his vehicle to keep his vehicle stationary for such period as is reasonably necessary to enable the Garda to discharge his duties. This clarification obviates the necessity of a Court implying such a power, as it did in the English case of *Lodwick v Sanders* and *Sanders v DPP* above. There, the driver of a defective articulated truck, having given his name and address, sought to move off after 30 seconds. The policeman grabbed the keys and was assaulted by the driver. It was held that the constable had a right to delay the vehicle for a reasonable time to effect an arrest, and that the driver would be convicted of assaulting a policeman in the due execution of his duty. See also para 4.13.4 above as to remaining stationary after an accident.

7.2.3.3 *Offence.* A person who does not stop or remain stationary is guilty of an offence to which the general penalty applies (para 7.1). There is, of course, discretionary power to impose disqualification and endorsement (see paras 2.9 and 2.10).

7.2.4 Disposition of vehicles

(1) *Power*
It is provided by s 110 of the 1961 Act that where a Garda arrests without warrant (see para 7.2.5) a person in charge of a mechanically propelled vehicle, the Garda may, if the circumstances so require, take or cause to be taken such steps as he may consider proper for the temporary disposition of the vehicle.

(2) *Exemptions*
Section 4 of the 1961 Act provides that the need for compulsory insurance under Part VI of the Act does not apply to a Garda using a vehicle for the purposes of a test, or for the removal or disposition of the vehicle under the Act or regulations thereunder (see para 6.6.1).

Section 38 of the 1961 Act requiring a driving licence does not apply to a Garda driving in the course of his duty (s 38(6)) see Chapter 2.

7.2.5 Arrest without warrant

Any member of the Garda Siochana has power under the following sections to arrest without warrant under the Acts:

1961 Act, ss 19, 40, 49, 50, 51, 53, 55, 69, 82 (inserted by 1968 Act), 107 (see para 7.2.2.1), 112, 113; 1968 Act ss 16, 56, 59; 1978 Act ss 12, 15 and 17.

It will be seen that there are relatively liberal powers of arrest without warrant under the Acts. The Courts in Ireland, however, have taken a strict approach to these powers. In *DPP v Gaffney* (1988) ILRM 39 the Gardai chased the defendant to his home after alleged acts of dangerous driving. The defendant entered his house, having refused a Garda request to stop. The Gardai were refused entry by the defendant's brother, who was arrested. The Gardai entered the house looking for information under s 107 of the 1961 Act. It was held in the High Court that they were entitled to do so. The Supreme Court, however, held that the arrest was unlawful, that there was no implied invitation or permission, and that nowhere in s 107 is there authority to enter a private dwelling without the permission of the owner or occupant. It also held that there was a violation of Art 40.5 of the 1937 Constitution. The entry was illegal and so was the arrest.

The Irish provisions on arrest are more frequent and extensive than those in the English Acts. So far they have not really been seriously contested. The Constitution provides that no-one shall be deprived of his personal liberty 'save in accordance with law' (Article). With regard to this phrase—'save in accordance with law'—the 'due process' cases in the USA are not in vogue here fully, but there has been an increased awareness of limitations on the legislature by the Constitution since 1961.

The Criminal Procedure Act 1967 deals with what happens to a person so arrested, e.g. charged before a District Justice or Peace Commissioner, etc., although the powers of a Peace Commissioner are now suspect since *State (Lynch) v Ballagh* [1986] IR 203 and *State (Clarke) v Roche* [1987] ILRM 309 (see para 4.13.9(2)).

Reading

On these subjects generally, see criminal law texts, e.g. Ryan & Magee, 'The Irish Criminal Process' (1983); Kelly, '*The Irish Constitution*'; and also The Criminal Justice Act 1984 (commentary in Irish Current Law Statutes Annotated) and, in relation to complaints against the Gardai, the Garda Siochana (Complaints) Act 1986 and the commentary thereon in the Irish Current Statutes Annotated series.

7.2.6 Identification of Garda

As seen above, the Gardai have been afforded wide powers under these Acts. To enable the motorist to be sure that the person stopping him or exercising the powers under the Acts is a Garda, s 111 of the 1961 Act was passed.

Section 111 requires that where, in the exercise of any power or the performance of any duty conferred or imposed by or under the Acts, a Garda makes in a public place a request, requirement or demand of, or gives an instruction to, any person, such person shall not be bound to comply with the request, requirement, demand or instruction unless the member of the Garda either:

(a) is in uniform; or
(b) produces, if requested by such person, an official identification card or such other evidence of his identity as may be prescribed.

As to 'public place' see para 7.9.

7.2.7 The Commissioner

Throughout the text the rights (e.g. to make Bye-laws) and duties of the Commissioner are set out. See also para 7.6.8 below and the Acts referred to which give him control of the Garda Force.

There is a specific saver of his general power and duty, and that of the Gardai, to preserve order in public places and to regulate and control traffic therein. This is in s 126 of the 1961 Act, and it is to the effect that this power and duty is in no way prejudiced or derogated from by the Road Traffic Acts.

7.2.8 Garda legislation

As to Garda appointments, uniforms, and regulation of the members, see

Garda Acts 1924 to 1979. Offences are created under these Acts for the misuse of uniforms, etc.

7.2.9 Traffic wardens

(1) *Power to employ*
To relieve the Gardai of many of the routine duties under the Road Traffic Acts, power is given to local authorities to employ traffic wardens. This power, and the general powers of the traffic wardens, is contained in the Local Authorities (Traffic Wardens) Act 1975. This Act has been slightly amended by s 12 of the Dublin Transport Authority (Dissolution) Act 1987.

Under the 1975 Act, a local authority, after consultation with the Commissioner of the Garda Siochana, may employ traffic wardens or enter into an agreement with another local authority to exercise its power so to do. County Councils, the Corporation of a County or Borough, Urban District Councils or Town Commissioners are local authorities for the purposes of the Act. The Minister for the Environment can make grants towards the expenses of a local authority.

(2) *Functions*
The functions of traffic wardens are those in relation to:

(a) the prohibition, restriction of stopping or parking of mechanically propelled vehicles under Road Traffic Act 1961, s 84 (see para 1.16);
(b) not displaying tax discs under the Roads Act 1920, s 73 and Finance Act 1976, 73, which state the need to have a licence disc (tax disc) displayed, and that the offence of non-display under the 1976 Act is to be covered by ss 2 and 3 of the 1975 Traffic Wardens Act, as amended by s 12, of the Dublin Transport Authority (Dissolution) Act 1987 and SI 187/1976 (para 1.11);
(c) fixed penalty procedures under s 103 in relation to ss 84, 86, 89 and 90 (see para 5.11.4 above);
(d) such other functions as may be prescribed by the Minister after consultation with the Minister for Justice, and different functions maybe so prescribed in relation to the functional areas of different local authorities.

(3) *Exercise of functions*
Where a traffic warden has reasonable grounds for believing that:

(i) a person is committing or has committed such an offence; or
(ii) a vehicle is being used to commit an offence in relation to those functions above;

He may deliver a notice on a prescribed form (see para 5.11) stating in that notice that:

(i) the person or vehicle is alleged to have committed the offence;
(ii) the appropriate fine specified can be paid to the local authority named within 21 days (the notice should be sent with the payment); and

(iii) no prosecution will be taken for the offence if so paid. The form of notice is prescribed in SI 261/1975.

The local authority issues a receipt for such payment. The fines may vary for different offences under the Act (1975). In the 1988 Act they range from £10 to £50, depending on the type of offence. If a prosecution does follow, the onus of proof of payment of the fine rests on the defendant. See para 5.11.4 above generally and as to the level of fines.

The only person who can remove the notice is the person the warden apprehends or the user of the vehicle. It seems that the Act is a bit vague on this latter point and on the point of who is to be prosecuted when no-one is apprehended at the time of having committed or committing an offence. Removal of the notice by a person other than the person to whom it applies is an offence with a fine of up to £150. (See s 12 of the Dublin Transport Authority (Dissolution) Act 1987.)

A traffic warden can demand a person's name and address when he believes him to have committed or to be committing an offence to which the Act applies. If the warden fails to produce official identity on request, the person requested to give the information need not do so. However, if that person is lawfully requested and fails to comply, or if he gives a false or misleading name or address, then an offence is committed, the fine for which is £150 maximum (see s 12(b)(ii) of the Dublin Transport Authority (Dissolution) Act 1987. A similar fine can be imposed on a person who obstructs a traffic warden in the course of his duty.

(4) *Prosecutions*
A local authority may prosecute in offences of unlawfully:

(i) removing a notice placed on a vehicle;
(ii) obstructing a traffic warden; or
(iii) refusing to give a, or giving a false or misleading, name or address to a traffic warden.

(5) *Regulations*
The Minister for the Environment has wide powers to make regulations under the 1975 Act. These must be laid before both houses of the Direachtas. They can be annulled by resolution of either House within 21 days.

The following regulations have been made—

Local Authorities (Traffic Wardens Act) 1975 (Section 3) (Offences) Regulations 1975 (SI 261/1975);

Local Authorities (Traffic Wardens) Act 1975 (Disposal of Monies) Regulations 1975 (SI 262/1975);

Local Authorities (Traffic Wardens) Act 1975 (Section 3) (Offences) (Amendments) Regulations 1976 (SI 187/1976);

Local Authorities (Traffic Wardens) Act 1975 (Section 3) (Offences) (Amendment) Regulations 1979 (SI 168/1979);

Local Authorities (Traffic Wardens) Act 1975 (Section 3) (Offences) (Amendment) Regulations 1985 (SI 256/1985)

Local Authorities (Traffic Wardens) Act 1975 (Section 3) (Offences) (Amendment) Regulations 1986 (SI 444/1986).

(6) *Disposal of fines*
Under SI 262/1975 above, moneys that accrue to a local authority under the Act go to the County or Municipal fund to (i) defray costs of operating the Act and then (ii) to capital moneys for car parks, road improvements and traffic controls.

7.3 Notice of intention to prosecute

A preliminary warning to a driver (known as a Notice of Intention to Prosecute) is, in relation to certain offences, necessary under s 104 of the 1961 Act (as amended by s 6 and Sch, 1968 Act). It must be proved that s 104 was complied with before conviction of dangerous driving and other offences (see para 7.3.6 below) can be imposed, unless the Notice is waived for one of the reasons in the section. The rationale of the section is to give the accused notice of a possible prosecution while the events are still clear in his mind.

7.3.1 Manner of warning

The section can be complied with in four ways:

(i) By service of the summons for the offence within 14 days of commission, i.e. by early delivery of the summons. Normally the prosecution has six months in which to make the complaint on which such a summons is based under the Petty Sessions (Ireland) Act 1851 or the Courts (No 2) Act 1986. In *Sage v Townsend*, *The Times*, 27 May 1986 it was held that if the defendant is charged within 14 days and given a copy of the charge sheet this is sufficient.

(ii) By verbal warning that, within 24 hours of the event in question (including being warned at the time), the question of a prosecution will be considered. Such verbal notice must be an effective warning which is understood by the person to whom it is given. It is not sufficient for a mere formula to be recited—the accused must be aware of its meaning (*Daly v Quilty* [1955] IR 14, where warning to a doctor preoccupied with the injured in an accident was insufficient). See a similar result in *Gibson v Dalton* (1980) RTR 413, where it was held it was not enough merely to address the warning to the defendant—it had to be a real warning and get through to the defendant.

It is not necessary that any details of the alleged offences should be stated in the verbal warning (*A-G v Foley & O'Toole* 86 ILTR 30). A qualified warning may be sufficient, e.g. *A-G v Baily* (1957) Ir Jur R 75, where, after the accident the accused was told by the police 'you are liable to be prosecuted under the Road Traffic Act 1933. I'll give you a week to fix up the business between you'. The accused swore he understood some further step would be taken before a prosecution would be brought. It was held to be a sufficient warning.

The onus of proof is on the defendant to prove, on the balance of probabilities, that he did not understand the warning (*Offen v Ranson* (1980) RTR 484). The question as to whether the defendant knew or understood the warning, or that it was sufficient, is based on an objective test, i.e. whether a defendant would reasonably be expected to have understood the warning or the words to be a warning (*Gibson v Dalton*, above).

(iii) A notice in writing stating (a) the time and place of the alleged offence, (b) brief particulars of the act or acts alleged to constitute the offence, and (c) the intention to prosecute, is served personally or by registered post on the accused or, in the case of a mechanically propelled vehicle, on the registered owner of the vehicle. See further below as to the specific items of this notice.

(iv) Waiver (see para 7.34 below).

Cases

The following decisions are of help in dealing with methods of complying with the section, particularly by written notice.

Place and time: In *Duffy v Lovegrove* [1956] IR 82 the notice of intention to prosecute set out that the alleged offence occurred at 'Stillorgan Road, Dublin' which was $1\frac{1}{4}$ miles long. The place could have been more particularly described. There was no accident. *Held*: notice insufficient. See also similar English decisions noted at ILTR & Sol Jo (1963) 75. In *Young v Day* (1959) 123 JP 317 and in *Shield v Crighton* (1974) Crim LR 605 a similar result to that in *Duffy*'s case was obtained. The fact that 'pm' was used instead of 'am' in the time stated makes no difference unless the accused shows he was misled (*Carr v Harrison* (1967) Crim LR 54).

In *A-G v McDonnell* (1952—unreported—High Court) a notice which did not refer to the place as being a 'public place' was held sufficient.

Act or Acts: In *A-G v Carroll* [1949] IR 344 the notice stated that Carroll drove 'In such a manner that it collided with a pedal cyclist'. *Held*: insufficient, i.e. the notice did not set out the acts alleged to constitute the offence.

Name: *State v President of the Circuit Court and District Justice O'Sullivan* [1949] IR 439; 83 ILTR 130 held that if a person wrongly named (O'Loughlin instead of McLoughlin) in a notice is served with that notice, acknowledges receipt of it, signs it, and the Garda puts the correct name on it, the notice is sufficient. See also *McDonnell v Guerin* (Supreme Court, 22 June 1967) as to a wrong christian name not making a notice bad where the correct christian name appeared in one part. A notice served on a company but omitting the word 'limited' was held good in *Springate v Quester* [1952] 2 All ER 21.

Wrong registration number: In *A-G v Callahan* (1958) ILTR 74 the notice and first summons had a digit wrong in the registration number. *Held*: sufficient.

Irish: A notice of intention to prosecute in Irish is sufficient, even though the defendant does not know Irish (*A-G v Wallace* (1964) ILT 117 and *A-G v Coyne & Kelly* (1967) ILTR 17).

Charges: If a notice refers only to s 52 of the 1961 Act (careless driving), the court cannot convict under s 53 (1966 ILT & Sol Jo 401), but one notice can cover both sections (*A-G v Edwards* 83 ILT & Sol Jo 125). The opposite does not apply, i.e. quoting s 53 and convicting under s 52 (*Russell v Read* (1948) 113 JP (J) 111) is sufficient.

7.3.2 Proof of notice

It is not necessary for the prosecution to serve a Notice to Produce for the Court as to the Notice of Intention on the defendant (*Sharkey v Cooke*, unreported, High Court, 3 June 1957).

7.3.3 Service

(a) As the notice is not a process, it can be served on a Sunday (*Maher v Prendergast* [1948] IR 339 83 ILTR 123).

(b) It can be served on either defendant who was in control of the vehicle at the material time, or on the registered owner, by registered post (*A-G v O'Keefe* (1952) ILTR 73). If the letter by registered post is received by someone authorised to receive mail it is a valid service (*Burt v Kilcaldy* [1965] 1 All ER 74).

(c) Any aider and abettor must be served with notice before a conviction can be sustained (*A-G v Carroll* (1950) Ir Jur R 20).

(d) If notice is served by registered post while the defendant is on holiday it is sufficient, provided the packet is accepted by an authorised person (*Layton v Shires* 94 ILT & Sol Jo 24). This also applies if the notice is served on the defendant while in hospital as a result of the accident (*Hosier v Goodall* 96 ILTR 171), even if it was sent to his 'ordinary' address (*Phipps v McCormich* (1971) Crim LR 541). Placing the notice in the letter box of the accused's residence is not sufficient (*Hallinan v O'Reilly* 87 ILTR 160). Service on the office of the owning company was held to be sufficient in England, even though the office was not the registered office. Posting it on the fourteenth day (see para 7.3.1) is not sufficient (*Nicholason v Tapp* (1972) RTR 313). However, if the notice is posted within the 14 days, although it arrives later that is sufficient (*Groome v Driscoll* [1969] 3 All ER 1638).

(e) Oral evidence of service is not necessary unless the Court or the defendant requires it (*State v O'Nunane* [1958] IR 178. The driver must show that neither he nor the owner was served with notice (*Archer v Blacker* (1965) Crim LR 165).

7.3.4 Waiver of notice

The fourth way of 'complying' with the section is set out in the proviso contained therein (s 104 of the 1962 Act, as amended by the 1968 Act).

It provides for four situations where failure to serve is not a bar on conviction. These are as follows:

(a) If the accused by his own conduct contributed to the failure. What is the extent of such contribution? Presumably the accused must be the substantial cause of the failure. In (1959) Jo Crim L 2 an instance is cited of a person giving an address he knows he will not be at.

(b) If the accused was at all material times aware of the occurrence in respect of which the prosecution is brought (inserted in 1968 Act). This was a somewhat unfortunate insertion. It seems to overlook the kernel of the need for these warnings. The early warning given by notice helps the accused.

(1) to collect his witnesses;
(2) to recollect the events when fresh in his mind;
(3) to record physical evidence, e.g. braking marks; and
(4) to obtain legal and other advice.

This insertion goes a long way towards nullifying the section. The purpose of the notice was shortly put in *Milner v Allen* [1933] KB 698—'To take the recollection of the motorist to the facts upon which reliance is to be placed'—and in *Venn v Morgan* [1949] 2 All ER 562—'to call attention of the driver to the time and circumstances in respect of the vehicle which he may be charged and give him an opportuniry in good time while memories are fresh to prepare his defence'.

(c) Where a mechanically propelled vehicle is involved, the name and address of the registered owner or accused could not be ascertained with reasonable diligence (see (d) below) within the 14 days. In *R V Bolkis* (1932) 97 JP 10 where the accused drove away he was acquitted because the police actually ascertained his identity in time to serve the notice.

The definition of 'registered owner' is set out in s 3 of the 1961 Act as being that assigned to it by the Road Vehicle (Registration and Licensing) Regulations 1958 (SI 13/1958) or any substituted regulation. The 1958 Regulations have been replaced by SI 311/1982 (see para 1.11). The present meaning of registered owner under the 1982 Regulations is defined as shown in para 7.9 below, i.e. as the person by whom the vehicle is kept, etc. Under Part I of the statutory instrument the owner has a duty to register his vehicle and, on such registration, presumably is the registered owner. See para 7.9 as to 'registered owner' and 'owner'.

(d) Where no mechanically propelled vehicle is involved, the name and address of the accused could not be ascertained with reasonable diligence within 14 days. 'Reasonable diligence' refers to the activity of the officer in charge of the prosecution (*R v Bolkis* (1933) 97 JP 10, above). See also *Haughton v Harrison* (1976) RTR 208 where, failure to discover the driver's or owner's name, etc within 14 days, having used reasonable diligence, was not a bar to conviction.

7.3.5 Practice presumption

The section provides an important presumption, i.e. that the requirement of the section has been complied with until the contrary is shown by the defendant. The word used is 'requirement', so presumably that means it is presumed that a notice is given or a notice or summons served within the required time. If the defendant shows it is not, the State must then show that the failure is overcome by one of the reasons given in para 7.3.4 above. The onus is on the defendant to show it is not on the balance of probabilities (*Offen v Ranson* (1980) RTR 484).

It is not necessary (though it is convenient) to raise the question of non-compliance before evidence is called. If no such question is raised as a preliminary matter, then the proper thing to do is to cross-examine the appropriate State witness (*R v Edmonton Justices* 95 ILT & Sol Jo 87).

7.3.6 Offences requiring notice

The offences requiring notice of the offence are:

(1) s 47—exceeding speed limit (see Chapter 3);
(2) s 51A—driving without reasonable consideration (see para 4.4);
(3) s 52—careless driving (see para 4.3);
(4) s 53—dangerous driving (see para 4.2); and
(5) aiding and abetting any of above (*The People (A-G v Carroll* (1950) Ir Jur R 20).

7.4 False declaration

As control is a basic concept in the Acts, with its corollary of licensees, permit plates, certificates, badges, etc. are methods or symbols of control, it is necessary to ensure, with criminal law sanctions, that information given for and by these symbols is correct. It is also important to ensure that the information on which they are based is correct, and that they are issued properly and in proper form.

To deal with false or misleading information, forgery and other fradulent practices, s 115 of the 1961 Act delcares that certain such actions are offences and attract a special penalty. Section 115 is slightly amended by Sch, 1968 Act and, as to the penalty, by the 1984 Act, s 3 and also by the Dublin Transport Authority Act 1986, s 46 (which in turn has been amended by the Dublin Transport Authority (Dissolution) Act 1987.

As to the position of disclosure and fraud in obtaining insurance, see para 6.4.3. However, s 115 also applies to the use of a certificate of insurance which ceased to be valid because of cancellation constitutes an offence under a similar section (*R V Clegharn* [1983] 3 All ER 671).

7.4.1 Offence

To be guilty of an offence under s 115 of the 1961 Act, as amended, a person either:

(a) where he is required by the Acts or regulations thereunder to furnish particulars in connection with an application for the grant or issue of a licence, or a plate or certificate, or otherwise, furnishes a particular which he knows is false or in any material respect misleading (subs (1) (as amended); or
(b) forges or fraudulently alters, uses, lends to or allows to be used by any other person, any licence plate, badge, certificate or special permit under the Acts or regulations thereunder (subs (4)).

In an English case relating to a similar section (*R v Howe* (1982) RTR 45), production of a drivers licence for purposes unconnected with driving on the road was not 'user' under that Act.

These offences are fraught with technical terms, such as 'knows', 'in any material respect', 'fraudulently', etc. The reader should refer to standard works on criminal law for these terms, but some help may be obtained from the following cases.

Two offences
In *State (Carther) v Carr* (unreported, Supreme Court, 11 November 1968; SI 185/1967) (see below also) the following extract from the judgment throws some light on the section. The court quashed a conviction. It stated:

> 'Section 115(1) creates two offences stated distinctly but shortly; These are (i) furnishing particulars which are false to one's knowledge (ii) furnishing particulars which to one's knowledge are in a material respect misleading. The particulars in question are particulars in connection with an application for the grant or issue of a licence or certificate. But the particulars in question are not merely particulars in connection with an application for the grant or issue of a licence or certificate; they must also be particulars which the defendant is required to furnish by the Act of 1961 or, as the case may be, by Regulations or Order. Let me now enumerate the other infirmities. First there is a failure to allege that particulars were false or misleading to the knowledge of defendant; second, in so far as misleading is concerned, there is a failure to allege that it is misleading in a material respect; third there is a failure to allege that defendant was required by the Act or Regulation thereunder to furnish the particulars. The summons grounding the proceedings is also bad for its failure to recite the list of these requirements.'

Knowledge
In *A-G (Comer) v Shorten* [1961] IR 304; 93 ILTR 168, a case under the Roads Act 1920, the principles of this type of knowledge were considered. The defendant, when applying for road tax, declared that for a period the vehicle had not been used by him or with his consent. At the hearing evidence of use by an unidentified person in said period was adduced. The defendant was charged that he did 'knowingly' make a false or misleading declaration. On a case stated it was held:

(1) Where evidence could not be adduced as to the actual knowledge of the defendant that the declaration was false when he made it, evidence of his means of knowledge that it might be false was admissible.
(2) Evidence of means of knowledge would be sufficient to support a prima facie case where the circumstances were such that the only reasonable inference which could be drawn from the fact that the defendant had means of knowledge was that he in fact must have used them to acquire actual knowledge.
(3) Having regard to the means of knowledge as to the truth of the declaration made by the defendant in the possession of the prosecution and the defendant respectively, the evidence adduced by the prosecution was not such as to entitle the District Justice to hold that the burden of proof had shifted to the defendant.

The English decision of *R V Cumerson* [1968] QB 534 runs counter to the Irish decision—it stated that these offences were absolute, i.e. no need for conscious falsity. It is necessary to prove this knowledge or lack of it in Ireland. Thus, a certificate issued by an employee while a sole director is on holiday may be insufficient (*Essendam v Maile* (1982) RTR 260).

Falsity

In *Roper v Taylors Limited* (1951) 2 TLR 284 knowledge was held to be either actual or second degree knowledge, i.e. 'where a man deliberately shuts his eyes to information which he fears will give him knowledge he does not wish to acquire'. However, in *Bloomfield v Williams* (1970) Crim LR 292, where the *Roper* case was referred to, an acquittal was achieved of a defendant who signed an application form completed by his daughter which contained a false statement but which he did not read.

In *State (Carthew) v Carr* above the High Court set aside a conviction under s 115 for a false declaration made to obtain a driving licence (which stated incorrectly that the applicant was not disqualified) as the Justices' minute book did not contain a reference to the 1961 Road Traffic Act, even though the charge showed it did.

The question of whether gain or advantage resulted from the false statement is immaterial (*Jones v Meatyard* [1939] 1 All ER 140 and see also *Welham v DPP* [1961] AC 103).

A statement that your name is A, when in fact it is B, is a false statement (*Clark v Chalmers* (1961) SLT 325). A backdated certificate is false in a material particular if backdated before the vehicle is examined (*Murphy v Griffiths* [1967] 1 All ER 424). Where the condition of a vehicle changes between the date of examination and the date of issue, the certificate can be false (*R v Evans* [1964] 1 WLR 1388).

Fraudulently

In *R V Terry* [1984] 1 All ER 65 it was held not necessary to prove an intent to avoid payment. It is sufficient to show that the defendant's purpose was to deceive a person responsible for a public duty and that the intended means of achieving this was dishonest.

7.4.1 *False declaration*

Forge
Making or altering something with the intention that it be regarded as genuine was the basis of conviction in *Clifford v Bloom* (1977) Crim LR 485, e.g. altering the digits in a number plate.

The document must be one to which the Act applies. As to an example of one which was not, see *R v Pilditch* (1981) RTR 303.

7.4.2 Presumption

Section 115(3) raises a presumption to ease the prosecution's proofs. It states that in a prosecution of an offence as to particulars for the application for the grant or issue of a licence, plate or certificate described in para 7.4.1(a) above, when the grant or issue of a licence, plate or certificate is proved, then the person to whom it was granted or issued is presumed to have made the application for it. Such person is, of course, at liberty to prove the contrary.

7.4.3 Penalty

Section 115(6) prescribes special penalties for nearly all offences under the section (but see s 115(4) below). These are, on summary conviction, a fine of up to £350 and/or up to six months' imprisonment. These are the penalties for furnishing false or material particulars, in reality. Disqualification and/or endorsement are optional. (see paras 2.9 and 2.10).

The general penalty (para 7.1) applies in the cases under s 115(4), however, i.e. forging, fraudulently obtaining, using, lending or allowing use of a vehicle plate, badge, certificate or special permit.

It seems unnecessary to have made this distinction in the offences.

7.4.4 Time limit

The normal six months limitation on commencement of proceedings by the Petty Sessions (Ireland) Act 1851 is extended to one year for offences under s 115 by subs (5) of the section. The year runs from the date of the offence and not from its detection. A similar provision would apply in prosecutions under the Courts (No 2) Act 1986.

7.5 Regulations

7.5.1 General powers

The Minister for the Environment is given general power to make regulations prescribing any matter or thing which is referred to in the Acts as prescribed or to be prescribed. This power is given in s 5(1) of the 1961 Act. No such power was found in the 1933 Act. The power is in fact widely used.

A myriad of regulations exist, as has been seen throughout the text and in index of statutory instruments at the beginning of this book. The general power of s 5 is regularly quoted in regulations. It is also specifically used in making regulations under sections where matters have to be prescribed, e.g. s 93 of the 1961 Act, as amended by s 61 of the 1968 Act.

7.5.2 Specific powers

Throughout this book the specific and detailed powers to make regulations have been discussed. These usually give a general power under the section in question, and then go on to detail items the regulations may deal with, without prejudice to the general power. Such powers to make regulations are found in 35 sections:

(a) in the 1961 Act, ss 11, 12, 13, 18, 31, 32, 33, 34, 38, 42, 44, 45, 46, 75, 82, 83, 86, 90, 95, 101A, 101B, 101D, 103 and 114;
(b) in the 1968 Act, ss 8, 9, 10, 11, 12, 13, 14, 17, 18, 55 and 60;
(c) in the 1978 Act, ss 4 and 26;
(d) in the 1984 Act, none;
(e) in the 1987 Act (see under (a), ss 101A, 191B and 101D);
(f) under s 10 of the 1961 Act, regulations under the 1933 Act and other repealed Acts continue in force until repealed. Most have been repealed and replaced. Where they are still extant they are referred to in the text and in the index of statutory instruments.

7.5.3 Road Act regulations

The 1961 Act (s 123) and 1968 Act (s 17) both extend the powers in s 12 of the Roads Act 1920 to make regulations. This is in respect of application for a licence (road tax) under the 1920 Roads Act and the Finance (Excise Duties) Vehicles Act 1952, as amended.

The 1961 Act extension provides power to make regulations dealing with an application for such a licence when the vehicle is not compulsorily insurable or not tested under s 18 of the 1961 Act. The 1968 Act extension gives power to require regulations not made under s 18 of the 1961 Act, but the European Communities Vehicle Testing Regulations provide for the compulsory road worthiness testing of certain vehicles (see para 1.8) and the production of a certificate as to weight, condition, etc. under Part II of the 1968 Act (see para 1.11 above).

7.5.4 Laying before Oireachtas

The 1961 Act, s 5(2) requires that all regulations under the Acts shall be laid before both Dail and Senate as soon as may be after they are made. A regulation becomes final unless annulled by a resolution of either house within 21 sitting days of such laying. If it is so annulled, the validity of anything done up to that date under it is not affected.

7.5.5 Proof of regulations

By the Documentary Evidence Act 1925, proof of all Ministerial regulations or rules is given by producing the Iris Oifigiuil or a copy printed by the Stationery Office (s 4). Such a copy is presumed lawful (s 5) until the contrary is proved. It is a criminal offence to unlawfully print, publish or tender as evidence any purported regulations not valid in source.

In *State (McColgan) v DPP and DJ Clifford* (unreported, 25 March 1980, noted in *Solicitors Gazette*, October 1981, green page XXVI) it was held that regulations made under the 1978 Act (now repealed), which had been passed but had not yet come into operation were valid, provided the making of such regulations was necessary and expedient to give the Act force and effect immediately on its coming into operation under s 10(1) of the Interpretation Act 1937.

7.5.6 Statutory Instruments Act 1947

This Act applies to regulations under the Road Traffic Acts 1961-84, as above. The 1947 Act requires that:

(a) copies of the regulations must be sent to the National and other specified libraries, the Law Library and other bodies;

(b) the regulations are printed and notice of them put in the Iris Oifigiuil. If a person is charged under a regulation with an offence, a copy of the Iris Oifigiuil showing publication is prima facie evidence of the Notice of Publication and, therefore, the valid making of the regulation. In DPP v Collins (1981) ILRM 447 it was held that the judge was entitled to take judicial notice of regulations about the Medical Bureau (see para 4.9.6.12).

7.5.7 Judicial Notice

The doctrine of Judicial Notice also relieves the onus of proof. Under this doctrine a court can accept the validity of well-known facts without formal proof. The reader is referred to books on Evidence for further details of this matter.

7.5.8 Commencement regulations

Section 2 of the 1961 Act allows the Minister for the Environment to bring the Act into operation piecemeal—on different days or for different purposes. Section 4 of the 1968 Act gives identical powers for that Act.
The following are the commencement regulations under these sections:

(a) *1961 Act*

SI No 173 of 1961
SI No 11 of 1962
SI No 17 of 1963
SI No 188 of 1963
SI No 28 of 1964

The net result of these is that all the 1961 Act is now in force, except as repealed or amended or unused.

(b) *1968 Act*

SI No 169 of 1968	SI No 244 of 1970
SI No 139 of 1969	SI No 6 of 1971
SI No 195 of 1969	

The net effect of these has been, in reality, to bring all the Acts into operation, except as repealed or amended or unused.

(c) The *1978 Act* came fully into operation on 20 July 1978 under SI 192/ 1978.
(d) The *1984 Act* came fully into operation without a special Commencement Order on 18 July 1984.
(e) The *1987 Act* (Dublin Transport Authority (Dissolution) Act 1987) came into operation under its s 15(5) on 1 January 1988.

7.6 Bye-laws and temporary rules

Bye-laws
A distinction is made between regulations and bye-laws under the Act. Regulations are made by the Minister for the Environment and may be annulled by either House of the Direachtas. Bye-laws are made by the Commissioner of the Garda Siochana or local authorities and usually have only local application. They normally must be approved by the Minister for the Environment.

In respect of one section (i.e. s 88 of the 1961 Act), which was repealed by s 60 of the 1968 Act, bye-laws were continued and deemed to be regulations. Since those bye-laws were in force for more than 21 days, the annullment procedure did not apply, as the Oireachtas was not involved.

Often these bye-laws are made after consultation under the Acts with relevant local authorities. Local authorities themselves are given powers to make bye-laws, and s 62 of the 1968 Act gives the Minister for the Environment power to transfer to specified Road Authorities (local authorities) the Commissioner's functions in certain areas under the Acts. Such orders would increase the local authority power to make bye-laws. No such orders have been made to date.

Temporary rules
The power of the Commisioner to make temporary rules is limited to ss 84, 89(3) and 90(7) (see paras 1.16, 5.4 and 5.5). These are made with the consent of the Minister for the Environment.

Many such rules were made over the years. They were experimental rules lasting for a period of one year, and normally effecting control over local situations. A series of 1985 temporary rules on parking, etc. were replaced on a County basis in 1986 by bye-laws for each County (see para 5.9 for a list of these). Where existing arrangements are unsatisfactory and new arrangements are to be tried out, new rules, usually temporary rules first, will be made.

7.6.1 Power to make bye-laws

Sections 84, 89 and 90 confer power on the Garda Commissioner to make bye-laws (see paras 1.16, 5.4 and 5.5):

(1) s 84—deals with stands for street service vehicles (see para 1.16);
(2) s 89—deals with bye-laws for the general control of traffic and pedestrians in specified areas (see para 5.3);
(3) s 90—deals with local parking of vehicles on public roads (see para 5.5).

Local authorities are given power to make bye-laws (1) by s 92 of the 1961 Act for fairs and markets in their area (see para 5.7) list (2) as above under s 101 for certain car parks (see para 5.14). (3), under s 101C of the 1961 Act (inserted by s 9 of the Dublin Transport Authority (Dissolution) Act 1987), a local road authority can, after consultation with the Minister, make bye-laws for the regulation and control of access to and egress from construction sites.

By s 10 of the 1961 Act, bye-laws under the 1933 Act and other repealed Acts continue in force until themselves repealed.

7.6.2 Procedure

This is set out in s 6 of the 1961 Act and SI 219/1961 (Road Traffic (Bye-laws and Temporary Rules) Regulations 1961, as amended by SI 60/1962.

Bye-laws made by the Commissioner which require *Ministerial consent* (i.e. those under ss 84, 89 and 90) must, before they have legal force:

(a) be submitted to the Minister for the Environment in the manner prescribed by SI 219/1961, R 3(1), i.e. the Commissioner must send two copies of the bye-laws to the Minister for his consideration. The Minister has the right to modify the bye-laws, or refuse approval, or approve of them;
(b) be published in the prescribed manner, which is specified by SI 219/1961, R 4(1). This is done by the Commissioner publishing, in at least three newspapers circulating in the area (one of which must be a daily paper) where the bye-laws are to have effect, a notice of the making of the bye-laws.

The notice mentioned in (b) above must contain statements that the bye-laws have been made, as to the sections under which they are made, the name of the functional area of the local authority which the bye-laws will affect, and a statement of where, and for how much, copies can be bought (SI 219/1961, R 4). In the case of general bye-laws under s 86 of the 1961 Act, the statement of the area could be in general terms (SI 60/1962, R 2—amending regulations which insert this into R 4 of the 1961 Regulations).

Under the 1968 Act, s 60 the Commissioner's powers under s 88 of the 1961 Act are replaced by the Minister's powers to make regulations under s 60 of the 1968 Act as to the general control of traffic and pedestrians (see para 5.3.3).

A bye-law made by the Commissioner which requires consultation with the *local authority* concerned must be dealt with as follows:

(a) The Commissioner must give notice to the local authority (or authorities) of his intention to make the bye-law affecting its area. If it is an area which is not a Borough, Urban District or Town (with Commissioners), then the County Council is the appropriate local authority.

(b) The Commissioner consults the local authority's representatives about the proposed bye-law. The making of these representations is a reserved function under the County Management Acts 1940-1955, as amended, i.e. the elected councillors deal with the matter and pass the resolutions, not the Manager or officials.

(c) The Commissioner submits the bye-law to the Minister for the Environment. Notice of the submission is given to the local authority. The Commissioner must submit two copies of the bye-law to the Minister, with such evidence as the Minister shall require to prove that the local authority has been consulted (SI 219/1961, R 3(2)).

(d) The Minister, having allowed one month after notice of the submission has been given to the local authority, may approve of the bye-laws.

(e) In the case of temporary rules, by ss 84, 89(4) and 90(7):
   (i) the Minister's consent must be obtained as above;
   (ii) the rules may not operate for at least seven days after their making;
   (iii) during those seven days the Commissioner must give notice of their making;
   (iv) they can be of not more than one year's duration, during which period they can be revoked;
   (v) they operate in lieu of any other bye-laws, under ss 84, 89 or 90 as appropriate, made under those sections for that period;
   (vi) different rules can be made for different classes of traffic and for different circumstances.

Otherwise, the same procedure for making and enforcing bye-laws applies.

7.6.3 Proof of bye-laws

Section 7 of the 1961 Act applies the Documentary Evidence Act 1925 to every bye-law made under the Road Traffic Acts by either the Commissioner or a local authority. They became documents of an official nature to be furnished under s 6 of the 1925 Act as proof, i.e. in a court they are presumed valid on formal production (see para 7.5.5 above).

7.7 Finance, fees and fines

7.7.1 Finance

All expenses by the Minister for the Environment or Garda Commissioner under the Acts are to be defrayed from moneys provided by the Oireachtas, subject to the control of the same by the Minister for Finance. These can be the actual amount of expenses or the estimated amount. The expenses of administering the Road Fund Act 1920 and the Finance (Excise Duties) (Vehicles) Acts 1952-1960, as amended, are similarly dealt with (s 8 of the 1961 Act, much of which has been repealed by SI 230/1980, R 2 and Schedule).

Road Grants or Loans may be made to local authorities for various purposes, e.g. s 101 of the 1961 Act for car parks; s 129 of the 1961 Act for road safety promotion.

7.7.2 Fees and fines

Fees and fines collected under the Acts are to be paid into the Exchequer, unless otherwise specifically stated in the Acts (s 9 of the 1961 Act). The Minister for Finance, in regulating the Exchequer, disposes of such moneys as he sees fit. Section 7 of the 1968 Act states that the Public Offices Fees Act 1879 does not apply to fees under the Road Traffic Acts. This 1879 Act provided generally for the disposal, etc, of fees payable to any public office.

An example of a contrary provision to the general rule of moneys going to the Exchequer is found in s 90 of the 1961 Act. This section deals with car parks, and subs (17) states that the Minister for the Environment may, by regulation, provide for the disposition of any fees collected under the section. By SI 169/1969, i.e. Road Traffic (Parking Fees) Regulations 1969, it is provided that the fees collected by the local authority are paid into the local authority's fund and applied primarily to paying the administrative costs of maintaining car parks, meter and disc car parking places, and secondly to capital funds for capital expenditures (approved of by the Minister) in providing and extending car parking facilities, road improvements and traffic controls and improvements, and the purposes specified in s 101 of the 1961 Act (car parks), as amended by s 6 of the 1968 Act (see para 5.14).

7.8 Application to the State

7.8.1 General application

By s 4(1) of the 1961 Act, the Acts apply to persons in the public service of the State and to vehicles owned by the State, except as set out below.

See also *Byrne v Ireland and A-G* [1972] IR 241, which, in reality, abolished much of the doctrine of Royal Prerogative.

7.8.2 Exceptions

(a) By s 4(2) of the 1961 Act, Part VI of the Act (dealing with insurance) does not apply generally to State vehicles or State employees during their employment or to a vehicle seized by the State, or to a Garda or Ministerial Officer testing, removing or disposing of vehicles under the Acts or regulations (see paras 6.6 and 7.2.4 above).

(b) Certain sections contain exemptions for State employees or vehicles, e.g. s 38(6) of the 1961 Act as to driving licences, i.e. not required by Gardai driving in the course of their duties.

(c) Certain exemptions also arise in connection with excessive periods of driving under s 114(8) of the 1961 Act (see restriction of s 114 application by SI 16/1979, R 10). These are mentioned in the text in the appropriate places. See para 4.1.2.

As noted in the text Defence Duties usually have special exemptions.

7.8.3 Negligent use

It is appropriate to mention that s 116 of 1961 Act was repealed before it came into operation by the Civil Liability Act 1961, s 59. Section 59 places responsibility on the Minister for Finance for the negligent use of State-owned mechanically propelled vehicles i.e. it is the Civil Liability Act that places the responsibility.

7.9 Definitions and phrases

Inevitably, in complex modern legislation technical and specialist definitions and phrases are used. Many of these are forged from the history of experience, and were introduced to change or modify abuses that developed or court decisions which were seen to allow loop-holes to emerge. The Acts themselves contain many such definitions, in particular in s 3 of the 1961 Act. Other Acts have special definitions for their particular Parts, e.g. Part III of 1978 Act on intoxication. Wherever possible, these have been referred to in the text.

The regulations under the Acts also abound with specialist definitions. Brief reference to these is made in the text, but the reader would have to peruse the regulations and their amendments to pin down a particular phrase. They are too numerous to deal with in this section.

Many relevant words, phrases and definitions have themselves been interpreted by the Courts. Where thought helpful, these are referred to in the text or this section. Sometimes reference is made to the meaning of words as used in other cases. In these, and, indeed, in all cases, the words of caution issued in *Sopp v Lang* [1920] 1 QB 518 should be borne in mind—'One may obtain some help from cases in which the construction of similar words in other statutes has had to be considered, but particular care must be taken'.

This section attempts in a brief way to deal alphabetically with some of these words, definitions or phrases. The list or treatment is not exhaustive. Reference may be made to works such as Stroud's 'Judicial Dictionary' or 'Words and Phrases Judicially Defined' published by Butterworths, and other sources.

'Adapted'
In *Taylor v Meade* [1961] All ER 426 it was stated that 'adapted' means some amount of alteration of the original construction, either initially or later. In that case it was held that putting rails in a van to hold dresses, which, when not there, still allowed passengers to be carried, were small fittings and attachments and not 'adapting'. In *Maddox v Starer* [1962] 1 All ER 831 it was said that adaptation could be by original construction or subsequent alteration.

The question of the permanence and extent of the changes was emphasised in *Westacott v Centaur* (1981) RTR 182, where four of the 11 seats on a minibus were rendered unusable for the carriage of passengers, but it was held not to have been 'adapted'. See also *Backer v SS of Environment* [1983] 2 All ER 1021.

'Analysis'
This is referred to at para 4.9 above in relation to intoxicated driving offences. In relation to Part III of the 1978 Act, it includes any operation used in ascertaining the concentration of alcohol in a specimen of breath, blood or urine, and any operation used in ascertaining the existence of concentration of a drug in a specimen of urine, and cognate words shall be contrued accordingly.

'Ancillary disqualification order'
This is dealt with by s 27 of the 1961 Act and in the text at para 2.9. It is a discretionary order.

'Appointed stand'
This is dealt with by s 84(1) of the 1961 Act and in the text at para 1.16. It is a standing or hiring place for taxis.

'Appointed weighbridge'
This is dealt with by s 15 of the 1961 Act and in the text at para 1.7. It is an official place for checking vehicle weight.

'Approved policy of insurance'
This is dealt with by s 62 of the 1961 Act and in the text at para 6.4.

'Arrest'
As to a Garda's rights generally, including the power of arrest, see para 7.2.5.

Many sections give a power to arrest without warrant to the Gardai. These sections are:

(a) 1961 Act, ss 19, 40, 49, 50, 51, 53, 55, 69, 82, 107, 112 and 113;
(b) 1968 Act, ss 16, 28, 56 and 59;
(c) 1978 Act, ss 12, 15 and 17.

Arrest is normally a result of the observation by a Garda of the commission of an offence, or of the formation by him of an opinion regarding the condition of the driver. The specific powers for various offences are set out in the text.

The Gardai and others (e.g. Excise Officers) have, of course, power to arrest under other statutes and limited powers of arrest at Common Law.

'Attempt'

The concept of an 'attempt' to do certain actions arises in several sections. There is no statutory definition. This is a difficult legal concept, and each case must largely be decided on its own facts. See a general article on 'Attempts' in (1968) ILT & Sol Jo 1968. See also general criminal law books.

In the *State (Prendergast) v Porter* (1961) 27 Ir J 14 the defendant, in front of a stationary van, commenced turning the starting handle. He then went to the right hand side, opened the door, leaned into the cab, and appeared to touch the dashboard instruments. He repeated these acts. It was held in High Court that these acts amounted to an attempt with an intention to drive. In *R v Cook* (1964) Crim LR 56 a man caught sitting in the driver's seat, with the dashboard lit and fiddling with the ignition, was found guilty of an attempt to drive.

In *Edkins v Knowles* [1973] 2 WLR 977 it was held that a man cannot be attempting to drive when he is effectively prevented or dissuaded from driving (see also *R v Neilson* (1978) RTR 232). However, an attempt to drive was made in *Kelly v Hogan* (1982) RTR 352 by a man who was sitting in the driver's seat. He did not have the ignition key, but was endeavouring to put other keys into the ignition.

A person who has committed the full offence can be convicted of committing an attempt (*Webley v Buxton* [1977] 2 All ER 595).

'Built-up area speed limit'

This is specified in s 45 of the 1961 Act and is dealt with in the text at para 3.1.

'Bureau'

The meaning of this i.e. medical Bureau of Road Safety, is covered in s 37(1) of the 1968 Act. This is the Bureau for testing blood and urine samples. It is discussed at paras 4.9.6 and 5.16.3. See also the Motor Insurance Bureau of Ireland at para 6.8.

'Bye-laws'

These are discussed at para 7.6 above, i.e. procedure for making. The specific powers of various persons (the Garda Commissioner or local authority) to make bye-laws and the extent of these powers are covered in the relevant sections e.g. ss 89 and 90.

'Carriage for reward'

This phrase occurs in various parts of the Act, e.g. as to public service vehicles (Chapter 1, part 2), as to tax (para 1.11), etc. See *A-G v Brogan* 87 ILTR 181, where it was held that a horse trainer carrying the horse for its owner was not carrying for reward, even though the owner was liable for the expense. See also 'Reward' below.

'Causes or permits'

In *Ross Allman Ltd v Bond* (1974) RTR 279 it was held that the offence of causing unlawful use requires proof of *mens rea* as to knowledge of the facts rendering the use unlawful. When a company is involved, the knowledge has to be by someone exercising a directing mind over the company's affairs (*Knowles v Russell* (1975) RTR 169). Charges in the alternative of causing/permitting or using can be brought against a company.

'Causing' involves some degree of dominance or of control, or some express or positive mandate; 'permitting' means giving leave or licence to somebody (*Shave v Rosner* [1954] 2 QB 113). See also *Houston v Buchanan* [1940] 2 All ER 179.

To constitute 'permitting', the person must be in a position to forbid use (*Goavarne v Buck* [1940] 1 KB 771). In *Keene v Muncaster* (1980) RTR 377 it was held that permitting means allowing someone else to do something, and one cannot be charged with permitting oneself. In *Jones v Smee* [1954] 3 All ER 273 a vehicle left the company's premises in good condition. A wrong coupling by employees during the journey damaged the brakes. *Held*: the company was not 'permitting'—no responsible officer had knowledge or was involved.

A supervisor of a learner driver does not necessarily permit the driving (*Thompson v Lodwick* (1983) RTR 76).

It is necessary for the prosecution to establish a command or a direction to establish that a company caused an employee to use a vehicle's tachograph improperly. Its transport manager's acquiescence may amount to permission but not to causation (*Redhead Freight Ltd v Shulman* (1988) Crim LR 696).

Some further cases on causation can be found at paras 4.2.7 and 4.12.2 *supra*.

'Certificate of competency'

This is specified in s 33(4) of the 1961 Act and is covered at para 2.5. These are the certificates issued on passing driving tests. They are necessary in relation to applications for drivers licences in certain circumstances (see para 2.3).

'Certificate of exemption'

This is specified in s 68 of the 1961 Act and is dealt with in the text at para 6.6.

'Certificate of fitness'

This is specified in s 34(4) of the 1961 Act and is dealt with in the text at para 2.6. It is a medical certificate, in reality, required in certain drivers licences applications, etc.

'Certificate of insurance'

This is specified in s 66(1) and covered at para 6.4.4. It is evidence to be produced to a Garda and others of the existence of insurance cover.

'Combination of vehicles'

This means a mechanically propelled vehicle and a vehicle or vehicles drawn thereby (s 3(1) of the 1961 Act). The expression is used regularly in Part

II of the Act (Chapter 1), dealing with the construction, equipment and use of vehicles. See, in particular, the regulations at para 1.5. See 'Vehicle' below.

'The Commissioner'
This means the Commissioner of the Garda Siochana (s 3(1)). He has various functions under the Acts, including making bye-laws (see para 7.6 above). He is in charge of the Gardai generally. See Act No. 7 of 1925 ss 5 and 8 of the Garda Siochana Acts 1924-79 generally.

By s 126 of the 1961 Act it is stated that nothing in the Road Traffic Acts prejudices or derogates from the general power and duty of the Commissioner and Gardai to preserve order in public places and to regulate and control traffic thereon. See generally para 7.2 above.

'Consequential disqualification order'
This is specified in s 26(1) of the 1961 Act and is covered at para 2.9, dealing with disqualification from holding a drivers licence.

'Contravenes'
This word is stated to include refuses or fails to comply with, and 'contravention' shall be construed accordingly (s 3(1) of the 1961 Act).

'Designated'
This phrase is assigned a special meaning for the purpose of Part III of the 1978 Act. In that context it means a doctor designated by a member of the Garda Siochana. This is in relation to intoxicant offences. It is dealt with in para 4.9.

'Drawn vehicles'
See 'Vehicles' below.

'Driving'

(1) *Generally*
The definition in s 3 states that 'driving' includes 'managing' or 'controlling', and driving therefore is extended beyond the ordinary meaning. It also includes riding a bicycle.

As to what 'managing' means in this definition, see the judgments in the civil case of *Neill v Minister for Finance* [1948] IR 88, where it was held that a postman closing the door of a van was not 'managing' the van within the criminal definition of driving in the 1933 Act.

Contrast a number of cases on driving:

(i) *R v McDonagh* (1974) RTR 372. 'The essence of driving is the use of the driver's controls in order to direct the movement, however that movement is produced'. Two factors were of particular importance; (1) that the alleged driver must be in the driving seat or in control of the steering wheel, and (2) his activities do not amount to driving unless they come within the ordinary meaning of that word. The action here held not to be driving was pushing the vehicle and steering with one hand.
(ii) *Hill v Baxter* [1958] 1 QB 278, where the defence of automatism was accepted, provided the 'driver' was unexpectedly deprived of all thought

from circumstances or happenings he could not anticipate. (See (2) below further about automatism).
(iii) *R v Kitson* (1955) 39 CAR 66. The accused was drunk and asleep in the car of his brother-in-law, who was the driver in the usual sense. The accused woke up to find the vehicle was moving. There was no-one in the driver's seat and no ignition key. He steered the car downhill and on to the grass margin. He was convicted.
(iv) *Edkins v Howles* (1973) RTR 257 has a useful review of English authorities. This review states these rules: (a) It is not necessary for the vehicle to be in motion, e.g. if driver is releasing the handbrake, applying the handbrake, etc. over a short period after the vehicle comes to rest the vehicle is still being 'driven' at the end of that journey. The interval need only be brief. (b) Similarly, stopping at traffic lights, and similar purposeful stoppings of a short nature, will be interpreted as driving. The longer the stop the less likelihood of 'driving'. (c) If a motorist has been effectively prevented or persuaded from driving he is no longer to be considered driving. (d) If stopped by Police and the suspicion arises, the motorist is still driving unless an appreciable time elapses before suspicion is aroused.
(v) *Samuelson v NIGG Limited* [1984] 3 All ER 107. The difference between the two concepts of using and driving is illustrated in this case. The plaintiff's insurance policy covered use of the vehicle. He was not covered, therefore, when the car was stolen when being driven by a motor trade repairer.
(vi) *Coll v Bool* [1940] 3 All ER 83. It is not necessary to start the engine. In this case, where accused was seated in the driver's seat, released the brake and let the car with no petrol run down a hill, it was held to be 'driving'.
(vii) *Owner*. See 'Owner' below as to cases when he may be asked to show he was not the driver. See also para 7.2.2 as to giving information about user. See also 'use' below.

(2) *Mental incapacity/Automatism*
A number of personal conditions affecting the driver can remove the voluntary nature of driving. These are a matter of evidence, and it is a matter of law to decide if such condition exists. Examples of these conditions are:

(i) automatism rendering the driver unconscious, e.g. an epileptic fit—*Hill v Baxter* [1958] 1 QB 277—unless he is prone to fits. See also *Roberts v Ramsbottom* [1980] 1 All ER 7;
(ii) a blow on the head rendering the driver unconscious (see *R v Spruge* [1961] 2 QB 205; [1961] 2 All ER 688);
(iii) an attack by a swarm of bees (*Farrell v Stirling* (1975) SL 771);
(iv) a severe attack of pneumonia causing loss of memory (*Police v Beaumont* (1958) Crim LR 620);
(v) insanity (see, generally, criminal law books and *Bratty v A-G* (1963) AG 388);

(vi) diabetes where specific intent involved (*R v Bailey* [1983] 2 All ER 503).

It is not sufficient merely to say the driver's mind was malfunctioning (*R v Isitt* (1978) RTR 211). In *Broome v Perkins* (1987) Crim LR 271 the court held the defendant was driving and should be convicted, even though he suffered a hypoglycaemic episode while driving. It did so because there was evidence that during the episode he exercised conscious control over the vehicle. The burden of proof is not upon the defence (*Bratty*'s case above), but the evidence must be considered with the other evidence (see *Moses v Winder* (1980) Crim LR 322). Necessity can provide a defence (*R v Miller* (1987) RTR 22).

(3) *Garda powers*
In s 107 of the 1961 Act (see para 7.2.2) the right is given to a Garda to demand the name and address of the user of a mechanically propelled vehicle. Exercise of this right normally results in an admission of driving. It has been interpreted to prevent, during a follow up in hot pursuit, entry to a private house in certain circumstances (*DPP v Gaffney* (1988) ILRM 39).

Where a police officer questioned a defendant, without administering a caution, in order to ascertain whether he was the driver, evidence of this conversation was held admissible (*Hennel v Cathbert* (1962) Crim LR 104). See para 4.13.9 on powers to locate vehicle.

(4) *Animals*
Under BL 31 of the General Bye-laws for the control of Traffic 1964 (SI 294/1964), the duties of the drover (driver) of animals is set out. In this regard 'driving' means conducting without rein or lead (see para 5.3.3).

(5) *EEC Provision*
In Art 1 of EEC Regulation 3820/85, dealing with drivers' hours, etc. (see para 4.7.11), 'driver' is defined as meaning 'any person who drives the vehicle, even for a short period, or who is carried in the vehicle in order to be available for driving if necessary'. Some consideration of this type of dual 'driver' position was given in *Pearson v Rutterford* (1982) RTR 54 and *Williams v Boyd* (1986) RTR 185.

(6) *Two drivers*
In *Langman v Valentine* [1952] 2 All ER 803 it was held there could not be two drivers of a motor cycle at the same time; but in *Wallace v Major* [1946] 1 KB 473 it was stated that a somewhat wider definition in the English Act should be interpreted as allowing two persons to be capable of being considered to be the driver at the same time. Thus, in *Tyler v Whitmore* (1976) RTR 83 a girl passenger leaning across with both hands on the wheel and steering was driving, as was her companion in the driver's seat who was controlling the propulsion. The degree of control in that type of case amounts to driving in the ordinary sense (*Jones v Pratt* (1983) RTR 54).

(7) *No driving or no likelihood*
See 'Attempting to drive' and 'In charge'.

Martin v Confer [1963] 2 All ER 765 decided that the Court should consider the defendant's intention as relevant evidence, but it must be considered with the other circumstances to establish whether, on the balance of probabilities, there was no likelihood that the intention would be departed from. In *John v Bentley* (1961) CLY 78/8 a man in a drunken stupor was held unlikely to drive.

'Driving or attempting to drive'
See above re 'Attempt' and 'Driving'. In particular, note *State (Prendergast) v Porter* (1961) Ir Jur R 15, where using a starting handle, dashboard controls, etc. was an attempt to drive.

In *R v Masters* (1972) RTR 492 a motorist was stopped on suspicion of not lawfully driving the car (police officer took the keys and motorist had left the car). The motorist was asked five minutes later to take a breath test. *Held*: at the time of the request it could not be said he was 'driving or attempting to drive'.

If a defendant is charged with 'driving or attempting to drive', then, under *State (Taylor) v CC Judge of Wicklow* [1951] IR 311, the conviction should only be for one of the offences, otherwise the conviction will be bad for duplicity.

In *R v Farrance* (1971) RTR 225 a defendant found revving up a motor car, which could not in fact be driven because the clutch was burnt out, was held to be attempting to drive.

'Driving licence'
This is specified in s 22 and is dealt with in the text at Chapter 2. There are different classes of driving licences and detailed requirements for getting them. EEC legislation is endeavouring to harmonise them throughout Member States.

'Excepted persons'
These are covered by s 65 of the 1961 Act and in the text at para 6.7. There are a number of limited classes of persons who can be excepted from the need to be insured by vehicle insurers under approved policies of insurance.

'Exempted persons'
These are dealt with at s 60 of the 1961 Act and in the text at para 6.6. They are certain State or semi-State bodies that are not subject to the normal insurance requirements.

'Footpath'
This means that portion of the highway provided primarily for the use of pedestrians (s 3 of the 1961 Act). In *A-G v Moss* (14 January 1959, High Court) a footpath was held to be a public place and part of a road.

See para 5.3 (General Bye-laws) as to the use and non-use of footpaths and para 5.5 as to parking on footpaths.

'General speed limit'
This means the speed limit specified in s 44A of the 1961 Act (see para 3.1). It is a limit which applies to all vehicles on all roads, unless a lower limit specifically applies.

'Hire and Reward'
See 'Reward' *infra*. See *McCarthy v British Oak Insurance Co* (1938) 3 All ER 39 as to hire at para 6.4.10.

'Hire-drive agreement'
By s 3(1) of the 1961 Act, this means, in relation to a mechanically propelled vehicle, an agreement under which the vehicle is hired from its registered owner, other than (a) a hire-purchase agreement, (b) an agreement merely for the carriage of persons or goods, or (c) an agreement under which the registered owner of the vehicle drives, or provides a driver for, the vehicle.

Certain sections apply to vehicles hired out so as to place liability on the hirer, e.g. certain parking offences as in s 90(10) (see paras 4.7 and 5.5).

See the special definition under the Litter Act 1982 at para 1.2.9.4.

'Hire-purchase'
The position of hire-purchase agreements is regulated by the Hire-purchase Act 1946, as amended (see para 1.3). In relation to the Road Traffic Act, however, the hirer in possession is deemed the owner by s 3 of the 1961 Act (see 'Owner' below).

See para 1.3, also as to the condition of the vehicle in relation to these agreements.

'In charge'
Also included in this commentary is 'In charge with intent to drive or attempt to drive'. This is a concept particularly important to s 50 of the 1961 Act, as inserted by s 11 of the 1978 Act and amended by the 1984 Act as to the penalty for intoxication. It is also relevant to other provisions in the Acts. Thus, the defendant must be shown to be 'in charge' and then he is presumed to be driving or attempting to drive under s 50(5) of the 1961 Act until the contrary is shown. It is a question of fact and law. There is no statutory definition of 'in charge' but there are a large number of decisions. However, s 90(14) stated that a licensed car park attendant is not considered to be in charge of the vehicles in the parking place at which he is an attendant.

A number of contrasting decisions which may help to illustrate the meaning of the phrase follows:

(a) *Held 'in charge'*

Walker v Rowntree (1963) NI 23. Defendant lying partly in and partly outside car, ignition key missing. *Held*: in charge.

R v Paul (1952) NI 61. Held—

(a) a vehicle incapable of being started because of a mechanical breakdown was nevertheless a motor car within a Road Traffic Act;

(b) the jury could find the appellant was in charge of the car, even if they accepted his case that he was neither the driver nor the owner of the car, when he was found sitting on it while awaiting the return of the driver who had gone for assistance.

The supervisor of a learner driver is in charge (*Clark v Clark* (1950) SLT 68 and *Sheldon v Jones* (1969) 113 Sol Jo 942).

Leach v Evans [1952] 2 All ER 164. A person who was in possession of ignition keys and looking for his car was arrested before he could enter it. *Held*: in charge.

(b) *Held not 'in charge'*

DPP v Joyce (1985) ILRM 206. Two Gardai went to a private yard to examine a motor vehicle and were there approached by the defendant. They alleged to him that this vehicle was involved in an offence 30 minutes earlier. As he gave off a smell of drink, a Garda, being of the opinion he was unfit to drive, breathalysed him. This was positive. He was arrested. A subsequent blood sample was over the limit on analysis. *Held*: he was not lawfully arrested. The request for a breath test has to be made in a public place (which the yard was not) and the person must then be in charge of the vehicle (which the defendant was not).

Crichton v Burrell (1951) SC 170. The owner was standing by the open car with a friend, with the ignition key in his possession, waiting for an employee to come to drive him away. *Held*: not 'in charge'. According to Lord Keith 'The words in charge mean being responsible for the control or driving of the car—The person who is for the time being in control of the vehicle'.

Dean v Wishart (1952) SC 9; *Williams v Osborne* (1975) RTR 181. An insensible drunk sleeping off the effects in the back of an (immobilised) car was not in charge. See also the similar case of *John v Bently* (1961) CLY 78/8, where, due to drunken stupor there was no likelihood of driving.

Winter v Morrison (1954) SC 7. Car owner in front passenger seat. His wife, who was the holder of an expired provisional licence, was in the driver's seat with the engine running. Owner held not in charge.

A mechanic repairing a fault on the roadside was not in charge (*Adair v McKenna* 1951 SLT 40).

It will be seen that the border line is often difficult to discern. It is a question of fact (*R v Hartnett* (1955) Crim LR 793).

The intention of driving, etc. is presumed against the defendant in subs (4). It is the duty of the defendant to upset this presumption, presumably on the balance of probabilities (*Northfield v Pinder* [1969] 1 WLR 50).

In *R v Jephcott* (1966) 110 Sol Jo 812 the facts that the vehicle was damaged so that it could not be driven and that the accused took drink thereafter were held to be matters to be considered.

In *State (Prendergast) v Porter* (1961) Ir Jur R 14 it was held that a person who turned the starting handle, used the dashboard, and sat in the vehicle when the engine did not start but turned over, had an intention to drive.

The onus on the defendant is, on the balance of probabilities (*Neish v Stevenson* (1970) Crim LR 161), to show that he was not in charge in certain circumstances.

'The insured'
This is specified by s 62(1) and is dealt with in text at para 6.4, i.e. a person covered by a vehicle insurer under an approved policy of insurance.

'Large public service vehicle'
Under s 3(1) of the 1961 Act, this means a public service vehicle having seating passenger accommodation for more than eight persons exclusive of the driver.

As to 'public service vehicle', see below. As to 'small public service vehicle' see below.

By s 121 of the 1961 Act the Minister for the Environment is given power to regulate the method of calculating passenger accommodation (seating and standing). See Chapter 1, Part 2 in particular, dealing with public service vehicles and see 'Passenger accommodation' below.

'Licensed parking attendant'
These are specified in s 90(15) and are discussed at para 5.5.

'Local authorities'
There are 27 County Councils, 5 County Borough Corporations, 6 Borough Corporations, 49 Urban District Councils, and 31 Town Commissioners. They have various functions under the Road Traffic Acts, as set out in the text e.g. parking control etc.

'Mechanically propelled vehicle'
See 'Vehicle' below. Under s 3(1) of the 1961 Act a mechanically propelled vehicle is a vehicle intended or adapted for propulsion by mechanical (including electrical or partly electrical) means, including:

(a) a bicycle or tricycle with an attachment for propelling it by mechanical power, whether or not the attachment is being used;
(b) a vehicle the means of propulsion of which is electrical or partly electrical and partly mechanical, but not including a tram car or other vehicle running on permanent rails.

Section 3(2) of the 1961 Act exempts a vehicle substantially disabled (by accident, breakdown, engine or vital part removed) so that it is no longer capable of being mechanically propelled from being a mechanically propelled vehicle for the purpose of the Acts. Thus, if parts are removed or a fault develops so that there is no reasonable prospect that it will be made mobile again, it is no longer a mechanically propelled vehicle (*Smart v Allan* [1963] 1 QB 2891). However, in *R v Challinor* (1985) RTR 373 it was held that mere towing of a broken down vehicle is not necessarily evidence of its no longer being a mechanically propelled vehicle. In *Bink v Department of Environment* (1975) RTR 318 it was stated that the test to be followed was whether the vehicle had reached such a stage that it could be said there was no reasonable prospect of its ever being mobile again.

In dealing with the question of whether a fork-lift truck was a 'motor vehicle' in *O'Brien v Anderson* (1979) RTR 388, it was held that as the vehicle was used, and intended to be used, on the road it was a motor vehicle. The court in *McEachran v Hurst* (1978) RTR 462 held, however, that the test to be applied is essentially one of construction rather than use. In *Percy v Smith* (1986) RTR 252 a fork-lift truck was held to be a motor vehicle which was a mechanically propelled vehicle.

The onus of proof that a vehicle is a mechanically propelled vehicle is on the prosecution (*Reader v Bunyard* (1987) 85 Cr App R 185—vehicle with no engine or gearbox not a mechanically propelled vehicle). A car with a flat battery was a motor vehicle (*R v Paul* (1952) NI 61). A moped whose engine could not start due to a temporary defect was a mechanically propelled vehicle (*R v Takson* (1970) Crim LR 160). Similarly, a moped is a mechanically propelled vehicle while being pedalled (*Floyd v Brush* [1953] 1 All ER 265), but not if vital parts are removed (*Lawrence v Howlett* [1952] 2 All ER 74).

'Minister'

This means the Minister for the Environment. The original designation in the 1961 Act was Minister for Local Government. The title of the Minister of his Department was changed subsquently to the Minister for the Environment, and the name of his department to the Department for the Environment.

The Minister has various powers, e.g.:

(a) to make regulations (see para 7.5);
(b) to control the making of bye-laws (para 7.6);
(c) to have accidents investigated (para 5.13);
(d) to regulate conditions of insurance (para 6.4);
(e) to regulate vehicle supply, equipment (Chapter 1);
(f) to regulate speed (Chapter 3), etc.

These are set out in text where appropriate.

Other Ministers have some functions under the Act, e.g. Minister for Labour as to excessive periods of driving (see para 4.11).

'Omnibus'

This means (s 3 of the 1961 Act) a large public service vehicle which is for the time being used on a definite route for the carriage of passengers, who are carried at separate fares and are picked up and set down along such route, whether on request or at a fixed stop. The position of omnibuses, or 'buses' as they are generally known, as is discussed at Chapter 1, Part 2, in particular, but the Road Traffic Acts generally apply to them. See below re public service vehicles also.

'Ordinary speed limit'

This is specified in s 44(3) of the 1961 Act and dealt with in the text at para 3.1. This is a limit that applies to certain types of vehicles, e.g. station wagons.

'Owner'

'Owner' means, by s 3(1) of the 1961 Act, when used in relation to a mechanically propelled vehicle which is the subject of a hire-purchase agreement, the person in possession of the vehicle under the agreement. See also 'Registered owner' and 'Use/user' below and 'Hirer' and 'Hire-purchase agreement' above.

In *Stickings v George* (1980) RTR 237, where the defendant made a statement at the scene to the police, and the statement was put in evidence, she had a case to answer as being the owner. Similarly, in *Scraby v Beskeen* (1980) RTR 420, where the defendant admitted owning a blue Range Rover and being at the place in question at the relevant time, he had a case to answer as being the driver on a careless driving charge. *Elliott v Loake* (1983) Crim LR 36 reviews many earlier English cases. In it, the owner had not furnished the required information and told lies. *Held*: he was the owner and had a case to answer as being the driver at the time of the accident.

'Parking'

(1) By s 3 of the 1961 Act, 'park' in relation to a vehicle means to keep or leave stationary, and cognate words shall be construed accordingly. See the general Index under 'Parking', where various aspects of parking are listed with reference. See also 'Use' below.

A number of sections deal with parking, e.g. s 55 on dangerous parking (see para 4.7); s 90 on the control of parking on public roads (see para 5.5); s 101 as to the provision of car parks (see para 5.14). See also para 4.8 as to obstruction. These provisions and others are dealt with in the appropriate places in the text. Where possible in the text, mention is also made of regulations, bye-laws and temporary rules governing parking.

(2) 'Parking meter'/'parking disc'/'parking attendant'. These are specified in s 90(15) of the 1961 Act and are discussed at paras 5.5.2, 5.5.3 and 5.5.4 *supra*.

'Passenger accommodation'

Section 121 of the 1961 Act enables the Minister for the Environment to make regulation stating how passenger accommodation can be calculated for mechanically propelled vehicles or classes of the same. These regulations may distinguish between seating and standing accommodation.

The Road Traffic (Passenger Accommodation of Mechanically Propelled Vehicles) Regulations 1962 (SI 143/1962) lay down these rules. The main rules for calculating passenger accommodation standards are:

(a) 16 inches for separate seat or continuous seat;
(b) driver's seat not to be counted.

Various of these rules are mentioned in text, e.g. regarding school buses.

'Pedal vehicle'

Special provisions in relation to pedal vehicles are found throughout the Acts and regulations, e.g. s 51 of the 1961 Act on intoxicants (see para 4.9); s 108 of the 1961 Act on the name and address of a cyclist (see para 7.2.2.2). As to cyclists holding on to other vehicles, see para 4.11, and as to taking without authority (s 112(3)), see para 4.10. The General Bye-laws regulate cycle tracks (para 5.3).

The definition of 'Driving' above states it includes riding a bicycle or tricycle.

Sub-definitions:

(1) *Pedal bicycle* means a bicycle which is intended or adapted for propulsion solely by the physical exertions of a person or persons seated thereon (s 3 of the 1961 Act);

(2) *Pedal cycle* means the vehicle is a pedal bicycle or pedal tricycle, under s 3(1) of the 1961 Act;

(3) *Pedal tricycle* means a tricycle which is intended or adapted for propulsion solely by the physical exertions of a person or persons seated thereon (s 3(1) of the 1961 Act).

'Pedestrian controlled vehicle'

This means a mechanically propelled vehicle:

(a) which is neither intended nor adapted for use for carrying the driver or a passenger; or

(b) which is intended or adapted so that there are alternative methods of driving it, namely, by a person carried on it or by a pedestrian, except during the period during which it is driven while carrying the driver or a passenger. (s 3 of the 1961 Act, as amended by Sch, 1968 Act).

As to 'Adapted', see above.

These vehicles have special provision made for them in the Acts and regulations. These provisions are mentioned in the text where appropriate, e.g. as to insurance exception under s 79, as specified in SI 14/1962 (see para 6.3.6) and as to the brakes on such vehicles (para 1.5.5.2), etc.

'Permitting'

See 'Causes or permits' above. See 'use' below.

'Person'

Includes a limited company where appropriate (*Briggs v Gibsons Bakery* (1948) N Ir 168).

'Prescribed'

This means prescribed by regulations under this Act (made by the Minister) (s 3(1) of the 1961 Act).

As to regulations, see para 7.5 above.

'Public place'

By s 3 of the 1961 Act this means 'any street, road or other place to which the public have access with vehicles whether as of right or by permission and whether subject to or free of charge'. Section 22 of the Air Navigation and Transport Act 1950 declares (to remove doubts) a state aerodrome as being a public place for the purpose of any enactment. See para 1.29.4 for the special definition under the Litter Act 1982.

There has been a good deal of case-law on what is or is not a public place. This is because most offences under the Acts have as an essential proof that the alleged offence occurred in a 'public place'. It is necessary to contrast this definition with 'public road' (below).

Case-law

In *Stanbridge v Healy* (1985) ILRM 29 the grounds of a hotel were held not to be a public place.

In *DPP v Joyce* (1985) ILRM 85 it was held that, as the defendant and his car were in a private yard, a breath test (which is to be done as a result of being in charge in a public place) was invalid and subsequent acts by Garda illegal.

In *A-G (McLoughlin) v Rhatigan* 100 ILTR 37 it was held that the onus was on the prosecution to prove the place was within the statutory definition. In the case itself, the place was held to be a private car park near licensed premises, and that there was insufficient evidence to show the public had a right of access. Contrast *Elkins v Cartlidge* [1947] 1 All ER 829, where the opposite conclusion was reached.

In *A-G v Moss* (High Court, 14 January 1959, unreported) it was held that a footpath, being part of a road, was a public place under s 3 of the Road Traffic Act 1933. See 'Footpath' above. See *A-G v Farrell* (1954) 88 ILTR 174 for a detailed definition of a public 'place' and 'road' (in this case, a road in hospital grounds).

In *R v Waters* (1963) 107 Sol Jo 275, Lord Parker CJ said 'Before a public place can become a private place, there must at some given point of time be some physical obstruction to overcome, for example, when someone entered in defiance of an order not to do so'. In the case it was held that a pub owner ordering a certain person to leave his car park did not constitute an obstruction or a prohibition. In this case also a proposition was stated that it is a question of degree and fact whether a place is public or private; if only a restricted class was excluded the place would be public.

The onus is on the prosecution to prove that it is a public place (*Pugh v Knipe* (1972) RTR 286). A piece of ground can be a public place at times and not at other times (*Sandy v Martin* (1974) Crim LR 258, where there was no proof it was a public place one hour after the pub closed).

As to 'Access' and 'Public', see *Montgomery v Looney* (1959) NI 171. Also see 'Road' below on this case and *A-G v Fanell.*

'Public road'

This means a road, the responsibility for which rests on a Road Authority (defined below). Some provisions of the Acts apply to public roads, others to the broader concept of public place (above) (s 3 of the 1961 Act).

The onus is on the prosecution to prove a road is within the Act (*Williams v Boyle* (1962) 106 Sol Jo 939).

Contrast with 'Public place' above, and see 'Road' below.

The Public Roads (Notice of Declaration) Regulations 1988 (SI 118/1988) specify the details required in a Road Authority's notice of intention to declare a road a public road.

See 'Road' below and cases referred to.

'Public Service vehicle'
This means a mechanically propelled vehicle used for the carriage of persons for reward (s 3 of the 1961 Act). As to 'Carriage for reward', see above and *A-G v Brogan* 87 ILTR 181, where it was held that a trainer carrying a race horse for its owner was not carrying for reward, even though the owner was liable for the expense. See Chapter 1, and in particular Part 2 thereof, dealing with, *inter alia*, these classes of vehicles. See also 'Small public service vehicles', 'Street service vehicles' and 'Omnibus' in this section. See also para 1.12.1.

'Registered owner'
Under s 3 of the 1961 Act the registered owner had the meaning assigned to it by SI 13/1958 (The Road Vehicles (Registration and Licensing) Regulations 1958). These regulations have now been repealed, as set out below, but the 1961 Act, s 3 provided that, in the event of such a repeal, the meaning of 'registered owner' would be that assigned by corresponding regulations for the time being in force.

The repealing regulations and those now in force are the Road Vehicles (Registration and Licensing) Regulations 1982 (SI 311/1982). These are dealt with at para 1.11 *supra*. They specify at Art 24 that the 'registered owner' of a vehicle should be:

(a) in the case of a vehicle used under a trade licence, the holder of such licence. A trade licence is issued under s 9 of the Roads Act 1920, as amended by s 15 of the Finance Act 1922;
(b) in the case of a vehicle in respect of which a declaration (in the form RF 6 in the 1982 Regulations) in respect of more than six vehicles of uniform type in the same ownership is current, the person shown on the declaration made in respect of such vehicle as the owner thereof, i.e. the fleet owner;
(c) in the case of a State-owned vehicle not being a military vehicle, the Department referred to in the declaration filed as to the vehicle under the regulations;
(d) in the case of a military vehicle, the Department of Defence;
(e) In any other case, the person whose name is most recently entered in the register maintained in respect of the vehicle under Art 22 of the 1982 Regulations.

In relation to (b) and (e), and indeed generally, it is important that the Licensing Authority has a note of a change of ownership. Article 9 provides for it, and failure to notify is an offence.

As to the registered owner of trailers, see para 1.5.2. As to 'Owner', see above.

'Reward'
In *A-G (Holland) v Hurley* 1960 Jo Crim L 59 the conflicting views as to what Reward is are discussed. In that case a lorry owner when charged with carrying scaffolding 'for Reward' stated he was merely doing so to oblige the owner of same was acquitted. See also cases referred to at 1.11.3. See 'Carriage for Reward' above and 'Hire and Reward' above.

'Road'

'Road' is stated by s 3 of the 1961 Act as including any bridge, pipe, arch, gully, footway, pavement, fence, railing or wall forming part thereof. In the English 1960 Act 'road' means any highway and any other road to which the public have access, and includes bridges over which a road passes.

In *Montgomery v Lomey* (1959) NI 171 it was held that, in respect of private property, 'access' meant access by permission, expressed or implied from acquiescence or other conduct, of the owner or occupier. It does not mean access in fact and irrespective of the will of the owner or occupier. Further, 'the public' means the public at large or a substantial section thereof, which is determined as a matter of fact or degree, having regard to the dominant object of the statute, namely the protection of the public. Those allowed to enter private property for personal reasons (e.g. pass holders, employees) will not be regarded as the general public because of the relationship between them and the owner or occupier. In the case itself it was held the forecourt of a filling station was a 'road or other public place'.

See *A-G v Farrell* (1954) 88 ILTR 174 for discussion of the differences between a public place and a road. A cul-de-sac can be a road (*Bass v Baynton* 1960 Crim LR 497). In *Griffin v Squires* [1958] 3 All ER 468 a car park was held not to be a road. See also 'public place', 'public road' and 'Roadway' (below).

'Road Authority'

Under s 3(1) of the 1961 Act this means (a) the Council of a County, (b) the Corporation of a County or other Borough, or (c) the Council of an Urban District. Reference to their functions and powers is made in the appropriate place in the text. See 'local authority' above.

'Road traffic weighbridge'

This is a weighbridge maintained by a Road Authority, as specified in s 15(3) and (4), and discussed at para 1.7. It can be a fixed weighbridge or a mobile one (s 15(7)).

'Roadway'

This means that portion of the road provided primarily for the use of vehicles (s 3 of the 1961 Act). In the General Bye-laws 1964 (SI 294/1964) roadway is stated as not including a cycle track. See 'Public place', 'Public road' and 'Road' above. See also para 4.8 and *A-G v Mayo Co Co* [1902] IR 13.

'Rules of the Road'

These are mentioned in the Acts. By s 3(4) of the 1961 Act, any reference to these is to the publication issued under that title by the Minister for the Environment, being the edition thereof which, at the relevant time, is the latest edition. The edition in use today is still the May 1979 edition.

The subsection confers no special legal status on these rules. In England the equivalent Highway Code has been considered. There, it has not been accorded any legal status either, but is said to have an evidential effect. In *R v Chadwick* (1975) Crim LR 105 it was stated that the Code and its provisions were inadmissible as hearsay, but that the braking distance tables could be used in cross examination. There are a number of cases where Courts have refused to convict of careless or inconsiderate driving merely because the Code was breached, e.g. *Scott v Warren* (1974) RTR 104; *Webster v Wall* (1980) Crim LR 186.

'Small public service vehicle'
This means a public service vehicle which is not a large public service vehicle, i.e. less than eight passengers accommodation. See Chapter 1, Part 2, especially paras 1.12 to 1.16. See also 'Large public service vehicles', 'Passenger accommodation' and 'Public service vehicles' above.

By SI 273/1968 licensed public hire vehicles became small public service vehicles.

'Special disqualification order'
This is specified in s 28(5) of the 1961 Act is dealt with in the text at para 2.9.

'Special speed limit'
This is specified in s 46(4) of the 1961 Act and is dealt with in the text at para 3.1.

'Street service vehicle'
This means small public service vehicle, the driver of which offers in a public place himself and the vehicle for hire, and for that purpose stands or drives the vehicle in a public place (s 3(1) of the 1961 Act, as amended by Sch, 1968 Act).

These vehicles are considered in Chapter 1, Part 2, paras 1.12–1.16 especially.

As to 'Small public service vehicles' and 'Public service vehicles' see also above.

'Traffic'
'Traffic' is not defined in the Acts. Some sections say that in their provisions it does not include pedestrians. These instances are mentioned in the text. It does include pedestrians as a general rule (see also their inclusion in many dictionary definitions). In the 1964 General Bye-laws (SI 294/1964) pedestrians are excluded from the definition of 'Traffic' (see para 5.3.1).

'Test certificate'
This is specified in s 18(8)(b) of the 1961 Act and is dealt with in the text at para 1.8. It is a certificate issued as a result of a test carried out under the section and regulations. EEC legislation now prescribes the testing of many vehicles (see para 1.8).

'Unladen weight'
This is dealt with in s 14(1) of the 1961 Act and covered in the text at para 1.7. It is normally the weight unladen of a vehicle or combination of vehicles with additions, but excluding certain items such as fuel. See also 'Weight' below.

'Use'

By s 3(1) of the 1961 Act, 'use', in relation to a vehicle, includes park, and cognate words shall be construed accordingly. The definition of 'parking' is set out above, i.e. as keeping or leaving a vehicle stationary. As to giving information as to user, see para 7.2.2 above. See also 'Driving' above.

By s 3(5) of the 1961 Act, use of a vehicle with the consent of a person includes a reference to use with his implied consent and to use of his order. See also s 118 of the 1961 Act, discussed at para 6.4.7. As to taking and using (joy riding) see para 4.10 and the cases therein cited.

A jacked-up vehicle with its wheels off and battery removed was in 'use' as a mechanically propelled vehicle requiring insurance according to *Williams v Jones* (1975) RTR 433. A vehicle being towed and steered was also in 'use' (*Milstead v Sexton* (1964) Crim LR 474). A partner who is a passenger in a van hired by the partnership and driven by his partner is not 'using' it (*Bennett v Richardson* (1980) RTR 358; In *A-G (O'Gara) v Cunningham* 84 ILTR 76). The Circuit Court held under Roads Act 1920 that to have an unlicensed car parked on the public highway is not proof of 'user'. This case also held its mere presence was not proof that it was a mechanically propelled vehicle. *Note:* the definition of 'use' above now includes 'park', but, of course, the prosecution must show who does the parking to prove the user.

A vehicle is in use when stationary on the road for loading or unloading (*Andrews v Kershaw* [1951] 2 All ER 765). A vehicle owner who hired a vehicle out was held not to be the user while the hirer had it; and the hirer also, when not in the vehicle, was held not to be using it (*Hamilton v Blair and Meecham* (1962) SLT 69).

In *Crawford v Haughton* (1972) 136 JP 234 it was held inappropriate to charge the owner of a vehicle with its illegal 'use' where the vehicle was being driven by someone who was not an employee. The Court stated that 'permitting' was appropriate.

In *Carmichael v Cottle* (1970) 114 Sol Jo 867 it was held that it is the hirer and not the car hire firm who uses the vehicle (similar type case to *Hamiliton* above). It was also held that only the employee may be convicted of 'using' when driving and not the employer (permitting would be the proper charge).

In *Leathley v Tatton* (1980) RTR 29 a person who sat in the passenger seat to see how vehicle performed with a view to purchasing it was held to be 'using' it.

Where an employee is driving a vehicle on behalf of a partnership, it is normally being used or permitted by all the partners (*Passmoor v Gibbons* (1978) Crim LR 498). The distinction between 'use' and 'driving' was dealt with in *Samuelson v National Insurance* [1984] 3 All ER (see above under 'Driving'). The distinction is often difficult to draw. In *Brown v Roberts* [1965] 1 QB 1 a person opening the door of a car was not using it for insurance purposes (this is probably a narrow construction). In *Mickleborough v BRS Ltd* (1977) RTR 389 the court said:

> 'Using applies on the authorities to the driver of the vehicle; it applies to the

vehicle, provided, first, the driver is employed under a contract of service and secondly at the material time the driver was driving on the employer's business.'

In *Carnish v Ferry Masters Limited* (1975) RTR 292 a drum fell off a lorry due to an unexplained inherent defect. It was held that both driver and owner could be convicted of using, even though there was no fault.

In *Garrett v Hooper* (1973) RTR 1 two partners were joint owners of a mobile crane. An appeal was allowed against the conviction of one partner who was not present when the crane was unlawfully used by the other partner. See also *Bennett v Richardson* (1981) RTR 358.

In *Thompson v Hooper* (1986) RTR 1 it was held that the term implied 'an element of controlling, managing or operating the vehicle'. A car with its steering locked, brakes seized, etc. is 'an inanimate hunk of metal'.

See also cases at para 4.10.2.

'Vehicles'

See 'Mechanically propelled vehicles', 'Pedestrian controlled vehicle', 'Public service vehicles' and 'Street service vehicles' above. See also para 1.2.4 as to the special definition of 'motor vehicle' under the 1980 Sale of Goods and Supply of Services Act.

The word 'vehicle' is not defined in the Acts, but 'mechanically propelled vehicle' is (see above), as are other types of vehicles in terms related to their use in the Acts. In *Fallon v Ferns* (High Court, 13 July 1962) it was held that there was no doubt that 'vehicle' includes a motor vehicle; it is not necessary to define every important word in a statute and, in the absence of such definition, the word must be read in accordance with the usual canons of interpretation. A dictionary definition of vehicle is 'any kind of carriage or conveyance'.

A similar line was followed in *Boxer v Snelling* (1972) RTR 472 under the English legislation where there is no definition. The Court said that in a borderline case the factors to be considered were, *inter alia*, the construction, nature and function of the contrivance, and the circumstances of use.

Drawn vehicle

Section 3(3) of the 1961 Act states that, save in relation to animal-drawn vehicles, any reference in the Acts to a drawn vehicle is to a vehicle attached to another, including attached by way of partial superimposition, for the purpose of being drawn thereby or actually drawn thereby.

Combination of vehicles

Section 3 says a combination of vehicles means a mechanically propelled vehicle or vehicles drawn thereby.

In *Dixon v BRS Limited* [1959] 1 All ER 449 the term 'vehicle' was held usually to mean one vehicle, not two linked together.

In *Ellis v Not-Bower* (1896) 60 JP 760 it was held a bicycle was a 'vehicle'.

EEC legislation is introducing various nominated types of vehicles (see para 4.12). As to control of vehicles generally, see Chapter 1.

'Vehicle insurer'
This is specified in s 58 of the 1961 Act and is dealt with in the text at para 6.5. They are authorised insurance companies who can issue approved policies to comply with the s 56 requirement for insurance.

'Weight'
There is a distinction between 'laden' and 'unladen weight' (see above). These two concepts are dealt with at para 1.7 above. The EEC legislation is introducing a new concept of 'permissible maximum weight' e.g. in the classes of driving licence (see para 2.3.3). Some regulations (e.g. at para 1.5) specify other types of weight criteria, e.g. axle weight, gross weight.

Certain vehicles must show the appropriate types of weight on a plate (see para 1.2.5).

Index